Robert Morgan

Robert Morgan

Essays on the Life and Work

Edited by Robert M. West
and Jesse Graves

McFarland & Company, Inc., Publishers
Jefferson, North Carolina

Library of Congress Cataloguing-in-Publication Data

Names: West, Robert, 1969– editor. | Graves, Jesse, 1973– editor.
Title: Robert Morgan : essays on the life and work /
edited by Robert M. West and Jesse Graves.
Description: Jefferson, North Carolina : McFarland & Company, Inc., Publishers, 2022
| Includes bibliographical references and index.
Identifiers: LCCN 2022001004 | ISBN 9780786448630 (paperback : acid free paper) ♾
ISBN 9781476641348 (ebook)
Subjects: LCSH: Morgan, Robert, 1944—Criticism and interpretation.
| Morgan, Robert, 1944—Interviews. | American poetry—20th century—
History and criticism. | Poets, American—20th century—Biography. |
Appalachian Region, Southern—In literature. | BISAC:
LITERARY CRITICISM / American / General
Classification: LCC PS3563.O87147 Z86 2021 | DDC 811/.54 [B]—dc23/eng/20220207
LC record available at https://lccn.loc.gov/2022001004

British Library cataloguing data are available

ISBN (print) 978-0-7864-4863-0
ISBN (ebook) 978-1-4766-4134-8

On the cover: Robert Morgan, 1993, Ithaca, New York. Dede Hatch took this picture for the jacket cover of *The Hinterlands*, which was published in 1994 (courtesy Robert Morgan); *background* © 2021 Konstanttin/Shutterstock

Printed in the United States of America

McFarland & Company, Inc., Publishers
Box 611, Jefferson, North Carolina 28640
www.mcfarlandpub.com

Table of Contents

Preface

Robert M. West

In 1969 Lillabulero Press—a small press founded by Russell Banks, Newton Smith, and William Matthews—brought out Robert Morgan's first book, *Zirconia Poems*. The title refers to a rural western North Carolina community near the author's childhood home, the smaller community of Green River. Both places are in Henderson County; drive south on U.S. 25 from the county seat, Hendersonville, and you pass through the village of Flat Rock, then through unincorporated Zirconia, and finally arrive at Green River not long before the road crosses into upstate South Carolina. When Morgan was born in 1944, the area was genuinely remote, and even today it would strike many as an unlikely starting point for a distinguished writer. Yet just thirty miles north (as the crow flies) is Asheville, once home to novelists Thomas Wolfe, Wilma Dykeman, and John Ehle. About the same distance to the northwest is the town of Canton, where novelist and poet Fred Chappell grew up. (Chappell taught Morgan in the mid–'60s, in the M.F.A. program at the University of North Carolina at Greensboro.) Go thirty miles northeast instead and you come to Black Mountain College, where poets Charles Olson and Robert Creeley famously taught, and where Asheville-born poet Jonathan Williams studied and founded his influential small press, The Jargon Society. Right in Flat Rock is Connemara, the retirement estate of the poet, Lincoln biographer, and raconteur Carl Sandburg. By 1969 the region did have more than one claim to literary fame.

Now, of course, in Morgan it has another. Half a century after the publication of *Zirconia Poems*, he has brought out sixteen books of poems, four books of short stories, seven novels, a book of essays and interviews on poetry, a biography of Daniel Boone, and a book on ten other figures crucial to the settlement of the American West. His books have been positively reviewed in such nationally and internationally respected venues as *Poetry*, *The Southern Review*, *The Washington Post*, and *The New York Times*. His poetry and fiction have garnered awards including four National Endowment for the Arts fellowships, a Guggenheim fellowship, *Poetry*'s Eunice Tietjens Prize, the North Carolina Award in Literature, and the James G. Hanes Poetry Prize of the Fellowship of Southern Writers. His poems and short stories have been reprinted in many anthologies, including *The Best American Poetry*, *New Stories from the South*, *Prize Stories: The O. Henry Awards*, *The Best Spiritual Writing*, and the Penguin anthologies *Good Poems*, *Good Poems for Hard Times*, and *Good Poems: American Places*. *Publishers Weekly* named his novel *The Truest Pleasure* one of the ten best books of 1995, and his novel *Gap Creek* was a *New York Times* bestseller, an Oprah's Book Club selection, and a winner of the Southern Book Critics Circle Award for Fiction. In 2007 the American Academy of Arts and Letters presented him with an Academy Award in Literature.

There are several kinds of achievement that count for literary success; given his reception by reviewers, his book sales, his awards, and his appearances in noteworthy anthologies, it is easy to describe Robert Morgan as a successful writer. Those who make a profession of academic literary study might ask for one more criterion of success, however, one that may count more than any other: does the writing invite extended, thoughtful discussion? Does it reward rereading? Is it rich enough to sustain the interest of serious readers with divergent critical perspectives—those interested in purely aesthetic dimensions, certainly, but also those drawn to, say, matters of psychology? Of social history? Of the history of ideas? Of human impact on the natural environment? When a writer's work proves multidimensional, when it begins to appear inexhaustible to serious readers, we rate that writer most highly. The greatest praise that academic literary critics have to bestow on an author is their repeated, sustained attention.

Robert Morgan's work earns that attention, and some of it—particularly the poetry—has received a portion of its due. Fred Chappell's early appreciation, "A Prospect Newly Necessary," from a 1976 Robert Morgan special issue of *The Small Farm*, salutes Morgan's poetic achievement and vouches for the accuracy of his portrait of western North Carolina. The most sweeping early assessment, William Harmon's kaleidoscopic "Robert Morgan's Pelagian Georgics: Twelve Essays," appeared in *Parnassus* in 1981. Rita Sims Quillen's 1989 *Looking for Native Ground: Contemporary Appalachian Poetry*, the first book on the poetry of the mountain South, devotes a quarter of its discussion to Morgan, considering his accomplishments alongside those of Chappell, Jim Wayne Miller, and Jeff Daniel Marion, three of his most respected Appalachian elders. Special Robert Morgan issues of *Iron Mountain Review* (1990), *Pembroke Magazine* (2003), *Appalachian Heritage* (2004), and *Southern Quarterly* (2010) offer many valuable assessments; one of the best is Michael McFee's *Iron Mountain Review* essay "'The Witness of Many Writings': Robert Morgan's Poetic Career." This collection gathers Chappell's, Harmon's, Quillen's, and McFee's articles to chart some of the major contours of the poetry's academic reception. Reprinted from a 2015 issue of *The Yale Review* is "The Elegiac Strain in Robert Morgan's Poetry," a comprehensive discussion by the poet Bhisham Bherwani, who studied under Morgan at Cornell University. Also appearing are two previously unpublished essays: Jim Clark's "Music's Mirror: Robert Morgan's *Musica Speculativa*" and an essay of my own, "'The Missing as Muse': Treatments of Absence in the Poetry."

Here are also several previously unpublished essays on Morgan's prose, which, coming along as it did much later than the poetry, has yet to receive as much academic consideration. In "Mountain Time: History and Forgetting in *The Mountains Won't Remember Us*," Paul Lincoln Sawyer pays special attention to the pivotal novella that lends Morgan's second story collection its title, and Suzanne Booker-Canfield offers an overarching reading of Morgan's short fiction in "Blood Soil Field: The Physicality of *The Balm of Gilead Tree*." In "'The Little Clearing of Now': Storytellers in *The Hinterlands*," Rebecca Godwin considers the trio of related narratives often billed as Morgan's first novel, identifying their "lessons in how to live." George Hovis, author of *Vale of Humility: Plain Folk in Contemporary North Carolina Fiction*, contributes "Faith, Sex, Talk, and Work: The Cornerstones of Community in *The Truest Pleasure* and *This Rock*," two of Morgan's novels about the Powell family. Martha Greene Eads argues in "The Work of Love in *Gap Creek*" that Morgan's most widely read novel asks us "to re-think our notions about what constitutes meaningful work and what constitutes meaningful marriage." In "Tunes from the 'Madrigal of Time,'" Harriet C. Buchanan shows how an awareness of madrigal form helps us appreciate the structure of Morgan's Revolutionary War novel *Brave Enemies*. In "Acting in Faith: Robert Morgan's *The Road from Gap Creek*," Thomas Alan Holmes charts the growth of Annie Richards Powell, the daughter of *Gap Creek*'s Hank and Julie Richards. These essays on the fiction are followed by "Robert Morgan's Nonfiction Books: Crossing Over the Mountains," Ted Olson's assessment of *Boone: A Biography* and *Lions of the West: Heroes and Villains of the Westward Expansion*.

While this is the first book entirely devoted to the study of Morgan's writing, and while it gathers together a great deal of essential commentary on his work, it omits some noteworthy previously published assessments. Among the factors weighed in deciding what to reprint here was a reader's likely ease or difficulty in accessing the previous publications. For instance, two insightful essays not included are John Lang's "Coming Out from Under Calvinism: Religious Motifs in Robert Morgan's Poetry," which first appeared in the journal *Shenandoah*, and Cecelia Conway's "Robert Morgan's Mountain Voice and Lucid Prose," which first appeared in *Appalachian Journal*. In addition to having been published in those widely circulated periodicals, both essays have also been reprinted in a well-distributed volume essential to anyone interested in Appalachian writing: *An American Vein: Critical Readings in Appalachian Literature*, edited by Danny L. Miller, Sharon Hatfield, and Gurney Norman, and published in 2005 by Ohio University Press. Readers interested in Morgan's poetry should also know of the chapter on him in Lang's book *Six Poets from the Mountain South*, which LSU Press published in 2010 and which, like *An American Vein*, has seen wide distribution. These and many other helpful and thought-provoking considerations are listed in the bibliography with which this book concludes.

Also here, thanks to Jesse Graves, are many photos of Morgan family elders and ancestors, as well as lists of their appearances in Morgan's oeuvre—either as themselves (in the poetry, usually) or as fictional avatars (usually in the short stories, novellas, and novels). Here too are remarks by Morgan himself: first, an essay titled "A Sense of Place," and then an interview ranging over his life as a reader, writer, and teacher.

Several factors contributed to a long delay in the preparation of this manuscript. The contributors have my deep gratitude not only for all their brilliant thinking and writing, but also for their extraordinary patience. I am also grateful to McFarland, of course, and especially to Gary Mitchem, Dré Person, Sonya Tedder, and Lisa Camp, who saw the book through to publication. Without their interest, their patience, their flexibility, and their expertise, this book would likely never have become a reality.

The same can be said of Jesse Graves, an excellent poet and former student of Morgan's. When it became clear that I needed a partner on this project, I knew who the perfect one would be, and I was right.

Jesse and I are both grateful to Robert Morgan for answering many questions and for his generous support of our work.

We hope readers will find this book an enlightening and enjoyable companion to a large and varied oeuvre of true distinction. We also hope that those familiar with only part of that oeuvre—the poetry, the prose fiction, or the nonfiction—will here find compelling reasons to explore the rest.

I

On the Poetry

A Prospect Newly Necessary[1]

FRED CHAPPELL

And now in Robert Morgan's poetry a whole landscape begins to come together. There was always landscape present, of course, but it was there as a generalized setting we mostly took for granted, a natural scenery through which each poem went hunting separately, each with one thing only on its mind. Homer thought of eyesight as more like a searchlight than like a camera; rays of intelligence went out of the head and captured those objects and processes to be fixed in the heart. This is pretty nearly how Morgan's earlier poetry worked: on this side was mind, on that side was an element of the natural world, and there was projected from the one to the other a metaphor of such clear exactitude that the forces on both sides seemed fixed forever, immutably in balance. *Vision as a thrown spear.*

These were brilliant poems. But the method of seeing seemed almost to preclude the possibility of a large and cohesive vision; the subjects seemed to hang separate in timeless space, each transfixed by its metaphor. Taken as a whole, these poems gave a picture of the universe analogous to the one contemporary science gives us, a gallery of discrete events, of isolate facts, every one of them true but every one autonomous. It has for a long time been the legacy of Imagism that its precision—which no honest poet is willing to forego—debilitates synthesis. *The Cantos*, *Paterson*, *The Maximus Poems*, *A*, are catalogues of stubborn particulars.

Now Morgan is changing all that. A broadly implicative background is taking shape, one which can accommodate perhaps an infinite set of separate metaphors and still assure cohesion. The outlines of this landscape are primitive; they consist of the enormous and imperious operations of nature, of a society of poor, narrow, and proudly embittered people, and of fundamentalist religion. This landscape is, in short, contemporary southern Appalachia, which Morgan sometimes widens out as a simile for earlier American history. I cannot guess how this intensely shaped background will strike other readers; they may find it willfully grotesque, or even artificial, but for me it is entirely naturalistic. I grew up in the mountains of western North Carolina and will testify on any soot-black Bible that Morgan's presentation is completely accurate. The culture of the mountains also informs my own conceptions of American history; surely this is how it was. The poem "Signs" tells how it was, how it is: "Swimmers on the sabbath / would be taken by suckholes / and whirlpools down."[2]

"Between a rock and a hard place"—a cliché I heard all my life in the mountains, and it describes sharply enough the bit of margin in which lives can take place. Between the exigencies of nature (the steep flinty fields, floods and hailstorms. the late and early frosts) and the imperatives of fundamentalism a man's life, a woman's, a family's, squeezes to its end. Human spirit is characterized by a sort of tormented recklessness, always on the blade-edge of violence. One of the local prison camps is Craggy; and the almost involuntary formula to be uttered when you see a handsome young girl walking along is, "There goes How-do-you-do-Judge-and-Good-morning-Craggy." … Not much leeway.

Is it true that if a man must diet on wormwood continually he accustoms himself and finally comes to prefer it? "Double Springs" is one of the best poems I have ever read, and the occasion Morgan recounts must have happened to him. That command in the bloodstream which ensures that the drinker will dip from the sweet poison southern spring rather than from the cold clean northern spring is not merely a perverse impulse; it is the fatalistic recognition of the fallen state of the soul. The drinker no longer has fear of God; it has been replaced by zero-at-the-bone terror of God. To drink the southern water, to carry that "ungodly taste" home, is to acquiesce wearily to the hard-shell Baptist vision of the soul's condition. The ironic knowledge that this one is the true water of life, "leaves and spiders / and aquatic mosses," is a secret to be held deep and silent in the breast during the long church service.[3]

The people are still there, live and kicking. I read in the Waynesville newspaper that So-and-so was arrested for drunk driving while riding a mule; in September you can go out to Hayesville and see the quilts and preserves and hear the music the tourists don't hear; in Hazelwood a local group has managed to get its recording of "The Fox Hunt" on the juke in two lonesome beer joints. But already the whole scene radiates *pastness*. The women still have prominent noses and chins and not the melted-off Barbie-doll faces that slide the TV screen. It's as if you are looking at a Victorian photograph album. Not picturesqueness, but the harsh capacity for leaning forward into present time and imposing features upon it. The *Mountain Lily* was never going to be a successful steamboat.

> There's a picture someone made
> of the sidewheeler stranded on mud
> near the bend at Arden,
> swaybacked and listing, stack
> tilted like a gun.[4]

It was stranded in history, in a photograph at the top of the mountain, before the boilers got well warmed. If it had been an Atlas rocket its fate would have been the same, or pretty nearly. And finally it is absorbed by that third element of the landscape, the white frame church with its rust-streaked tin roof:

> some of the planks in Horse Shoe Church
> once steamed through the gap
> into the stadium of mountains
> with the Sunday bell warning of departure.

(In Hamlet, North Carolina, the roof of the Methodist church is a ship's hull, keel forming the ridgepole.)

Works both ways, of course; present time in these poems hungers for the past as much as the past for the present. And the purpose is the same on both sides: to destroy. Just as the past is going to smash that Steamboat of Progress, present time mounts its counterattack.

With one blow of his light
hammer
the tongues-speaking auctioneer
will transform to rubble.[5]
But always and everywhere the final thrust belongs to the past.
It's the sight
of the still-wooded ridge that hurts.

But it is worth pointing out that here is no simple-minded identification of nature with the past, one of the staple strategies of all the newly ecological poets who clutter the magazines. Morgan underlines the persistence of nature into the present, and will view its operations with the understanding eye of the moonshine-runner's car mechanic. In "Sunken Treasure" the fallen timber is seen as a wrecked locomotive—a more familiar sight, perhaps:

Holes
have been blown in the boiler
by groundhogs and a fox sleeps
in the stack. Debris from the
crash scatters downhill gloved
in moss.[6]

Or, insouciant as Marianne Moore, Morgan will note that a spring lizard is "shiny as vinyl"[7] and that hornet larvae burning will "drop off whole postoffices of trout bait."[8] In pointing up these passages I intend simply to underscore the fact that Morgan is less conventional and less sentimental than one expects nowadays; he does not belong among the truckle ruck of poets who think that *pollution is a doggone shame!* His sensibilities are more flexible and more discriminating than that, and he has a larger feeling for time-scale.

Having said so much, may I now admit that I am disturbed by parts of *Trunk & Thicket*? I am thinking of such undeniably brilliant passages as this one:

With this accretion of language
I want to build up an atoll
you can come ashore on and
rest for awhile. Something that
might last long enough above
the surface for dirt to form[9]

and this one:

I want a powerful enjambment
like a stream carried on and over
its rocks, sometimes pausing
in deep pools and then darting
in a channel...[10]

Lines like these make me want to say to the poet, "Don't explain; explanation colors into apology. You can't establish intelligence and sympathy in any kind of reader by showing how you do what you do. Don't go to them; make them come to you." Here at the ash-end of the century, I begin to seek a poetry without manifesto; let the critics make their own precious mistakes.—But even as I object, I feel an empathic impulse, thinking, "But is it not cheating not to admit self-consciousness? If the poet cannot use his notion of poetry to hold the elements together, then probably he must use his ego, a method much worse."

When I pose a dilemma such as this, I begin to see more clearly the magnitude of Morgan's ambitions and the thousand stumbling-blocks.

It is obvious, though, that *Trunk & Thicket* is going to be one of the achievements of the decade. This "powerful enjambment" of people, place, and force already hints its final lineaments. The characters of the poem, their hard lines honed savage by trouble and weariness, cast shadow and more than shadow; their profiles discharge sheets of electricity. The uncle in his old Army truck, the father with his weighty toolbox, Jones obsessed with his bottom land: these men stand defining the natural weathers and the weathers of temperament which surround them, as magnets pull the gray iron filings into determined arabesques.—What will the women in this poem be like when we see them? Already for me they are hugely present, and energies begin to collect to those spaces in which they will appear.

An exhilarating prospect opens before us. It cannot have been often that readers could take a stance so early in a poet's career and, looking both backward and forward, see such fearsome accomplishment. To be truthful, I'm not certain how much of the responsibility that Morgan's poetry generates in the world of letters will be taken up. Every day I distrust more the responsiveness of readers to writers whose thrust is experiential. Every new issue of the magazines clouds the ear with systemic jargon, and the chatter of pretentious intellects more and more opaquely fends away from the nerve ends the touch of immediate language. But still I'm going to have confidence that Morgan will burst through. This poetry is too genuine, too urgent, not to be felt, admired, possessively clutched.

Because Morgan's aesthetic rests on a basis of faith in the necessity of poetry. I don't mean a mildly liberal confidence that poets will go on poetizing, but that poetry as an object will keep turning up among the other objects in the universe. This poetry may have the momentary accidental appearance of sparks shot off when stones knock stones, but there is nothing accidental in that kind of occurrence. These bits of matrix-flame are as inevitable as any other necessity, as inevitable as ice, as germination. Many of these poems refer to the secret heats in the cores of objects, and partake of the nature of that fire. But Morgan recognizes that it is not the poet's prerogative to break open the objects, to unveil those fires, but instead to stand away and to watch the effects within phenomena, shock wave on shock wave riding outward. Actually to pretend to enter the wood and water and stone is to reduce one's poetry to rhetoric. It is very nigh blasphemy, pretending to say the unknowable, but to cherish perception is a form of worship.

I am insisting upon Morgan's poetry as experiential and even as naturalistic because some of his contemporaries—not knowing nature and science as well as he does—have described his precisely observed lines as surrealist. They are not; Morgan is not licentious. Simone Weil spoke of surrealism in this way: "Men have always been intoxicated by licence, which is why, throughout history, towns have been sacked. But there has not always been a literary equivalent for the sacking of towns. Surrealism is such an equivalent."[11]

Another such equivalent is the fashionable con game in which the poet claims that he has actually entered into the anima of his subject and is speaking the language of quartz, oak, starlight, or whatever. Making this claim he enters into nothing except a self-indulgent fog, an autocracy of merely verbal impulse.

Robert Morgan resists this easiness; he observes and compares. I have no notion of what his writing habits actually are, but when I imagine him in the act of composition I see him in a real workshop, surrounded by unvisualable tools of different sorts, turning over lists of measurements and analogues, and always comparing what he finds there to three or four enormous formulas (to me unreadable) written out on a curtained-off blackboard. And all this labor is characterized by an intense patience and a fever for accuracy. Like Faraday, like von Helmholtz, like Dirac…

Notes

1. "A Prospect Newly Necessary" first appeared in *The Small Farm 3* (Spring 1976): pp. 49–53. The essay quotes and comments on several poems by Morgan published in the same issue of *The Small Farm*. For this collection, the editors have added the following endnotes, which locate the poems in the books where they later appeared.
2. From "Signs," in *Land Diving*, p. 26.
3. From "Double Springs," in *Land Diving*, p. 5.
4. This and the following indented quotation are from "Real and Ethereal," in *Groundwork*, p. 13.
5. This and the next indented quotation are from "Surveying," in *Land Diving*, p. 17.
6. From "Sunken Treasure," in *The Small Farm* 3 (Spring 1976), p. 10. The poem remains uncollected.
7. From "Mountain Alligator," in *The Small Farm* 3 (Spring 1976), p. 9. This poem also remains uncollected.
8. From "Burning the Hornet's Nest," in *Groundwork*, p. 41.
9. From the excerpt of "Trunk & Thicket" appearing in *The Small Farm* 3 (Spring 1976), pp. 27–30. These lines were omitted from the poem before its collection in the 1978 book of the same title.
10. From "Trunk & Thicket," in *Trunk & Thicket*, p. 19. There the passage is revised and begins, "See the powerful enjambment…."
11. From Richard Rees' translation of Weil's essay "The Responsibility of Writers," in *On Science, Necessity, and the Love of God*. London: Oxford University Press, 1968 (p. 167).

Robert Morgan's Pelagian Georgics

Twelve Essays[1]

WILLIAM HARMON

1

Let us have a legend:

Z = *Zirconia Poems* Lillabulero Press 1969. 40 pp. $1.50 (paper).
R = *Red Owl* Norton 1972. 73 pp. $6.95. $1.95 (paper).
L = *Land Diving* Louisiana State University Press 1976. 70 pp. $9.95. $4.45 (paper).
T = *Trunk & Thicket* L'Epervier Press 1978. 43 pp. $3.75 (paper).
G = *Groundwork* Gnomon Press 1979. 56 pp. $8.50. $5.00 (paper).
B = *Bronze Age* Iron Mountain Press 1981. 25 pp. $12.50 (paper).

As any fan of maps will know, the legend alone speaks volumes, a continent: New Hampshire, New York, Louisiana, Colorado, Kentucky, Virginia, New England, Middle Atlantic, Gulf, Rocky Mountain, South: no two states the same. One large commercial house, one university press, several provincial publishers. The titles speak, too: out-of-the-way minerals that give names to even more out-of-the-way places; wild creatures; savage rituals one inch short of suicide; trunk of a tree, trunk in the attic; the notion of *ground* and *work*, each term an old solid noun and verb alike. In Greek, *ground* would be *geo-*, *work* would be *ergon* (both from one root, **werg-*). Together they make *geōrgos*, "farmer." All of Robert Morgan's poems are georgics.

The legend needs some supplementing, because not all of Morgan's poems have been collected in books. With a supplement, the legend would attest to much writing, scores of poems, some fairly long. Morgan (b. 1944) began young and has continued steadily.

And consistently. He seems to have been born with most of his materials and techniques, as shown in "High Country," the first poem in his first book:

> In the hills, dead springs, blue flame of sky.
> The horizon goes all the way around.
>
> When it comes the darkness sprouts from rocks and fills
> the valley with wine. Splinters of ice form in the sky,
> cold air stoking light.

A crystal trills at the bottom of a well
blasting tunnels upward.

It is the blue sun rising all night under the sea [*Z* 3].

It is all there already: poetry built up on a foundation of *data*, things given. They are georgic elements, sky and sea, light and night. Among them, no "I" or ego-persona interferes with the scene. (Later, Morgan will shift to an imperative mood in which both the first-person speaker and the implied second-person interlocutor are subdued; he could be talking to himself.) The first line is nine monosyllables, six of them stressed and long, and it is also the first sentence. There is a progress, from no verb in the first sentence, through a succession of increasingly vivid intransitive verbs ("goes," "comes," "sprouts"), to a sudden salvo of metaphors detonated by verbs mostly transitive ("fills," "stoking," "trills," "blasting"). Not until the last line does the poem put forth a linking verb, and then the assertive equation ("It is the blue sun") seems to have earned its clear voice so convincingly that "the blue sun rising all night under the sea" overwhelms a reader with a force that might as well be true, it is so beautiful.

Morgan shows in this early poem some other features that have lasted. He avoids regular rhyme and rhythm, but the result is not mere prose. As one looks and listens, subtle connections emerge. Certain words at ends of lines ("fills," "light") resonate to rhymes inside lines ("hills," "trills," "night"), "horizon" finds an echo in "rising," and internal repetition of one vowel-consonant pair threads through "Country" (in the title), "tunnels," "sun," and "under."

Here and in many other poems Morgan orchestrates such resonances on several frequencies at once, all scrupulously tuned and harmonized. He does not often explicitly allude to the work of others, but he seems, maybe subliminally, to re-inscribe the vocabulary of earlier poems. The first section of *The Waste Land*, for example, may donate something to our sense when we read Morgan's "In the hills," "dead," "spring," and even "sprouts." Robert Lowell's translation of a Rimbaud line ("The whole / valley bubbled with sunbeams like a beer-glass") may have been the inspiration of Morgan's vision of darkness that "fills / the valley with wine."[2] This sort of alcohol-landscape almost became a habit with Morgan, who resorted to it in two other poems in his first book: "valley in sherry" and "vodka air" (*Z* 15 and 18); but he got over it.

2

Toward the back of *Zirconia Poems* Morgan put some poems that I think must be earlier than "High Country." I say that because, while they show his customary virtues of clarity and originality of vision, they lapse into perfunctory verse expressing perfunctory feelings. This is "Awakening":

A stone is cracked open in the mountain pasture
and a thousand birds escape, imprisoned since the Ice Age.
Water strokes the silence of the air and falls
through valleys lined with fir.
The air above me sings a thousand miles.
I run along the icy streams and fall in darkness
where moments tick like dripping sleet above a campfire.
As far back as Wales
my family farmed the red clay hills of fear [*Z* 33].

There is a good deal to admire here, but a few things to lament. "The red clay hills of fear" is exactly the misalliance of concreteness and abstraction that Ezra Pound had justifiable fits over. "I run along the icy streams" makes clear, by contrast, the achievement of "High Country," which does without an "I." The first two lines move with unmechanized ease, but the iamb begins to encroach in the third line, and "The air above me sings a thousand miles" hums a Morse tip-off, "Not so, not so, not so." (It may also hum, "Gary Snyder, Gary Snyder, Gary Snyder.") Very quickly, Morgan was to abandon such determined iambic writing: good riddance.

"As far back as Wales" reminds one that "Morgan" is an ancient Welsh name. A Morgan in the Royal Welsh Fusiliers would probably have to be known by number, like the star-crossed 99 Davies in *Goodbye to All That*; and Dylan Thomas' celebrated creature "Organ" Morgan comes to mind.

3

In the eighteenth century, there was an Anglo-Welsh satirist named Macnamara Morgan (d. 1762) whose pseudonym was Pelagius Porcupinus. He evidently shared the traditional belief that the fifth-century heresiarch Pelagius, about whom almost nothing definite is known, was a Welshman named something like "Morgan," which means "by the sea" and can be turned into a credible Greco-Roman name meaning "by the sea," which is Pelagius.

Saint Augustine attacked Pelagianism, and it was condemned as a heresy in 416, when Pelagius may still have been alive. He may even have mended his ways. But his doctrines, concentrating on the denial of Original Sin, have continued as an unofficial article of faith among many who are, in other details, orthodox Christians. And in modern thought the dogma of Original Sin has migrated from theology into literary criticism, introduced there first, I believe, by T.E. Hulme just before the First World War. In his bitchy but simpleminded way, Hulme distinguished between "the two views": "One, that man is intrinsically good, spoilt by circumstance; and the other that he is intrinsically limited, but disciplined by order and tradition to something fairly decent. To the one party man's nature is like a well, to the other like a bucket. The view which regards man as a well, a reservoir full of possibilities, I call romantic; the one which regards him as a very finite and fixed creature, I call the classical.... One may note here that the Church has always taken the classical view since the defeat of the Pelagian heresy and the adoption of the sane classical dogma of original sin."[3] (It is easy to see Hulme's connection with Irving Babbitt, Eliot, Pound, Wyndham Lewis, Auden, and Winters.)

In 1949, Randall Jarrell called William Carlos Williams "as Pelagian as an obstetrician should be: as he points to the poor red thing mewling behind plate glass he says with professional, observant disbelief: 'You mean you think *that's* full of Original Sin?'" A few years later, with the aptly breezy tone of a man throwing open a window in exasperation, crying for fresh air, and dumping out a fair number of babies with a great number of baths, Karl Shapiro, pondering the "suicides, alcoholics, and mental cases" among modern poets, judged, "The textbook explanation will give you an equation of poet-versus-society, poet-in-the-industrial-world, poet-and-Original-Sin, or some such thing. I do not agree...." That was in "The Critic in Spite of Himself," and thousands cheered (well: *dozens*). But it was not too long before Shapiro was practicing what he had preached against so potently. He said that Pound, Eliot, Yeats, and Stevens, as different as their opinions of religion seem to be, all "observe one or another version of the central religious doctrine of Original Sin. It is at this point that Modern Poetry differentiates itself from 'Romantic' poetry, whether by Whitman, Blake, Lawrence, or Williams."[4]

The subtitle of T.S. Eliot's *After Strange Gods* is *A Primer of Modern Heresy*, which suggests that Eliot is nominating himself for an office he had already tried out in *The Waste Land*, that of a contemporary Augustine. (James Augustine Aloysius Joyce, who admired Eliot's poem "The Hippopotamus," made a note, "Eliot: Bishop of Hippo.") It seems that *the* modern heresy that Eliot is anxious to condemn is Pelagianism, traces of which he finds in Lawrence, Pound, and several others. Better than Hulme, Eliot clarifies the importance of a religious doctrine for literary art. One's acceptance or rejection of original sin will directly determine one's notion of tragedy, character, destiny, history, and language. An extreme case of acceptance of original sin (and Eliot was such a one, even before his public profession of faith) will produce an artist nearly asphyxiated by his sense of the past adding burden after burden to his back and at the same time foreclosing his chances of redemption. At the other pole, rejection of original sin (and Whitman is such a one) produces an artist with almost no sense of evil at all and consequently, it may seem, no sense, period. Without some sense of evil—what Pound came to call "the nature of error"—a poet will be motivated only by a defective notion of cause and effect, beginning and end, what we deserve and what we get. When one's sense of evil is lost, so is all chance of tragedy and comedy of the deepest and most moving sort.

We may see Eliot and Joyce as Augustinian artists whose works are complex and often obscure but, in formal and technical senses, clear and finished. In Yeats—who asked, "What theme had Homer but original sin?"—we may make out another unofficial Augustinian. But in Lawrence, Pound, and Williams, the clarity and finish are lacking, however heroic the energy.

According to the entry on Pelagius in the *Oxford Dictionary of National Biography*, "attempts to interpret his name as a Hellenization of the Welsh 'Morgan' or the Irish 'Muirchu' represent philological wishful thinking." Although Pelagius may not have been named Morgan, and Robert Morgan may not be connected to Pelagianism except in general tendency, I feel justified in calling his poems "Pelagian georgics" because of their refusal of the easy equations between grief and doom. He never says "I told you so"; instead, subjecting language to an impassioned microscopy, he converts "need" back into "eden"—

> The sun never sets on this brief empire
>
> of creation compressed so small
> every molecule's candescent and all
> seasons rub hot like brushes
> of a generator dusting and cutting
> lines of force. Where
>
> the magnetic fountain rears
> I crowd my exhilarations
> into a camera flash. Shunned
> by the long deliberate year
> I make these few midnights solar
>
> and strike into the long night of need
> a rank garden, an eden ["Midnight Sun," *L* 69].

On the next page, in a poem called "Paradise's Fool," he embraces, espouses, and proclaims the Pelagian folly of bestowing a prelapsarian splendor on the maligned fruit:

In the appletree abloom at the field's
edge and the hummingbird's
nest of moss and plantdown,

in the canticles of the star maiden
and the subtle
aesthetics of failure,

the severalty of tidelands, duff
of fencerows, word amulets, stench of traffic
in the electron, I

am paradise's fool [*L* 70].

Audible here, I think, in the harmonies of "appletree" and "hummingbird," is the presence of another Welsh-connected voice, the Gerard Manley Hopkins who paid attention and devotion to the Scotist details of kingfisher and dragonfly. Since Hopkins was a loyal Jesuit, it would be far-fetched to identify his thought absolutely with that of either Pelagius or Duns Scotus; but all of them are British, with a British habit of concentration on minute particulars. In Hopkins' verse, this attention to words' inscape demands an unprecedented reliance on the Welsh device of compound alliteration called *cynghanedd*, which radiates from the sonnet I have mentioned already:

As kingfishers catch fire, dragonflies draw flame....[5]

The closing lines of Morgan's "Paradise's Fool" [also the last words of *Land Diving*] continue his customary play on "spring" (season, water, device, motive, leap, origin, resilience) and provide, in "surview nor sweet veld," a rare modern instance of *cynghanedd*

Lo, worlds without beginning in
the spring's contact lens,
the haunted well and camphorwood.

Neither in surview nor sweet veld
do I escape the terror,
the presence of the comforter [*L* 70].

4

A poet writing a poem will not have his mind on Duns Scotus or Pelagius, or Appalachian variations on the American character, or Hans-Georg Gadamer's revaluation of Heidegger's "equiprimordiality" (*Gleichursprünglichkeit*). A good poet in the act of writing a real poem is somebody worried about where the next word is coming from. The next word comes from a lexicon tipped over on its side and opened to the magnetic field of acoustic connections that matter almost as much as semantic connections. A *really* good poet possessed and absorbed by his work is somebody worried to death about where his next phoneme is coming from. Sameness or likeness of sound is the Virgil in this realm. Having said "upon" in the first line of "The Raven," Poe puts "pondered" in the second; in each line, the second stress is on the syllable *pon*. Having said "disobedience" in the first line of *Paradise Lost*, Milton puts "forbidden" in the second, so that each line contains a stressed syllable built on *b* and *d*, the unvoiced articulation of the same sounds found nasalized in "man," a bilabial followed by an apico-alveolar.

With nothing more than rudimentary sophistication, these potentials are harnessed and regulated. Regular rhyme tends to make connections between ideas that are not connected; the primary relation of rhyme to reason (to tip my hat towards W.K. Wimsatt's profound essay) is difference. "Hire" and "fire" rhyme but mean opposite actions. "King" and "thing" rhyme but belong at opposite ends of an axis; this rhyme in the first and eighth lines of "The Windhover" is one source of its dramatic power. On the other side of the syllable, alliteration tends to connect ideas that are already connected, words from the same page of the dictionary. Regular alliteration—as in virtually every poem in Old English and all of its counterparts among the Germanic languages—becomes insistent and monotonous. The medieval Welsh device of *cynghanedd gytsain* (ably described in Joseph P. Clancy's *Medieval Welsh Lyrics*) complicates and enriches the alliteration so that monotony surrenders to surprise. English adaptations of these patterns appear in isolated spots in poetry before Hopkins, as at the end of Wordsworth's "England 1802," where the poet says to Milton, "And yet thy heart / The lowliest duties on herself did lay."[6] But it was Hopkins, in just about every poem, who employed the device with both regularity and ease. There are many patterns and permutations involving two or three consonants or consonant clusters. Morgan's "surview" and "sweet veld" represent the simplest combination; his line-end connection of "terror" and "comforter" is more complex.

5

De minimis non curat lex: the law is not concerned with trifles. You will not be arrested for driving 35.001 miles per hour in a zone marked "35 MPH." The law glows with grace periods and benefits of the doubt. But great poetry is concerned with trifles and minute particulars; there are no generous etceteras, grace periods, benefits of doubt. Great poetry *curat de minimis* and *de maximis*, anything extreme and superlative. Our ears wake up when a preamble promises information about *first* disobedience, *last* duchess, *cruellest* month, *supreme* fiction. Caring insistently about superlatives and particulars, Robert Morgan has produced an ample corpus that may soon need a glossary of terms peculiar to Appalachian folklore, customs, material culture, and speech.

Throughout his poetry there runs a stream of the rather disgusting things that no attentive poet can ignore. A Morgan concordance is going to reveal many entries under "scab," say, and he devotes a good deal of description to the sick, deformed, and grotesque. (A handy guide to some terms and customs is Horace Kephart's *Our Southern Highlanders*, which I regard as a sorry and patronizing piece of work, though I admit it tells things that cannot be found elsewhere.) Morgan's narrative or descriptive poems often involve horror and the supernatural ("Mountain Bride" and "The Flying Snake" are especially fine—*G* 8–11); by the year 2000, folklorists will have to depend on writings such as Morgan's for information about practices and tales now nearly perished. He seems to feel a responsibility for preserving things in the attic trunk of his poetry, but in a poem like "Death Crown" he is a much nobler preserver than any mere antiquarian:

> In the old days back when
> one especially worthy lay dying
> for months, they
> say the feathers in the pillow would
> knit themselves into a crown
> that those attending felt in perfect
> fit around the honored head.

The feather band they took to be
certain sign of another crown,
the saints and elders of the church,
the Deep Water Baptists said.
I've seen one unwrapped from its
cloth in the attic, the down
woven perfect and tight for
over a century, shiny but
soft and light almost as light [*G* 19].

Although I am skeptical about expressive and imitative forms, I have to admit that the articulation of these lines shows a subtlety, delicacy, and strength that match those of the "death crown" itself. Poems of this sort can skid off the straight and narrow path into any number of gullies and ditches—cuteness, corniness, theology. But Morgan maneuvers the thing right down the middle, so that the play on two senses of "light," adjective and noun, added to the vernacular superlative ("light as light can be") ends the poem perfectly. The pace and tone are both exactly right, and the patterns of rhymes throughout the poem nudge it into shapeliness without ever stretching or pinching its fabric. (Morgan's art here resembles William Stafford's in some respects, but Morgan impresses me as a much more substantial and less sentimental poet.) After several readings, one sees more and more of the carpentry, but it is nowhere obtrusive. Each of the first four lines contains one word from the "days-lay-they-say" group; the last word of the first sentence rhymes with the last word of the second ("head" and "said"); the repeated "crown" rhymes with "down"; and the repeated "light" in the last line rhymes with "tight" two lines above, but the "tight" is set back from the end of the line, so that the rhyme does not pounce. "Death Crown" is Morgan's best short poem.

Morgan's best long poem is "Mockingbird" (*T* 35–43: about 350 roughly decasyllabic lines). It is his chief entry in the Sweepstakes of the Signifying Bird, which includes "Ode to a Nightingale," "The Raven," "The Windhover," "The Darkling Thrush," "Leda and the Swan," "Thirteen Ways of Looking at a Blackbird," Williams' versicle with white chickens, and "Burnt Norton." In the stratosphere of abstraction, these poems seem to ask, "What does the world say?" The answers range all the way from "Nevermore" to "Quick now here now always," with stops in between for uncertainty, ambiguity, and more questions. It seems common for the poet, in his flight of song, to become one with the bird that flies or sings; this union works well with the mimetic mockingbird, already something of an artist a step or two away from unmediated spontaneity. Mockingbirds do repeat what they hear. Morgan's "Mockingbird" begins, as "High Country" does, by omitting finite verbs in independent clauses, with the effect of subduing the time-sense in the overture:

While the bee sleeps in the southern night
and weeds weigh under dowries of dew,
above the distant honky tonk of falls in
the July dark, before the katydids, when
the only frost is lunar, a voice that
raises the hackles of mountains and chills
the barometric spine, that radios through
many channels in the crab orchard and from
maples above the road. What madrigalist
watering the night with polyphony [*T* 35].

Here Morgan seems to be continuing a motif already adumbrated in a slightly earlier poem, "Whippoorwill":

> The dead call at sundown from their places
> on the mountain and down by the old mill.
> ....
> The whippoorwill interprets the news
> from the dead, the unborn [*R* 31].

But the mockingbird has the aesthetic advantage of being peculiarly American. It is Whitman's best bird. Probably the oldest popular song still sung at all in this country is Septimus Winner's "Listen to the Mockingbird," which dates from before the Civil War. Morgan's sense of a bird's voicing of a present so concentrated that it collapses inward, black-hole-wise, to deliver the dead and the unborn from past and future, recalls Keats's "The voice I hear this passing night was heard / In ancient days," here and now issuing from *Mimus polyglottos*. What does the bird say?

> I will be what I will be. It is the
> dead speaking now from every petal
> of the compass, every atom in
> the dark traffic. The voice ascends at the
> wavelength of mountains out of swamp musk
> into the crypt of sky, builds loglog concision
> in the night of Babylonian weight,
> a table whose bulbed legs whirl gyroscopically
> vertical, with grain distinct as the
> thumbprint of a file or the ingots of
> a snake's belly. Say the statute of
> limitations has run out on original
> sin, take quiddity of tumbleweed, the
> medicine river, take fernbrakes and a
> mouse gnawing the atlantic cable to
> swill electrons, take rawhide and Cherokees,
> the county seat and demonology,
> take the stream going underground in late
> summer leaving puddles of fry thickening
> among the white rocks [*T* 40–41].

To ask, "What does the bird say?" is impudent, I suppose. Morgan's answer here implies a different wording of the question: "What does the bird's song sound like it is saying?" It is fanciful but not, I think, far-fetched to say that Morgan has begun here by recording some of the peculiar effects of a bird's singing, and the fidelity of the transcription is brilliant. If you listen to a bobolink or whippoorwill, say, you will not hear "bob-o-link" or "whip-poor-will." Those are conventions of transcription faithful less to acoustic actuality than to a stubborn insistence on "hearing" personal names in the language of animals. (As Wilhelm Wundt observed many decades ago, German birds say "David" and "Jakob"—in German, of course.) Here Morgan has arranged a persuasive spillway of words that, if you really listen and pay attention, do sound like a mockingbird. "I will be what I will be" records the repetition and front vowels, grouped around the contrasting moment of "what." The vowels of "I," "will," and "be" dominate the passage. The aptly "liquid" consonants *l* and *r* appear in virtually every line, most strikingly in "a table whose bulbed legs whirl gyroscopically / vertical." It is clear, furthermore, that the bird's vocabulary contains an unusual number of words that repeat some single consonant (a phenomenon that Indo-European languages tend to discourage and even to eliminate gradually by dissimilation—old "apricock" becomes "apricot" by a process of avoiding duplication). To my ear, a sort of articulatory artery runs through "dead," "loglog," "Babylonian," "bulbed," "distinct," "statute," and other words that contain a repeated consonant. If you listen with all your ears, mockingbirds say "quiddity" and "Cherokee" in exponential tapestries of combination. (Philosophically, a good Pelagian-Scotist would stress the "hæcceity of tumbleweed" and not the "quiddity." But mockingbirds do not say "hæcceity"; I can hardly pronounce it myself.)

Morgan's "loglog" impresses me as the most wonderful single moment in "Mockingbird." It is, first of all, onomatopoeia. (I conjecture that any salient reduplication in an Indo-European language departs from the norm of dissimilation and does so, moreover, in two opposite directions: downward to pure plural sounds that mimic those in nature and upward to pure singular concepts that distinguish unique individuals in culture. Onomatopoeia and special names flank the middle zone of significant language. Inventions like "Xerxes" and "Miami" will probably be either racket or a proper noun but not anything between.) "Loglog," second of all, means "log-log," the fitting together of two logs in building, in which Morgan aptly finds "concision." Third, "loglog" is a word from the obsolescent lexicon of slide-rule nomenclature and slang. Cheap pocket calculators have now replaced the slide-rule completely. The great firm of Keuffel and Esser, which made the celebrated "K & E" slide-rules, produces them no more. The slide-rule and its panoply of nicknames ("slipstick") and holsters and horror stories are gone forever into the limbo of folklore and collectibles. "Log log" refers to a scale on a slide-rule that yields, in effect, logarithms' logarithms, with concision.

Morgan and his "loglog concision" belong among a fair-sized company of recent American writers—Mailer, Ammons, Starbuck, Pynchon, McPhee, Snyder, the late Forrest Read, and others—who have some experience in mathematics, science, and engineering. Poe may be the progenitor of this dynasty, since he brought into literature, for better or worse, a vocabulary like those of geographers, mathematicians, and physicians. Pynchon—himself a sort of logos-logarithm of Poe, Hawthorne, and Melville—has gone most deeply into the mysteries of calculus, electronics, and rocketry. (Some engineers are indeed the hard-headed technocrats of the caricatures, but most that I know have a mystical streak a kilometer wide.) Morgan's "loglog" reaches back to "compass" (and "compass rose" is a cartographer's term) and forward to his later poem "Compass" (*L* 57). We can take his "wavelength of mountains" as a pretty, sinusoidal picture. One of these days, an annotator will compute that a mockingbird song of about 15 kHz will have a wavelength of about 20,000 meters, so that Morgan's "wavelength of mountains" is an accurate figure as well as a nice one. (My calculation may be off by one or two orders of magnitude; no matter.)

Morgan's "Mockingbird" is one of the most remarkable poems in American literature. It is a graph of the most scrupulous fidelity. Since it is utterly lifelike, its moral burden, validated by honesty, is easy to accept. The bird is Pelagian when it comes to original sin and Scotist when it comes to quiddity. The closing episode of the song repeats the *cynghanedd* that I associate with an antique "Welshness" of empirical vision:

> Reject the dryhides and
> take the holy dance. Take the land beyond
> the fall-line, beyond the corduroy road
> and depot, and ford the creek lengthwise to

get into town. Offer reticence and disapprobation,
follow no trade, and heading for deep cover
come to an opening in the canopy
where light shines from obscure places. Hide
behind a waterfall in congregation
with mist and rock. Take the justified
margin of cornfields. Inaugurate by
leaving, ordained by anonymity [*T* 42–43].

6

Morgan's is clearly a poetry that takes certain chances and runs certain risks. (I speak figuratively and relatively; nobody ever suffered a hernia while writing a poem.)

Even with his clarity of sight and delicacy of verbal engineering, he now and then lapses from his proper georgic altitude and goes to moralizing, sermonizing, and editorializing in a crackerbarrel style that has disfigured American literature since October 1492. James Thurber skewered this species of "backwoods Voltaire" in his story "A Friend of the Earth," which is humorous but not entirely light-hearted. Thurber's unbearable Zeph Leggin, who calls himself "a man of philosophy and easygoing nature," is stupid, lazy, and mean. He plays the rustic game of staying one-up on everybody by insisting on seeming two-down, or more. The Zephs of the world will say, "I never enjoyed the advantages of wealth, leisure, and education like you city fellers did, and I've had to work all my life, and I don't talk too good..." and they infiltrate even a canon as chaste as Morgan's with two or three poems like "Privilege":

The overly advantaged
remind me of the young birch
that planted by a seed floating
to rest on a stump
takes root in the damp

composting rings and sprouts
prodigious, drinking
even in dry weather from
its spongy mesa....

The problem manifests when
the privileging pedestal

erodes from its grasp
and the young birch,
stranded three feet out of dirt,
must trust its full weight to
slender roots exposed above soil [*L* 65].

To which I say, "Nuts." One or two generations back, on both sides, my people were mountaineers, like Morgan's. There's a place called Harmon's Den in the North Carolina mountains. One of the celebrated storytellers of the "Jack Tales" was named Council Harmon. Neither of my parents got beyond the eighth grade (there was no ninth); between them, they had twenty-three siblings. Et cetera. Just let me say that I do not think that anybody will be justified in complaining that Morgan tends, once every two or three years, to protest too little about the dismal poverty and absence of privilege in his background. I never had nothing neither, and I cannot see that it makes the least bit of difference. (Hell, Morgan wasn't even born until 1944. He should have been around in the 1930s, as I was, when things were *really* tough. You see what I mean.)

With the family farm eroded by New Deal boondoggles and now rebuilt as a slick agro-business enterprise all regulated and subsidized, it seems likely that georgic poems such as Morgan's may be the last dwelling place of oldtime agriculture and country life in general. One cannot help noticing the promotion of bucolic ideals by entertainers like Bob Dylan, Kris Kristofferson, and the Taylor kids, none of whom has very much true bucolic in his or her background. I think I smell—not a rat, but at least a sort of preppie pseudo-rural note of falseness in so many magazines and presses with names that all sound like *Blacksmith's Armpit*. That is probably all right. Calling a magazine *Harness Gall* when you don't know a harness gall from a saddle oxford. It's probably just my mountain mean streak coming when, with a dollar to spend on a poetry magazine, I reject *Watering Trough* in favor of *Mildewed Dildo*. (I think I made up all these examples; you know what I mean.)

7

I hope I have shown that Morgan's best poetry puts together a number of elements: a consistent freshness of vision, a high level of technical skill, a pervasive generosity of attitude and gesture (which I have called his unofficial Pelagianism), an engineer's sophistication, and much intelligence.

A poet with a high I.Q. is like a dog with a million dollars, the Zeph Leggin in me says. Book-learning is no different from anything else a poet finds to use. Some have gotten by with no particular intelligence, and others have taken pains to hide theirs, as Frost often did. There are few people more obnoxious than a sharecropper who reads Iamblichus by the light of a kerosene lantern. Frost, Faulkner, and Gary Snyder all have an extraordinary degree of intelligence and learning, and so do many other American writers, but almost all of them work like dogs to hide their lights. Sometimes I think that Charles Bukowski is the most American poet. The only horses he seems to know or care much about are those that wear numbers and carry wee men around a track.

Intellect is just one more thing for a writer to make his peace with. Morgan—unlike the dog who used his million for bedding or for breakfast—has a very fine intellect indeed and uses it intelligently almost all the time.

8

If you have never seen a Southern scholar, poet, politician, lawyer, surgeon, or industrialist trying to out-Mortimer-Snerd Mortimer Snerd, you've missed something. There are Oxford graduates (Oxford, *England*) in the South who spend three hours in the bathroom every morning to achieve the perfect effect of utter neglect, dishevelment; diamonds in the rough, salt of the earth. They send away to Manhattan for tape-recorded correspondence courses in Speech, Rustic (Lesson One: Droppin Yore G's). Faulkner's Snopes trilogy gives, in Lawyer Stevens (Harvard, Heidelberg), a transparently phony instance of all this. Styron's *Set This House on Fire* gives a more accurate picture of the sinister expatriate playboy who begins a sentence, "I hear tell...."

Having put on most of these acts myself, I think I can testify about why we do it. It keeps people out of your hair. Being Oscar Wilde was hard even for Oscar Wilde. He did it superlatively—never better than when he went to Leadville, Colorado, and kept his cool and distinguished himself as a gentleman and an aesthete among loutish miners. But being Oscar Wilde is also asking for trouble, so that it is much more expedient to put on the mask of Abner Yokum, Dogpatch, U.S. of A.

It is surprising, in a way, that Morgan's poems have not attracted more critical attention. (Being published by Norton is not exactly a case of neglect, but not much happened after *Red Owl* appeared.) It may be that the rustic manners of the poems achieve the purpose of keeping people out of their hair. Morgan has been interviewed and photographed, and his work has received some rather perfunctory critical notice, but none of this attention is commensurate with the great distinction of the poetry.

I have read three critical essays on Morgan's work. One of them begins, "This past week I have been watching and sometimes swimming in the surf on the south shore of Oahu between Pokai Bay and Maili Point."[7] Thus it begins and thus, for me, it ends. I have better things to do with my time.

Another begins, "Sir Kenneth Clark's book on *The Romantic Rebellion* notes that Delacroix was entranced with horses' manes and continually used them in his canvases as a kind of artistic doodle, a symbol of the painter's unbridled fantasy"—here we get the first of forty-six footnotes. Between footnotes 39 and 40 this text says, "Through telling scientific or technical metaphor, Morgan reaffirms man's place in the universe."[8] Gad!—to adapt what Carlyle said about Margaret Fuller's decision to accept the physical world—he'd better.

When something like that gets me down—and having somebody tell me about a reaffirmation of man's place in the universe gets me really down—I turn to some sentences in "The Sanction of the Illative Sense" near the beginning of Chapter Nine of *An Essay in Aid of a Grammar of Assent* by John Henry Newman, and I recommend them to you:

> We are in a world of facts, and we use them; for there is nothing else to use. We do not quarrel with them, but we take them as they are, and avail ourselves of what they can do for us.... I am what I am or I am nothing. I cannot think, reflect, or judge about my being, without starting from the very point which I aim at concluding. My ideas are all assumptions, and I am ever moving in a circle. I cannot avoid being sufficient for myself, for I cannot make myself anything else, and to change me is to destroy me. If I do not use myself, I have no other self to use.

The Church that made the man who wrote that a cardinal cannot be all bad.

9

The third essay on Morgan that I have read was written by his teacher and friend, Fred Chappell. Chappell comes from high country himself, and, sure enough, he indulges himself in Zeph's Snerdisms and Dogpatchese now and then. But those camouflage tarpaulins cannot hide the difference between Chappell's decency and intelligence and the vastly inferior worth of the Aloha-Delacroix commandos whose names, with exquisite diplomacy, I withheld above. Chappell says, "It has for a long time been the legacy of Imagism that its precision—which no honest poet is willing to forego—debilitates synthesis." I cannot quite see how that works. From the rocking chair on my porch, it looks as though there was no such thing as Imagism; if there were, it demonstrated no more genuine precision than any other school; if it did, plenty of honest poets would probably forgo it and spell the word right while doing so; if they would not, that still would not matter as far as the debilitation of synthesis goes. He says, "*The Cantos, Paterson, The Maximus Poems, A*, are catalogues of stubborn particulars." They are indeed; they also are not. He goes on, "Now Morgan is changing all that. A broadly implicative background is taking shape, one which can accomodate [sic] perhaps an infinite set of separate metaphors and still assure cohesion." Now we're getting somewhere, even if we don't want the Yankees and lowland millionaires and city-slickers to know that we can spell "accommodate."[9]

Chappell has done something, and he does some good. He calipered up a line from Morgan's *Trunk & Thicket*, then in progress—"I want a powerful enjambment / like a stream"—and put his finger plumb on the weakness, virtually unavoidable when a poet speaks in his own voice about what he wants in poetry. When *Trunk & Thicket* appeared, Morgan had made a small but decisive revision—now "See the powerful enjambment"—that rinsed off the flaw and left the rest of the passage intact. So we owe Chappell a debt, and I should not kid his prose so much. Besides, "forego" is an acceptable variant, and the misspelling of "accommodate" is probably not Chappell's fault.

10

In a forthcoming book, Alan Williamson mentions the recent blossoming of nicknames on title pages.

We never hear of Benjamin Jonson or Walter Whitman, but just about everybody else except Ben and Walt up to 1950 seems to stick to a full name or a pseudonym. But now the Contents and Contributors pages of *Harness Gall* and *Mildewed Dildo* read like the rosters of athletic teams and rock groups: Jack, Dave, Pete, Peggy, Skip, Flip, Chip.

Southern businessmen (including politicians) for generations have played a modest shell game with identity, and there gets to be some pretty active jockeying for position on ballots as the Johns and Jameses fade and the Jacks and Skeeters emerge. It's a dodge that everybody sees through; I wonder if the 1980 election was not just a way for the American people to say they preferred a man calling himself Ronald to one calling himself Jimmy.

Often, in the South at least, a child is christened with what seems to be a nickname. My mother's mother's name was Sallie, and my daughter is Sally. Ammons' name is Archie, but he sticks to initials on his title pages. Morgan is called Bob, but he is Robert Morgan to the world at large.

I think I prefer that kind of solemn approach: two initials and a last name, or a full first name and a last name. At anything else—pseudonyms, nicknames, three names, two names with an initial before or between, hyphenated names—I bridle.

Then what about X.J. Kennedy? He did not want to be another Joe or Joseph Kennedy, understandably. But Morgan stuck it out patiently while one of North Carolina's senators was named Robert Morgan. He was defeated in 1980, and the real Robert Morgan endures.

11

How can it be that two of the best American poets—possibly even *the* two best—are North Carolinians now teaching at Cornell? Maybe it says more for Cornell than for North Carolina, but it is a fact that Morgan comes from the remote mountains and Ammons from the rather washed-out low country much farther east. North Carolina is 550 miles wide, with a varied terrain and population, so that it may be only an accident that Morgan and Ammons—and Chappell and Jonathan Williams and Thomas Wolfe and Howard Cosell and poor old Andrew Johnson—happened to be born in the same state.

The late Guy Owen used to circulate questionnaires and attend symposia that had to do with the Problem of the Southern Writer and so forth. He was a North Carolinian distinguished as a novelist and as an editor of the *Southern Poetry Review*. He thought that terrain, population, vocabulary, and folklore made a difference. He was fond of sayings like "awkward as a hog upstairs" and "grinning like a mule eating briars." I used to respond to his questionnaires by saying that Southerners talk so funny they have to write things down if they want to be understood.

I was just being difficult, of course. Probably that peevish mountain blood. My father was a traveling salesman and my mother was a farmer's daughter, and neither character type is given to telling the whole truth and nothing but. One talks too much, the other too little. Tall tales and ironies may be the inheritance of people who have been on the losing side for so long. Quite a few North Carolinians, from one viewpoint or another, were on the "wrong" side in the Revolution and the Civil War: Tories and Unionists. Given that tradition, you do not need external enemies. Taciturn and secretive, Stonewall Jackson told no one where he was going, and on May 3, 1863, was shot by his own men, who were North Carolinians. He died a week later. For many years, North Carolina ignored May 30 as a holiday but observed May 10 as Confederate Memorial Day, by God.

There used to be a sign in Concord, my hometown. "Jefferson Davis, President of the Confederacy, fleeing south after Lee's surrender, spent the night of April 14, 1865, in this house." The house was torn down not long ago, and a new sign was put up that got rid of all the defeatist talk. "Jefferson Davis, President of the Confederacy, spent the night of April 14, 1865, in a house near here."

Whenever Owen would talk about pickup trucks and grits, I would remind myself that he was a member of roughly the same generation as Reynolds Price, also a North Carolinian from a small town. But Price went to Oxford and drives a Mercedes and writes critical essays of matchless elegance and sophistication on *Samson Agonistes*, *The Wings of the Dove*, and Rembrandt's etchings, not to mention Price's celebrated novels.

I do not know, then, why two of the best poets alive today should both come from North Carolina and both teach at Cornell. But those are facts, and we are in a world of facts, and we use them, for there is nothing else to use.

It is also a fact that Morgan, Owen, and Price are Welsh names; I wonder if a sort of Welshness may not matter more than incidental Southernness. The Welsh, like the Walloons and the Wallachians, have a name that seems to mean "foreigners" (a root present also in "walnut"). It seems that about four-fifths of the tribal names in Europe mean "us"; and the other fifth mean "them." Being Welsh may mean nothing special, but it may mean being like the fifth-century Morgan-Pelagius who rejected orthodoxy and was himself condemned by Pope Zosimus. Being a poet in Wales may mean belonging to an alien species in an already alien genus. When Dylan Thomas wrote his ornate and obscure lines and even when he wrote ornate and pellucid lines like "Deep with the first dead lies London's daughter," he was asserting his claim to membership in an atavistic dynasty of artists who, centuries ago, perfected Europe's most complicated verse-forms and the most demanding curricula for poets. Something of this potent spirit sings in

Frank Lloyd Wright's architecture (Wright named his houses for the legendary Welsh bard Taliesin) and Robert Graves's *The White Goddess*, not to mention the public personalities of Thomas, Wright, and Graves. (Graves, like David Jones, is not a genuine Welshman; that means speaking the language and being a Methodist. But the spirit is there even if the chromosomes are not.)

12

Three of Robert Morgan's most interesting poems date from about 1978 and have not yet been collected in one of his own volumes. "Humus" (*Cornell Review* 6, Summer 1979) superficially resembles "Mockingbird" in that it is in roughly decasyllabic lines (about 220) in which a commanding voice from nature dictates a succession of emblematic diggings, as though in preparation for a garden as well as the turning over of a new leaf of self. This voice sounds like Morgan's Mockingbird's with overtones from Mahler's *Das Lied von der Erde*:

> Turn east against the earth's inertial
> spin, through waves of corialis,
> against the clockwise drag. Turn to the first
> rising of the voice from dusk, back to the diamonds
> pressed from breathing ferns...

Such earth tones are fine, rather like the opening of Frost's "Directive," but I miss the alertness and fun of the poet's acute ear that hears "county seat" and "Cherokee" in the birdsong. Another difference between "Humus" and "Mockingbird" is that the former alternates the voice of the earth with the poet's own editorials that point the moral a good deal too self-consciously. This idiom runs the risk of developing into Zeph's reverse oneupmanship, as though one yokel were to say to another from a slightly less barbaric backwoods place, "That's nothing. I had pellagra and rickets and scarlet fever and malaria all at the same time and no medicine but a corncob soaked in kerosene and turpentine and a daddy (also my half-brother) crazed with white lightning coming at me with a butcher knife four feet long and the double-clutching E-flat Pentecostal Apocalyptic preacher coming at me from the other side threatening to put a very literal interpretation on 'baptism of fire' etc." To which the other replies, "That's nothing." I don't know why Southerners do this kind of thing. Their discourse breaks down to 40 per cent understatement and irony, 40 per cent exaggeration, and 20 per cent sullen silence. One wishes that Fred Chappell could stay by Morgan and prevent him from giving in to the temptation to write like this:

> I go way back to some remote settlement
> in the cradle of mountains that embodies
> history. Not the loamy patches along
> the Poor Fork of Roasting Ear Creek,
> but higher, further back above the hollows,
> where autumn pays the dirt in scrip good
> only washed to the valleys. Beyond where
> tar cakes the feet of telephone poles,
> where exertion is for fun. You too would be
> attentive to weather up where lightning
> finds its resolutions.

That's nothing. A much more eloquent use of personal materials dignifies Morgan's great "Chant Royal" (*Poetry*, May 1978) in which the diabolically difficult verse-form works to validate and brace the poet's voice, compounding his complexity with its own. I do not know of any other poet in English who has used the chant royal for a serious poem, and even its employment in light verse (such as by Don Marquis) is extraordinarily rare. It is as though Morgan, suspected of shirking his duties and loafing in easy free-verse forms, were to respond by producing a marvelous poem in one of the most challenging stanzas ever devised. (He also writes now and then in a six-line stanza rhyming *abccba* that he seems to have invented; if it doesn't have a name, I suggest "morganelle.") Chant royal consists of five eleven-line stanzas rhyming *ababccddede* plus a five-line envoi rhyming *ddede*; the last line of each stanza and of the envoi is a refrain. Apart from that, no rhyme-word may be repeated. Morgan allows himself some looseness of rhythm and latitude of rhyme, but not much. All his rhymes are vowel-consonant combinations, which are harder to handle than simple vowels (as "tree" and "sea"). Here is the first stanza:

> Born in a notch of the high mountains where
> a spring ran from under the porch, on
> the second of April just one hundred years
> ago this month, my grandpa was a weak one
> to start with, premature, weighed a scant
> two pounds twelve ounces. So fragile the aunt
> who tended him that first night feared to move
> him except for feeding and the changing of
> diapers. He slept near the fire in a shoebox
> with one end cut out. Against the odds he would prove
> adequate for survival, withstanding all knocks.[10]

There follows a fascinating biography of the grandpa, who was made healthy by a doctor's prescribing tobacco ("Give him a chew"). The brief life takes the reader through some unfamiliar terminology, but it seems justified. We can figure out what "yarb grannies" are (Thoreau once said "yarb" for "herb"); "frampold" is exceedingly rare but turns out to have been used by Shakespeare (*The Merry Wives of Windsor*); "sanghunting," we know from elsewhere in Morgan's poetry, is ginseng hunting.

Given the ornate verse-form, the rather prosaic writing works with elegant poise. Given the austere story, the exotic vocabulary glows with harmony and balance. (*Bronze Age* includes a pun on the German *Morgenland*, which means "morning-land" or "Occident." It also features a fine poem called "Earache," which is in the rare form of a "terza rima sonnet" that, as far as I know, has been used only by Shelley in "Ode to the West Wind" and Frost in "Acquainted with the Night.") "Chant Royal" and "Mockingbird" are among Morgan's most distinguished achievements and, I think, high among the finest poems by any American in a long time. The "Chant" ends with an envoi of which the assertions, pride, and resolution seem perfectly justified:

> Guardian ghost, inhere herein. Before Jove
> may this music honor his example, improve
> my time as he invested his, and no less unorthodox
> discover significance in the bonds his fate wove
> adequate for survival, withstanding all knocks.

(One will note the similarity between this conclusion and that of "Mockingbird": "Inaugurate by / leaving, ordained by anonymity.")

At the end of "Midnight Sun" Morgan linked "need" and "eden" (*L* 69) in a gesture of considerable ingenuity, using anagram to rescue paradise from necessity. This kind of practice always seems to have a peculiarly mixed effect. On the one hand, we distrust language and know that writing and sound are connected as arbitrarily as sound and sense. On the other hand, we have a sense that the shapes of letters and the inane sounds of phonemes come from mysterious sources fenced and hidden by centuries of taboo. One would think that the Bible would have better things to do than make jokes out of the names of Isaac or Peter, but it does just that. Samuel Johnson and Thomas Wolfe are both on record with gripes about Shakespeare's incurable punning, but he does it every chance he gets. What is Brutus up to when he plays "Rome" backwards and says "Rome more"? Why should Julius Caesar, probably for Shakespeare the greatest non-divine man who ever lived, a military, political, and literary genius, die with a near-palindrome in his mouth? Et tu, Brute? Why have we left it to two Slavs—Jakobson and Nabokov—to notice the palindromes and anagrams in "The Raven" and "Ulalume"?

Not just anywhere in literary works but in the most intensely solemn spots, the words seem to blow up, their atoms fly apart and re-form as though they were the determinants of the discourse—they and not some mere idea. Our naïve trust is more in sounds than in letters, and we seem more at ease in granting the writer his acoustic play than in tolerating graphic effects. Babble is better than doodle. Anagrams in general and palindromes in particular must be the humblest, silliest, and puniest of literary devices. A censor in the head keeps reminding us that "bedroom" and "boredom," "marital" and "martial," "casual" and "causal," "destiny" and "density," say, just happen by accident to share the same letters. In many such cases—classically in "canoe" and "ocean"—the graphic identity has nothing to do with the sound and the sound nothing to do with the sense. Forget it.

And yet we watch Keats at play with the shapes of M in Mountain, V in Valley; Valéry puts "ample" and "palme" side by side; Pound makes a square out of ROMA and AMOR. And Morgan, at the climax of "Chant Royal," says, "Guardian ghost, inhere herein."

One thinks of "atone" and "at one," or of "accord," "a cord," and "a chord." "Inhere herein" is the touch that makes me admire Morgan most enthusiastically. At the very nucleus of his poem, the pressure causes an explosion of echo in the words, which seem to be invested with a life and symmetry of their own. He could have said something like Kipling's "Be with us yet," which has the virtue of being to the point. But with "Inhere herein" the poet seems to step back from the text and let the sounds and letters carry the meaning themselves.

Extremes do meet: poetry at its sublimest height comes back to writing at its humblest level. These extremes are necessarily rare, and no poet can sustain such intense concentration for long. No language will bear it, and no reader can take it with full strength for more than about fifteen words. Robert Morgan has written a breathtaking twelve-word anagram poem (published only in a festschrift for Jonathan Williams' fiftieth birthday in 1979) that I want to quote as a conclusion. Let it be a vade mecum:

Spore Prose
for the author of "Slow Owls"

Mountain Graveyard

stone notes
slate tales
sacred cedars
heart earth
asleep please
hated death[11]

Notes

1. "Robert Morgan's Pelagian Georgics: Twelve Essays" first appeared in *Parnassus 9* (Fall-Winter 1981): pp. 5–30.

Given the essay's (or essays') introductory "legend" and the parenthetical page references keyed to it, the addition of MLA-style documentation would be redundant. For this collection, the editors have only added the following endnotes to help interested readers pursue the quotations from other writers, when the author has left the exact sources unidentified.

2. The reference is to T. S. Eliot's poem *The Waste Land* (1922). "The Sleeper in the Valley," Robert Lowell's translation of Arthur Rimbaud's sonnet "Le dormeur du val," appeared in Lowell's book *Imitations* (1961).

3. From Hulme's essay "Romanticism and Classicism," in *Speculations: Essays on Humanism and the Philosophy of Art*, edited by Herbert Read, first published in 1924.

4. The quotation from Jarrell is from his introduction to William Carlos Williams's 1949 *Selected Poems*; Jarrell reprinted it in his book *Poetry and the Age* (1953). Karl Shapiro's essay "The Critic in Spite of Himself" appears in his book *In Defense of Ignorance* (1960), as does the source of the second quotation from Shapiro, "W. B. Yeats: Trial by Culture."

5. The quotation is the first line of an untitled sonnet by Hopkins.

6. The quotation is the conclusion of William Wordsworth's sonnet to John Milton. The poem usually appears with the title "London 1802."

7. The quotation is from J. B. Merod's essay "Robert Morgan's 'Wisdom-Lighted Islands,'" in *The Small Farm* 3 (March 1976): pp. 54–62.

8. From Louis M. Bourne's essay "On Metaphor and Its Use in the Poetry of Robert Morgan," in *The Small Farm* 3 (March 1976): pp. 63–79. The second quotation is on p. 74.

9. In the original publication of Chappell's essay "A Prospect Newly Necessary," the word often spelled *forgo* appears as *forego*, and the word *accommodate* appears with only one *m*. In republishing Chappell's essay here, the editors have retained the spelling *forego*, a variant recognized by authoritative dictionaries (including the *Oxford English Dictionary*), but have corrected the spelling of *accommodate*.

10. The essay quotes "Chant Royal" as it appeared in the May 1978 issue of *Poetry*. A slightly revised version was first collected in *At the Edge of the Orchard Country*, pp. 65–67.

11. A slightly different version, titled simply "Mountain Graveyard," was first collected in *Sigodlin*, p. 27.

Looking for Native Ground

Robert Morgan[1]

RITA SIMS QUILLEN

In a letter to the author, Cornell University Professor Robert Morgan discusses his life and writing, noting,

> Appalachia has been called an island of the past, and while that is not entirely true by any means, there is a parallel perhaps between our sense of awakening and the relish of new freedom the New Englanders felt in the 1830s to 50s. There is that emerging from the rapt gloom of fundamentalism into the wide natural daylight.

Robert Morgan emerges into that wide natural daylight on every page of his 1979 book, *Groundwork*. The book is a journey, moving from high up in the mountains themselves, as Morgan contemplates the natural boundaries that have defined his unique mountain community, to the valley below where the people live and work.

Like Jeff Daniel Marion, Morgan is a clear-eyed, meticulous observer of nature. He constantly seeks to understand how man fits into the scheme of things. The two men are equally attentive to detail and appreciative of natural mysteries. But there is also a marked difference in perspective. Whereas Marion sees man's connection with seasons and the rituals of life and growth, decay and death as positive, even as an anodyne for the pain that is the price of vision, Morgan seems to view nature in a more adversarial role. For him, the value lies in the struggle, as two powerful forces attempt peaceful co-existence. Morgan has written, "I believe in the anarchic and creative soil, and stick to the fringes of society, out where it comes into collision with nature, in the chaotic backwashes and countereddies" ("The Transfigured Body" 37).[2]

Marion's world is an elemental order where knowledge, vision, and peace are possible; the darkness that we must acknowledge is "out there" beyond the creek, the woods, the garden. His relationship with the earth and his poetry is fiducial.

For Morgan, the darkness is everywhere: nature embodies chaos, but so does imagination, and reason can give order to both. In "The Transfigured Body: Notes on Poetry from a Journal," he writes,

> The marginal and chaotic have promoted more permanence than the institutions of the majority.... Out of desperation comes the recklessness to get near enough to chaos for some fire, and out of alienation the patience to husband and direct it for the community [32].[3]

"The Hollow," the opening poem in *Groundwork*, begins in the marginal, chaotic mountains, explaining why the first settlers stayed there, charmed and transfixed by the beauty of the peaks rising around them. The ridges were "a screen / sent up from the oaks and hickories / to keep them hidden from disease / and god and government, and even time" (1). In "Fear," Morgan continues describing the people and places who make up his mountain community. In this wild, natural world, superstition reigns, and the natural entwines the supernatural.

> A flea circus of dust thrown
> up in the yard means
> the haints are near
> and ghosties roost like cocoons
> in the appletree. I've seen bones
> underground burn like filaments
> when passed over by highwires from town,
> in torment with
> the suffering of the elements.
> Everybody knows the waterfall is
> haunted by a woman
> strangled in her wedding dress back then;
> mushrooms are the fingers
> of the dead reaching through
> and crickets their moving eyes.
> Trash around the spring means one
> has tried to get back in there [3].

After a contemplation of the boundaries, the high mountain divides that separate this particular place from everywhere else, Morgan moves down to where the people are. Like [Fred] Chappell, Morgan is a storyteller. He tells tales that have been told over and over. We sense that these stories are about real people. These are not the mythic, symbolic personages of some of Danny Marion's poems. Morgan's people have flesh and bone, and a little less beauty and grace. The flavor of oral tradition abounds; we picture evenings spent re-living these moments of family history.

In Morgan's first story-poem, a man named Revis and his bride come to their newly built cabin after their wedding to spend their first night together. Revis has built his cabin on a huge, flat rock, thinking this natural foundation would provide the best possible site for his home. But the rock was already home to a huge nest of rattlesnakes, and the first fire built for his new bride brings them out.[4]

> It was she
>
> who wakened to their singing near
> the embers and roused him to go look.
> Before he reached the fire
> more than a dozen struck
>
> and he died yelling her to stay
> on the big four-poster.
> Her uncle coming up the hollow
> with a gift bearham two days later
>
> found her shivering there
> marooned above a pool
> of hungry snakes,
> and the body beginning to swell [8–9].

There are serpents in this Paradise, and man must always be on guard. Morgan continues his contemplation of snakes in the next poem, "The Flying Snake," in which the snake takes on mythic proportions and his great-grandpa, the Snake Killer, becomes an epic hero. A giant rattler had killed four settlers and many farm animals. Attempts to stop the cruel killer had failed. Morgan imparts human or super-human characteristics to the rattler, suggesting it always knows when the hunters are coming. Morgan's great-grandfather finally conquered the snake. He got a brilliant idea of tying his seine net around his team, and he rode out to meet the snake, standing up in the wagon. When the snake made a lunge at him, it got caught in the net and the old man was able to shoot him. The memory of killing the snake became a haunting nightmare for the old man. For the reader the snake is a powerful symbol of the darkness of nature and of the deeper question of how we account for it in God's world. Morgan leaves us wondering with these last lines:

> Years later he'd imagine spiders
> falling from the sky like snowflakes,
> and mad dogs and angels in storms,
> and once in a nightmare he shot
> by mistake Jesus as he came
> through the east in Rapture light [11].

In that dark gloom of fundamentalism Morgan mentioned earlier, Jesus and his angels are a mystery in God's plan and arouse the same feelings of dread as spiders, mad dogs, and snakes, the dark sentries of the wild. There is danger in God's world, and Morgan constantly reminds us, not that we might pull away or limit ourselves, but that we might use the knowledge and heightened senses for greater awareness and self-knowledge. J.B. Merod writes,

> Despite the pretensions of intellect, wealth, or social position, nature equalizes us all; but Morgan goes beyond that knowledge to instruct us in the uses of disorder and catastrophe. In his view danger comes in many forms. Just as there is threat in privilege, there is also a threat in the status quo, in the weight of entrenched modes of thought and life. Against the inertia of habit, Morgan proposes to go with nature: to ride the waves and rhythms of natural process [57].

Morgan's personal and family history weaves in and out of various poems as he comes to terms with his feelings about his past. Like Chappell, [Jim Wayne] Miller, and Marion, he takes stock, as he approaches mid-life, of who he is and where he and his family have been. There is sometimes a glimmer of resentment for exploitive "outsiders," as in "Plankroad."

Adolescent longing comes to life in "Bean Money" where the young farm boy plots his escape from the hard work and isolation of his mountain farm. After a summer of aching, sweaty labor, the father pays him his share of the season's profits. It is greedily stored away to finance, he hopes, a new life for himself.

> That consecrated metal was an abstract
> drawn off the soil and sweat and
> cast into a jewelry of value.
> I meant those struck emblems to act
> as compact fuel, like nuclear pellets,
> to power my long excursion out of the sun
> and beyond the ridges ...
>
> ... the young summers
> become signs to be translated
> again into paper, ink and paper,

in the cool timeless leisure I saw
while washing my feet on the back steps [31].

But mostly, the talk of the past is gentle, tinged with pathos. "Mountain Page" is a re-evaluation or assessment poem. Here we see the speaker's understanding and sympathy for those who have gone before. We feel his sadness for the family—its hardships, suffering, unfulfilled dreams. Morgan writes,

My people came from South Carolina by
way of Mountain Page in the last century
and suffered here long enough
to build a church and leave
a dozen graves in the crab orchard.

One wasted years in search of
a secret lead mine the Cherokees
rumored was behind a cliff
...
Another shunned his fields to dig for
gold the millionaires at Flat Rock
must have buried in the Civil War [47].

Now the narrator sees himself in these lives, sees his own failures and accepts those of his forebears:

and I stop to let their haunt blow
past and dew out in the weeds
while I prospect and dig and bury
expectations; my people
prayed and dug and failed here too [48].

A dominant theme in *Groundwork* is man vs. nature, particularly the idea of the people in his family and community struggling with the forces of nature. In "Canning Time," the yearly rite of canning peaches becomes an ordeal, a trial that vexes body and soul. It is almost a battle scene. The canners do not partake in a religious ritual of communion with nature, as we might see in Jeff Daniel Marion's world. They are women at war, fighting for survival.

In that hell they sealed the quickly browning
flesh in capsules of honey ... [20].

In "Huckleberries" the suffering necessary to be part of nature is the underlying idea. The poet gathers berries with a friend called F.A., and he fears every buzz and hum: "*Never trust the innocent twig in high / berry country; it may be stingworm, / snake or walkingstick*" (32). As they pick the berries "so few, so tedious / to gather" (32), F.A. relates a tale which presents the most terrible image of nature invading the security of home—the darkness snuffing out the light and fire of the heart. A panther steals a baby from a cabin porch. A posse trails the animal to its den where the remains of the infant are found. This tragedy is contemplated as they sweat and ache in the hot sun, gathering their sweet treasure. When they finish, they have paid a price, both in the tale and in the tedium of the labor: "The morning has been said and won, / hands bloody with sweet sun" (33).

Another image that occurs in *Groundwork* is land left barren and useless. Morgan's memories of his childhood North Carolina are not a romanticized vision of lush, green fields and postcard mountain scenes. He remembers in "Milksick Pen" a place where a poison weed grows that will taint the milk of the cow who grazes there. A fence erected around the place allows the forest to flourish untouched by man or animal. And in "Smokehouse Dirt" the salt used to cure meat has created a sterile desert where neither animals, plants, snow, nor light can rest. Man and his appetites have left a scar.

> The shadow of the meat-hung roof puddles
> sterile as the site of Carthage. Rain will
> lick away the savor in about
> a century. The light cannot feel at
>
> home on this ground for a while, nor rabbits
> warm here at a hearth of vegetation.
> The scald won't even
> hold a drop of snow, but eats
>
> away the lush crystals fast as heat.
> Where the smoked ham sweated and fatback wept
> its oils, and molasses cooked
> down to plasma in jars, erosion
>
> rubs brine in the wound same as a pissburn
> in the pasture. The lye tub drooled its
> whey also. Hunger has left a tear
> track, recondite among the thickets [43].

Morgan's persona remembers the hard times and backbreaking work of the farm life, and he is willing to let it go. The farm boy knows too well the stubbornness of mountain land, its reluctance to yield up its bounty. In "Secret Pleasures" he returns to fields he once worked and seems to rejoice in the land that is now being left to nature; the poet enjoys knowing that no one works this field. Though everyone else has had the good sense to abandon it, Robert Morgan, the poet, returns to find a new use for the land.

> Let it
> scab and fur over on its own
> and offer no crop bigger than dew
> and the beadwork of berrypicking.
> My secret pleasure: to come and watch
> these shoots work up
> their honey from bitter clay.
> Lichen gardens improve the scars,
> patching over history. I offer
> the land my leisure [50].

Not all the interaction with nature is portrayed as negative or dangerous, however. One of nature's most destructive elements—fire—becomes for Morgan a life force, a symbol of renewal. Fire fascinates him: this powerful image occurs memorably in "Burnoff," "Baptism of Fire," and "Burning the Hornet's Nest." We are reminded of his statement, "Out of desperation comes the recklessness to get near enough to chaos for some fire" (Notes 32).[5] The fire is the imagination and the human spirit. Morgan has no patience with complacency; the poet must live and think dangerously. With his poetry, Morgan means to build a little fire under us, like a good Baptist preacher. With this seeking of the light, Morgan is reminiscent of Marion. But his light is the light of a raging fire, as his interest in the scientific gives metaphor to an obsession with fire's power.

In "Burnoff" fire is part of the work at hand, and it is a positive force. The fields are burned in the spring in order to kill the weeds and prepare the ground for planting. He presents and analyzes the event as if it were an experiment, some chemical process, a perspective that is pervasive in *Groundwork*. There is also a spiritual side, though, to the burning of the fields.

> As though the conflagration summons
> dirt syrup and fire ink out of clay
> to irrigate anemic soil
> to pave the slope tar-black.
> The shadow will need to be turned
> like frying ham, sweet with
> baked larvae, wormeggs, roots.
> We rub the season's minstrel char
> on skin, and ask the land to hold its
> charge until we plug in seeds [22].

Fire is not the only metaphorical element in this poem; the work involved is also significant. The value of physical work is a recurring theme in Morgan's poems, as it is in Marion's. These poets remind us of the writings of Simone Weil, the French philosopher who devoted much thought and energy to the contemplation of the relationship of work to the human soul. She believed that work and thought must combine to produce wholeness in society and the individual, writing, "If on the one hand the whole spiritual life of the soul, and on the other hand all the scientific knowledge acquired concerning the material universe are made to converge upon the act of work, work occupies its rightful place.... [I]t becomes a point of contact between this world and the world beyond" (94).

Preparing the field for planting becomes a point of contact with the world of the spirit through fire, literally and metaphorically, as the fire embraces the spirit seeking knowledge, wholeness, vision. The burning field offers its own revelation to the poet/seer/scientist. It connects with an image in the poem about the burning hornet's nest that Morgan describes as a great burning eyeball (41). As Stephen Marion says in his essay, "Fire sweeps life, death, and decomposition together in one swift vision.... A certain essence, a signal, is revealed, as if the fire threw vision as it throws light" (25).

That is why Gondan, the preaching fieldhand in "Baptism of Fire," argues with the conventional notion of water, symbol for the blood of Christ, as the only element with redemptive powers. Gondan says:

> "The Word says it takes the Baptism of Fire
> to see the Kingdom..."
> ....
> "Anyone that ain't rubbed clean by
> purifying flame better get his asbestos suit" [28–29].

Morgan's image of fire dovetails with Fred Chappell's here, as we remember the poem "Bloodfire" when the father says, "Maybe hellfire is good for the South, a kind / Of purgative. We could use a lot of that" (62). The key word is purgative because Morgan and Chappell share the idea of redemption made possible by fire. All of us need to feel the fire occasionally to shock us out of our smugness, our laziness, our vulnerability to self-importance. For Morgan and Chappell, nature's most violent element, fire, seems to offer more power to change and renew than its quieter sister, water.

Groundwork is no lament of the horrors inherent in the natural world or even the hell of burning imagination in the mind of a North Carolina farm boy. Morgan is not complaining. The voice is admiring, seeking understanding, questioning the source, and cataloguing the mysteries of the scientific world. Morgan is the scientist/poet in the tradition of Henry David Thoreau or, more recently, Loren Eiseley. As Stephen Marion has observed,

> For Morgan, science is a sense of new ground. He watches natural reactions and cycles and introduces human senses to form an experiment, a poem, to reveal the essential properties of all the elements involved. The poem is a field laboratory, where measurements are done by hand and eye. It is a place where the senses of nature are given life to react with the senses of man, to produce a glow that is essence [27].

Robert Morgan's latest effort, *At the Edge of the Orchard Country*, from Wesleyan University Press, is an even more developed expression of many themes and motifs found in *Groundwork*. In this book Morgan draws on memory, family stories, and local history of his North Carolina home, bringing grandparents, parents, aunts, uncles, and cousins to life in poem after poem, "recovering pieces of the morgenland" in a very thorough fashion (68).

The book opens with a poem about Horace Kephart working in his tent on a chapter of *Our Southern Highlanders*, writing he does as repayment to his parents for all the years of college and all the blessings life afforded him. The poem and its theme of indebtedness become a metaphor for Robert Morgan and *At the Edge of the Orchard Country*—a repayment of a debt to the people and places who made him. Every poem in the first section is a broken twig on the twisted path of Morgan's memory of his childhood and family. "Passenger Pigeons" and "Buffalo Trace" are about homing in and finding direction. The sleeper in "Feather Bed" dreams and drifts across space, time, years "[a]cross the troubled Atlantic and centuries / toward a white immaculate garden" (7). Thomas Wolfe feverishly writing in his Brooklyn apartment is juxtaposed with a moonshiner back home in "Looking Homeward," directing our attention to the final poems in the section. "Halley's Comet" and "White Autumn" feature women in the family album whose words and lives informed Morgan's own. Indebtedness becomes the dominant theme of the entire first section, gratefulness for having "yet another spring he'd been / privileged to remember..." (12).

One important image from *Groundwork*, fire, and one important idea, the value of physical work, continue in *At the Edge of the Orchard Country*. Fire, heat, and light provide the central image in poem after poem. The burning intensity of a creative genius like Thomas Wolfe is held up beside the moonshiner's fire in "Looking Homeward." A comet, a swirling bomb of gases jetting through the night sky, is "a kind of promise of the continuance / of things in a broken world—" (12). In "Manure Pile" and "Dead Dog on the Highway," the heat of fermentation is the focus. From the tiniest light of all, the lightning bug, to the emotional heat of a "hot and vivid" revival in a country church (29), fire of any kind is important to Morgan, suggesting the possibility of renewal, promise, and positive energy. In "Nail Bag" we learn of the pioneer practice of burning a barn down for the nails. This was necessary in order to move on to new, more fertile land. The settlers would arrive with their reclaimed nails, burn the logs that were cleared from the new claim, scatter the ashes and reap a bountiful harvest. Fire again brought a new beginning, a place for another generation.

> As though all husbandry and home
> were carried in that charred handful
> of iron stitches, blacksmithed chromosomes
> that link distant generations [61].

As in the work of the three poets previously discussed, the value of physical work is a predominant idea in Morgan's book. In the world of the farm, people do not sit idle, or worse, in front of the television. They do not have time for aerobics, jogging, or analysts. There is much to do, and the people Morgan brings to life for us are busy. They rake, sweep, plow, plant, clean off the cemetery, tend their land and animals. Even a little boy like the young Robert Morgan could not spend too much time dawdling. He says, "I had other lives also, and work to do" (42).

In "Harrow" the work of plowing takes on cosmic importance, as the finished new ground is "the planet's newest field" (38). And in "Field Theory" work as a preserver of sanity and innocence is the underlying idea.

> I like to think they found in work
> a soil subliminal and sublime.
> Their best conspiracies were two
> breathing in the night [68].

The second section of the book focuses on nature's sights, sounds, and smells—from manure to spring flowers, lightning bugs, the air itself—then the poet moves us easily, quietly into childhood memories of church services, hiding in potato holes, visits with relatives, a boy's first attempt to plow. Morgan is mining his memories for insights into his character, the whys of his own journey through life. There is the same exciting mix of scientific knowledge and terminology in the poetry that we saw in *Groundwork*. These lines from the poem "Brownian Motion" offer an example:

> The air is an aquarium where
> every mote spins wild
> and prisms the morning light.
> Lint climbs sparkling on
> convection's fountain,
> and magnetic storms boil away
> like gnats bumped by molecules.
> Every breath swarms
> the clear spores, ion seethe,
> magnified in playful flight [23].

Section three, the last, is a continued regression into the past, beyond Morgan's personal memories, to a historical tracing of a more cultural memory, and his indebtedness to the collective experience of his forefathers and mothers. These poems chronicle the life of the early pioneers, with descriptions of how the early settlements were set up, how land use was parceled out, and what role the Indians played in the past of the Appalachian Mountains.

Showing his mastery of complex poetic forms, Morgan writes about his grandfather using a very difficult old French form, the chant royal. The technically formidable form requires five stanzas of 11 lines each, followed by an envoi. Each section ends with a refrain. Morgan's "Chant Royal" is a hymn of praise and a prayer, a fitting close to any ceremony—hence its position as the next-to-last poem in the book. The poem recounts the life of Morgan's grandfather, born weak and fragile. Only determination on the part of his mother kept him alive. Her strength not only saved him but also prepared him for a hard life. When the grandfather was finally able to buy a piece of land of his own, Morgan tells us "he sank a well through rock, / weathered debt, depression, set groves, / adequate for survival, withstanding all knocks" (67). This last line becomes an underlying theme for the entire collection, as the envoi enlists the help of higher powers in living a life of integrity:

> Guardian ghost, inhere herein. Before Jove
> may this music honor his example, improve
> my time as he invested his, and no less unorthodox
> discover significance in the bonds his fate wove
> adequate for survival, withstanding all knocks.

Memory. History. Imagination. Science. These are the subjects of *At the Edge of the Orchard Country*, the entire collection a fermentation of Morgan's complex system of interests. Like the other poets discussed here, Morgan acknowledges and honors memory's place in literature. But his distinction lies in his successful blending of science and poetry. He may be the answer to I.A. Richards' ideal, discussed in his famous essay "Science and Poetry," in a book by the same name, published in 1926. As Richards pointed out, science alone can only tell us how things behave, how the universe exists and operates; it cannot tell us why. Science cannot tell us what we are, what the world is. That is the poet's job. Survival in the modern scientific world requires that the scientists and poets not turn away from each other, but instead become more alike.

In a letter to the author, Robert Morgan has written, "In my own case I feel equally moved by the old hymns at baptizing and quantum mechanics." That might serve as a motto for him in one sentence. His sense of adventure, his desire for order and understanding, and his quest for vision are equally satisfied in poetry and science.

Notes

1. "Robert Morgan" is the fourth and final chapter of Quillen's book *Looking for Native Ground: Contemporary Appalachian Poetry*. Boone, NC: Appalachian Consortium Press, 1989. Chapters one through three discuss the poetry of Jim Wayne Miller, Fred Chappell, and Jeff Daniel Marion.
2. "The Transfigured Body: Notes from a Journal" is reprinted in Morgan's *Good Measure: Essays, Interviews, and Notes on Poetry*. Baton Rouge: Louisiana State University Press, 1993, pp. 109–118. The passage quoted appears there on p. 115.
3. In *Good Measure* the passage quoted appears on p. 110.
4. Quillen's note: "This story is also told as part of John Ehle's novel *The Landbreakers*, a fact that Robert Morgan was surprised to learn. He told an audience at the Hindman Settlement School in 1987 that he heard that story growing up and believed it to be true. It was only a few years ago that he learned about the scene in the novel and realized the story was a 'tale.'"
5. In *Good Measure*, the passage quoted appears on p. 110.

Works Cited

Chappell, Fred. "Bloodfire." *Midquest: A Poem*. Baton Rouge: Louisiana State University Press, 1981. 53–94.
Marion, Stephen. "Gleaning the Unsayable: The Terrain of Vision in Poems by Robert Morgan, Fred Chappell, and Jim Wayne Miller." *Mossy Creek Journal* 9 (1985): 25–33.
Merod, J. B. "Robert Morgan's 'Wisdom-Lighted Islands.'" *The Small Farm* (1976): 54–62.
Morgan, Robert. *Groundwork*. Frankfort, KY: Gnomon, 1979.
______. *At the Edge of the Orchard Country*. Middletown, CT: Wesleyan University Press, 1987.
Weil, Simone. *The Need for Roots: Prelude to a Declaration of Duties Toward Mankind*. Trans. Arthur Wills. New York: G. P. Putnam's Sons, 1952.

“The Witness of Many Writings”

Robert Morgan’s Poetic Career[1]

Michael McFee

A few pages into “Mockingbird,” his polyglottal improvisation on “the southern night,”[2] Robert Morgan begins to slip into the imperative. In itself, this is nothing unusual, especially in his early work, which is striking for its many shifts of tense and diction and syntax, its “rough music.” But as he begins to warm to the imperative mood, it becomes clear that he is actually addressing *himself*, so that the ensuing passage becomes a kind of poetics, a summary of his technical and theoretical enterprise as a poet, and a convenient retrospective and prognostication of his poetic career. It is his “[a]udition for the future,” for us.[3]

“You will have / the witness of many writings,”[4] Morgan says, a prophetic statement for a man who—fifteen years later, in 1990—has eight first-rate books of poems, a ninth (*Green River: New and Selected Poems*) on the way, and a well-received collection of stories, *The Blue Valleys*. And what is the nature of that “witness”? What is Morgan’s credo in his “many writings,” according to the imperatives of “Mockingbird”? I count at least nine articles of poetic faith.

1. “Believe in the immaculate / conception of matter from energy.”[5] Morgan is obsessed with origins, with conceptions, with pursuing what he slyly calls “alma matter”[6] back to its beginnings. For some, this might be a religious or philosophical impulse; for Morgan, it is a scientific one, a question of physics rather than metaphysics. And so the language of his poetry is minutely focused and precise, literally profound. “Your work will be radical / as the springhead,” as he says.[7] “Keep the covenant / with bottomlands and shovel down into / the atom’s masonry.”[8] This is a powerful tropism, one that pulls the poet and his work deeper and deeper, further and further, until he reaches “The Music of the Spheres,” as a recent poem puts it, the innermost harmony, “the rings around / atoms singing,” “fireworks / of the inward horizons,” “the heavens / within every speck of substance.”[9]
2. Against this depth, Morgan counterposes a height: “Stay with high moor and / mountain, the ultraviolet region.”[10] This is exactly what he has done in his many writings, which have been consistently faithful to his place of origin, in the North Carolina mountains near Zirconia. “There’s about a square mile of land there I know every foot of,” Morgan once told the little magazine *The*

Small Farm. "I think my sense of place is very local indeed, not a culture, not a region, just one community. Since moving away I have found myself comparing everything I've seen to that archetypal acreage, soil, plants, climate, stream beds, as well as people."[11]

3. Morgan's witness is radically deep, and mountainously lofty; it is also characterized by astonishing attention to detail, by what one of his characters calls "biting focus," "detailed as a reconnaissance photograph under a microscope."[12] "Interpret literally the eros of detail,"[13] he commands in "Mockingbird": "Each rock and bit of trash is an avatar… / The virtual coil of dust is erotic."[14] When the least scrap of matter crackles with such energy, sexual and yet divine, the poet's passion for specifics is no surprise.
4. "Play with matches, / correspondences."[15] Once you get past the pun on "playing with matches"—a typical twist for Morgan, who relishes peculiar vocabulary and wordplay of all kinds, puns, anagrams, etymologies—you arrive at an essential ingredient of his work: correspondences, similarities in detail between one thing and another, an analogic link, the power of metaphor. Nobody wields more vigorous images than Morgan, in more concentrated fashion: in the fifteen-line poem "Lightning Bug," for instance (another poem about "the southern night"), I count a dozen sharp metaphors for that insect.[16] If metaphor is indeed "the greatest thing by far" for a poet, as Aristotle said, "the hallmark of genius," then Morgan is preeminent among his contemporaries.[17]
5. "Note nature's / formality and the million intersections / in a piece of cloth."[18] In focusing so intently on nature, what emerges for Morgan is not chaos and a poetics of entropy, but formality and an intricate poetics of order, which has become more evident in his technique as his career has progressed. Before there ever *was* a so-called "new formalism," Morgan was writing rhymed stanzas of subtle virtuosity; and his intricate "Chant Royal" simply blows the competition out of the formal waters.
6. "It's / difficult to leave the country where your / ancestors are buried."[19] This non-imperative is almost an aside in the verbal cataract of "Mockingbird," but it's a telling one. Literally, Morgan has had to leave that country, having lived and taught in upstate New York for decades: he is a writer in exile, which is "difficult." But in his writings, he's never really left that country at all: his work is a tenacious memorial to his buried ancestors, who live a new life in his lines. His work salvages their lost world. In fact, Morgan's distance from home may have lent keenness to his re-creation of home, to its picture on his inward eye and on the page.
7. "Feel the / church's talon in the night sky."[20] The presence of religion, of the fundamentalist faith of his upbringing, is so pervasive in the language and metaphors of Morgan's work that it barely needs mentioning. But I would note that, though clearly an outsider to this worldview, the poet never condescends to it or satirizes the urge to worship.
8. "Licensed to plead for yourself in / history bear to city-dump and fertilizer / plant the thermal waste and bilge of learning."[21] This is a complicated command, especially since Morgan's own poetry is so learned and so interested in history. But I think it may have to do with a certain *kind* of learning and attitude. What Morgan opposes is the fancy-talking lawyer for hire, the disembodied

knowledge that produces useless waste and nonsense. What he advocates in his work is pleading your own case and place in history, learning the durable lessons at hand. "Build with undressed / stone," he says. "An illiterate ancestor won the / battle of Cowpens. Reject the dryhides and / take the holy dance."[22] This is genuinely political poetry, from someone who understands "labor's playful war with time,"[23] from a man who has lived the lessons of history and social class, arrogance and ignorance.

9. Morgan's conclusion to "Mockingbird" is rich and oblique: "Offer reticence and disapprobation, / follow no trade, and heading for deep cover / come to an opening in the canopy / where light shines from obscure places. Hide / behind a waterfall in congregation / with mist and rock. Take the justified / margins of cornfields. Inaugurate by / leaving, ordained by anonymity."[24] The witness of Morgan's many writings is indeed reticent and yet confident, solitary and yet "in congregation" with the polyglot world, almost anonymous in its objectivity and yet wholly distinctive, marginal and yet absolutely central to Southern and American letters. The speaker of these poems may hide or head for deep cover, but he doesn't miss a thing: his perspective is practically omniscient, and he can find light in the most obscure places. And he is his own man, tough as that may be on his career: as he says elsewhere in "Mockingbird," "I will be what I will be."[25]

Having sketched out some of the general qualities of Robert Morgan's poetry, as concentrated in the lines of "Mockingbird," let me turn now to the witness of the many writings themselves. I'd like to trace the development of his career through some specific poems, ones that demonstrate not only his admirable consistency of vision and expression over a quarter century, but also his willingness to change as he matures, to try new things in his work, to develop as a poet.

Twenty springs ago, a young poet named Robert Morgan published three poems in a special "North Carolina Poetry" issue of *Southern Poetry Review*, a magazine in which he'd appeared since 1965, while still a mere undergraduate at UNC–Chapel Hill. The three poems—"Moon Wearing Antlers," "Cedars," and "Hot Day Ending"—fit easily on two-thirds of a page, and contain a *total* of thirteen lines and just over fifty words. That data should suggest just what kind of poems these are: short, obviously, but also compressed, condensed, distilled. One in particular, the five-line "Cedars," epitomizes Morgan's very early style, the style seen in *Zirconia Poems*, the scarce chapbook called *The Voice in the Crosshairs*, and—to a lessening degree—his first major collection, *Red Owl*.

Cedars

Fur tears
turret the hill, tips nervous,
pointing. Caves in the tight sky.
Stalagmites. Tacks.
Black sails move among cattle.[26]

In one way, this stripped-down little poem represents a young man working out his influences. Among those I would count: (1) the "deep imagery" practiced and preached by Robert Bly and others in the 1960s, those odd evocative dream-images from the subconscious—dark, quiet, subterranean; (2) the Japanese and Chinese poetry also fashionable at the time, especially as filtered through disciples like Gary Snyder—a spare, suggestive, somewhat elliptical mode; (3) the surrealism of French and other foreign poetry, which was being made available in translation as never before; and, underlying all these; (4) Imagism itself, the early modern movement as articulated by Pound and Amy Lowell, whose objectives included employing always the exact word; presenting a concrete, firm, definite image; suggesting rather than offering complete statements; and—above all—striving for concentration, which they believed to be of the very essence in poetry.

"Cedars" manages to satisfy most of the rules of most of those schools: it is an apprentice-poem. But in another, more important way, it is clearly a Morgan-poem, a distinctive and promising start. His metaphorical gift is unmistakable here: the cedar trees in silhouette are tears (and fur tears at that, a nice surrealistic touch, besides being more exact); they are turrets, caves, stalagmites, tacks, sails—six images in five lines. So is Morgan's gift for using words in surprising ways: I first read the beginning as "Fur *tears*," the second word as a verb, until I realized that there was some pretty fierce enjambment going on at the start, with the verb "turret" (another typical Morgan flourish, using a noun as a vigorous verb) emphatically planted at the opening of line two. After that, Morgan abandons verbs completely, until the last line, with "Black sails move." But above all, "Cedars" demonstrates Morgan's abiding gift for precision of seeing and saying, for being concise and incisive. "I tried to be true to objects," he has said of this early phase "I wanted poems terse and precise, yet as encompassing as mathematical proofs."

But while the image may be the essential unit of energy in any poem, a poem that is nothing but a pile-up of images is still not quite a poem. It may be interesting, it may be striking, it may be original, but somehow it just won't move: its very reductiveness does it in. And I think the maturing poet Robert Morgan began to sense that in his book *Red Owl*. It's still dominated by the "terse and precise" poems characteristic of his early phase, but it also includes poems where the lines seem more relaxed, extended, and musical than before. The images are no less brilliant, but the verbal context is more accessible; there is connective tissue as well as muscle.

Here's one of the best poems from the book. The title is very close to the title of the poem just explicated, but the tone and pitch represent a significant development.

Cedar

Smell the recorders buried here.
Music lies in the wood
as in the cat's entrails, in ore.
Faint musk of old arrows, canoe ribs.
Wood still giving
its breath, radioactive—releasing
a subtle verb for years
to fill whatever room or closet it lies in
till it's dark, inert
as the wood of cathedral carvings.
Weather leaches the glow
and withes of cool air plunder the fibers. The heat
is drunk off.
The wood reveals in lessening quanta the spice
from a country no one has seen,
leaking from a broken limb expanding to nonexistence.
But inside the scent's strong as light; it repels
the moth as two ends of a magnet

shun meeting.
For they are from the same country, the smell
lunar, musty, an ember so cool
you can hold it in your hand, and the moth
burning out of the dark, its semiquaver
weak as a photograph emerging in the darkroom pan.[27]

"Cedars" was tense, terse, "nervous," "tight," remote in perspective. "Cedar," on the other hand, is much more inviting and intimate from the very first word, the imperative "Smell." (An aside: Morgan is a superb poet of all the senses, but his olfactory range is particularly impressive. He may be the best poet of smell we've had since Roethke and his "congress of stinks."[28]) What we are invited to smell, in a nice synesthetic leap, is potential music, the recorder that might come from a piece of cedar, as fiddle strings come from catgut, as trumpets come from ore. In the fourth line, the poem threatens to fade into memory; but then, in the following five lines, it discovers the momentum that keeps it going until the last line, the twenty-fourth. The trigger is the word "radioactive," one that not only accommodates Morgan's scientific nature, but also is perfect for the slow release of that penetrating cedar odor. (Besides which, it is the first note in a chord of technical language that echoes through the poem, in the quanta and magnetic fields and semiquaver.) And note how this discovery seems to release the poem's syntax: three of the first four lines were end-stopped, but lines five through ten are beautifully run-on, fluid, breathing. The subsequent lineation is flexible and sharp, and it helps the poem build to a genuine conclusion, a satisfying sense of closure. Much of this has to do with Morgan's willingness to extend his images: whereas the young poet might have been satisfied to discover the moth/magnet connection or the "country no one has seen," the maturing poet develops both in the final lines. He yokes the moth and the cedar wood, returning to the initial "smell" (with a nice pun on "luna moth" in "lunar"); he revives the earlier "heat" in the oxymoronic "ember so cool / you can hold it in your hand" (note the inclusive pronoun "you") and the moth "burning out of the dark"; and he circles us all the way back to the opening lines with the poem's crowning word, "semiquaver." Besides the way the sixteenth note fleetingly sustains the poem's musical motif, the word is also a perfect description of a moth's half-quavering flight.

With such a build-up, the simile of the last wide line—"weak as a photograph emerging in the darkroom pan," which in a more minimal context might seem like mere deep imagism—becomes a wonderful figure for the poem itself, developing, steadily emerging, fading *in*.

"My dream," Morgan said of his writing at this time, "was to write a maquette-sized poetry, of bonsai complexity and detail. Each poem was a new beginning of perception, an atom of recognition, explosive in its transfers of bond and structure."[29] In a poem like "Cedar," though, I think the "atom of recognition" has been raised to at least the molecular level: there is a complexity and interconnectedness and movement that signals a new stage in Morgan's career. His early poetics seems to have been "Make something happen in every syllable": "build a syllable at a time / on the footing of silence," as one poem puts it.[30] But his new principle—one easier on writer and readers—is "Make something happen in every *line*."[31] And he is beginning to think and write in lines that move together down the page, not just in isolated sequences of phrases and fragments. He is developing a voice that is more than just sound, however striking: he is converting his natural reticence into a virtue. He is on the verge of a breakthrough.

Which, to me, comes with the book *Land Diving*, published in 1976, his thirty-third year. It's the ugly duckling among Morgan's many handsome volumes; it apparently received little critical attention at the time; but it is, I think, his first mature book, one whose poems proclaim to those with eyes to see and ears to hear: *This is the real thing.* Just what did Morgan discover in his third book of poetry? New possibilities, new challenges for his obvious talent, including (1) poetic form, "the carefully measured / bonds"[32] of tercets, quatrains, sestets—a new order for the old material; (2) character, which includes not only memorable family members but also the "I" speaking the poems, who emerges from hiding for the first time and takes on characteristics of his own; (3) narrative, the possibility of a story line around which the "tropes and turning" of a poem might accrete; and (4) the long poem—two, five, even six pages of typeset text, poetry that requires sustaining for what must have seemed a marathon length after the wind sprints of *Zirconia Poems* and *Red Owl.*

Consider this poem from the first section of *Land Diving*, framed by sestets and quatrains and the two-page "Dark Corner":

Face

The story went that once someone, an unbeliever,
looking into the clouds saw among the luminous
caravan of shapes and smokes, the usual sheep

and outcroppings of battlevapor, signals, choo-
choos, stretching fish, when suddenly in
one great chunk of the sky the Lamb himself,

the face of longhaired Jesus, looked sadly down
at him. Struck down on his way from that moment
he believed. Having a camera he snapped the

quickly dissolving icon. Advertised on radio
and at revivals that photo sold thousands. Looking
at the black and white you never found the image

at first, but when it came rushing out of the
wisps and puffs hardening into a perfect likeness
the recognition was beyond all expectation chilling.

For months I kept eyes ahead or to the ground out
of horror, feared looking back I would see
the Tiger clawing through eastern azure.[33]

Before you even read the words of this poem, you can look at it and tell there's something different about it. The lines are long, or wide; they are regular, at least visually, on the page; and they are arranged into unrhymed tercets, six of them. This may be a subtle development; but for Morgan, whose work had been a model of imagism and free verse and the jagged prosody that often accompanies those modes, it signals a new interest in the possibilities of verbal order.

And once you do read the first words of "Face," you know you're in for a new kind of Morgan-poem. "The story went," it starts; and what follows is indeed a story, a once-upon-a-time tale. It's not a conglomeration of images, though there are vivid figures when looking into the metaphorical clouds: it's a story *about* imagery, about the suggestive power of an image in the individual imagination. It's a Blakean moral tale, about taking an image too literally, about freezing and hardening and thus limiting and distorting it. Once the "unbeliever" is struck down on his road to Damascus and sees Jesus in the clouds and fixes the face in a photograph and begins selling it, an inescapable insidious cycle is set in motion. Once you see the picture, and the wispy "image" hardens "into a perfect likeness" (is there really any such thing?), you too are struck down and trapped; you can't see anything else. As the beautifully suspended last line of stanza five puts it, "The recognition was beyond all expectation chilling."

Most poets might stop here. I think the younger Morgan might have stopped here, letting the poem land on that last word "chilling," making the reader shiver. But he doesn't: the poet pushes the poem further, introducing another character, another "face." So far we've had the unbeliever looking up, Jesus sadly looking down, the collective "you" looking at the picture; but then in the last stanza, Morgan personalizes the story, moves all the way to first person, becomes the unbeliever and the you, his face averted. "For months," he says, giving the story time and tension, "I kept eyes ahead or to the ground out / of horror." He too has been infected by the image, the terrible epiphany; and the last lines are one long growl, a thunderhead of r's about to burst on the boy who "feared looking back I would see / the Tiger clawing through eastern azure." (More Blake-echoes: "In what distant deeps or skies / Burnt the fire of thine eyes?" "Did he smile his work to see? / Did he who made the Lamb [and 'the usual sheep'] make thee?") The allusion, the level of language, the fluidity of line and line-break, the handling of character and story and form—all bespeak a poet who has hit his stride, who has found his voice and his persona: that of a keen watcher and listener, an outsider who is nevertheless part of the community.

Land Diving was followed by *Trunk & Thicket* two years later, in 1978. The book is a kind of triptych, a central prose memoir ("Homecoming," about the annual church reunion in Green River and its decline) framed by two long poems, "Trunk & Thicket" and the previously discussed "Mockingbird." Both poems are loaded with rifts of ore, and could be mined for themes and motifs and subjects central to Morgan's poetry; but, as the title poem says, "the real world I guess, the / motif, is home. Homecoming. Homing. / How to touch base."[34] Which is a perfect description of Morgan's next book, the gorgeous *Groundwork*. For as the title implies, this is a book about working the familiar ground, about home and the homecoming possible in poems. "I prospect and dig and bury / expectations," says Morgan: "my people / prayed and dug and failed here too."[35] *Groundwork* is a book wholly focused on his people and his place and their stories: it is his most purely Appalachian book, and possibly the best single book of lyric poems ever to come out of the Southern mountains. Like any masterpiece, it creates its own secondary world—palpable, intriguing, and memorable.

The poems themselves continue to develop Morgan's interest in story (including history, an abiding and growing passion) and character and form: the balladic "Mountain Bride," that highlands Gothic gem, is a paragon of both. The voice and prosody in *Groundwork* are absolutely confident. And the "I" of the poems, whose appearances in the early poetry were so reluctant and self-conscious, has by now become a solid figure, as in this poem:

Zircon Pit

Just below the crest of Meetinghouse Hill
I used to climb the apron of spoil
into a digging long abandoned. Leaves
and saplings hid the raw dirt and the hole,
half-filled in fall, fit like a nest
from which to drowse and look

down the steepness and keep watch
on my century. One of the high places.
I spent hours there in late winter,
warmed by leaves and the solartrap, just
out of the summit winds compressing
across the rim. Caught the best sun, the new light
of February when the mountains
pressed clean by snow began to twitch
and trickle. From that blind
I watched the mailman on the creekroad
hours before he reached our box.
The only gem found where Great-grandpa dug
was the many-facet thrill and vantage of remoteness.
Sometimes the whole forest seemed to river
up and over my lookout and burn
vivid, then drain into the present.
I listened, close to the new sky.[36]

This poem is only a line shorter than "Cedar," that dark image-rich poem published at the other end of the decade; but it seems infinitely more spacious and at ease. The opening lines are specific (especially with the local place name), but their focus is not so "biting." And rather than merely commanding, "Climb the apron of spoil," the poet uses a more conversational syntax and tone: as a result, we naturally want to climb along with him. And when he does arrive at a simile, he doesn't just drop it or bury it: he lets it grow until it achieves a remarkable perspective, the pit "like a nest / from which to drowse and look / down the steepness and keep watch / *on my century*." As always in Morgan, there are no wasted words; but he seems more willing to use words that are not sheer distillate, for the sake of poem and subject and reader.

The most important thing about this poem is the "I," the speaker-persona, who—rather than the zircon pit itself—is really the point of the poem. Whereas Morgan was once interested in being true to objects and writing with mathematical precision, he seems increasingly willing to risk the subjective, to measure the emotional impact of an object on a character, including himself. And so we get the recurrent figure of the poet-in-hiding, taking to an abandoned or marginal place, a "blind" or "lookout," from which he can watch the world, wait, listen. Like Antaeus, Morgan seems to draw strength from contact with soil, dirt, earth, land: all of his poetry is a kind of ground-work, a land-diving, a geologos. There in the zircon pit he is high but low, and paradoxically rich: "The only gem found where Great-grandpa dug / was the many-facet thrill and vantage of remoteness." To the poet, especially perhaps in retrospect, that remoteness and the vantage-point it offers is true wealth. The poem builds to a quietly visionary moment: "Sometimes the whole forest seemed to river [great verb, as usual] / up and over my lookout and burn / vivid, then drain into the present."

That last phrase, "into the present," is curious but telling. Many of Morgan's poems have an archaic feeling, as if his subjects are remote not only in space but also in time, as if they were from another century, suspended outside the present like the boy in the pit enjoying the "vantage of remoteness." But against that great distance, Morgan juxtaposes great intimacy: the poem ends not with the time shift "into the present," but with a quiet single-sentence line: "I listened, close to the new sky." The poem lands firmly on its "I," reinforcing it with a terminal rhyme, "sky," the "I" and "sky" yoking the personal and universal in one line. And now the formerly reticent first-person speaker has adopted an almost prophetic pose, his ear tuned to heaven and his eye turned on the world below.

"Zircon Pit" may not be the best poem in *Groundwork*, but it's representative of the steady maturation of Robert Morgan as a poet. Even so, that fine book didn't bring Morgan the critical attention he by now deserved. That attention came, at long last, with *At the Edge of the Orchard Country*, published in 1987, eight years after *Groundwork*. But in the interim there was another small book, Morgan's sixth, a beautifully designed collection of nineteen poems published by Robert Denham at Iron Mountain Press in Emory, Virginia. *Bronze Age* is its title, and despite the chapbook size it's a fine sampler of Morgan's range at mid-career: there are short imagistic poems, long story poems, a couple of flawless poems in sestets, a rare terza rima sonnet, and a number of poems in what was coming to be Morgan's preferred form, the eight-syllable line. It's a book beautifully grounded in the mountains and "a soil subliminal and sublime," the poet secure in his "fundamental lair": "only way out to the sun is down," as he says in the hayloft, "through the exquisite filth."[37] And luckily, it's a book whose best poems are not impossible to find, despite its out-of-print status: eight are reprinted in *At the Edge of the Orchard Country*, and one is scheduled for the "new" section of the *New and Selected Poems*. Here is the last and longest poem in *Bronze Age*, which appears as the next-to-last poem in section two of *At the Edge of the Orchard Country*:

Man and Machine

Besides drinking and telling lies,
nothing interested my cousin Luther
like working with the tractor.
Astride that bright and smelly beast
he was a man inspired.
Revving and tearing the stubble
of early spring he cussed
the metal like a favorite mule,
parrying any stallout with the shift.
In too big a hurry to turn
at the end of a row he jammed
in a brake and spun around,
lowered the harrows
into the winter-bleached field
and blasted off for yon end.
Barely able to read, he took
dusters and bush hogs and diesel movements
apart with the skill of a surgeon,
hollering on the phone for parts
as far away as Charlotte or Atlanta.
Would stay on his ass at the filling station
or country store for weeks
while wife and kids and parents
picked in the heat the crops he'd
drive to market. Neither storm-threat
nor overripening could move him
to join their labor. Until time
for dusting with the homemade blower
mounted on a jeep. Or after the vines
were cut he'd windlass in the long wires.

> Winters Luther lived only for his truck,
> banging down the dirt road to Chestnut Springs
> for booze and women. But that was just
> occasional. Most days he'd brag at the store
> about his pickup, or be trading for another
> with even thicker tires, more horsepower
> and chrome, a gunrack in the window.
> At home he'd maybe tune a little,
> oil the plates of the planter.
> But off the machine he was just
> another stocky hoojer, yelling
> to make up for his lack of size
> and self-esteem, adding fat and blood
> pressure. Late February breaking time
> transformed him. He leapt on the big
> diesel and burned out its winter farts
> all the way to the bottoms, whipping
> the animal until it glowed, became
> his legs and voice and shoulders.
> To children and himself he tore up ground
> like a centaur. Plowing with the lights on
> all night in the river fields
> he circled more times than any race driver,
> shouting in the settling damp while
> we slept hearing the distant fury.
> And by morning the fields were new.[38]

One reason this is a great poem, more than just another eccentric Southern character study, is implicit in the title. The poem's not called "Cousin Luther"; it's titled "Man and Machine," which raises cousin Luther to another, more universal level. Morgan makes it a poem *about* Luther's elevation to another level, about his transformation, his redeeming change, from "just another stocky hoojer" (*Dictionary of Smoky Mountain English*: "a person native to the mountains, especially one considered ill-mannered or particularly rustic") off the tractor to something else entirely when "astride that bright and smelly beast," tearing up ground "like a centaur." Luther has been mythologized, immortalized: his passion for plowing not only transforms him, it transforms the land every spring, makes possible the crops that keep his family and community going. And his triumphant cries near the end, "shouting in the settling damp," represent a transformed speech for Luther, who throughout the poem has told lies, cussed, hollered ignorantly on the phone, bragged, yelled "to make up for his lack of size / and self-esteem." Now these violent turns and spins of "a man inspired" become a kind of poetry, an enjambment of lines (as implied in the root sense of the word "verse": "a turning of the plow"). The poem's self-contained last line recalls the quiet conclusion of "Zircon Pit," "I listened, close to the new sky": "And by morning the fields were new." The old fields, the old man, made new, born again: one of our oldest stories, given memorable local embodiment by the poet Luther and (later) his poet-cousin.

Technically, this is a modest poem, with none of the virtuosity of the book's penultimate "Chant Royal," a vernacular masterpiece honoring the tradition of that intricate Old French courtly verse form while making the poem sound wholly Appalachian. "Man and Machine" features the supple syllabic line that Morgan favors in his later books, an eight-beat framework on and around and through which the poem can grow. "A poem is structured freedom," as he once said, and syllabic verse seems to provide Morgan with a necessary skeleton without restricting his freedom too greatly.[39] It's an almost invisible discipline, which may be the best kind: the art is to hide the art, as Horace said and Morgan does. "Man and Machine" is much more capacious than early Morgan work, in tone and diction and vocabulary: it opens with a relaxed joke, and it's among his most reader-friendly poems. Its voice is more accommodating than ever; as Morgan commented in a 1985 interview, "I would like to see poetry achieve a classic balance between sophistication and precision, in a vocabulary that can say with great subtlety exactly what you want to say. I would not like to go to either extreme: poems that anybody can understand on first hearing or poems that are completely hermetic."

I would say that he has achieved that balance in "Man and Machine," and in many of the poems in *At the Edge of the Orchard Country*. I would say that this book is a cross-section of Morgan's style and themes and subjects: you can find hints of *Zirconia Poems*, his first book, published eighteen years earlier, and you can find hints of *The Blue Valleys*, his next book, published two years later. But I would also say that this is no self-satisfied magnum opus, no mere resting on long-deserved laurels. Like any first-rate poet, Morgan is still pushing himself, trying new things, developing new interests and directions. Even as he establishes himself as the greatest Appalachian poet of his generation, if not of all time, he is expanding his horizons beyond the merely regional: he is becoming one of the best American poets of his generation, indeed one of the best poets of his time, period. This is evident in several ways. One is the increasing number of poems about history, especially American history and myth: look at the first and third sections of *At the Edge of the Orchard Country*. Another way is evident in a poem like "Brownian Motion," and in poems like "Inertia" and "Radiation Pressure" from his new book *Sigodlin*, and in many of the "new" poems in his *New and Selected*: that is, poems of a theoretical scientific nature, poems whose verbal physics are not region-specific at all. And finally, as "Man and Machine" suggests, there is his newfound desire to universalize the local, to make it part of a much larger pattern, especially at the ends of poems: consider "Harrow," for example, where the poet remembers his "first plowing" and concludes, "I held in soaked / palms one great smelly horsepower / that leapt ahead to my voice / and sideways toward the eye of / the planet's newest field."[40]

That expansive impulse is most clearly seen in *Sigodlin*, which may be Morgan's least explicitly regional book since the first volume or two, and his most cosmopolitan: after all, it has two pantoums, and the definitive poem about the Vietnam Veterans' Memorial in Washington. But at the same time that Morgan avoids being labeled "merely" an Appalachian writer, *Sigodlin* proves that he is still a writer wholly rooted in that place, those people, their language: after all, he does call the book *Sigodlin* and not *Shadow Matter*. Particularly in the longer second section of the book, Morgan continues to develop his familiar world: "the real world," as he once wrote and apparently still believes, "is home. Homecoming. Homing."[41]

I'd like to end this survey of Morgan's poetic career with "Heaven," one of the poems from *Sigodlin*, perhaps my favorite among his new work. In its quatrains and level of language, in its tone and scope and subject matter, in its haunting voice, it's Robert Morgan at his best.

Heaven

And yet I don't want not to believe in,
little as I can, the big whoosh of souls

upward at the Rapture, when clay and ocean,
dust and pit, yield up their dead, when all

elements reassemble into the forms
of the living from the eight winds and flung
petals of the compass. And I won't assume,
much as I've known it certain all along,

that I'll never see Grandma again, nor
Uncle Vol with his fabulations,
nor see Uncle Robert plain with no scar
from earth and the bomber explosions.

I don't want to think how empty and cold
the sky is, how distant the family,
but of winged seeds blown from a milkweed field
in the opalescent smokes of early

winter ascending toward heaven's blue,
each self orchestrated in one aria
of river and light. And those behind the blue
are watching even now us on the long way.[42]

Will somebody please read this poem—so reluctantly doubtful about the afterlife, so apocalyptic and yet intimate, so gorgeous in image and imagination after the turn at "but," so heartbreakingly hopeful in its final sentence—at my funeral?

By way of conclusion, let me say a few words about Robert Morgan's new career, that of successful fiction writer.

First, I don't think we need to worry about a permanent defection from the house of poetry, or about Morgan being warped out of his poetic orbit by paperback deals and movie rights and a walk-on role in a Major Motion Picture made from his book, as happened with a fine Southern poet-turned-novelist of the previous generation.

Second, it's not so surprising, if you go back to Morgan's beginnings as a writer, which were in fact in fiction. While at North Carolina State as an undergraduate, he took novelist Guy Owen's celebrated writing class; and when he transferred to Chapel Hill as a junior, he continued to work mostly in fiction, taking an honors fiction class and serving as Fiction Editor for the *Carolina Quarterly* for three issues in 1964, one of which included a short story by him. And even in the hardback anthology *Chapel Hill Carousel*, edited by his teacher Jessie Rehder and published by UNC Press in 1967, his contributor's note to that latter volume concludes, "He is at present working on a novel." Fiction has been in his blood for decades.

And third, and most important of all, if you read *The Blue Valleys*, you will recognize it as part of the same "witness of many writings" as his poetry. This is not to say that these are self-consciously "poetic" stories: happily, they are remarkable for their quiet, unforced voice, which may be closer to Raymond Carver than Faulkner or Agee or Cormac McCarthy. These are not curiosity pieces, a poet's idle detour into fiction, fit only for footnotes in studies of the poetry: they work as stories all on their own. *The Blue Valleys* is as important as any of the nine books of poems because it is so clearly a part of the same witness: they address the same material—the place, the people, their stories—from a slightly different angle, less intense verbally but no less focused and true.

And the stories help clarify Morgan's relationship to his material, which has never been as simple and nostalgic as some readers have imagined. As a poet in exile, his attitudes toward home are necessarily complex, and not unlike those of Jones in "Tailgunner," who lives in Sumter, South Carolina, but hesitates to let his daughter and her family build a summer house on family land back home in the mountains. "He couldn't explain why he hesitated. He almost never went back there, even in summer. The pasture had grown up in blackberries and black pines. The old log barn had caved in and been swallowed by the brush and honeysuckle. The plum trees and apple trees of his granddaddy's orchard were surrounded by tall thin pines. And his cousins seemed like strangers. They represented everything he had tried to get away from and forget: the church quarrels, the ignorant disputes about theology, the suspicion of outsiders, the money grubbing of some and the embarrassing poverty of others, the beat-up pickup trucks and the dirty children. Yet at times he ached to be back there."[43]

In his stories and his poems, in the steady witness of his many writings, Robert Morgan transmits to us that "ache to be back," that homeward instinct we all know, so complicated and conflicted and yet satisfying like nothing else. I expect the scope of his poetry and fiction to grow for many years, outward and upward, yet backward and homeward. Like the "Writing Spider" in *Sigodlin*, Morgan will continue to "spell / a message to the world," one we can all continue to read and interpret and value: "That web / was strung significant as lines / in a palm and the little webster, / spinning out its monogram like / the fates, put the whole dictionary / of a life in one elaborate / letter to be abstracted from / the Jacob's ladder of floss and dew / in the eye of the beholder, / a lifetime's work for it and all."[44]

Notes

1. "'The Witness of Many Writings': Robert Morgan's Poetic Career" first appeared in *The Iron Mountain Review* 6 (Spring 1990): pp. 17–23. It also appears, with a few minor revisions, in McFee's *The Napkin Manuscripts: Selected Essays and an Interview*. Knoxville: University of Tennessee Press, 2006, pp. 164–80. The text here is that of the revision.
2. "Mockingbird" appears in four of Morgan's books: first included in *Trunk & Thicket*, it is reprinted both in *Green River: New and Selected Poems* and *The Strange Attractor: New and Selected Poems*, and Broadstone Books has since published the poem as a separate volume. For this essay's quotations from the poem, the editors of this collection have provided footnoted page numbers keyed to the poem's publication in *Trunk & Thicket*. McFee quotes "the southern night" from the poem's first line, p. 35.
3. From "Mockingbird," in *Trunk & Thicket*, p. 37.
4. *Ibid.*, p. 37.
5. *Ibid.*, p. 36.
6. From "Carved Seeds," an uncollected poem published in *The Small Farm* 3 (Spring 1976): p. 4.
7. From "Mockingbird," in *Trunk & Thicket*, p. 37.
8. *Ibid.*, p. 37.
9. "Music of the Spheres," a revision of the poem quoted, eventually appeared in the October 1993 issue of *Poetry* and was later collected in *Topsoil Road*.
10. From "Mockingbird," in *Trunk & Thicket*, p. 37.
11. From the 1976 "Interview by Jeff Daniel Marion," reprinted in *Good Measure*, p. 128.
12. Both quotations are from the short story "Blinding Daylight," in *The Blue Valleys*, p. 165.
13. From "Mockingbird," in *Trunk & Thicket*, p. 37.
14. *Ibid.*, p. 42.
15. *Ibid.*, p. 37.
16. "Lightning Bug," from *At the Edge of the Orchard Country*, p. 24.
17. From Aristotle's *Poetics*.
18. From "Mockingbird," in *Trunk & Thicket*, p. 38.
19. *Ibid.*, p. 41.
20. *Ibid.*, p. 37.
21. *Ibid.*, p. 42.
22. *Ibid.*, p. 42.
23. From "Overalls," in *Sigodlin*, p. 55.
24. From "Mockingbird," in *Trunk & Thicket*, pp. 42–43.
25. *Ibid.*, p. 40.

26. From *North Carolina Poetry*, a special issue of *Southern Poetry Review*, vol. 11, no. 1 (Spring 1970): p. 39.
27. From *Red Owl*, p. 39.
28. From Theodore Roethke's poem "Root Cellar."
29. From Morgan's 1984 essay "The Cubist of Memory," reprinted in *Good Measure*, p. 9.
30. From the title poem of *Trunk & Thicket*, p. 6.
31. From Morgan's 1980 essay "Some Sentences on the Line," reprinted in *Good Measure*, p. 3: "My first principle of versification was, Make something happen in every line."
32. From "Land Diving," in *Land Diving*, p. 33.
33. From *Land Diving*, p. 19.
34. From *Trunk & Thicket*, p. 13.
35. From "Mountain Page," in *Groundwork*, p. 48.
36. From "Zircon Pit," in *Groundwork*, p. 49.
37. The sentence quotes three poems first collected in *Bronze Age* (which omits page numbers) and reprinted in *At the Edge of the Orchard Country*: "a soil subliminal and sublime" is from "Field Theory" (*At the Edge*, p. 68), "fundamental lair" is from "Potato Hole" (*At the Edge*, p. 32), and "Only way out to the sun is down / through the exquisite filth" is from "Hay Scuttle" (*At the Edge*, p. 36).
38. From *At the Edge of the Orchard Country*, pp. 50–51.
39. From "The Transfigured Body: Notes from a Journal" (1970–1975), reprinted in *Good Measure*, p. 1[illegible]8: "A poem is structured freedom, appetitive."
40. From *At the Edge of the Orchard Country*, p. 38.
41. From the title poem of *Trunk & Thicket*, p. 13.
42. From *Sigodlin*, p. 30.
43. From *The Blue Valleys*, p. 116.
44. From *Sigodlin*, p. 49.

Music's Mirror

Robert Morgan's Musica Speculativa

JIM CLARK

Music, writing, history, and nature would seem to be Robert Morgan's poetic quadrivium. As the arc of Morgan's poetic achievement begins to come more clearly into view, these are, to borrow a phrase from that splendid narrative of obsession *Tristram Shandy*, his "hobby-horses." *Quadrivium*, of course, is Latin for "the four ways" or "the four roads" of medieval education which come after the *trivium*, those "four ways" being arithmetic, geometry, music, and astronomy. Readers of Morgan's poetry will no doubt recognize that given Morgan's scientific training, arithmetic, geometry, and astronomy also figure prominently in his writing. It is curious, then, that while Morgan has on numerous occasions written about the powerful influence of music on him and on his writing, he has written only a handful of poems that are actually about music. This study will examine that handful of poems in an effort to more fully appreciate the powerful but subtle influence of music on Robert Morgan's poetry.

The title of this essay, "Music's Mirror," is borrowed from the title of the second part of Morgan's collection of "essays, interviews, and notes on poetry," *Good Measure*. "Music's Mirror," however, is also the English translation of the Latin *Speculum Musicae*, the title of Jacques de Liège's seven-volume *summa* of medieval music theory written in the fourteenth century. Much of Jacques' masterwork is devoted to *musica speculativa*, theoretical discussions of music, mathematics, and mysticism, underpinned by Pythagorean notions. It is also a defense of the older *ars antiqua* against the newer *ars nova*. Clearly, Morgan knows his music history, and it is not surprising that Jacques might be a favorite, given the medieval writer's fascination with mathematics, history, and philosophy, as well as music. Jacques devotes a chapter of his treatise to a numerological discussion of the importance of the number four as the foundation of harmony, in music as in the world generally. Interestingly, among the poems this essay will consider is a suite of four poems in Morgan's collection *Topsoil Road* that all have to do with music and musical instruments.

Morgan's most succinct statement about the influence of music on his life and writing comes from his 1998 Harder Lecture at Cornell Plantations, "Nature Is a Stranger Yet," the text of which can be found on his personal website (www.robert-morgan.com). Rich in biographical detail, the passage is worth quoting in full:

> As I got into my teens I read and read and thought about writing. And I took piano lessons and studied music theory and harmony on my own. I listened to the New York Philharmonic on the

> AM radio on Saturday nights, and I fell under the spell of Baroque music, especially Bach and Handel. Before that, from infancy, I had been exposed to hymn and ballad singing. I grew up among people who could sing shaped notes, and old mountain ballads. My grandpa had been a banjo picker before he got married and joined the church. One of my great-great-grandfathers had been the most famous fiddle player in upper South Carolina in the 1850s and 60s. Before I could read, before I had ever studied music, I heard music in my head much of the time. When I looked at a mountain, or at a tree in the wind, or the sun on tall grass, I heard a musical equivalent to the scene in my head. As best I can remember, it was music made up of snatches of things heard on the radio and in church. I could play the music in my head for hours. There was a musical correlative to everything I saw or thought about, a melodic accompaniment, a harmonic enhancement to every mood or image. I looked at the clouds and heard the sweep of music. I thought of old, sad stories, and heard music. As I grew older I lost that ability to compose mentally and spontaneously. But in my teens I became convinced that I wanted to compose music.

Though it is clear that Morgan has a knowledge of and affinity for classical music, very few of his poems explicitly reflect that. Rather, more of them have to do with folk music—with banjos and fiddles and dulcimers—and with individual musicians.

"Concert," a fairly early poem from *Land Diving* (1976), is a portrait from memory of "Aunt Wessie," one of the members of Morgan's close-knit Green River valley community. The poem's carefully turned *aabb* quatrains with their subtle slant rhymes and its economical yet trenchant narrative illustrate why Morgan has said of *Land Diving*, "That book means the most to me because in some ways it cost me the most. I found I was able to incorporate narratives and history, folktales and science, monologue and traditional forms into my writing, and that gave me a gratifying sense of control and freedom" ("Interview by Suzanne Booker" 136). The poem begins with a neat conflation of musical performance and farm work:

> When Aunt Wessie played she
> reached into the keys with heavy
> arms as though rooting tomato
> slips, sinking hands in to
>
> the wrists and raking the dirt
> smooth, humming as she worked [*Land Diving* 10].

The poem emphasizes the physicality of Aunt Wessie's piano playing, noting that she would

> plunge onto the keyboard jamming the
>
> pedal in like an accelerator
> and slapping chords over
> the melody [10].

Morgan has spoken often about the importance of work. Having first sought to escape the hard labor that is the life of a mountain farmer, Morgan says, "I fell in love with work through words. I looked again and again at the details and discipline of work, at the drama of digging and hoeing, sawing and chopping, I had performed as a boy. The catharsis of work in the hot Southern sun, became the central experience in much of my writing" ("Writing the Mountains"). Even the heaving, halting line breaks in the poem are suggestive of the staggered rhythm of physical labor, and like many, Aunt Wessie hums as she works (or plays). The farm work motif is continued when the wires in the piano's sound board are described as a trellis, with the notes like vegetables or fruit (tomatoes, perhaps): "and every note on the trellis of wires blurred" (*Land Diving* 10). Sadly, as Aunt Wessie ages and her sight and hearing fail, those members of the community who "worked off in the fields" no longer hear her piano concert, but rather her TV, which "blasted soap tragedy / all over the valley."

Morgan's 1990 collection, *Sigodlin*, contains a sort of companion piece to "Concert" titled "New Organ," which again features Aunt Wessie, as well as tributes to two noted historical flute players: John James Audubon and Sydney Lanier. "New Organ" once more works the familiar ground of physical labor and music. In this case, however, the poem focuses on a man, seemingly Wessie's husband, who "[w]ithout a dollar in the house" offers a peddler "sixty / bushels of his finest sweet / potatoes, then seventy, eighty" for a pump organ (*Sigodlin* 44). The poem emphasizes his hard work—"A season / he'd given to the yield of those / great milky nuggets"—and, much like "Concert," elaborates intriguing connections between music and work:

> He picked each swollen
> root from the soil like a note
> and filled the basket eighty times,
> and then his wagon, thinking
> one hamper for each key[44].

Just as musical notes were compared to vegetables or fruit on a trellis in "Concert," here they are compared to the sweet potato roots, and of course filling the basket eighty times will just about pay for the standard eighty-eight keys of a keyboard. And one strategy of any type of manual labor is to divide the job into smaller tasks so that one does not become discouraged or overwhelmed by the scale of the job.

Wessie, too, works, in her way, as the poem describes the physicality of her musical endeavors:

> Wessie pulled the stops and pedaled,
> walking as she played, stepping
> on the red carpet treadles to
> the edge of another weather
> to look over [44].

Now that the summer is over and the crop harvested, winter is drawing near ("the edge of another weather / to look over"), the time when Wessie does her work, playing the organ as

> the family sang and the young
> gathered to the heat of his labor
> transmuted into a movement
> of the air [44].

although we find that the man who bought her organ "frowned / and never spoke approval" in regard to the organ and Wessie's music. It would be easy to infer that he does not approve of the luxury of the organ and views it as frivolous, a grudging concession to Wessie's eccentric passion. However, the poem is at pains to emphasize the transformation of his labor into Wessie's music—"the heat of his labor / transmuted into a movement / of the air, a stir of air in / the shudder and breath of the pedals." And when he looks outside to see the hillside where he had harvested the sweet potatoes "frozen over / and snow shawling over the clay" (45) (a nice echo of the earlier "white / convolvulus vines shawling on / the hillside" [44]) we find the frozen furrows each "become a phrase," also transformed into music, "while / the carpet wore out on the pedals / as from a long pilgrimage" (45). The earlier description of Wessie's music as "a dance of color in sadness / of the hymn's expectations" (44), coupled with the last line's image of "a long pilgrimage," evokes not just the hard life and fatalistic outlook of many mountain people, but also their yearning, fervent faith. The hymn mentioned might be one like Isaac Watts' "We're Marching to Zion." Just as in the poem, where "the family sang and the young / gathered," the hymn urges "Children of the heavenly King"[1] (11) to "Join in a Song with sweet accord" (3). Similarly, the Christians in the hymn are "marching thro' *Immanuel's* Ground / To fairer Worlds on high" (39–40), while in the poem the carpet on Wessie's organ pedals wore out from her tireless playing "as from a long pilgrimage." And finally in the poem, just as the man's hillside field yields not only sweet potatoes, but ultimately beautiful music, so, in the penultimate verse of "We're Marching to Zion," "The Hill of *Zion* yields / A thousand sacred Sweets / Before we reach the heavenly Fields / Or walk the golden Streets" (33–36). Perhaps the man's taciturn frown is only the mountain farmer's acknowledgment that life is harsh and hard, a frown of "sadness / of the hymn's expectations."

"Audubon's Flute," a pastoral pantoum, is about as thoroughly *musical* a poem as Morgan has ever written. With its lulling, insistent *repetons* carried over from quatrain to quatrain, its profusion of alliteration, and its rhythmically varied octosyllabic lines, the poem is a tour de force in which Audubon's musical performance—"his breath modeling a melody"—is in perfect concert with the idyllic natural world "two hundred miles from any wall," where "sunset plays the stops of river" (*Sigodlin* 4). Like an American Pan with his "silver pipe," Audubon charms the "deer and herons," his melody "coloring the trees and canebrakes." Whether he intended it or not, Morgan's poem contains many of the central elements of Pan's story—the pipe, the river, the canebrakes, the moon, the echo of the *repetons*. Pan made his pipes from river reeds, one of which was the water nymph Syrinx (daughter of the river-god Landon) who had been transformed into a river reed to help her escape from Pan's amorous advances. Another time, Pan disguised himself with a sheepskin in order to draw down the moon goddess Selene from the sky and seduce her in the forest. In one story, Pan, jealous of the nymph Echo, had his followers kill and dismember her, strewing the pieces of her body over the earth. Only her voice remains, repeating the last words of others.

Finally, the interlinked imagery and the twisting, turning rhythmic repetition, a necessary feature of the pantoum, is reminiscent of Wallace Stevens' poem "Domination of Black," which Morgan says was one of the first modern poems he came to cherish: "But the one that made the deepest impression was Wallace Stevens' poem 'Domination of Black.' ... The repetitions and music of the poem thrilled me" ("Nature Is a Stranger Yet"). Though the mood of "Audubon's Flute" is ecstatic and celebratory—almost the polar opposite of "Domination of Black," which seems anxious and fearful—both poems evoke their moods by incantation. Both poems also contain similar natural imagery (trees, leaves, twilight, solitude, vastness) which seems to partake of the Romantic sublime; both focus on an insistent sound that is related to the imagery ("the cry of the peacocks" in Stevens' poem [8], and the "silver notes" of Audubon's flute in Morgan's poem); and both at the end rise skyward ("I saw how the planets gathered" [9] in Stevens' poem, and "the whitest moon is rising / to the horizon and beyond" in Morgan's).

"Sidney Lanier Dies at Tryon 1881" is a very different sort of poem—a conventional lyric narrative composed in a type of versification Morgan calls "the simplest I know, an eight-syllable line with no regular meter, no counting of stresses. It is almost-free verse broken into arbitrary length, based vaguely on four-beat common meter: a kind of humble blank verse" ("Good Measure" 6). The form's humble simplicity provides an ironic contrast to the poem's subject, Sydney Lanier, a noted musician and next to Poe perhaps America's most prodigiously ornate and musical poet, and one whose poems Morgan had committed to memory in elementary school ("Nature"). Morgan alludes to Lanier's mastery of prosody, and his study of it, *The Science of English Verse*, early in the poem:

> Two months of camping on the peaks
> only made the world more hazy,
> ghostlike, and the summit winds had
> sucked away his breath, and stolen
> his voice, the form and duration
> of English phrasing he'd worked so
> to make measurable, to set down [*Sigodlin* 33].

It is here, after this allusion to prosody and verbal music, that the poem's focus on Lanier as a musician begins:

> And the current pouring from his lips
> into the flute had vanished
> and only turbulence and coughs
> and random winds were left gusting,
> subsiding in his head [33].

The poem then lyrically describes the dying Lanier's feverish, nearly hallucinatory memories of his life as tuberculosis inexorably steals the last of that life away:

> The one
> oratorio, all notes and language,
> seemed red as coals, red as his
> syllables, while the night he'd married
> hovered near, and his son the shadow,
> and the world somewhere gaudy and
> subtle as Shakespeare drew further
> back, swam on the higher oceans [33–34].

"The one / oratorio" may well refer to *The Centennial Meditation of Columbia*, a cantata commissioned for the 1876 American centennial for which Lanier wrote the words, while "red ... syllables" refers back to the earlier "blood he / spat" (33). The world that "swam on the higher oceans" prepares for "The black peaks beyond the house" (34), which the dying flutist tries to imaginatively reconstruct in his memory through his memories of past musical performance—"a little turn on / the flute he must try to recall, / that ran the same as the dark ridge." Alas, unlike the vigorous naturalist Audubon, Lanier is too weak to summon the creative energy to body forth the mountains in either music or memory.

"Audubon's Flute" and "Sidney Lanier Dies at Tryon 1881" each in its own way embodies Morgan's notion of the artist achieving a sort of *participation mystique*[2] in the rendering of nature. Morgan articulates his own youthful yearning for such a creative enterprise in "Nature Is a Stranger Yet":

> As I looked across the Green River valley at the Cicero Mountain looming dark lavender in winter and tipped with ice on its cliff, I knew I wanted to compose a poem or piece of music as grand as the mountain. It would be an epic, or something like an oratorio, or fantasia and fugue

> for organ. I heard vast, deep chords like engines and heavy machinery inside the earth, and crisp notes sparkling in the high registers as though from beyond the Milky Way. My composition would be heroic, and it would be in the measure and wavelength of the mountain.

One is reminded of Wallace Stevens' poem "The Poem that Took the Place of a Mountain," which perhaps bears quoting in full:

> There it was, word for word,
> The poem that took the place of a mountain.
>
> He breathed its oxygen,
> Even when the book lay turned in the dust of his table.
>
> It reminded him how he had needed
> A place to go to in his own direction,
>
> How he had recomposed the pines,
> Shifted the rocks and picked his way among clouds,
>
> For the outlook that would be right,
> Where he would be complete in an unexplained completion:
>
> The exact rock where his inexactnesses
> Would discover, at last, the view toward which they had edged,
>
> Where he could lie and, gazing down at the sea,
> Recognize his unique and solitary home [Stevens 512].

Audubon and Lanier, each having imaginatively "recomposed the pines" through his music, end their poems "complete in an unexplained completion" each recognizing "his unique and solitary home"—Audubon through an ecstatic *participation mystique* "in the summer woods" (*Sigodlin* 4) and Lanier through an acceptance of his imminent death, almost remembering "the precise fingering, the pause / and the continuing line, just as the world became visible" (*Sigodlin* 34).

Despite his love of classical music and knowledge of music theory, it really comes as no surprise that Morgan's most sustained exploration of music in poems focuses on Appalachian folk music and its instruments—the fiddle, the dulcimer, and the banjo—and not on Bach or Handel or the clavier and the violin. Near the end of *Topsoil Road* (2000) Morgan features a quartet of poems about musical instruments—their materials, their makers, and their masters. In "History's Madrigal," "Tail Music," "Mountain Dulcimer," and "The Grain of Sound," Morgan combines music and myth and history and a little Pythagorean mathematical mysticism to create his own modern, homegrown *musica speculativa.*

In "History's Madrigal" Morgan begins with the simple notion of "fiddle makers and dulcimer / makers" looking for the "best material" from which to craft their instruments (*Topsoil Road* 48). "[T]hey / prefer old woods, not just seasoned / but antique," we are told, for "the older wood has sweeter, more / mellow sounds, makes truer and deeper / music." This leads to the poem's central conceit—that the old wood is itself a kind of recording medium, registering and storing history in its grain:

> as if the walnut or
> cherry, cedar or maple, as
> it aged, stored up the knowledge of
> passing seasons, the cold and thaw,
> whine of storm, bird call and love
> moan, news of wars and mourning, in
> its fibers, in the sparkling grain [48].

This stored litany of history can then be "summoned and released by / the craftsman's hands and by careful / fingers on the strings' vibration," resulting in a polyphonic, contrapuntal voicing of the inscribed events of "decades and generations," or, as the poem says, "the memory and wisdom of / wood delighting air." Morgan's choice of the word "madrigal," with its etymology going back to the Latin "matrix" and "mater"—"womb" and "mother," respectively—is especially apt here in that the polyphonic voices released by the craftsman and musician create a sort of womb-like, mystically unified simultaneity of time in which "century / speaks to century and history / dissolves history" (48).

In "Tail Music" Morgan continues his exploration of music and history, and now also folklore, by writing of the habit of some old-time fiddlers who put a rattlesnake rattle in the sound box of their fiddle. Given the common characterization of the fiddle as "the devil's instrument," it is truly a tempting subject. Morgan begins with a mundane explanation of the practice:

> they meant to swell
> the resonance of the sound box,
> give the wood vibrations added
> flavor [*Topsoil Road* 49].

"[T]hresh and shiver-hum" is vivid aural imagery for the sound produced by the rattle, with "thresh" being nearly onomatopoeic and the compound "shiver-hum" having a bit of the flavor of a kenning. Not content to remain on the level of the mundane, Morgan brings the real subject of his poem into focus by introducing folklore and mythology with the phrase "serpent's tail-music," the synonym "serpent" for "snake" providing an almost guaranteed allusion to Satan, and the talismanic "presence of the rattles" that "must have made the fiddlers feel more / daring." Bringing up the centuries-old criticism of rhythmic music as being carnal and sensual and provocative, the notes of "the devil's instrument" are described as "hypnotic as a snake's / stare, and stirring evil in young / bodies." Indeed, the title "Tail Music" itself seems fashioned to suggest not only the whirring of the rattlesnake's rattle, located in its tail, but also the effect of the forbidden music on humans and their anatomy—after all, we use phrases such as "shake a tail feather" and the more recent "shake your booty" to rather crudely describe some types of dancing. "[T]he inclination / to dance all night and the next day" provoked by the music proves that "the serpent had its way / again," and Morgan's final, somewhat surprising image of "those days when young men / ate the heart of any rattler / they killed raw, to give them courage" suggests that perhaps each of us has at least a little "snake blood soaring" in our veins, waiting to be awakened by the right combination of sounds (49).

"Mountain Dulcimer" returns to some of the themes explored in "History's Madrigal"—time, history, and how human experience and emotion may somehow inhere in the very materials from which a musical instrument is made, and the sounds it produces. The poem begins with two questions: "Where does such sadness in wood come / from? How could longing live in these / wires?" (*Topsoil Road* 50). The third sentence elaborates a lovely and evocative simile, suggesting something of an answer: "The box looks like the most fragile / coffin tuned for sound." The word "coffin" brings up various connotations of death, suffering, and sorrow; these connotations, and the circumstances of the poem—a woman playing the dulcimer and holding the instrument in its traditional pose, "laid / across the knees"—inspire the brilliant imaginative leap "it looks less like a baby nursed / than some symbolic Pietà." From this point on, the poem consists of one long, proliferating, concatenated sentence requiring an unusual quality and degree of attention of the reader. The sounds produced by the dulcimer, then, are those of the emotions associated with the Pietà:

> and the stretched body on her lap
> yields modalities of lament
> and blood, yields sacrifice and sliding
> chants of grief [50].

"Modalities" is an especially apt word for a poem about the mountain dulcimer as the dulcimer's frets are typically arranged in a diatonic scale, and tuning the strings to different notes produces different modes, such as Ionian, Aeolian, etc.[3] The word also functions as a bridge between music and emotion since "mode" and "modality" are employed to discuss both the psychology of emotion and the theory of musical harmony. As well, certain musical modes are sometimes described as sounding "happy" and "vibrant" (major modes) or "sad" and "wistful" (minor modes). "Sliding chants" is careful description as well, as the dulcimer is usually played by pressing a "noter" (often something like a Popsicle stick or a dowel) to the melody string and sliding it up or down the fret board to change the pitch, and "chants" connotes the Gregorian "modal" sound of the instrument. The musical and emotional "modalities" previously described

> dance and dance toward
> a new measure, a new threshold,
> a new instant and new year that
> we always celebrate by
> remembering the old and by
> recalling the lost [50].

This conflation of new and old is very similar to the simultaneity of time we find at the end of "History's Madrigal." Added to this simultaneity of time is a simultaneity of emotion—"voices join in sadness and joy"—evoked by loss, by "honoring / those no longer here to strike these / strings like secrets of the most / satisfying harmonies." And of course "secrets of the most / satisfying harmonies" also hints at the Pythagorean mysteries[4] of music and mathematics which if rightly apprehended are capable of telling us "again what we already / know, have always known but forget," even if only played on a "fragile / coffin tuned for sound" and coming "from way back in the farthest cove, / from highest on the peaks of love" (50). Thus the poem resolves its long final sentence with the sure sense of closure provided by the slant-rhyme couplet.

The final poem of this quartet, "The Grain of Sound," focuses on a different instrument, the banjo, perhaps the quintessential voice of the mountains. The poem begins much like "History's Madrigal," with a search for "wood to carve / an instrument" (*Topsoil Road* 51). Walking in the mountains, the banjo maker will "hit / the bark and listen for a note." "[H]ickory," we find, "makes the brightest sound," while "poplar has a mellow ease." The quality of the wood is essential, however, as "only straightest grain will keep / the purity of tone, the sought—/ for depth that makes the licks sparkle." Morgan's synaesthetic, onomatopoeic descriptions of the banjo's sound are reminiscent of some of Wallace Stevens' enchanting, alliterative experiments in pure sound such as "Life Is Motion" and "Bantams in Pine-Woods": "A banjo has a shining shiver. / Its twangs will glitter like the light / on splashing water." Morgan marvels at the sounds produced by the banjo "even though / its face is just a drum of hide / of cow, or cat, or even skunk." Again, as in

"Mountain Dulcimer," the music produced by the banjo conjures emotion: "the sad of honest pain, the chill / blood-song, lament, confession, haunt." In the banjo's music, the

> tree will sing again from root
> and vein and sap and twig in wind
> and cat will moan as hand plucks nerve,
> picks bone and skin and gut [51].

One notes the insistent monosyllabic rhythms of these lines which are evocative of the banjo player's bright, fast, discrete plucking of individual strings. The "song of materials" implicit in all four of these poems—the music made from what the instruments are made of—is fascinatingly similar to one of the old traditional folk songs collected and published by British musicologist Francis James Child in the late nineteenth century, a rather macabre one called "The Twa Sisters" (Child ballad #10), also sometimes called "The Cruel Sister." Though there are endless variants, the basic narrative of the song is that two sisters both love the same man. The elder sister should have precedence over the younger because of her age, but the man loves the younger sister and gives her a "gay gold ring" while he "didn't give the elder one anything." In a jealous rage, and in the midst of the "wind and rain" of a storm, the elder sister pushes her sister in the water to drown. The younger sister's body floats down to "the miller's mill pond" and the miller removes her body from the water and lays her on the shore. Next comes "a fiddler fair" (or in some versions "a harper") who constructs a fiddle from the younger sister's body parts ("He made fiddle strings from her long yellow hair," "He made fiddle pegs from her long finger bones," "He made a little fiddle body of her breast bone"). The song concludes with the repetitive, mournful refrain played by the fiddle:

> And the only tune that fiddle could play
> Was Oh, the Wind and Rain
> The only tune that fiddle could play
> Was Oh, the cruel Wind and Rain.

There seem to be elements of ancient myth, like that of Philomel and Procne, at work in such a song, where the victim is transformed into something else (a fiddle, or a bird) in order to tell, or sing, her fate, and also perhaps of Orpheus, where music and musical instruments (the lyre) have a profound magical power. "The Grain of Sound" ends with the elemental "blood" and "love" (ingredients of so many human stories) as the banjo music "pricks / the heart as blood will answer blood / and love begins to knock along the grain," just as the banjo maker earlier knocked on the tree bark to "listen for a note" (51).

In these poems of music, musicians, and musical instrument makers, music can easily be seen as an analog for poetry. Music is the "master metaphor" that allows Morgan to synthesize and unify his poetic quadrivium of music, writing, history, and nature into a harmonious whole. Just as the fiddle maker in "History's Madrigal" knows that the older wood contains "stored … knowledge" that can be "summoned and released" by the instrument maker and the musician (48), so the poet knows, as Emerson says in "The Poet," that "language is fossil poetry" (457) and that fossil record can be "summoned and released" by the poet. With his keen interest in science, his eye for detail, and his penchant for narrative, Morgan would seem to be more of a sharp-eyed, precise and objective realist, but music is his route to the Orphic, the Pythagorean. His poems about music comprise his own unique metaphysical *musica speculativa* revealing "secrets of the most /

satisfying harmonies" (50) and demonstrating how "century / speaks to century and history / dissolves history" (48).

Notes

1. Watts' original line was "But Favorites of the heavenly King" but nearly all modern versions of the hymn substitute "But Children of the heavenly King." Watts' original title for the hymn was "Heavenly Joy on Earth."

2. In *How Natives Think* (1910) French anthropologist Lucien Lévy-Bruhl employs the phrase *participation mystique* to help describe the nature of the primitive mind which he said was characterized by prelogical "mystical thinking" as opposed to modern Western logical thinking. *Participation mystique* means that the primitive experiences the world (object) as an extension of himself (subject), so that his consciousness is a seamless "mystical participation" with nature that is indifferent to contradictions. C.G. Jung adopted and refined this notion of *participation mystique* for his own purposes, and his student Erich Neumann applied it particularly to the process of artistic creativity in his essay "Art and Time," from *Art and the Creative Unconscious* (1971).

3. A *mode* is a term used in music theory to denote the seven available fixed orders of diatonic notes within a given octave. The modes are Ionian, Dorian, Phrygian, Lydian, Mixolydian, Aeolian, and Locrian. The Ionian mode is the natural major and the Aeolian mode is the natural minor. The Greek mathematician and philosopher Pythagoras is generally credited with discovering the relationships of musical intervals on which harmonic theory is based. For example, expressed as a mathematical ratio, a unison note would be 1:1, an octave 2:1, a harmonic fifth 3:2, etc.

4. Though a full accounting of the "Pythagorean mysteries" is probably impossible—they are "mysteries," after all, and Pythagoras was apparently very secretive about them, supposedly never writing anything down—they might include the fact that Pythagoras felt that mathematics was the key to all reality. He extrapolated his discovery of the musical harmonic interval to cosmic proportions, believing that the heavenly bodies had mathematical relationships to each other which produced the fabled "music of the spheres." He believed in the transmigration of souls as well, and advocated vegetarianism and other ascetic disciplines. Christoph Riedweg's *Pythagoras: His Life, Teaching, and Influence* (Cornell University Press, 2008) is a good basic study.

Works Cited

Emerson, Ralph Waldo. "The Poet." *Essays and Lectures*. Ed. Joel Porte. New York: Library of America, 1983. pp. 447–68.
Morgan, Robert. "Good Measure." *Epoch* 33 (Fall–Winter 1983): pp. 80–81. Rpt. in *Good Measure: Essays, Interviews, and Notes on Poetry*. Baton Rouge: Louisiana State University Press, 1993. pp. 5–7.
______. "Interview by Suzanne Booker." *Carolina Quarterly* 37 (Spring 1985): pp. 13–22. Rpt. in *Good Measure: Essays, Interviews, and Notes on Poetry*. Baton Rouge: Louisiana State University Press, 1993. pp. 131–43.
______. *Land Diving*. Baton Rouge: Louisiana State University Press, 1976.
______. "Nature Is a Stranger Yet." *Robert Morgan Official Author Website*. 17 June 2016. <http://www.robertmorgan.com>.
______. *Sigodlin*. Middletown: Wesleyan University Press, 1990.
______. *Topsoil Road*. Baton Rouge: Louisiana State University Press, 2000.
______. "Writing the Mountains." *Robert Morgan Official Author Website*. 17 June 2016. <http://www.robertmorgan.com>.
Stevens, Wallace. *The Collected Poems*. 1954. New York: Knopf, 1989.
Watts, Isaac. "Heavenly Joy on Earth (We're Marching to Zion)." *Isaac Watts Hymns and Spiritual Songs 1707–1748: A Study in Early Eighteenth Century Language Changes*. Comp. and ed. Selma L. Bishop. London: The Faith Press, 1962. pp. 188–90.

The Elegiac Strain in Robert Morgan's Poetry[1]

Bhisham Bherwani

Robert Morgan's substantial poetic oeuvre is pervaded by an appreciation for his forefathers, as in the concluding lines of "Mound Builders," with which he closes his fourteenth poetry volume, *Terroir*:

> ...all of us rely, and must,
> on our traditions and the deep
> ancestral memories and ways
> to bear us up and get us through
> the deadly and uncertain days,
> sustaining breath and sight and hope
> on residue and legacy
> of those beloved who came before
> and watch us from the glittering stars [92–93].

The poem—in which the speaker considers how Georgia's Creek Indians "deposited their dead, their kin, / in ceremonial heaps"—is an apt metaphor for Morgan's work, populated as it is from his earliest volumes to his most recent ones by "ancestral memories" of great-grandparents, grandparents, parents, aunts and uncles, and others who inhabited, literally and in spirit, the rural Appalachian landscape of his childhood. "The dirt is our ancestors," he concludes in an earlier "Mound Builders," from *Red Owl*, his third volume, which precedes *Terroir* by forty years (17).

Morgan is keenly tuned to his legacy: his speakers are profoundly sympathetic to family and tradition, to filial continuity. "Family Bible," from *Topsoil Road*, his twelfth volume, in which he recalls the "leather of the book," "soft / and black as that of Grandma's purse," notes the passages, through generations, of life's customary rituals:

> The marriages recorded, births
> and deaths set down in pencil and
> in many inks and hands, with names
> and middle names and different dates
> and spellings scrawled in berry juice
> that looks like ancient blood. And blood
> is what the book's about, the blood
> of sacrifice, the blood of Lamb,
> two testaments of blood, and blood
> of families set in names to show

> the course and merging branches, roots
> of fluid in your veins this moment [26].

The poem repeats *blood* six times in five lines (and twice again in its penultimate line), stressing the web of family associations and traditions, "the course and merging branches, roots / of fluid" in Morgan's veins. In "Books in the Attic," from *At the Edge of the Orchard Country*, Morgan's eighth volume, the poet and his father visit on a Sunday afternoon the decrepit loft of "the Morgan house," where "Dozens had been born and died" and "All of Daddy's / renovations before the war / for his bride were peeling, moldy"; there,

> sprawled the books of the family
> smelling of must and old tobacco,
> silverfish and pages tinged by time,
> the fat histories Great-grandpa
> got in Augusta when he wagoned
> hams and produce down the Winding Stairs [17].

The ancestral continuity of "Books in the Attic," which includes Morgan and, by reference, his father and great-grandfather, is reinforced, five volumes and twenty years later, in *October Crossing*'s "The Years Ahead," which begins, "When my grandpa took his produce / down the Winding Stairs to Greenville / to peddle door-to-door, he left / the day before and camped somewhere / near Travelers Rest just north of town" (37). The two poems embrace four generations, two on the same road, a grandpa retracing literally a great-grandpa's footsteps, and Morgan in turn retracing theirs through his poems.

The reference to the great-grandfather in "Books in the Attic" is followed a few years later by a reference to him in "The Road to Elmira," from *Sigodlin*, Morgan's ninth volume. The great-grandfather recalled, Frank Pace, was an important presence in Morgan's life. He served in the Confederate Army and was incarcerated at Elmira Prison in 1864–65. He never returned to Elmira—a short drive, ironically, from where Morgan, Kappa Alpha Professor of English at Cornell University, has made his home since 1971—but lived as a farmer on the family land, telling stories to the poet's father about history and the Civil War.

His own work's "pages tinged by time," Morgan's predecessors are rendered vivid through their outmoded and esoteric codes and customs. Rooted in place and tradition in a world of preachers and natural healers, they resist modernization, living simultaneously with and in awe of the natural and the supernatural, fathoming and interpreting their existences through biblical allegory and superstition: the grandfather on his journey in "The Years Ahead" "watched above / the trees the comet fling its ghost, / portending either ruin or / a century of wonder" (*October Crossing* 37). The premonition mirrors that in *Orchard Country*'s "Halley's Comet," where Morgan's father, haunted by the recollection, remembers the comet—which appears once every seventy-six years or so—being pointed out to him by Morgan's grandmother: "He often tried / to recall what she said it portended: flood? / famine? war?" He thinks,

> if he saw its milky breath again he'd be eighty-one,
> and the century old and time's conclusion
> near, for all preachers agreed the century would see
> the end of this dimension [11].

In *Sigodlin*'s "Writing Spider," "When Uncle Wass had found the spider's / W woven between the limbs / of a dead chestnut [...] / [...] he said he knew / there would be war." Morgan goes on to note that

Grandpa, his brother, told
how the writing spider's runes could spell
a message to the world, or warn
of the individual reader's own
end with an initial [49].

And in a crescendo as far as elicitations of the extraordinary go, in *Orchard Country*'s "The Gift of Tongues," the "father looking at // the altar as though electrocuted" speaks in tongues, conjuring the past beyond bloodline: "It was a voice I'd never heard / but knew as from other centuries."

It was the voice of awful fire
"What's he saying?" Ronald hissed
and jabbed my arm. "Probably Hebrew."
The preacher called out another
hymn, and the glissade came again,
high syllables not from my father's
lips but elsewhere, the fire of
higher language, sentences of light [29].

Unsurprisingly, given his lifelong proximity to nature—especially to mountains (the Blue Ridge and, beyond, the Appalachian range at large, extending to upstate New York) and their rivers and trees and creatures (the birds, bees, crickets, rattlesnakes, and spiders that inhabit his poems, often ominously)—Morgan imbues the elements with the ability to speak ("the voice of awful fire"), write, and even sing. His intimacy with perennial decay and renewal seems to underlie his urge to revive in poems what is in other ways irretrievable (his childhood, its people, the past in general).

Morgan's *ars poetica* is *Sigodlin*'s ingeniously pithy, concrete "Mountain Graveyard," a tombstone epitaph visually by virtue of its shape:

stone notes

slate tales

sacred cedars

heart earth

asleep please

hated death [27].

Nature both observes (in the context of "notes" as a verb) and sings (in musical "notes") above the buried dead, the song building on stories ("tales"), from sources perhaps religious or ancestral (both "sacred"), made possible by enduring life ("cedars," rooted in "earth"), resilient despite its uneasy ("hated") and unalterable relationship with death, grounded below. The "notes," "tales," "sacred," and "heart" imply human engagement, human interpretations of the words' counterparts ("stone," "slate," "cedars," and "earth"). The "stone notes / slate tales" identify nature's vocal as well as textual (the pun on "slate") potential, its lyric as well as narrative aspects. The "notes," aligned closest in the poem's configuration to "the glittering stars," the ultimate residence of the dead past the graveyard in "Mound Builders," suggest a psalm ("sacred") or a requiem that amplifies human grief, individual and universal, stemming from the "heart."

The transformations in the anagrams in each line of "Mountain Graveyard" are as much metaphorical as rhetorical. The general tone of reticence in the poem is countered by the intemperance of the all-too-human "please" and "hated," through which it invites in the reader. A fugue as it traverses its tiers from the delight of music to the dread of "hated death," the poem juxtaposes a word conjuring presence human ("notes," "tales," "sacred," "heart," "please," and "hated") with one conjuring presence extra-human. Of the latter, the inanimate "stone" and "slate," outliving death, are durable recorders and testimonies of the "notes" and "tales."

Between the last two lines of stasis and the first two of transcendence, are the two pivotal centrally located lines, where the generative ("earth" and "cedars") propagate the emotional and the spiritual ("heart" and "sacred"): the two fugal strains cross here, implying in counterpoint a complementary, inevitable, and necessary relationship between nature and man, present and past, life and death, and song and silence.

"Mountain Graveyard" has a biographical subtext. Simultaneously Christian and pagan, it emblematizes Morgan's straddling in his childhood stringent religious orthodoxy and nonjudgmental natural grandeur. The passivity that permeates the poem—even though it is a meditation on a subject no less severe than death—contrasts with the anxiety inherent in the conclusion of "The Gift of Tongues": "My hands hurt / when pulled from the pew's varnish / they'd gripped and sweated so." "Later," however,

> standing under the high and plain-
> sung pines on the mountain I clenched
> my jaws like pliers, holding in
> and savoring the gift of silence [29].

"When young," Morgan said to Suzanne Booker (in a conversation in *Good Measure*, a compilation of essays and interviews edited by the poet), "I remember being extremely frightened of [my father] and others speaking in tongues, shouting [...]. But mostly I remember the great relief when the service was over, and we could go back out into the sunlight and the sweet breeze among the pines. There seemed a wonderful poise in nature, as it merely went about its business, with no interest or designs on us" (133). What Morgan, while alluding to the religious orthodoxy of his childhood, has noted about William Cullen Bryant in his essay "Bryant's Solitary Glimpse of Paradise" (in *Good Measure*) is embodied in "Mountain Graveyard": "After the terror and exclusions of Calvinism, what an assurance to see the infinite cycles of decay and growth, incorporating human compost in fertile progression. Most great poems touch somehow the figure of resurrection, but 'Thanatopsis' succeeds [...] in evoking communion through death and collective loss" (25).

Devoid of people and pronouns, "Mountain Graveyard" is a meta-elegy. While his poetry, in different ways in different periods, is normally restrained, allowing nature in its largesse to overshadow the self in offering voice and metaphor, when the singular, subjective first-person speaker does surface in Morgan's work—as it does in the elegies and in poems of childhood (such as the many in *Orchard Country*)—it can disarm the reader with its voice of delicate, human intimacy. For example, in "Cowbedding," in which the speaker recalls his grandmother raking leaves in the fall, "I want to go back" is repeated ("I want to go back there and help / hold the sack open while she / feeds the burlap sack of gold / and stuffs in more," and "I want to go / back and stand on the frost" on the swept patches), irrationally in the face of overwhelming memory of love and loss, by adult transformed into child and straining to reach into his past (*Orchard Country* 35). In contrast, it is unsettlingly the adult who speaks, with a tone of resignation, in *Sigodlin*'s "Heaven," in which Morgan recalls his grandmother and two uncles:

And I won't assume,
as much as I've known it certain all along,

that I'll never see Grandma again, nor
Uncle Vol with his fabulations,
nor see Uncle Robert plain with no scar
from earth and the bomber explosions [30].

The late Uncle Vol's "fabulations" represent concretely the abstract "tales" of "Mountain Graveyard"—as do the invocations of Uncle Robert. In fact, nowhere in Morgan's work is the bonding of his life with those of his predecessors more deliberately and definitively forged than through his relationship with his namesake uncle, an engineer-gunner in the Second World War whose aircraft caught fire on takeoff and crashed in England. In Morgan's earliest memories, recounted in his essay "The Cubist of Memory," "over all the paraphernalia and talk [of the war] was the spoken and unspoken presence of my Uncle Robert[,] who had been killed in a B-17 in 1943, the year before I was born. He cast a shadow almost as large as the biblical figures' over my play and daydreams. The pigeons in the attic, the toolboxes and paint set; even my name had been his. [...] He had been an athlete, a martyr, an artist, and I had no choice but to rebel, then follow" (*Good Measure* 11).

An occasion similar to the one recounted in "Cowbedding" ("While we raked leaves / for the cowstall Grandma told me how / you came up here on summer afternoons") opens *Orchard Country*'s long, touching elegy "Uncle Robert," an ode with an epigraph that is an epitaph with his air force credentials. Subsumed by his ancestry through a mysterious mode of initiation, Morgan is secured a place in his family's legacy:

It was hinted I was "marked" somehow,
not only by your name, but in some way
unexplained was actually you [*Orchard Country* 45].

The uncle's life foreshadows Morgan's life as an artist—as a poet, a short story writer, and a novelist—the bequest being handed down, item by item, in spirit:

Your paintings watched me
from the bathroom wall and mantel
and your poem clipped from the paper
yellowed among the rationbooks. I inherited
your Testament with its boards of carved cedar,
and the box of arrowheads you picked
from the dust of bottomlands on Sunday afternoons [45].

It ends—the presence of the mother highlighting the closeness of the family and the continuity of ancestral narratives—

Mama liked to take out
of the cloth a clay statue of a naked man
face down in the dirt which you once
modeled and called "The Dying Warrior."
I marveled at the cunning work of leg
and tiny arm and spilling hair, and touched
your fingerprints still clear on the base [47].

* * *

While resurrecting and honoring his past, Morgan's elegies also exemplify and embody over five decades his poetic impulses and interests in terms of subject and prosody. Their consideration therefore provides an illuminating perspective for the examination of his poetry in general and leads to a deeper appreciation of and insight into it. For example, the subject of "The Gift of Tongues" is revisited, in a lighter vein in two poems from *October Crossing*, "Holy Cussing" and "The Holy Laugh." In the former, with a particularly spectacular twist,

> Sometimes a man who spoke
> in tongues and leapt for joy would break into
> an avalanche of cursing that would stun
> with brilliance and duration [9].

In the latter,

> In services they say she would
> not only speak in tongues and dance
> the holy dance and shout the shout
> but sometimes laugh the holy laugh [26].

The exorcism through dance, witnessed in the swearing man and the laughing woman, is enacted in "Care," from *Topsoil Road*. The dance, however, is a metaphor for the father's breath as Morgan invokes him blowing over his children's hot breakfast.

> He would pant
> the steam away and huff until
> we laughed at his choo-chooing chant
> to drive away the haunt, expel
> the fire ghosts that stung our tongues [13].

Then he'd "bring the dishes / back exorcised by his lungs' / performance of burning frenzies" (13).

When animating the elements, Morgan not only permits them to speak, write, and sing, but also empowers air—the omnipresent medium of transport for the spirit world in his poems, for "the fire ghosts" to be "exorcised" by the "burning frenzies"—with supernatural qualities. Several poems—such as "Radio," "Church Dust," "Natural Radio," and "Time's Music," the first from *Orchard Country*, the others from *The Strange Attractor*, Morgan's thirteenth volume—build on this conceit. In "Radio" the speaker recalls his grandfather tuning the instrument, "where the languages of the air / are trapped and spoken" (*Orchard Country* 28). Arguably an elegy, the poem is tinged with the wistfulness of "Cowbedding" ("I want to go back there") through its use of the first person:

> I want to reach in there
> and find the jars that sing,
> and watch through a gap in the back
> the vials glowing in the muck of wires,
> a throbbing in the metal
> where the languages of the air
> are trapped and spoken [28].

The poem, which identifies the radio with a cathedral, its "gothic windows stretched with cloth," showcases Morgan's resourcefulness with metaphor; with "the muck of wires" it underscores the ubiquity of nature even in a product of modern technology.

The "gothic windows" and "the languages of the air," along with the dance of exorcism, are implicit in "Church Dust," where the debris from the floor launches into "a shiver dance / that shows the air is troubled in / the stillest house, the quietest room" (*The Strange Attractor* 16). The dance is reenacted when the settled dust is again stirred to "swirl away like words / from long-forgotten sermons, hymns." The poem ends with "time," entirely abstract and intangible, personified, "coolly"—unperturbed by timeless mortal struggle and grief—"counting dust."

"Radio" is also complemented by "Natural Radio." By turning on a metaphorical "radio," or tuning your senses, in the wilderness, the speaker declares, you

> Hear the signals from
> electric currents in the earth,
> magnetic wells and fountains, storms
> of northern lights and southern lights.
> You catch the whistle of a bolt
> shriek of lightning, chatter of
> auroras. Birds are calling to
> each other from the nests of atoms [6].

Even distant "Emissions from the surface of / the sun come in as trills. But listen," he advises,

> to the hum of older spaces
> a hush of the beginning worlds,
> as steady as tall water on
> a mountain's rocky lip, that
> speaks of time and matter's first motet [6].

"Natural Radio" is about "the languages of the air" of "Radio," but outside its title it shares little with the contraption, or with the latter poem. The two poems differ in important ways. In the unpeopled "Natural Radio," addressed to "you," the first-person speaker is absent; and while Morgan evokes the natural world in "Natural Radio," he does so conspicuously with the dialect of science—earth's "electric currents," "magnetic wells and fountains," "nests of atoms," the sun's "emissions," "spaces," "time," "matter"—even as he summons celestial creation ("time and matter's first motet"). Not only do terrestrial and cosmic elements "shriek" and "chatter," "time," together with "matter," is (as in "Church Dust") personified, and communicates through music ("motet"), while solar emissions become trills and atoms talk. Be it biblical or the Big Bang, creation's (and time's) "hush" lingers.

Something similar is evident in "Time's Music," where "grasshoppers / and crickets effervesce" "ticking away the summer" (*The Strange Attractor* 13). Each like a tuned "natural radio,"

> Insects in an August field seem
> to register the background noise
> of space and amplify the twitch
> of partners in atoms [13].

The creatures sweep across fields, "whispering of / frost and stars overhead and chatter / of memory in every bit / of matter, of half-life in / the thick and flick of creation" (13). The poem, spoken in neither first nor second person (and without an imperative, to "listen," for instance), is yet another step removed from the personal.

The titles "Church Dust," "Natural Radio," "Time's Music," and *The Strange Attractor* (and diction such as "half-life" and "amplify") indicate that for Morgan the natural, the supernatural, and the scientific are complementary, residing cozily together on his palette, all reasonable candidates for metaphorical manifestation, one not necessarily dominating the other. While *The Strange Attractor* is motivated by the relationship between the cosmic and the scientific, scientific idiom is present throughout his work. In "Π," from *Topsoil Road*, the volume that precedes *The Strange Attractor*, Morgan puns on "transcendental" (the relation between "line and circle" "cannot be written out / in full, … but / is exact and constant, is / eternal and everyday" [40]); in "Music of the Spheres," also from *Topsoil Road*, atoms are ingeniously rendered as representative of the cosmos (each region of an atomic spectrum "voicing its wavelength with / choirs in the tiny stadiums / of harmony of the deeper / galaxies, ancient octaves" [39]); and in the opening poem, "Big Talk," of his latest (sixteenth) volume, *Dark Energy*, following *The Strange Attractor* by a decade, the geologists' explanation of ancient mountainous echoes is interpreted by Morgan on his own terms, "as part / of the tectonic conversation / among the continents as old / as planet earth or starry birth, / the gossip of creation's work" (3).

However, for all its pervasiveness, science, unlike the natural, the supernatural, and the religious, does not make even a cameo appearance in Morgan's elegiac poems. ("Radio," though it invokes a product of modern technology, has imagery rooted in nature and religion, not physics and electrical engineering.) In an oeuvre characterized more often than not, volume after volume, by a pattern of accretion and consolidation of his interests and his thinking—with the natural and the supernatural insinuating the spiritual, and the scientific insinuating the natural and the supernatural—the absence of science in a particular strand of Morgan's poetry stands out.

This may reflect the dominance in the poet's memory of his earliest childhood experiences, permeated with religion and superstition (as in "Halley's Comet"), over his adult education, which included the study of engineering and mathematics as an undergraduate at North Carolina State University. But it may, in light of Morgan's long and prolific career, also reveal a more disquieting conflict—that of the virgin and the dynamo—perhaps to date unresolved in his mind.

"Natural Radio" ("the nests of atoms") and "Time's Music" (grasshoppers and crickets effervescing, amplifying "the twitch / of partners in atoms"; the "memory in every bit / of matter") are Lucretian, with science subjugating religion, replacing it as the source of Morgan's customary idiom and metaphors (*The Strange Attractor* 6, 13). In fact, the most cursory survey of Morgan's poetry reveals more poems that, like *De Rerum Natura*, are unpeopled than peopled. While sidestepping the elegiac poems, this Lucretian instinct straddles his work from his earliest volumes to *Dark Energy*, a title that contrasts with that of the preceding volume, *Terroir*, as the earlier *The Strange Attractor* contrasts with the preceding *Topsoil Road*. Notably, in "Binary," in the latest volume, two yellow butterflies pursuing in flight their "ritual / of courtship, mating minuet" are "flowers that spin like particles / at love and matter's deepest core"; and the air plant of the eponymous poem in the same volume is an "Ascetic epicurean" (*Dark Energy* 49, 51).

The absence of science in Morgan's "personal" poems may also reveal something about his childhood kin. Despite their intense denominational and provincial skirmishes—which Morgan's *Trunk & Thicket* explores—they were welded by religion and history, the latter including conflicts with Native Americans, the Civil War, two World Wars, and the Cold War. History and religion were often intertwined through the shared fear of the spread of communism and nuclear holocaust as manifestations of the impending Apocalypse. In *Topsoil Road*'s "Heat Lightning" Morgan recollects being unnerved at the age of four by any sudden noise, "gunshot or backfire / or clap of thunder": "And all the talk of nuclear war / did not soothe me" (18). In *Sigodlin*'s "Uranium," Morgan's grandfather and his friend take a Geiger counter around the fields and woods to measure radiation emitted by rocks, something seemingly amusing ("Each time they found / a specimen they put the mike / to its gritty form and listened"); but the young speaker "knew the Russians might blow us / up any day ... and what / they looked for bombs were made of" (46). Morgan recounts how later "the old men talked of wealth and sure / Armageddon and the Bible's / plans for our annihilation."

The entanglement between history and religion is brought to light in "Homecoming," an essay from his 1978 book *Trunk & Thicket*. There he tells of a "distant cousin who rose during worship one Sunday to declare 'that in a vision it had been revealed to him Uncle Robert's death in Europe had been sent as punishment for family sins.'"

Even though radio, TV, and automobile did not threaten plough, spirit level, and wagon, for Morgan's people science would naturally have been symbolic of an alien, and maybe hostile, realm—at odds with their lives of religious orthodoxy and rusticity, understood through the prophecies of the Bible, the arc of Halley's comet, and the genius of the "Thrush Doctor" (*Topsoil Road*). For Morgan to introduce science in poems that evoke his childhood and its denizens would perhaps be instinctively unnatural, imposing a dialect foreign to the premise, a violation of memory.

The sanctity of Morgan's childhood—including the soil of its terrain and the beliefs of its people (even as he was at times terrified by the beliefs, and rebelled against them)—is preserved in ways more than just by his omission of science in certain poems that resurrect his past. Several of Morgan's poems, such as *October Crossing*'s "Clogging" and *Dark Energy*'s "Carpet Tacking," are about purposeful, communal activity that enforces kinship and foster bonding. And though such poems seem to contrast with the several that invoke fiercely independent and competitive pioneers (such as Audubon and Thomas Wolfe), explorers, and frontiersmen—of which his forefathers were a kind—in reality they are both two sides of the same coin: the affinity of the individualists to their land—be it Appalachia (which it usually is) or America at large—is unassailable. Morgan's subsistence-seeking great-grandfather of "The Road to Elmira" and grandfather of "The Years Ahead" naturally or premeditatedly retrace their steps home, as, eagerly, does his amusement-seeking father in *Dark Energy*'s "Escape Route":

> When Daddy drove his pickup truck
> south from the hills, across the Piedmont,
> to Greenville, South Carolina, he
> took care to park on the north side
> of town, the truck already aimed
> toward home [28].

The father, who "thrilled to crowds / and stores at first, to spectacle, / electric buses, higher buildings," and so on, was eventually "elated to / retrieve his truck still pointed at / the distant range, and freedom from / congested, smelly streets," and drove back "toward higher, cleaner air, / the intimate familiar" (28). "I know," Morgan has observed (in *Good Measure*'s "Conversation with William Harmon"), "in my own family, my uncles moved away and then returned, except the one who was killed in World War II. My dad tried to leave the mountains several times to be a trapper in Canada, to go to Minnesota and raise wheat, but he always came back. It's very hard to escape that repulsion and attraction" (168).

The same innate sensibility and sensitivity that respect and guard the past—enmeshed in religion, meshed by history—and regard the encroachment of anything outside it (such as science) as something extraordinary, also render that past tenuous, susceptible to impingement. A number of Morgan's poems allude to the dislocation of Native Americans, and may reveal an underlying wariness, indeed an anxiety, of the precariousness of any way of life (including his ancestors' way), of "the deadly and uncertain days" ("Mound Builders"), which we resist by "our traditions and the deep / ancestral memories and ways," on which "all of us rely / and must" (92). Similarly, poems that reflect on the disappearance and extinction of species, such as *Orchard Country*'s "Passenger Pigeons," point to a similar concern with a way of life's endangerment. More broadly and chillingly, in *Dark Energy*'s "Big Bone Lick," where explorers discovered colossal Pleistocene skeletons, "Eden once gave way and shrank / to just a regular promised land / to fit our deadly, human scale" (4).

Morgan's awareness of this vulnerability, compounded by his affinity with the past, may explain his evocation and delineation in meticulous detail of curios, mementoes, and relics in his poems: the Geiger counter, the radio, the books in the attic, the family Bible, Uncle Robert's paraphernalia. In *Sigodlin*'s "Grandma's Bureau," he conjures "the great black comb fine as / the sieve of a whale's mouth"; "the coffin-wardrobe"; the "steel brush" that "held a few gray strands among its / thousand stingers"; "the tortoiseshell mirror"; the hatpins ("There was a / mystery to such thin strength"), "Some ... long as witches' wands / with fat pearl heads"; and even the dust on the furniture (58).

This protective instinct may influence Morgan's response in some poems to modernization and urbanization, which in our times of both epidemic exploitation of natural resources and environmental awareness and activism have unprecedented significance. A number of such poems define the first section of *Dark Energy*. "Ancient Talk" recounts Thomas Wolfe considering a sequoia; it ends bemoaning his premature demise and speculating

> His gift to us, I think, is the
> suggestion that we find our own
> communion with the noble trees
> and rocks and diamond peaks, and pause
> to see and listen to the whisper
> of our now fragile hemisphere [7].

In *Dark Energy*'s "Jaguar" we're reminded that "such speed and power and prowess" as that of the tiger "once / patrolled these forests, mated, drank / from creeks and branches, screamed afar" in the Carolinas, "where fastest killer's now the car" (5). His consciousness tuned not only to the power of nature, but also to its fragility, Morgan, if ever political in his poetry, is so as an ecologist, a reluctant conservationist. What Robert Frost brazenly addresses in "The Line-Gang," Morgan does so delicately, but assertively, in poems such as *Topsoil Road*'s "Atomic Age," which concerns the depletion of Green River topsoil, the "greasy / savings of centuries of leaf rot, forest mold / nursed by summit fogs and isolation, / sold to decorate the cities of the plain" and "fissioned to the suburbs" (17).

* * *

In Morgan's first volume, *Zirconia Poems*, the title of which refers to the North Carolina region in which he grew up, a sequence, "Dream," contains a haunting two-stanza lyric, "Distances," where, recalling a solitary home in a "short valley," the "Mind wanders down the long slope of trees," "[c]lear through the distance of memory"

> into the cabin where my great grandmother, a bride,
> sits by the fire smoking her clay pipe
> and watching through the door the gap in the mountains
> where her man may come at any moment
> with gun on shoulder and quail swinging
> and steps so rhythmic
> they leave tracks in the mind [32].

The same word, "mind," opens and closes the poem, preceded in neither case by a noun or a pronoun. The possessive "my great grandmother" suggests it is the speaker's mind that navigates "down the long slope of trees / ... / into a short valley / with only a cabin and a juniper / and one horse nibbling the dried grass / around an Indian grave" to a real or imagined past (32). The subject of the second "mind," however, is more abstruse, open to the possibility of its referring to the speaker, the great-grandmother, or "her man," or some combination of these, making the poem enigmatic. Such instances of inscrutability are not uncharacteristic of Morgan's early poems.

Morgan has acknowledged Ezra Pound's *Cathay* as a formative influence, and, like the poems in that volume, Morgan's engender a place complete with its natural surroundings and its people and their culture. Deeper associations are also evident. For example, the theme (a wife anticipating her husband's arrival) and mood (of wistfulness) of "Distances" parallels that of Pound's famous Rihaku (or Li Bai, or Li Po) translation, "The River Merchant's Wife: A Letter," a modernist archetype; and the opening line of "Distances" echoes Pound's "Mind like a floating white cloud" from "Taking Leave of a Friend," another *Cathay* poem after Rihaku (Pound 141).

But despite these occasional associations, Morgan's early poems appear to embrace more of Pound's imagist doctrine than emulate the transparence and end-stopped lines of *Cathay*, as in "Great-Grandmother," from his second volume, *The Voice in the Crosshairs*:

> Her skin like the gray paper of a hornet's nest
> is frightening to touch.
> As though you might receive a shock
> this close to the strange meat of death [n.p.].

The intimacy so effectively apprehended in Morgan's later poems—with his kin conjured, often by name, as flesh, blood, and spirit—in the earlier poems "is frightening to touch. / As though you might receive a shock...." This tentativeness toward terrifying intimacy (the use of "you" rather than "I") is exemplified in *Zirconia Poems*' ostensibly dismissive "Elegy," with an unidentified third-person actor:

> Guess I'll light a rag out of here, he said
> and blindness rose in his open eyes.
>
> Tilted chessmen, tombstones graze on a hill,
> drag shadows at the setting moon.
> Eighty years go down
> like a ship [12].

An unattributed quote is followed in "Elegy" by a corroborating observation, which is followed by a consequent image, which is followed by a summary conclusion, the four parts logically related. "I wanted poems terse and precise, yet as encompassing as mathematical proofs," wrote Morgan in "The Cubist of Memory" (*Good Measure* 8). In an earlier essay, from 1980, "Some Sentences on the Line," he remarked, "I like poems in fragments, things with rough and sharp edges that sometimes cut unexpectedly, that cannot be handled too easily and always with safety. One piece of broken quartz can shave an ax handle, same as an expensive plane. Lines are the gathered bits of the original shattered diamond" (*Good Measure* 4).

Morgan's early poems, wittingly delivered obliquely, are often definitional. Channeled by the juxtaposition of images—fragmentary and splintered by brusque enjambments and varying line lengths—they consider and develop various aspects of something that cumulatively circumscribe the full thing, shaping in the process a thought, an idea, a mood, as if the poet had taken on the role of a "cubist of memory." In "Copper," from *Red Owl*,

> The meat of the sun is still pink inside.
> But the skin's deceptive,
> growing mossy barnacles
> on bullets.
> Drinks electricity.
>
> Squeeze the juice out.
> The lights are still on inside.
> Molecules beating like pistons.
> Hypnotic presence.
> All metal is evil [45].

In pithy sentences and fragments, Morgan niftily steers the poem in his treatment of the metal from its physical description ("pink," "barnacles") to its uses (to make bullets, to conduct electricity) to its metaphorical potential (the "evil" of money, its most basic unit, the penny, made of copper), while animating the element ("The meat ... still pink inside," "the skin ... / growing," the drinking).

The juxtaposition may also be an outcome of the early influence of Whitman. "It was the contrast between 'soul' and that one 'spear of grass'" in the opening lines of "Song of Myself" ("I loafe and invite my soul, / I lean and loafe at my ease observing a spear of summer grass") "that really struck me," Morgan noted in an interview ("The Rush of Language," *Good Measure* 147). He recalled his encounter with the poem as an adolescent in his elder sister's college anthology. "It was the juxtaposition that first started me thinking about poetry."

Morgan's early influences, interests, and experiments cast a well-defined shadow across his volumes through *Red Owl* (published in 1972), a shadow that spills into later volumes, including the 1987 *Orchard Country*, with poems such as "Brownian Motion" and "Lightning Bug," and the 1990 *Sigodlin*. The experiments were influenced by modernism not only in poetry, but also in music and visual art: his senior year in college in 1964, "I felt that I too could write poetry," Morgan explained to Booker, "by being true to the world of experience beyond the ego, and true to the plainest, most honest voice. I heard a lucid, modern measure I wanted to learn to use, lean as Webern, subtle as Bartok, crisp as Pound's *Cathay*" (136).

Morgan's approach must have impelled him to actively explore the possibility of metaphor (the tombstones "tilted chessmen" that "graze on a hill"; the "meat" of malleable copper, its "barnacles," its "Molecules beating like pistons," its animal qualities), the active use of which continued to permeate his later work. Consider, almost two decades after "Copper," *Sigodlin*'s definitional "Spirit Level," where "Shifty-eyed as an auctioneer, the bubble / hides quick" and "The nervous little fish / of emptiness backs, then rushes forward / in the vein of elixir" until it is "Put to sleep by accuracy" (22). In fact, along with his plain, honest early voice and his early subjects, Morgan's rhetorical strategies too have endured—and matured—over decades. Even *Cathay* appears to inform Morgan's later work, which resonates with the "valleys full of voices and pine-winds" of Pound's "Exile's Letter," another translation from Rihaku (Pound 138).

While the rough-hewn quality of the earlier poems is replaced by regular prosody as Morgan's poems start to settle into formally defined grids of verse that are metrically and syllabically sensitive, his lyric poetry abandons neither the prismatic nor the metaphorical qualities of the early work. However, no longer "fragments, things with rough and sharp edges," they are subsumed by the newer approaches. *Terroir*'s title poem, for example, begins plainly enough, with a straightforward definition of the distinctiveness of a vineyard's environment,

> The quality that seems unique,
> as thriving from a special spot
> of soil, air flow and light specific,
> and also frost and winter sleep,
> conditions of particular year [5].

But this distinctiveness is then associated with "what Hopkins chose to call inscape, / or individuation" (5). Then, semi-punning on the poeticized "terroir," which "sounds / so close to terror you'd confuse / the two," he infuses wine with deadly, supernatural potency,

> as if the finest and
> the rarest blend would come with just
> a hint of fear or pain, the sting
> and shiver of revulsion with
> the savor of the earth and sun [5].

The metaphors are less conspicuous and more complex in this later poem than in the preceding examples, absorbed organically into the lyric; though charging the poem with dimensions of meaning, they appear not premeditated but offhanded. The lines, too, are marked by consistency: almost all of them eight syllables in length, each with four stresses, they are loose tetrameters that, more often than not, are iambic.

While Morgan has experimented with many forms—*Orchard Country*'s "Chant Royal"; the pantoums of *Sigodlin*'s "Audubon's Flute" and *Topsoil Road*'s "Hearth"; the latter volume's sonnet "Care"; the villanelle "Subduction" from *Green River*, his tenth volume; *Strange Attractor*'s "Triolet"—his mode has converged to the unrhymed tetrameter line: just about every poem in *Dark Energy* is composed in this meter, as are most in *Terroir*; the line sustains even his longer narrative poems, such as the elegiac "The Years Ahead." He has further calibrated the four feet in poems such as "Clogging" and *The Strange Attractor*'s "Legends," both composed in trochaic tetrameters.

Morgan has addressed in the essay "Good Measure" his transitional explorations with syllabics in the context of "Grandma's Bureau": "The versification is the simplest I know, an eight-syllable line with no regular meter, no counting of stresses. It is almost-free verse broken into an arbitrary length, based vaguely on four-beat common meter: a kind of humble blank verse" (*Good Measure* 6). But the evolution to lines *with* regular meter, i.e., the convergence to relatively short (typically seven to nine syllables to accommodate four beats) metrically charged lines, engenders poems celebratory and ecstatic, such as "Terroir," or, for that matter, the earlier "Holy Cussing," "The Holy Laugh," "Care," "Natural Radio," and "Time's Music."

The ecstasy is well complemented, if not heightened, in his lyric poems by the intensely metaphor- and simile-imbued, mature trademark Morgan lines, orchestrated by wordplay from clever, attentive diction (as in the implication of "mote," appropriately complicating and enriching the context, in "motet" in "Natural Radio"), often through the use of subtle puns (the spirited "effervesce," for example, both scientific and emotive, in "Time's Music"), that infuses poems with riddle-like qualities—all transported by the routine, accelerating enjambment (particularly effectively in lines ending in verbs, such as "chant," "expel," "dance," and "shout") of already speedy, rhythmic lines and by the resonances of rhymes and slant rhymes ("pant," "chant," and "haunt"; "stung" and "tongues"; "chatter" and "matter"; and "thick" and "flick"), alliterations ("choo-chooing chant"), consonances ("choo-chooing chant"; "chatter" and "auroras"; and "matter" and "motet"), assonances ("tongues" and "stun"), and repetition ("dance / the holy dance and shout the shout / but sometimes laugh the holy laugh"). Even poems with sobering themes, such as "Church Dust," embody these rhetorical flourishes (as in the two iambic lines, "[t]he salts and silts of human hope / and human sweat and human mourning," not to mention "forgotten sermons"; "floor," "altar," and "shiver"; and "shiver" and "shows"), which make them immensely readable, delightful, and memorable (*The Strange Attractor* 16).

Morgan's tendency to describe and define often encompasses process ("Cleaning Off the Cemetery" in *Orchard Country*; "Moving the Bees" in *Sigodlin*; "Sharpening a Saw" and honey-harvesting, the latter by way of the georgic "Honey," in *Topsoil Road*; "Clogging" and "Singing to Make Butter Come" in *October Crossing*) and method (*Orchard Country*'s "Harrow," *Sigodlin*'s "Hayfield") through poems not only on doing something or making something, but also on changing something into something else with a memory of its origins. In "Terroir," wine betrays its terrestrial roots. *Topsoil Road*'s "The Grain of Sound" begins with the speaker explaining a banjo maker's practice of hitting the barks of trees to find the best wood for the instrument ("A hickory makes the brightest sound; / the poplar has a mellow ease"), which is then defined ("A banjo has a shining shiver. / ... / ... the face / of banjo is a drum of hide / of cow, or cat, or even skunk"); then, in an incantatory, hypnotic, monosyllabically rich sentence that integrates performance and provenance,

> The hide will magnify the note,
> the sad of honest pain, the chill
> blood song, lament, confession, haunt,
> as tree will sing again from root
> and vein and sap and twig in wind [51].

Similarly, in "History's Madrigal," also from *Topsoil Road*, fiddle and dulcimer makers seek out old wood for their instruments because (in a sentence nineteen lines in length) "the older wood has sweeter, more / mellow sounds, makes truer and deeper / music," "as if the walnut or / cherry, cedar or maple, as / it aged, stored up the knowledge of / passing seasons, the cold and thaw, / whine of storm, bird call and love / moan, news of wars and mourning, in / its fibers, in the sparkling grain," to be evoked "decades and generations" later (48).

The transformations from trees to musical instruments parallel that in "Atomic Age," where, however ecologically destructive the depletion of the soil, it is reshaped as structures of modern cities and suburbs. "Old stone to new building," wrote T.S. Eliot, an influence on Morgan, "old timber to new fires" ("East Coker," Eliot 182). All matter, organic and inorganic, tends in Morgan's poems to corroborate the laws, from physics, of conservation of mass and energy. In *Orchard Country*'s "Nail Bag," as another illustration, the poet observes how after a patch of land had been exploited to its potential, "the soil / bleached and threadbare," the farmers, before moving on, burned down the barn for its nails; then, after clearing the next patch of lush land, used the nails ("blacksmithed chromosomes / that link distant generations") to "summon / wilderness into new structure" (61).

Morgan's impulse to resuscitate his near and dear ones and assemble them in his volumes can be seen as a manifestation of the same dynamic that informs poems of process and method and transformation. In "Singing to Make Butter Come," once the milk has been appropriately coaxed, "soon the bits appear," like the departed returning in flesh from the spirit world, "like flakes out of the depths and more / rise like the dead at resurrection, join / their lips and soaring bodies in the light / to form ... / a sweet and firm and perfect gathering" (*October Crossing* 29).

Following *Red Owl*, the volume after which Morgan's composition significantly changed, "I found I was able to incorporate narratives and history, folktales and science, monologue and traditional forms into my writing," he said to Booker. "I could write poems longer than a page, and integrate more levels of language and experience" (136). Longer, narrative poems underlie *Trunk & Thicket* and *Groundwork*, the volumes that follow *Land Diving*, which follows *Red Owl*. In subsequent volumes, such poems are often elegiac. "The Years Ahead" has 55 lines; "Chant Royale" has its 60 lines; "The Road from Elmira" has 80 lines; and "Uncle Robert" has 90 lines.

Morgan's newfound expansiveness starts to embrace the expansiveness of the nation and its people. Influenced by pioneering explorers and chroniclers of the continent—"Among my favorite writers are Bartram, Alexander Wilson, Audubon, André Michaux, Lewis and Clark" ("The Cubist of Memory" 10)—Morgan's kindred extend beyond his blood relatives as his poems start to honor those who share his Welsh and his Appalachian, Southern, and American inheritances. In *Green River*'s "We Are the Dream of Jefferson," "The great Welshman where he lies in / his blue ridge dreams our continuing" (4). Around his grave in the vicinity of the Blue Ridge Mountains of the Appalachian range—where, prefiguring Whitman ("I am large, I contain multitudes"), the Founding Father "creates through / the text of his thought ... / the multiple and possible"—"the pasture hills roll / on to highway and crowded mall, / city and refinery, slum and / harbor, to the Rockies, to space" (4). Morgan invokes Thomas Wolfe in "Legends," "Ancient Talk," and *Orchard Country*'s "Looking Homeward," in the first of these, mirroring "Jefferson," through the novelist's grave ("From the ghostly page of stone script / spills a thread of foxfire language" across America) (*The Strange Attractor* 11).

Morgan's catapulting references to his Welsh roots can be seen as an extension of his summoning of his immediate family. In his first volume, in a sequence, "Zirconia," following "Dream," the poet observes in the somewhat cryptic lyric "Awakening" that "As far back as Wales / my family farmed the red clay hills of fear" (33). Conversely, in Scotland, far from home but close to his ancestral roots, he notes in *Sigodlin*'s "Hawthornden Castle" "the line of distant blue hills / sad as the Carolina mountains" (16).

In *Terroir*'s "Go Gentle," an elegy that recalls his father dying ("No greater horror could / be thought than witnessing a loved / one angry and in fear scream out / and hopelessly resist, deny / the step into a mystery"), Morgan evokes Dylan Thomas (by first name even) to challenge the legitimacy of poetry:

> That Dylan's powerful poem thrills
> those far from any scene of death
> can't be denied, and proves as truth
> Plato's contention that verse lies,
> and mostly feeds our vanities [45].

"Go Gentle," like "Cowbedding," has a first-person speaker, who, to great effect, speaks plainly. The poem begins,

> Was only when I watched my dad
> approach his end I understood
> how little Dylan Thomas knew
> of death and dying

Terroir in fact opens with a first-person elegy, the prefatory "In Memory of William Matthews," dedicated to Morgan's poet friend and colleague:

> Your death keeps on
> astounding me with jolts of sadness,
> as I think I'll never hear your voice
> again [xv].

The poem's pattern and tone resemble those of "The River Merchant's Wife"; it ends, like Pound's poem, suggesting the possibility, and in anticipation, of another encounter: "Send / no flower, bub, but maybe some / good claret might not be unwelcome" (xv).

Besides Jefferson, Wolfe, Thomas, and Matthews, Morgan's extended family, elegized or recalled in his poems, includes Horace Kephart (*Orchard Country*'s "Horace Kephart"), Audubon, Sidney Lanier, and Elisha Mitchell ("Audubon's Flute," "Sidney Lanier Dies at Tryon 1881," and "The Body of Elisha Mitchell," respectively, from *Sigodlin*), and Attakullakulla (*Topsoil Road*'s "Attakullakulla Goes to London"). Their treatment, like the elegies for members of his immediate family, was enabled by the same influences.

Referring probably to the early and mid–1970s (*Land Diving* was published in 1976), Morgan recounts to Booker how "It was just sheer good luck that a number of things came together for me around that time, from my reading of Smart's 'Jubilate Agno,' and discovering the rich textures of Geoffrey Hill's poetry, and beginning to fumble around with my own memories and childhood, with stories my grandfather and father had told, and a new coming to terms with the rhetoric of the New Testament" (137). These influences have followed Morgan into the present, not only in the use of "narratives and history," but also with regard to form and rhetoric. "On first reading any of Hill's poems," wrote Morgan in "The Reign of King Stork" (*Parnassus: Poetry in Review*, Volume 4 Number 2), a 1976 essay on the poet's early work, "one is struck by his fresh and functional use of forms, and by the almost incredibly dense connotative textures" (31).

Morgan's poetry about his family, immediate and extended, could be argued to be operating under the auspices of part V of Hill's "Genesis" (by way of Christopher Smart's riffing on the Bible): "By blood we live, the hot, the cold, / To ravage and redeem the world: / There is no bloodless myth will hold" (4). Morgan's "Family Bible" rhetorically mirrors Hill's lyric (in which "blood" is used four times in five consecutive lines), though, in the larger scheme of things, the "no bloodless" connotes as much the blood-forged family—the likes of Great-Grandfather Pace and Uncle Robert, whom the poet, in the process of recalling, mythologizes—as it does the spilled blood of the continental settlement of the New World: "the fifth day," Hill concludes part IV of his "Genesis," "I turned again / To flesh and blood and the blood's pain" (4).

Despite his admiration of the early Hill's formal dexterity and dense allusion, beyond its intersection with "Genesis," Morgan's work proceeds in a direction orthogonal to Hill's. Morgan directs his poems toward elucidating rather than obfuscating idiom.

The poems in *Dark Energy*, loosely organized by Morgan's preoccupations, reflect the durability of his interests and his thematic consistency. In the first section they invoke an Arcadian past as they look toward an ecologically endangered future; the second section comprises personal poems, many of them elegies, recalling Morgan's childhood and family; the final, fourth section is laced with poems informed by science.

The subtext of the third section is vanity—"beneath the stars' indifference," as in "Chance" (38). In "Clockwork," "The seconds count off yet another year / advancing toward infinity, which we / will never see but still can contemplate, / inside the clockwork of creation / in steady progress toward oblivion" (37).

Neither devoid of joy ("Be Drunk") nor stripped of the promise of another sunrise or another year, the images of isolation render this section, and, in turn, the volume, tragic, a document testifying, despite earth's enduring beauty, to an unfortunate milestone in our "steady progress toward oblivion." "All wait the grime" in "New Year," "the wound, the signature of time" (39).

Embedded in this section is a self-elegy, the ironically titled "Living Tree." It follows somewhat the theorem pattern of Morgan's early approach. Its long concluding sentence, preceded by three short ones, states, "I like to think / that when I'm gone the chemicals / and yes the spirit that was me / might be [...] / [...] raised with sap through capillaries / into an upright, fragrant trunk" [...]

> to
> the sunlight for a century
> or more, in wood repelling rot
> and standing tall with monuments
> and statues [46].

Morgan's poetry continues the important "living" tradition rooted in Hesiod and Theocritus, inherited by way of Virgil, the Romantics Blake, Clare, Shelley, and Wordsworth, and Frost. "Living Tree," a pastoral as much as an elegy, and as much an elegy as a paean to earth's regenerative potential—"to decay and growth, incorporating human compost in fertile progression"—embodies Morgan's peculiar conceits: the natural, the scientific ("capillaries"), and the metaphysical coexist in the lines ("the chemicals / and yes the spirit ... / might be searched out by subtle roots") (46). But there is also something novel in this reticent poet's making himself the instrument of his poem: the single-minded artist who early on resisted the "I" now entertains it in the most personal of contexts.

"Living Tree" ("that's pointing toward infinity" in the poem's conclusion) communicates the poet's wish not to be forgotten, to be indefinitely ("for a century / or more"), even eternally, recollected. Horace's first ode concludes (associating, like Morgan's "Mound Builders," the afterlife with celestial stars), in David Ferry's translation,

> The cool sequestered grove in which I play
> For nymphs and satyrs dancing to my music

> Is where I am set apart from other men—
> [...]
> But if *you* say I am truly among the poets,
> Then my exalted head will knock against the stars [5].

In his characteristically unassuming manner, admitting nature as his ambassador, Morgan's lines resound with the same profound ambition as the classical poet's.

Note

1. "The Elegiac Strain in Robert Morgan's Poetry" first appeared in *The Yale Review* 105.1 (January 2017): pp. 80–106.

Works Cited

Eliot, T. S. *Collected Poems 1909–1962*. San Diego: Harcourt Brace Jovanovich, 1963.
Hill, Geoffrey. *Selected Poems*. New Haven, CT: Yale University Press, 2009.
Horace. *The Odes of Horace*. Trans. David Ferry. New York: Farrar, Straus and Giroux, 1997.
Morgan, Robert. *At the Edge of the Orchard Country*. Middletown, CT: Wesleyan University Press, 1987.
______. "Bryant's Solitary Glimpse of Paradise." 1985. *Good Measure: Essays, Interviews, and Notes on Poetry*. Baton Rouge: Louisiana State University Press, 1993. pp. 25–26.
______. "Conversation with William Harmon." 1990. *Good Measure: Essays, Interviews, and Notes on Poetry*. Baton Rouge: Louisiana State University Press, 1993. pp. 158–70.
______. "The Cubist of Memory." 1984. *Good Measure: Essays, Interviews, and Notes on Poetry*. Baton Rouge: Louisiana State University Press, 1993. pp. 8–11.
______. *Dark Energy*. New York: Penguin Books, 2015.
______. "Good Measure." *Good Measure: Essays, Interviews, and Notes on Poetry*. Baton Rouge: Louisiana State University Press, 1993. pp. 5–7.
______. *Green River: New and Selected Poems*. Middletown, CT: Wesleyan University Press, 1991.
______. "Interview by Suzanne Booker." 1984. *Good Measure: Essays, Interviews, and Notes on Poetry*. Baton Rouge: Louisiana State University Press, 1993. pp. 131–43.
______. *October Crossing*. Frankfort, KY: Broadstone Books, 2009.
______. *Red Owl*. New York: W. W. Norton, 1972.
______. "The Reign of King Stork." Rev. of *Somewhere Is Such a Kingdom: Poems 1952–1971*, by Geoffrey Hill. *Parnassus* 4.2 (1976): pp. 31–48.
______. "The Rush of Language: Interview by William Heyen and Stanley Rubin." 1985. *Good Measure: Essays, Interviews, and Notes on Poetry*. Baton Rouge: Louisiana State University Press, 1993. pp. 144–57.
______. *Sigodlin*. Middletown, CT: Wesleyan University Press, 1990.
______. *The Strange Attractor: New and Selected Poems*. Baton Rouge: Louisiana State University Press, 2004.
______. *Terroir*. New York: Penguin, 2011.
______. *Topsoil Road*. Baton Rouge: Louisiana State University Press, 2000.
______. *Trunk & Thicket*. Fort Collins, CO: L'Epervier Press, 1978.
______. *The Voice in the Crosshairs*. Ithaca, NY: Angelfish Press, 1971.
______. *Zirconia Poems*. Northwood Narrows, NH: Lillabulero Press, 1969.
Pound, Ezra. *Personae: The Shorter Poems*. Rev. ed. Edited by Lea Baechler and A. Walton Litz. New York: New Directions, 1990.

The Missing as Muse

Treatments of Absence in the Poetry

ROBERT M. WEST

Most of the best writers on Robert Morgan's poetry have noted its preservationist or commemorative aspect: that is, they see Morgan as a documentarian of a disappearing—or disappeared—Appalachian culture and landscape, a poet who portrays a distinct world that exists (at first) largely apart from modernity, but gradually becomes assimilated into homogeneous modern America. That readers could trust Morgan's vision was asserted early on by his best-known teacher, the poet and novelist Fred Chappell: in a 1976 essay titled "A Prospect Newly Necessary," Chappell, who, like his student, had grown up in western North Carolina, declared that he would "testify on any soot-black Bible that Morgan's presentation [of the region] is completely accurate" (49). In 1981, in an essay titled "Robert Morgan's Pelagian Georgics," William Harmon speculates that "by the year 2000, folklorists will have to depend on writings such as Morgan's for information about practices and tales now nearly perished," though Harmon takes care to say Morgan is "a much nobler preserver than any mere antiquarian" (13). Reviewing the 1987 collection *At the Edge of the Orchard Country*, Robert Schultz notes that "as Morgan increases his reach, he writes now of his home region's history and lore," creating "poems of memory" (187); in a review of the same book, P.H. Liotta notes, "His work is filled with a glossary of folklore, terms, customs, speech, and cultural life peculiar to the Appalachians" (34). In his 1990 essay "The Witness of Many Writings," Michael McFee says that Morgan's poetry "redeems [his ancestors'] lost world from decay, salvages it" (17). These responses all highlight what is indisputably an important aspect of Morgan's oeuvre, beginning especially with those poems gathered in his books of the late 1970s; anyone browsing through his collections from then on will discover that "lost world" put on fine display.

It needs to be said, though, that a poet documenting a lost world—even one to which he traces his own origins—isn't necessarily nostalgic for it. Although he writes about aspects of rural Southern Appalachia that are gone or nearly gone, and although he does sometimes heroize his forebears, Morgan usually stops short of suggesting that the past was *better* than the present.[1] In this regard, he differs from another fine poet of the rural South, Wendell Berry: ten years Morgan's senior, Berry unambiguously laments the development of an industrial, high-tech society that he argues has been detrimental to nonhuman nature, small farming, local culture, and human life generally. While Morgan doesn't celebrate the arrival of such a society, he doesn't go so far as to condemn it, either: when addressing changes that time has brought to his home region, he usually avoids striking explicit notes of approval or disapproval. True, when he writes a poem about something now gone—an aspect of rural or wild landscape, say, or a distinctively regional cultural practice—he represents the absent element with great vividness, conjuring it back into the world; an important part of such a poem's performance is the momentary restoration of something or someone now gone. To the extent that Morgan editorializes on that disappearance, though, whether in such restorative poems or in poems otherwise revolving around absence, he is much likelier to marvel at it than to bemoan it: some of his best poems treat disappearances as sources of wonder and even inspiration.

His poem "Fasting," first collected in *The Strange Attractor: New and Selected Poems*, explains this habit in abstract terms. Adopting a prophetic voice much like that of Morgan's early long poem "Mockingbird," and savoring paradox as much as anything by John Donne and George Herbert, "Fasting" asserts that "Nothing is delicious as absence," that "Nothing satisfies like / nothing" (4). The poem not only acknowledges life's ephemerality, as when it declares, "The green tracts of tree and hill are read out / and snatched away," but also goes so far as to embrace deprivation, paradoxically claiming that "To feast on nothing, / to feast on time / itself ... thrills welcome to flesh." "Fasting" testifies to the exhilaration of a radical asceticism. But whereas literal fasting is for many a means of spiritual revitalization, a turn away from the body's demands and toward the nourishment of the soul, this metaphorical fasting is less ethic than aesthetic. That is, for Morgan, the recognition of an absence—a going without—presents an occasion for the making of a poem, and this fact has led to the composition of much of his best and most memorable work in poetry.

A case in point is "Passenger Pigeons," from the 1987 collection *At the Edge of the Orchard Country*. The poem meditates on the old migrations, which were so large they became the stuff of 18th- and 19th-century lore. Here it is in full:

> Remembering the descriptions by Wilson
> and Bartram, and Audubon and other
> early travelers to the interior, of the sky
> clouded with the movements of winged pilgrims
> wide as the Mississippi, wide as the Gulf
> Stream, hundred-mile epics of equidistant wings
> horizon to horizon, how their droppings
> splashed the lakes and rivers, how
> where they roosted whole forests broke down
> worse than from ice storms, and the woods floor
> was paved with their lime, how the settlers
> got them with ax and gun and broom
> for hogs, how when a hawk attacked
> the endless stream bulged away
> and kept the shift long after
> the raptor was gone, and having read how
> the skies of America became silent, the fletched
> oceans forgotten, how can I replace
> the hosts of the sky, the warm-blooded jetstreams?
> To echo the birdstorms of those early
> sunsets, what high river of electron, cell and star? [*Orchard Country* 5].

The poem certainly doesn't celebrate the eradication of the pigeons, but it doesn't express sorrow over their disappearance either: given the ways it evokes them—the recollection of the broken forests, the image of the ground "paved" with their excrement—it's hard to imagine that anyone would want them back. Although hunting and destruction of habitat led to their extinction, the poem doesn't offer either of those explanations or any other. We read only that "the skies of America became silent."

At least three things are happening in this poem. First, it's teaching us about something that was once widespread but is now gone, briefly bringing it back to life in our imaginations. Second, by following that vivid evocation with an abrupt reversal, a quick reinstitution of the absence ("how / the skies of America became silent"), the poem not only informs us of the disappearance, but does so in such a way that we experience it as a sudden vanishing: we marvel over the size of the flocks, but we're also invited to marvel over the fact that something once so unmistakably present could now—not so much later, to anyone with much sense of history—be wholly gone. Third, Morgan here takes the pigeons' absence not as cause for lamentation, but as a challenge, and in that sense as inspiration.

Once, in a review of Morgan's 1996 chapbook *Wild Peavines*, I looked back at the closing lines of "Passenger Pigeons" and saw in them "a gesture of helplessness," a characterization that failed to do them justice (43). In fact, they announce the poet's sense of a calling, a vocation, and they deserve close attention. "Passenger Pigeons" consists of twenty lines but only two sentences, both of which are questions. The first is periodic, running sixteen and a half lines before introducing its short independent clause: "[r]emembering the descriptions" of the passenger pigeons by the early naturalists, and "having read" of the pigeons' extinction, Morgan asks, "how can I replace / the hosts of the sky, the warm-blooded jetstreams?" "Replace" is an interesting verb there, and the context allows us to interpret it in at least two ways. We can read "replace" as "re-place," meaning to "put in place again": thus understood the question is, how can the poet put the pigeons back into the sky and the forests? That question answers itself: in one sense, for the readers of this compact but evocative poem, he already has.[2]

On the other hand, "replace" can also be read to mean "find a substitute for." Considered that way, the question may be surprising: who would expect a poet to find or invent a substitute for the pigeons, to replace them in that sense? *Is* there any "high river of electron, cell and star"—any broadcast signal, any other creature's flight, any starry night sky—that can "echo [those] birdstorms"? Anything so amazing? Whether the answer to that question is "Yes" or "No," the answer to the question "how can I replace / the hosts of the sky … ?" is not simply "I can't." Morgan can and does provide an echo, one he makes with his own "high river" of thought and expression—the metaphor lends itself both to the movement of verse and to the flow of ink—as he does in his many other meditations on disappearances and absences.[3]

Following "Passenger Pigeons" in *At the Edge of the Orchard Country* is "Buffalo Trace," which deals with absence in a way best appreciated with the whole poem—a single sentence—in view:

> Sometimes in the winter mountains
> after a little snow has blown in the night
> and nothing's alive in eye-range
> but the clouds
> near peaks frozen clean
> in the solstice sun,
> the white finds a faint depression

> to stick in out of wind
> and makes visible for the first time
> through woods and along the slopes
> to where it nicks the rim
> perceptibly, a ghostpath
> under brush and broomsedge,
> merging in the pasture with narrow
> cowtrails but running on through fences
> and across boundaries, under branches
> in tattered sweep out to the low
> gaps of the old migrations
> where they browsed into the summer mountains
> then ebbed back into the horizon
> and back of the stars [*Orchard Country* 6].

Two definitions of the title word "trace" apply: the poem describes a trace (a path) once followed by the old wild buffalo herds (sticklers would call the animals "bison," as the setting is presumably American), but it also suggests that that trace is the only trace (i.e., sign) of themselves that they left behind.[4] Instead of just reporting the facts, though, Morgan spends his first six lines leading us into the wintry mountain setting, and then through the next twelve directs our attention to the track subtly marked out by the light snow, as if we were actually walking with him beside us as our guide. Only in the nineteenth line of this twenty-one-line poem, and only that one time, does Morgan directly refer to the buffalo themselves; even then he only uses the pronoun "they," counting on readers to "trace" the antecedent back to the title. By the time we have found them in the poem, they are long gone: "ebbed back into the horizon / and back of the stars." They have become a haunting absence: we have followed the trace's "ghostpath" and aptly found only ghosts.

More like "Passenger Pigeons" is "Wild Peavines," first collected in the 1996 chapbook of that title and then reprinted in Morgan's next book, 2000's *Topsoil Road*. Just as "Passenger Pigeons" begins by evoking the unavoidable birds, "Wild Peavines" opens by conjuring up the formerly ubiquitous spread of wild peavines over the mountain landscape, as reported by early explorers and settlers. Description and awe (to the point of near disbelief) are paired right from the start:

> I have never understood how
> the mountains when first seen by hunters
> and traders and settlers were covered
> with peavines. How could every cove
> and clearing, old field, every
> opening in the woods and even
> understories of deep woods
> be laced with vines and blossoms in
> June? [*Topsoil Road* 7].

As with the pigeons, Morgan doesn't describe the vines in terms that would suggest he regrets their disappearance. "They say," he writes, "the flowers were so thick / the fumes were smothering"; he calls their spread a "sprawling mess" and notes that it would "choke out other flowers." Again, then, this is a poem that recalls a former reality, but not one that bewails its going. Incredulity, not sadness, is the note the poet strikes in his response: "But hardest of all is to see / how such profusion, such overwhelming lushness and lavish, could vanish." The conclusion delivers a memorable simile: to find a wild peavine now, we read, is like running across "some word from a lost language / once flourishing on every tongue" (7). "Flourishing" there is an etymological pun, since, like "flora," it derives from *flōs*, the Latin word for "flower." Whereas "Passenger Pigeons" ends with the poet challenging himself to compose a body of work equivalent to the vanished flocks, "Wild Peavines" ends on a fitting note of pure wonderment—with, so to speak, a figurative flourish.

For a more recent example in a similar mode, consider "Canebrake," from the poet's 2015 collection, *Dark Energy*. "The fertile valley floors first seen / by Europeans flourished with / tall cane stalks twenty feet or more," it begins, before describing the rich animal life for which the canebrakes provided habitat (10). As he evokes what that habitat must have felt like to the hunters stalking game there, Morgan writes, "a human felt no more / than mouse or rabbit trapped within / the cage of stalks"; the predator is recast as prey. That passage more or less parallels the descriptions of the overwhelming lime in "Passenger Pigeons" and the smothering odor of "Wild Peavines" and performs a similar function: that is, it resists an easy sentimentality toward the now-vanished aspect of wild nature, waxing neither nostalgic nor misanthropic. That said, whereas "Passenger Pigeons" and "Wild Peavines" both report their erasures without addressing the causes, "Canebrake" does attribute the brakes' disappearance to human activity: hunters set fires,

> and soon the brakes were just a scar
> and then a memory, and then
> not even that, as vanished as
> the pigeon, panther, painted face [10].

"Canebrake" is written in iambic tetrameter, and that form emphasizes the poem's plot: that is, the insistent rhythm underscores the unstoppable march of white settlement in North America, and the short lines sweep us down the page with a speed like that of the change those settlers wrought upon the landscape.

Some of Morgan's most memorable poems are those that contemplate human absences. One such poem is "Uncle Robert," which takes its title from the uncle for whom the poet was named, Robert Levi. Levi, who served in the Eighth Air Force during World War II, died in a mid-air explosion over England in 1943, the year before Morgan was born. The poet thus had no acquaintance with him, and the poem works up no false emotion about his uncle's short life. Rather, Morgan describes the personal items that Levi left behind, and explains the role they played in his own life as a boy: among these were Levi's chevron patches, his mess kit, his fly-fishing gear, his canoe, and his bugle. Driving Morgan's childhood interest in those items was the family's identification of him with the dead man:

> It was hinted I was "marked" somehow,
> not only by your name, but in some way
> unexplained was actually you. Aunts and cousins
> claimed we favored and I spoke with your stammer [*Orchard Country* 45].

> They said
> I had the high-arched "Levi foot"
> like you, and your quick laugh [47].

Having circled his uncle's absence as a boy, as an adult he continues that circling by writing the poem, and the intensity of his continuing interest is suggested by the use of apostrophe: the poem is not just *about* his uncle, but is addressed *to* him. The closing lines have a subtle power:

> Mama liked to take out
> of cloth a clay statue of a naked man
> face down in the dirt which you once
> modeled and called "The Dying Warrior."
> I marveled at the cunning work of leg
> and tiny arm and spilling hair, and touched
> your fingerprints still clear on the base [47].

What a revelation, here in the poem's final moments: the fact that Levi, who had died in war, had once produced a remarkable sculpture he had titled, of all things, "The Dying Warrior."

However, Morgan doesn't actually conclude the poem on that note of pathos. The poem has revolved around his boyhood grappling with his uncle's absence. The family may have seen the boy as a reincarnation of his uncle, but here he (or rather the adult poet writing the poem) resists that identification. Although his fingertips meet his uncle's fingerprints, in an image of contact and communion, any mention of fingerprints also necessarily invokes their uniqueness. The uncle is irrevocably gone, and Morgan in the end is his own person: even if their fingerprints happen to be similar, they won't match. The point seems to be underscored by the scansion of the last three lines, which carry the final sentence: the first two of those lines easily scan as iambic pentameter, five *daDUM*s each,

> x / x / x / x / x /
> I marveled at the cunning work of leg
> x / x / x / x / x /
> and tiny arm and spilling hair, and touched

but the final line diverges from the pattern:

> x / x x / / x x /
> your fingerprints still clear on the base.

One may hear stress or not on "-prints"; the same is true of "still." Regardless, at least by its end, that last line departs from the consistent strong rhythm that precedes it—just as the poet undermines a potentially stifling identification with his absent uncle. Asserting his uncle's distinctiveness—his individuality—the poet implicitly asserts his own.

Another poem about Morgan's deceased elder kin is "Heaven." No more an expression of grief or nostalgia than "Uncle Robert," it tightly choreographs an inner conflict between rationalist hopelessness and supernaturalist hope. On the one hand, there is what the poet—a cosmopolitan man of the world, a student of science, an Ivy League professor—says he knows: that any reunion with the dead is impossible. On the other hand, there is what he—someone who grew up in an intensely religious rural community in the Bible Belt—was raised to believe, and what he would in fact prefer to believe: that he *will* be reunited with his elders in the afterlife. The poem's beginning ("And yet") suggests that this is an ongoing debate, and the double negative that immediately follows ("I don't want not") hints that the conflict may run too deep to be resolved[5]:

> And yet I don't want not to believe in,
> little as I can, the big whoosh of souls

upward at the Rapture, when clay and ocean,
dust and pit, yield up their dead, when all

elements reassemble into the forms
of the living from the eight winds and flung
petals of the compass [*Sigodlin* 30].

The afterlife Morgan describes here is one explained by the Apostle Paul at length in I Corinthians 15 and more briefly in I Thessalonians 4, and it would certainly be a familiar idea to anyone immersed in Protestant fundamentalism, as Morgan was throughout his youth.[6] The poem's second sentence starts with a contradictory promise that only deepens our sense of the poet's dividedness:

And I won't assume,
much as I've known it certain all along,

that I'll never see Grandma again, nor
Uncle Vol with his fabulations,
nor see Uncle Robert plain with no scar
from earth and the bomber explosions [30].

The third sentence begins, "I don't want to think how empty and cold / the sky is, how distant the family" (30). Not "how empty and cold / the sky *seems*," but "how empty and cold / the sky *is*"; not how distant the family *seems*, but how distant, how completely absent, they *are*. The general point is that he prefers not to face facts—but we could come closer to capturing the profundity of the inner conflict by putting it this way: he doesn't *want* to accept what he *does* accept as fact. Unable to embrace fundamentalist dogma, and just as unable to find comfort in the rationalist's "empty and cold" perspective, he develops an imaginative alternative:

I don't want to think how empty and cold
the sky is, how distant the family,
but of winged seeds blown from a milkweed field
in the opalescent smokes of early

winter ascending toward heaven's blue,
each self orchestrated in one aria
of river and light. And those behind the blue
are watching even now us on the long way [30].

Preferring to think of us all as "winged seeds" eventually finding our way to "heaven's blue," he imagines that the souls of the dead, having completed that journey, are now "behind [that] blue" and "watching even now us on the long way." The doctrine of the Rapture is traded for a concept of the afterlife less dramatic and less dogmatically correct, a more continual process based on the poet's observation of nature. The dead are still absent, but he imagines their absence as an occlusion behind a one-way window, a window we approach as we near life's end. The old spatial concept of heaven as "up" is retained, so that our life's journey is figured as a steady climb to that exalted realm. Each of us is a "winged seed," rising but not yet transformed into our mature, more spiritual state.

That consoling notion is first introduced as wishful thinking ("I don't want to think how empty and cold / the sky is, how distant the family, / but of winged seeds ..."), yet the poem closes with a separate sentence emphatically affirming it: "And those behind the blue / are watching even now us on the long way." The verb is "are," not "would be" or "may be." In "Coming Out from Under Calvinism: Religious Motifs in Robert Morgan's Poetry," John Lang has argued that that last line's "deliberately awkward syntax" and its "unidiomatic phrasing" suggest a lack of conviction (54).[7] One might also say that, given the fact that the prior quatrains all tie together their second and fourth lines (as they do their first and third) with relatively clear slant-rhymes—*souls/all*, *flung/along*, *fabulations/explosions*, and *family/early*—the difficulty of crediting any kind of rhyme between *aria* and *way* may subtly undercut the last sentence's believability: that is, the last quatrain's formal disjuncture underscores the disjuncture in its logic.[8] Looking at that passage a little differently, we could also view its departure from the established rhyme scheme as a defiant evasion corresponding to the poem's final defiance of comfortless fact. Regardless of how those technical aspects inflect the poem's conclusion for attentive readers, the final sentence says what it says, and it *is* the final sentence, resolving (or at least setting aside) the poem's central conflict by offering a third way in terms of a solacing metaphor.

Like the poems discussed previously, "Heaven" appears to germinate from contemplation of an absence—in this case, that of Morgan's deceased elder kin. The poem doesn't actually lament their disappearance: whatever the poet's private feelings, we find no direct expression of sorrow over their deaths. Instead, we witness and take part in an elaborate performance for which their absence is the inspiration—a performance that articulates nuanced feeling through hairsplitting grammar, pairs traditional poetic form with sophisticated and subtle sound effects, and concludes with the invention of a metaphor that suffices (to use Wallace Stevens's term) better than either the fundamentalist or the materialist view of life after death.[9] All of which is to say that this poem, too, as acutely personal as it is, is a complex work of art inspired by absence, not a report of sadness over loss.[10]

"Field Theory," first collected in the 1981 chapbook *Bronze Age* and then in *At the Edge of the Orchard Country*, also meditates on the absent dead, invoking an unspecified earlier "they"—presumably the poet's ancestors and other predecessors in the mountain South, what the poem calls "the upland atoll." Morgan knows well—and has made clear in many poems, essays, short stories, and novels—that life in rural Appalachia has never been easy, but the world evoked by "Field Theory" sounds like a pleasant one indeed:

> In those days they grew sweet potatoes
> big as newborn babies, and discovered
> the power of clouds in boilers.
> The spring said its diamonds under the poplars
> and the spine[11] twinkled like a milkyway.
> Children shouted kickball and tag
> from early evening until dark in the pasture.
> I like to think they found in work
> a soil subliminal and sublime.
> Their best conspiracies were two
> breathing in the night. They lived
> on the upland atoll and didn't care
> to step on horizons [*Orchard Country* 68].

Whereas Kentuckian James Still sometimes characterizes the highlands as a trap for those who grew up there,[12] this poem's "they" were content to stay where they were: like the inhabitants of Voltaire's utopia Eldorado in *Candide*, they "didn't care / to step on horizons."

Where are they now? Like the great flocks of passenger pigeons and the sprawling wild peavines, the people of that happy world have disappeared, and their exit (like those of the pigeons and the peavines) is evoked in such a way that it seems both sudden and total:

> [they] left no more
> trace than a cloud shadow when I woke
> from the coils of the cell's heart,
> in the non-euclidean mountains,
> recovering pieces of the morgenland [68].

The poem's last line sounds like the invocation of a birthright, a claim to "the Morgan land," but the spelling there puns on *Morgen*, the German word for *morning*: that happy earlier world thus becomes the "the morning-land."[13] The definition of the poet's vocation as "recovering pieces" recalls a line near the end of T.S. Eliot's poem *The Waste Land*: "These fragments I have shored against my ruins" (*Collected Poems* 69). However, whereas Eliot's poem repeatedly evokes the spiritual barrenness of its present without exalting a previous golden age (or at least not explicitly), Morgan's portrays a happy past while only gently suggesting its difference from the present: the phrase "In those days" implies a contrast with *these* days. Whether "those days" were quite as they're imagined here is something the poem itself may incline us to question: half the title *is* the word "theory," and any declaration beginning with "I like to think [that] ..." asserts something other than cold, hard fact. Schultz credits Morgan with "celebrating (or inventing) an Appalachian past that is Edenic and heroic" (187), and parts of "Field Theory" may earn that parenthetical caveat. Regardless, the poem offers itself (and others) as a response to the disappearance of a culture, idealized or not.[14]

Although probably best known for his poems of Appalachia, Morgan has written many poems with other settings and subjects. Another inspiring absence, one far from the mountains, is an old puzzle from the eastern end of his home state: the Lost Colony, the vanished 1587 English settlement on Roanoke Island. After a few weeks, the settlers' leader, John White, sailed back to England for much-needed supplies; unable to return until 1590, White found no sign of the colony, except the word "CROATOAN" (a variant of "Croatan," the name of a local Native American tribe) carved on one tree, and the letters "CRO" carved on another. With virtually nothing being known about the colonists' experience after White's departure, Morgan was free to invent a plausible account of his own. Here is the poem in its entirety:

> **Lost Colony**
>
> The first spring they watched the east every day
> for the ships, and planted what seed they
> had saved from mold and rot in the island
> sand with fish as the heathen had said.
>
> But even by the sea it rained little
> and their island gave just a trickle
> of fresh water. Many died of fever
> or bad air, especially children and expectant
>
> wives. Evenings in the stockade
> they prayed for the Captain to return with bread.
> A cow was stolen by the Lumbees,
> or maybe Croatans—by day professing

> friendship, even interest in the Faith.
> Often the men rowed out into the Sound
> to fish and look for higher ground
> up the tidal creeks, and found only
>
> further marshes, a catarrh of mud squeezed
> out of reeds, and alligators
> bellowing in brakes. Two died of snakebite
> while inspecting a hummock above the flats.
>
> The season came foul again. One saw
> in a dream their Knight beheaded in the Tower.
> By Christmas with the biscuit gone
> and powder for their fusils, the meager
>
> magazines of grain now bare, they lived,
> the dozen left, by snaring an occasional
> duck, or fishing when the cold wind
> abated and they could take oars
>
> to the deep channels of the Sound.
> And entered the new year, Indians now
> paddling to their shore and mocking
> with baskets of maize to be exchanged
>
> for wives and daughters. An elder
> ordered they start rowing in the skiff
> for England and at least die bravely at sea,
> not teased by infidels
>
> and hunger tempting with each other's flesh,
> nor wandering the wilderness to the west
> where they understood the Spanish had,
> through sin's alchemy, extracted base gold [57–58].

A dream of "their Knight beheaded in the Tower" would have been prophetic: the settlement's major backer, Sir Walter Raleigh, a favorite of Queen Elizabeth I's, was imprisoned in the Tower of London by her successor, King James I, and eventually executed for treason. For all the details the poem offers, it stops short of accounting for the colony's final disappearance. Did the remaining settlers starve to death? Did they, in the end, join the "infidels"? The poem doesn't presume to say. What it *does* do—like "Passenger Pigeons," "Wild Peavines," and "Canebrake"—is vividly evoke something long gone, something whose disappearance has long been a matter of bafflement.

Many appreciative critics have addressed the frequent engagement with science in Morgan's poetry, and here too, especially in his poems relating to astrophysics, absences (or what at first seem to be absences) serve as inspiration. Noting that astronomers find some celestial bodies behaving as if they were responding to bodies otherwise undetectable, Morgan has written poems that describe those mysteries and explore their significance. Those and other recent poems suggest not only a continuing interest in absence, but also a new embrace of mystery *per se*. For example, "Shadow Matter," from *Sigodlin*, begins,

> Those looking further into space,
> and closer, find evidence of
> unseen matter everywhere, dark
> bodies not only dust storms
> obscuring other stars and voids

> between clusters and superclusters,
> but long black strings and gravities
> unexplained except by presences
> invisible [...] [20].

Later, the title poem of *The Strange Attractor: New and Selected Poems*, from that book's section of new work, describes the theory of an enormous, interstellar body of dark matter undetectable but for its gravitational effects on what we can observe around it: this "strange attractor" (known to astronomers as the Great Attractor) is "a heart that holds the spinning / bits of glitter of the seen in / their coherent scatter" (12).[15] "Still unproved," the phenomenon is "substantiate / only in attraction of lesser / bodies to the unknown greater"; that is, although it "cannot be found"—indeed, although it is "unseen, as yet unheard," and even "unplaced"—"our gravity [...] tells us it is there." Everything revolves around this missing matter, in much the same way that Morgan's young life seemed to revolve around his missing uncle. What directs us to it is "our gravity"—in the literal sense of the physical force, yes, but also "gravity" in the sense of *gravitas*: it takes a serious mind to contemplate the paradox of an absence exerting such an effect that it seems a kind of presence. Later still, the poem "Dark Matter" (from *Dark Energy*) asserts that its titular mystery—the fact that observable mass behaves as if affected by mass we can't perceive—shouldn't be *too* surprising, since we've long known "what we know is just / a fraction of what is." Acceptance of that

> may be the start of our
> intelligence, may be
> the launch of honest awe
> and curiosity,
> and lesson of humility [67].

It's worth noting that, although Morgan's poems generally don't sorrow over absences, there are a few exceptions; one is the opening poem to *Terroir*, "In Memory of William Matthews." There Morgan addresses with conversational transparency his old friend and fellow poet, who died almost a decade and a half earlier at the age of fifty-five. The poem limns an appealing portrait, first hailing Matthews as a "veteran insomniac," always reading and thinking and writing—someone of superior "alertness / and [...] articulateness," "both old before [his] time / and younger than the rest of us" (xiv). "Of our generation," Morgan says, "you were the most / generous behind the mask of irony." With unusual emotional directness, he admits that Matthews' absence still brings him "jolts of sadness," and goes on to declare, "I want to note that you / were loved and that your work is loved / and will be" (xv). "In Memory ..." may surprise readers who encounter it after immersing themselves in Morgan's other poetry: it's the exception that proves the rule. The poem's placement and formatting in *Terroir* underscore its exceptionality: following as it does the book's dedication to the poet's mother, but preceding the rest of the poems' groupings into numbered sections (starting with "One"), it seems neither dedicatory poem nor part of the collection proper—and the fact that it's printed entirely in italics sets it further apart.

That said, "In Memory ..." isn't entirely different from Morgan's other absence-inspired poems. Though addressed to Matthews, it includes details that help bring him to life for those who never knew him, details that the man himself wouldn't need to be told: "You were a connoisseur / of wines, of things Italian, of / custom shoes, who would forget / to match or even to wear socks," who produced "quick snarls about the nature / of nature poetry," and who lived in "smoke that hung like incense in / a Hindu temple everywhere / you lived" (xiv-xv). And the disappearance of one so alive is—like the disappearances of the passenger pigeons and the wild peavines—itself cause for wonder, however sorrowful: Morgan says that Matthews' "death keeps on / astounding me" (xv). In the end he goes so far as to ventriloquize his friend, letting him have the last word (including a sly rhymed couplet): after laying a "final flower / ... at the place of / memory," Morgan imagines Matthews snickering in response, then saying, "Send / no flowers, bub, but maybe some / good claret might not be unwelcome" (xv). As different as this poem is from most of Morgan's oeuvre, here too he finds inspiration in an absence, pondering it and teaching us about who or what is missing, sharing wisdom and evoking wonder along the way.

Notes

1. For other perspectives on the relationship between Morgan's work and nostalgia, see "The Politics of Nostalgia: Uses of the Past in Recent Appalachian Poetry," by Frank Einstein, and "Many Returns: Forms of Nostalgia in the Poetry of the Contemporary South," Chapter 3 of Daniel Cross Turner's *Southern Crossings: Poetry, Memory, and the Transcultural South.*

2. This reading of the question invites a comparison to Samuel Taylor Coleridge's poem "Kubla Khan." After offering an evocative and memorable portrait of Kubla Khan's realm of Xanadu, the poem concludes with a wish for the power to do what it has already done.

3. Morgan's "Passenger Pigeons" invites comparison with two earlier poems by an older Appalachian poet, James Still: "Passenger Pigeons" and "Year of the Pigeons." Both appeared in Still's 1937 collection, *Hounds on the Mountain*, and are now included in his *From the Mountain, From the Valley: New and Collected Poems*, edited by Ted Olson. Neither of Still's poems includes any reference to the poet himself.

4. According to the U.S. Fish and Wildlife Service, wild bison were hunted nearly (but not quite) to extinction in the late 19th century. Certainly there was nothing anymore like "the great migrations."

5. For the uninterrupted, complete text of "Heaven," see Michael McFee's "'The Witness of Many Writings': Robert Morgan's Poetic Career," reprinted in this volume.

6. For this discussion, the most relevant part of Paul's explanation to the church at Corinth is as follows, as rendered in the King James Version: "Behold, I shew you a mystery; We shall not all sleep, but we shall all be changed, In a moment, in the twinkling of an eye, at the last trump: for the trumpet shall sound, and the dead shall be raised incorruptible, and we shall be changed. For this corruptible must put on incorruption, and this mortal must put on immortality. So when this corruptible shall have put on incorruption, and this mortal shall have put on immortality, then shall be brought to pass the saying that is written, Death is swallowed up in victory. O death, where is thy sting? O grave, where is thy victory?" (I Corinthians 15:51–55).

To the church at Thessaloniki, Paul promises that "the Lord himself shall descend from heaven with a shout, with the voice of an archangel, and with the trump of God: and the dead in Christ shall rise first: Then we which are alive and remain shall be caught up together with them in the clouds, to meet the Lord in the air: and so shall we ever be with the Lord. Wherefore comfort one another with these words" (I Thessalonians 4:16–18).

7. Lang makes the same point using the same terms in *Six Poets from the Mountain South*, p. 92.

8. The final quatrain also breaks another pattern the poem has established: instead of rhyming its first and third lines, it ends both with the word "blue."

9. In his poem "Of Modern Poetry," Stevens suggests that a modern poem cannot simply repeat old ideas and techniques, but must instead find "what will suffice" now.

10. The conclusion of a fine later poem, "Mound Builders," combines the endings of "Buffalo Trace" and "Heaven" when it refers to "those beloved who came before / and watch us from the glittering stars" (p. 93).

11. "Spine" here refers to grass-covered ground. The *Oxford English Dictionary* dates that use of the word to 1786, and offers as synonyms "greensward," "sward," and "turf."

12. See, for example, references to the "prisoning hills" in Still's poems "Heritage" and "Journey Beyond the Hills," both of which were first collected in his 1937 book *Hounds on the Mountain* and now appear in *From the Mountain, From the Valley: New and Collected Poems*, ed. Ted Olson.

13. That said, *Morgen* is also the German word for "tomorrow." For the reader aware of both definitions, the line may suggest a Janus-like perspective, attentive to both past and future.

14. Before leaving off with poems set or possibly set in Appalachia, I should point out that I have elsewhere examined the treatment of absence in another such poem, "Church Dust," from the "new" section of *The Strange Attractor: New and Selected Poems* (2004). Like the poems discussed up to this point, "Church Dust"

draws a sharp contrast between past and present—in this case between, on the one hand, the passionate life of one of "[t]he oldest wooden churches" in its heyday, and, on the other, its silent emptiness today, "as time goes cooly [sic] counting dust" (16). Again, the predominant tone is one of wonder rather than sorrow. See "'Here's the Church, Here's the Steeple': Robert Morgan, Philip Larkin, and the Emptiness of Sacred Space." *Southern Quarterly* 47.3 (2010): pp. 91–97.

15. The poem's title reflects some poetic license: the mathematical term "strange attractor" designates a dynamical system (that is, a system with a precisely defined relationship to time) where coordinates tend over time toward a fractal structure. That said, the Great Attractor is indeed strange, in the lay sense of that word, and so the poem earns its title.

Works Cited

Chappell, Fred. "A Prospect Newly Necessary." *The Small Farm* 3 (1976): pp. 49–54.

Einstein, Frank. "The Politics of Nostalgia: Uses of the Past in Recent Appalachian Poetry." *Appalachian Journal* 8 (1980): pp. 32–40.

Eliot, T.S. *Collected Poems 1909–1962*. Orlando: Harcourt Brace Jovanovich, 1963.

Harmon, William. "Robert Morgan's Pelagian Georgics: Twelve Essays." *Parnassus: Poetry in Review* 9 (1981): pp. 5–30.

Lang, John. "'Coming Out from Under Calvinism': Religious Motifs in Robert Morgan's Poetry." *Shenandoah* 42.2 (1992): pp. 46–60. Rpt. in *An American Vein: Critical Readings in Appalachian Literature*. Ed. Danny L. Miller, Sharon Hatfield, and Gurney Norman. Athens: Ohio University Press, 2005. pp. 261–74.

______. *Six Poets from the Mountain South*. Baton Rouge: Louisiana State University Press, 2010.

Liotta, P.H. "Pieces of the Morgenland: The Recent Achievements in Robert Morgan's Poetry." *Southern Literary Journal* 22 (1989): pp. 32–40.

McFee, Michael. "'The Witness of Many Writings': Robert Morgan's Poetic Career." *Iron Mountain Review* 6.1 (1990): pp. 17–23. Rpt. in *The Napkin Manuscripts: Selected Essays and an Interview*. Knoxville: University of Tennessee Press, 2006. pp. 164–80.

Morgan, Robert. *At the Edge of the Orchard Country*. Middletown, CT: Wesleyan University Press, 1987.

______. *Dark Energy*. New York: Penguin, 2015.

______. *Sigodlin*. Middletown, CT: Wesleyan University Press, 1990.

______. *The Strange Attractor: New and Selected Poems*. Baton Rouge: Louisiana State University Press, 2004.

______. *Terroir*. New York: Penguin, 2011.

Schultz, Robert. "Recovering Pieces of the Morgenland." *Virginia Quarterly Review* 64 (1988): pp. 176–88.

Stevens, Wallace. *Selected Poems*. Ed. John N. Serio. New York: Knopf, 2009.

Still, James. *From the Mountain, From the Valley: New and Collected Poems*. Ed. Ted Olson. Lexington: University Press of Kentucky, 2001.

Turner, Daniel Cross. *Southern Crossings: Poetry, Memory, and the Transcultural South*. Knoxville: University of Tennessee Press, 2012.

Wildlife Biologue: American Buffalo (Bison Bison). U.S. Fish and Wildlife Service, 1997. At https://www.fws.gov/uploadedFiles/American_Buffalo.fws%20biologue.pdf.

West, Robert. "'Here's the Church, Here's the Steeple': Robert Morgan, Philip Larkin, and the Emptiness of Sacred Space." *Southern Quarterly* 47.3 (2010): pp. 91–97.

______. Rev. of *Wild Peavines*, by Robert Morgan. *Carolina Quarterly* 49.3 (1997): pp. 43–45.

II

Robert Morgan's People and Places

An Essay and Photo Gallery

Jesse Graves

Robert Morgan was born October 3, 1944, in a rural corner of Henderson County, North Carolina. Green River runs through the valley, and Cicero Mountain casts a long shadow over the landscape. Morgan's childhood took place in an idyllic setting, and its influence was so pronounced that he titled his first book, a collection of poems in 1969, *Zirconia Poems*, and a volume of *New and Selected Poems* was titled *Green River*. Through his written recollections, Morgan has salvaged a world that might otherwise have been lost to the quick and unfeeling advances of history, and a culture more focused on the present and future than the past. In his essay, "The Uses of Photography," John Berger says, "Memory implies a certain act of redemption. What is remembered has been saved from nothingness. What is forgotten has been abandoned" (54). Robert Morgan's poetry and prose preserve people and places that have been regarded with very little interest or attention in the national media. Many of the most memorable and recognizable characters in Robert Morgan's body of work are based on real people, members of his family and community. In the photo of Morgan's grandmother Julia Capps Levi, for example, we see the real-life model for Julie Harmon, the narrator of *Gap Creek*; in the photo of Morgan's uncle Robert G. Levi, we see the real-life inspiration for at least half a dozen of Morgan's works.

Though mostly the hard times and hard work of life in Southern Appalachia have been documented in Morgan's poetry and fiction, a sense of literary possibility would have been palpable in the region during Morgan's childhood. A great western North Carolina writer, Thomas Wolfe, would have turned 44 years old on the day Morgan was born, had he not died of tuberculosis in 1938, at the very height of his literary promise. Wolfe's early death created a kind of tragic mythos around the writer, and his literary and cultural reputation grew steadily throughout the time of Morgan's youth. Morgan has spoken of the intensity of his experience in reading Wolfe's *Look Homeward, Angel* in his introduction to Scribner's 2006 reissue of the novel:

> One of the great events of my teen years was the appearance of the Henderson County bookmobile in the parking lot of Green River Baptist Church every first Monday of the month in the late 1950s.... From those shelves I picked *Farmer Boy*, Jack London's *White Fang*, James Oliver Curwood's *The Valley of the Silent Men*, as well as *Oliver Twist* and *David Copperfield*. But one afternoon in 1960 I saw a huge volume in gray cloth with *Look Homeward, Angel* printed on the spine. I'd seen Thomas Wolfe's photograph in the Hendersonville newspaper, along with a photograph of a stone angel in the local cemetery that was supposed to have inspired him. I knew that was the book I had to read [xi].

Not only did the young Morgan have a literary role model, this passage also shows his access to books, which would have been quite remarkable even one generation earlier. The Green River Baptist Church, where the bookmobile visited, is pictured in the following gallery of photos. The church is less than a quarter mile from Morgan's home place, where he lived after 1948.

While the legend of Thomas Wolfe expanded to the north, in cosmopolitan Asheville, another famous American writer, Carl Sandburg, made his home in Flat Rock, just to the north of Morgan's Green River valley. Though Sandburg was not a native North Carolinian, it is where he chose to spend his later years, moving there in 1945, just one year after Morgan's birth. Sandburg was one of the most popular writers in America, winning three Pulitzer Prizes. His poems about Chicago and his biography on Abraham Lincoln had already become permanent features of twentieth-century Americana. The proximity to the Wolfe and Sandburg legacies surely made the prospect of becoming a writer more viable for Robert Morgan than would have been common in most parts of southern Appalachia.

In "The Sense of Place," an essay on the role of landscape and local custom in Irish poetry, Seamus Heaney says the following:

> I think there are two ways in which place is known and cherished, two ways which may be complementary but are just as likely to be antipathetic. One is lived, illiterate and unconscious, the other learned, literate and conscious. In the literary sensibility, both are likely to co-exist in a conscious and unconscious tension: this tension and the poetry it produces are what I want to discuss [p. 131].

Like Patrick Kavanaugh and the other Irish poets to whom Heaney refers, Robert Morgan writes in a manner that must be faithful to both insider and outsider knowledge and experiences. He has lived among people like those in his poetry and prose, so he shares with them the illiterate and unconscious knowledge of their place and time, yet he has also acquired the literary learning which they mostly lack. The writer has a literary-historical sensibility that would seem alien to many of his subjects, even those who are better read than others, and he must be able to apply this learning without imposing it on his characters. Mostly this happens through form and technique, the organization and deep structures of a literary text.

Morgan has written celebrated works in varied forms, yet three elements emerge as constant presences, regardless of the particular genre: family, landscape, and history. These themes do not divide up neatly into categories. For instance, family may appear to dominate Morgan's fiction, and landscape his poetry, but the flood scene in his novel *Gap Creek*, and the presence of Uncle Allen in his poem "Bellrope," and his father in "When He Spoke Out of the Dark," are among countless examples that remind us of the intricate intertwining Morgan performs in his writing. Even in his non-fiction historical and biographical writing, family plays a role just as integral as national or civic history in the lives of Daniel Boone, and many public figures, such as Nicholas P. Trist and Kit Carson, in *Lions of the West*. Photographs in this gallery resonate with all three of Morgan's major themes, as they convey family brought together in time and place, with all the particulars of dress and manner of that historical moment, covering several generations of images.

Reading a writer's work through the lens of a gallery of photographs presents the possibility for an overly subjective interpretation, an evaluation of how well the author depicts the "real-life" counterparts in the pictures. While the photographs of Robert Morgan's family and home life provide a valuable context for interpreting his writings, the accomplished work of imaginative poetry and fiction must attain a more objective quality of representation as well. At the peak of New Critical, non-autobiographical interpretation, Dorothy Van Ghent reminds the reader of the importance of authenticity in the world a writer creates. In her 1953 volume, *The English Novel: Form and Function,* Van Ghent stakes a claim for intertwining of form and content:

> The sound novel, like a sound world, must hang together as one thing. It has to have an integral structure.... Finally, we judge a novel by the cogency and illuminative quality of the view of life that it affords, the idea embodied in its cosmology [p. 6].

Robert Morgan's individual collections of work "hang together as one thing," as Van Ghent requires, yet his entire body of writing could also be said to "hang together" in a similar way. The faces and places in the following photographs make up the fabric of what hangs together in Morgan's work, his aesthetic commitment to how lives are actually lived, and the extent to which geography affects those lives.

An appendix follows the photo gallery in which names of particular Morgan family members are listed, along with the corresponding works in which they are portrayed. The list should have excellent value for scholars looking to compare different versions of the portrayals, especially useful for such notable figures as Clyde R. Morgan, the author's father, who is represented in many different works, and whose character and personality are revealed in rich and sometimes conflicting manners.

The photographs in this gallery are intended to show an element of the lived experience of Robert Morgan's background, and to provide a more complete picture of his family life and upbringing. The early photographs reveal many characteristics familiar to the time and place: firm, unsmiling faces above Sunday-best clothing, and the guarded, formal poses of people unused to being photographed. Several of the pictures show people in nature, outside, taking part in their local landscape. The photos complement what Robert Morgan says in his accompanying essay, "A Sense of Place":

> It is important to remember that place primarily means people, the people on the land, the people who have been on the land. Our greatest interest in a place derives from those who are there, their struggles, failures, joys. A place is about stories, and stories are about encounters, people encountering people, encountering the elements, or fate [p. 3].

Few writers bind people and place more intimately than Morgan. Equally in his poems and prose, one finds people working the land with great care to meet their own physical and emotional needs. One also finds people in conflict with the land they live on, struggling against its indifference and occasional ferocity. Morgan explores the paradox of a beautiful and bountiful land presenting imposing dangers to those who attempt to live on it, to pursue their destinies in harmony with the natural world. The photographs that follow show different stages of Morgan's own life, and images of his forebears, who provided so much inspiration for his writing.

Works Cited

Berger, John. *About Looking.* New York: Pantheon, 1980.
Heaney, Seamus. *Preoccupations: Selected Prose, 1968–1978.* New York: FSG, 1981.
Van Ghent, Dorothy. *The English Novel: Form and Function.* New York: Holt, 1953.

Top: Green River Baptist Church, Second Building, 1890. The first Green River Baptist Church was a log building. This frame structure survived into Morgan's childhood. Later wings were added to the building, and around 1975 the church was covered with brick.

Above: From left to right, Clyde, Dwight, Pearlie, Grandfather John Mitchell Morgan, Mae, and Great-Grandfather Frank Pace. Old Morgan House, 1914. Robert Morgan's first house (1944–1948). Morgan says, "This family photo was taken by a traveling photographer after the death of my Grandmother Morgan. My dad was nine, Dwight was twelve, Pearlie, fifteen, and Mae six. They had just come out of the field."

Right: Wessie, Julia, Robert Hampton Levi, William Levi, 1907. This photograph was taken on Gap Creek, five years before Morgan's mother was born. Wessie (1904–1994) was three, and William (1906–1993) was one.

Opposite page: Annie Capps, Carola Capps, Fidele Capps, Rose Capps, and Delia Johnson Capps, c. 1915. Morgan says, "Annie (1882–1960), Carola (1895–1984), and Rose (1889–1981) never married. They stayed home to take care of their parents, Delia Johnson Capps (1860–1953) and Fidele Capps (1850–1933). I loved to visit them at the old Capps house on Pleasant Hill because Aunt Rose, who had dozens of cats lurking around, always had a fresh coconut cake to share with us."

Top—left: Great-Grandmother Delia Ann Johnson Capps, age 14, 1874. Morgan says, "This photo was taken when Delia was a student at Judson College in Hendersonville, North Carolina. I used it on the cover of *The Strange Attractor*." *Right:* Aunt Wessie Levi Corn, 1904–1994. This photo was made around 1925, when Aunt Wessie was courting in the Roaring Twenties. She played the foot-pump organ for services at the Green River Baptist Church.

Top—left: Grandfather John Mitchell Morgan, 1863–1941. Morgan says, "John Mitchell Morgan was begotten when his father, John E. Morgan, deserted from the Confederate Army to come home and put in a crop for his wife. John was a notably successful farmer on Green River. He could remember smelling the scent of burnt leather in the air after the Great Chicago Fire of 1871." *Right:* Grandfather Robert Hampton Levi, 1877–1955. Morgan recalls, "Hamp Levi was born on top of Cicero Mountain, so premature no one expected him to live. But he survived and grew up to be a strong man, called 'Big Hamp' by the community. When he married Julia Capps in 1901 they moved to Gap Creek in South Carolina."

Right: Grandmother Julia Capps Levi, 1883–1948. Morgan says, "My grandmother Julie was the inspiration for Julie Harmon in the novel *Gap Creek*. I remember her well for her kindness and tireless work to help others."

Opposite page—bottom, left: Delia Ann Johnson Capps, Great-Grandmother, 1860–1953. Morgan says, "Born in 1860 to George Johnson (1824–1900) and Rebecca Ann Blocker Johnson (1832–1924), Delia was taken to Walterboro, South Carolina, to be safe during the Civil War. She could remember Sherman's army coming through, and bodies piled on their porch." *Right:* Great-Grandfather Frank Pace (1838–1918), Confederate Army. Frank Pace was a lifelong Republican, who enlisted in the Confederate Army for six months, but was then kept in the army for the duration of the war. Captured in 1864 near Petersburg, Virginia, he was sent to Elmira Prison, where he almost died of diphtheria, but survived to return to North Carolina and marry Mary Ann Jones (1839–1880).

Top—left: Grandmother Sarah Matilda Pace Morgan, 1871–1912. Tildy Morgan was the inspiration for Ginny Peace in the novel *The Truest Pleasure*. Morgan says, "She was an intense, intellectual woman, who became involved in the Pentecostal Holiness movement in 1905, much to the chagrin of her husband John. She died of measles in 1912." *Right:* Grandparents Robert Hampton Levi and Julia Capps Levi, c. 1930. Morgan says, "In this photo we get a sense of my Levi grandparents as they looked in middle age, before the grief for the death of their son Robert in 1943 prematurely aged them."

Top—left: Clyde R. Morgan, 1990. Morgan says, "Born in 1905, in Theodore Roosevelt's administration, my dad loved to study history and geography, and he lived through a lot of history. As a boy he had sat at the feet of his grandpa Frank Pace, listening to stories about the Civil War and Elmira Prison Camp, the Cherokee Indians, and the old days on Green River." *Right:* Robert Morgan with his mother Fannie Levi Morgan (1912–2010) and sister Evangeline, 1946. This picture was taken by his father in the yard of the old Morgan house down by Green River. He was not yet two years old.

Right: Robert Morgan, first grade, 1951–1952, Tuxedo Elementary School. Morgan started school a year late because his birthday came after October 1st. His mother taught him to read and write and count at home in 1950–1951.

Opposite page—left: Uncle Robert G. Levi, 1942. Morgan says, "I grew up listening to stories about my Uncle Robert, who died in a B-17 crash in East Anglia, England, on November 10, 1943. The family thought he was a mechanic, but I later found out that at the time of his death he was serving as an engineer/gunner on a top secret Pathfinder aircraft." *Right:* Clyde R. Morgan, Father, 1924. Morgan says, "My dad always loved to dress up, and he was proud of his looks. He drove a Model T Ford Roadster in the 1920s and spent much of what he made from trapping furs on fine clothes from stores in Asheville."

Top—left: Robert Morgan, second grade, 1952–1953, Tuxedo Elementary School. Morgan says, "My teacher in first and second grades was Ruth Hill Mullinax. She was a patient, caring teacher. Because I had already learned much of the material of the first and second grades, I was the class smart aleck." *Middle*: Robert Morgan, fifth grade, 1955–1956, Tuxedo Elementary School. Morgan's teacher in Fifth Grade was Laura MacDonald. That was the year he got out of class each day to work in the lunch room to pay for his meal, saying, "It was glorious to get out of class, scrape dishes for the dishwasher, and burn trash in the incinerator behind the school. When I returned to class, Miss MacDonald would snarl, 'There comes Robert after gallivanting around the world.'" *Right:* Robert Morgan, ninth grade, 1958–1959, Flat Rock High School. Morgan skipped the seventh grade at Tuxedo School and entered Flat Rock High School in 1958. The young writer hoped to catch sight of the poet Carl Sandburg, who lived just across the road from the school, but never did. He was away in Hollywood, working on the film *The Greatest Story Ever Told*. Morgan left high school in 1961, without graduating, to enter Emory College at Oxford, Georgia.

Robert Morgan, 1976, Rogersville, Tennessee. This photo was taken at Nance Ferry on the Holston River by Jeff Daniel Marion, just after the Robert Morgan issue of *The Small Farm* was published. Morgan gave a reading at Carson-Newman College to celebrate the occasion.

Robert Morgan, 1993, Ithaca, New York. Dede Hatch took this picture for the jacket cover of *The Hinterlands*, which was published in 1994.

An Appendix of Family Members Appearing in Morgan's Writing or Serving as the Basis for Characters in His Fiction

Father, Clyde R. Morgan (1905–1991)

Poem: "Getting Out Rock" (*Land Diving*)
Poem: "Trunk & Thicket" (*Trunk & Thicket*)
Poem: "Walnutry" (*Groundwork*) [with R.M.'s sister Evangeline]
Poem: "Baptism of Fire" (*Groundwork*)
Poem: "Bean Money" (*Groundwork*)
Poem: "Elevation" (*Bronze Age*) [with R.M.'s sister Evangeline and especially their mother]
Poem: "The Gift of Tongues" (*At the Edge of the Orchard Country*)
Poem: "Halley's Comet" (*At the Edge of the Orchard Country*) [The back of a photograph including his father identifies him as the "he" in this poem.]
Poem: "Sunday Toilet" (*At the Edge of the Orchard Country*)
Poem: "When He Spoke Out of the Dark" (*Sigodlin*)
Poem: "Working in the Rain" (*Wild Peavines, Topsoil Road*)
Poem: "Mowing" (*Wild Peavines, Topsoil Road*)
Poem: "Care" (*Topsoil Road*)
Poem: "Oranges" (*Topsoil Road*)
Poem: "Go Gentle" (*Terroir*)
Poem: "Great Day in the Morning" (*Terroir*)
Essay: "Homecoming" (*Trunk & Thicket*)
Essay: "Work and Poetry: The Father Tongue" (in *Southern Review* 31 [1995]: 161–179.)

Mother, Fannie Levi Morgan (1912–2010)

Poem: "Canning Time" (*Groundwork*) [with his Aunt Wessie]
Poem: "Elevation" (*Bronze Age*)
Poem: "Vapor Salve" (*Wild Peavines, Topsoil Road*)
Poem: "Heaven's Gate" (*Dark Energy*)
Essay: "Homecoming" (*Trunk & Thicket*) [brief mention]

Uncle Robert G. Levi (1915–1943)

Poem: "Pigeon Loft" (*Groundwork*) [with "Grandpa" and RM's mother]
Poem: "Uncle Robert" (*At the Edge of the Orchard Country*) [with RM's mother]
Poem: "Podington Air Field" (*Sigodlin*)
Poem: "Heaven" (*Sigodlin*)
Poem: "Heat Lightning" (*Topsoil Road*) [with mention of RM's mother]

Aunt Wessie Levi Corn (1904–1994)

Poem: "Concert" (*Land Diving*)
Poem: "Canning Time" (*Groundwork*) [With RM's mother]
Poem: "New Organ" (*Sigodlin*)

Uncle Allen Corn (1899–1979)

Poem: "Bellrope" (*At the Edge of the Orchard Country*)

Great-Grandmother Delia Johnson Capps (1860–1953)

Poem: "White Autumn" (*At the Edge of the Orchard Country*)

Grandfather Robert Hampton ("Hamp") Levi (1877–1955)

Poem: "Cold Friday" (*Land Diving*)
Poem: "Radio" (*Bronze Age, At the Edge of the Orchard Country*)
Poem: "Chant Royal" (*At the Edge of the Orchard Country*)
Poem: "Uranium" (*Sigodlin*)
Poem: "The Years Ahead" (*October Crossing* and *Terroir*)
Poem: "Hole in Water" (*Terroir*)
Novel: *Gap Creek* [He is the model for Hank.]

Grandmother Julia Capps Levi (1883–1948)

Poem: "When the Ambulance Came" (*Groundwork*)
Poem: "Cowbedding" (*Bronze Age, At the Edge of the Orchard Country*)
Poem: "Bare Yard" (*At the Edge of the Orchard Country*)
Poem: "Grandma's Bureau" (*Sigodlin*)
Poem: "Besom" (*Topsoil Road*)
Novel: *Gap Creek* [She's the model for Julie.]

Grandfather John Mitchell Morgan (1863–1941)

Poem: "Snowlight" (*Groundwork*)
Novel: *The Truest Pleasure* [He's the model for Tom, though it was his wife and not he who died of measles in 1912.]

Grandmother Sarah Matilda Pace Morgan (1871–1912)

Poem: "The Holy Laugh" (*October Crossing*)

Novel: *The Truest Pleasure* [She's the model for Ginny, though it was she and not her husband who died of measles in 1912.]
Novel: *This Rock* [She's the model for Ginny.]

Great-Grandfather John Benjamin Franklin Pace (1838–1918)

Poem: "Zircon Pit" (*Groundwork*)
Poem: "Books in the Attic" (*At the Edge of the Orchard Country*) [Also mentioned there: R.M.'s father.]
Poem: "The Road from Elmira" (*Sigodlin*)
Novel: *The Truest Pleasure* [He is the model for Ginny's Pa, Ben Peace.]

Great-Grandmother Mary Ann Jones Pace (1838–1880)

Short Story: "Martha Sue" (*The Mountains Won't Remember Us*)

Aunt Pearlie Morgan Capps (1899–1972)

Poem: "Parlor" (*At the Edge of the Orchard Country*) [Morgan there invents the name "Aunt Florrie."]
Poem: "Ghosts in the Carpet" (in the new poems section of *Green River*)

Uncle William V. Levi (1906–1994)

Poem: "Roost Tree" (*Land Diving*)
Poem: "Sunday Keeping" (*Sigodlin*)
Poem: "Concert" (*October Crossing*)

Uncle Volney Pace (1873–1958)

Poem: "Heaven" (*Sigodlin*) [He is also Locke Peace in *The Truest Pleasure*.]

Uncle Wascinura Levi (1887–1941)

Poem: "Writing Spider" (*Sigodlin*) [He is the brother of Robert Hampton.]

Cousin Horace Pace (1903–1938)

Poem: "Horace Pace" (*Land Diving*)

Cousin Ida Pace Jones (1894–1978)

Poem: "Appleglow" (*Green River*) [She is first cousin to RM's father, and sister of Horace Pace.]

Cousin Harold Corn (1945–)

Poem: "Appleglow" (*Green River*) [He is the grandson of Ida Pace Jones.]

Aunt Tharmuthias Morgan Staton (1876–1960)

Poem: "Aunt Tharmuthias" (*Terroir*)

Great-Grandfather John E. Morgan (1836–1864)

Story: "A Brightness New and Welcoming." [He is the model for John.]

Uncle Dwight Morgan (1902–1973)

Poem: "Oranges" (*Topsoil Road*) [He is also (in Morgan's words) "loosely, perhaps very loosely, Moody in *The Truest Pleasure* and *This Rock*."]

III

On the Prose

Mountain Time

History and Forgetting in The Mountains Won't Remember Us

Paul Lincoln Sawyer

> "I have tried to create verbal spaces in which other *things* and animals, not just people, can be heard. Maybe what I've tried to voice most is how: institutions, artifacts, the dirt."
>
> —Robert Morgan, "Interview by Jeff Daniel Marion" (*Good Measure* 130)

I

The shortest epitome of all Robert Morgan's work can be found in the twelve words of the poem "Mountain Graveyard":

> stone notes
> slate tales
> sacred cedars
> heart earth
> asleep please
> hated death [*The Strange Attractor* 105].

The six anagram pairs reduce to an extreme point of terseness the genre of graveyard elegy, and a tradition at least as old as Christianity: the conception of nature as the divine handwriting, God's other scripture. Disembodied of syntax, the words seem to stand motionless and thing-like on the page. But who or what utters them? We could think of the first three pairs as the thoughts of a casual visitor to a place of burial, listing what s/he sees, but the last three might just as easily be fragments of inscriptions or the voices of the dead. "Slate tales" and "stone notes" describe, of course, both landscape and gravestones, while "heart earth" blends the human perspective and the inhuman (the earth is a kind of heart, the human hearts below are earth). Looked at in another way, the anagrams resemble geological rather than human syntax: the letters shuffle the way stones and earth slip over time, creating accidental combinations that are nevertheless legible to the geologist. As Morgan put it in an earlier poem, "Mockingbird," "the law / of conservation means the world's / an anagram of each stage of evolution" (*The Strange Attractor* 54). Thus, by lining up words in a double column of six that issue from no determinate, conscious or intentional source, he wittily captures what it might feel like not just to read gravestones but to hear behind and through them "books in the running brooks, / Sermons in stones"[1]: the speech of the great, mute presences that surround human life—the dead, the earth. For a post-structuralist, the sense of presence inhering in writing is an illusion dependent upon the structural properties of language; we could also say, then, that "Mountain Graveyard" generates meaning as the effect of a geo-social system of signs. By imitating in his letters the shift of impersonal processes—creating as it were a flicker by which the words seem now "full" (voiced) and now "empty" (inscriptions, or marks on a page), Morgan gives us the sense not of hearing the voice of a particular poet, but of decoding on our own a fragmentary record without authorship. Yet amidst it all, we hear most loudly the whisper of finite creatures and their needs ("hated death," "asleep please").

I begin with these six anagrams not just to notice Robert Morgan's double identity as poet and fiction writer but to point to an even more dramatic duality: a poet of nature whose fiction contains an unusually complex view of human social history. The key to the paradox, for me, lies in his ability to disturb and confuse the conventional boundary between the human and the natural. Both geologist and historian, he writes out of an acute sense of the surface, textures, pitted accidents and events of the earth that are also the records of the human communities that alter it. As a poet of nature and of material culture, he writes of ranges and rivers, of whippoorwills, orchards, and lightning bugs, but also of slop buckets and manure piles, dank cellars and toolsheds re-opened after fifty years, odometers and rearview mirrors—richly detailed visual meditations through which one intuits the lineaments of a complex human community. Earth becomes the ground or support of human communities—their institutions and artifacts, their ways of building, coping, eating and sheltering, surviving, rearing and dying—as well as the region of nonhuman existence that stands as the other of human knowledge and will, eluding and ultimately outlasting it. Similarly, in his fiction he constructs the lineaments of a social history which is also a kind of geology—a record of the endurance and decay of the earth as well as humans and their products.

The Mountains Won't Remember Us occupies, in my view, a central place in Morgan's work as a whole. All eleven stories take place in a single region—the ridges and valleys that ripple out of the Carolinas towards Virginia and Tennessee, the region known locally as "the mountains" and nationally as "Appalachia"; but they extend widely in time, from the decades just after the Revolution to the present day, covering two hundred years of human habitation. Thus, although each story stands on its own, as a group they form a whole that exceeds the sum of the eleven parts—nothing less than the [a?] narrative of the region's history. Morgan's most ambitious historical work [fiction?] to date, *The Mountains Won't Remember Us* is a meditation on the history of the earth as well as those that dwell in it, and on the relationship between Memory (which for the Greeks was the mother of history) and memory's opposite, the forgetting that surrounds life as sleep surrounds waking. Since the time of the earth can be grasped by humans only implicitly, in the mute spaces where human presences break off and resume, the stories also contain within them the hush of "Mountain Graveyard." All of their themes and effects are amplified in the climactic novella that gives the collection its title, to which I'll turn in the third section of this essay after an overview of the shorter pieces that lead up to it.

II

The first three stories take place in the wilderness near the turn of the nineteenth century; the next two are post–Civil War; the next two cluster around the middle of the twentieth century; the last four are roughly contemporary. The cycle of changes the stories record begins with the building of a stone bridge across a gap in the mountains that opens the region to settlement and commerce. Mountain life in these years is lived close to the unbroken earth, under austerely difficult conditions—travelers disappear and homesteaders are killed by Indians or robbed by bushwhackers; nevertheless, triumphs can come to the spirited and the independent. Ten years after the Civil War, the railroad comes in, promising a new era of prosperity and a new influx of vacationers. By the late twentieth century, of course, this "underdeveloped" region has become overdeveloped. Industrial civilization, ameliorating the harsher forms of destitution, danger, and isolation, does so by a succession of assaults both on the earth and on the ways of life it nurtured. Roads are clotted with traffic, the soil has been bulldozed into shopping malls; people drift through jobs, nestle in mobile homes, and compete for parking space with Cadillacs from Miami. In the seventh story, a woman discovers that her old homestead has been flooded with red mud because the developer next door has razed the surface of a hill; in the ninth story, a man swindled out of his land discovers that the new owner is illegally burying chemical waste near a riverbed.

The first thing to note about these events is that, like geological process, human time strictly speaking possesses no forward direction or telos. It's history without leaders, founding families, popular movements, proud traditions, great events, great crimes or battles; it's also, as we'll see, history without a male bias. Morgan depicts people and their practices in the process of passing from youth through various stages of endurance and decay and (if renewal is too strong a word) replacement—a process that contains causes and effects—but he does so without either regret or celebration. Although his narratives begin in the wilderness, he conjures up no giants in the earth, no "old people" half-shrouded in legend, not even an idealized race of yeoman homesteaders, and therefore no devolution into a spawn of Snopeses; Appalachian time, in other words, is neither progressive nor elegiac. In the powerful story "The Watershed," Morgan's second narrator expresses an almost mystical sense of pre-existence in the woods ("I've often thought the woods was haunted by the Indians.... Every time you hear a waterfall or shoals you think you can hear an Indian talking in it" [30].) But as a boy, the same narrator takes part in an attack on a sleeping Indian village; when he and the God-fearing adults have slaughtered all the Indians they can catch, they return past a group of new-built houses, built by the newest race of inhabitants: "I don't reckon any had been built during the night, but it seemed they was more cleared ground and trails, and the houses and barns had multiplied" (38). The word "watershed," the narrator points out, can describe "the place a decision is made close up in just a matter of a fraction of an inch yet it has such a long-range consequence" (28), a comment that describes his own last-minute shooting of a defenseless Indian girl, but the definition also seems to describe Morgan's view of human agency in general and therefore the processes of history, which unfold as a set of unforeseen consequences for better or worse.

A second feature of Morgan's historical narrative is that once the settlement period is over, the material conditions of his characters' lives come increasingly under the control of distant centers of power. The first narrator, the young mason who helps build Poinsett's

Bridge, is nearly overwhelmed, at the end of his story, by the flood of human traffic crossing the gap that includes not only country folk like his neighbors but a party of wealthy tourists from the Low Country: "I stood back and let them pass, and they ignored me just like I was air" (21). The wealthy Charlestonians and investors of this opening story become the forebears of the developers and resort-owners of the later stories. In "Caretakers," set a hundred and fifty years later, an affluent couple from Virginia exploits local labor at the same time they appropriate local history, fabricating through a resort called "the Mountain Manor" a fake image of antebellum gentility. This story is narrated by the exploited servant of the owners; when she learns on the radio of the end of World War II, she responds in this way:

> It meant things would no longer be rationed and my brothers would come home. It meant that building supplies would be available again, and that the loan might come through to build a house on the land my daddy deeded us. Me and Roy would no longer have to work as caretakers for the Mountain Manor [94].

The great moments of American history and its celebrated triumphs take place, so to speak, offstage and far away; instead of the official story, in other words, Morgan gives us history experienced from below.

Western fiction has often attempted to depict the impoverished and powerless, but typically through the mediation of a sophisticated narrative language that contrasts with the characters' rudimentary education and non-standard speech; the effect is to picture the poor condescendingly in terms of lacks: lack of psychological interiority, self-consciousness, agency, or articulate speech. Morgan in contrast depicts the struggles of plain people—farmers and laborers, shopkeepers, mechanics, artisans, housewives—without sentimentalizing them as the salt of the earth nor pitying them as victims nor mocking them as hillbillies or white trash, but by presenting them from within. Or rather, he lets his characters present themselves.[2] Every story in *The Mountains Won't Remember Us* is narrated in the colloquial first-person idiom that has become the hallmark of Morgan's fiction—a feature of his work so well-known it's easy to take it for granted. Yet skill in fashioning speech that's both plain-spoken and lyrical, yet capable at times of psychological complexity and moments of extraordinary emotional power, is in my view his most remarkable achievement as a writer of fiction. His success here is hard to miss; what's easier to miss is the relationship between the first-person idiom and the form of the stories themselves.

Most generally, the stories are constructed as a compromise between oral and print modes. On the one hand, the narrative convention Morgan favors is one common in short fiction today, which I call here the temporal loop: the story begins in the midst of an ongoing event (a crisis or developing conflict) that's deferred by a movement of retrospection which in turn circles forward to the crisis developing in the present. The technique combines the largeness of process with the intense focus of a "breaking" event that, framing the past in the present, can reveal the meaning of a whole stretch of a person's life. But this is not the usual way people tell stories. Morgan also imitates in his narrative shapes the movements of oral history, with its spontaneity and associativeness. Like one person speaking to another, these narrators mix anecdotes, explanations, interjections, and occasional sententious reflections; they sometimes explain too much, take too many words, and offer too many maxims. (The first two narrators actually speak from a space of years, one addressing his audience as "Son," the other as "Boy.") The trick is to manage the contradiction between the well-crafted loop and the tendency of oral recall to meander between chronology and digression.

Morgan's life-narratives therefore contain a complex interplay between personal memory and the accumulation of historical time, a fact that's reflected in their arrangement. As the stories move from the remote past into the present, the protagonists tend to age. The first three are young men or boys faced with heroic (or comic-heroic) challenges, while the tenth protagonist is barely surviving at eighty-five, and the last one, an elderly woman, lives mainly in her memories. As the older narrators reflect on the personal past, they cast an indirect light on the past time of the collection itself, so that we re-visit in fragmented form some of the temporal territory we have already traversed. On the other hand, the two stories told from a deathbed occupy the middle of the collection. The relationship between human aging and the aging of the region is therefore only one dimension of the stories' temporal patterning.

Colloquial narration is one way Morgan represents the lives of the poor up close; the other is to describe their labor.

In a certain sense, work has always been the "other" of the proper subject of fiction. We expect novels to be about love, war, intrigue, adventure, or complex reflection—whatever takes place outside of workday lives—except insofar as work is construed as something other than work (statecraft, soldiering, social climbing, creating); *Robinson Crusoe* stands almost alone in the European (and American?) literary canon as a narrative of labor (alongside, perhaps, *Moby Dick*). Although the processes of work (building a house, tilling the soil) have to be explained in sequence, as a story does, we understand this kind of exposition to be different from narration. And a character's inner life, we tend to assume, can only unfold when abstracted from the work he or she does. But Morgan's characters—true to the tendency of oral history—*talk intimately about the work they do and cannot be understood separately from it.*[3] Appropriately, the earliest description of a job in *The Mountains Won't Remember Us* is a boy's first try at a chimney—the core of any human habitation, which in this case is constructed from a calculated re-arrangement of the mountain elements (mud, stones) that we might also think of as the first, most primitive form of human making, or *techne*. By explaining the details of his job, Morgan's narrator reveals himself, as it were, externally, and as fully as an interior monologue might do:

> But then I seen in my pile a rock that was perfect for a cornerstone, and another that would fit against it in a line with just a little chipping.... I put the cornerstone in place, and slapped on some wet clay, then fitted the next rock to it. It was like solving a puzzle, finding rocks that would join together with just a little mud, maybe a little chipping here and there to smooth a point or corner. But best of all was the way you could rough out a line, running a string or a rule along the edge to see how it would line up, so when you backed away you saw the wall was straight in spite of gaps and bulges [4].

No adequate literary view of life from below can fail to represent the processes of work—as both a physical and mental activity and as a form of social relationship. And no living writer is more deeply concerned than Morgan with the material processes of his characters' lives, or with the ways specific work forms part of an overall labor economy. Redemption through work has of course been a constant theme in Morgan's writing; as he noted in a lecture delivered ten years ago, "I came to see that work was a purifying ritual, and the baptism of sweat a sacrament in the quest for meaning" ("Nature"). By the same token, he has been much admired for his dazzling accuracy in depicting the material conditions of pioneer life. But we've seen that the stories in *The Mountains Won't Remember Us* stretch far beyond the early settlement period, which means they also record the changing social and material conditions of work as a source of value. The plot of the first story presents this theme with fable-like clarity. Robbed of the silver that had been a season's pay for working on Poinsett's Bridge, the young mason spies in the road ahead of him the glitter of something more precious than silver—his light mason's hammer, which he picks up and pockets. Nearly two hundred years later, a farmer's son turns the family acreage into a shrub nursery in order to make a quick profit on a new consumer trend. He tells his father, "there's money in this ground.... I always thought it was just dirt" (134). The old man muses sadly, "I never was able to communicate to Everett that the only real wisdom is in the work itself" (135). Work as an end in itself and money as an end in itself here stand opposed as God to Mammon, an opposition signaled historically by the shift in the region's economy from subsistence farming to production for an abstract marketplace.

But if there's wisdom in work, work is also the prime means of human subjugation. The profoundest social change Morgan chronicles is the shift in the social nature of work, from production for the homestead or immediate community to wage labor for others or for an abstract market. Morgan's later narrators have a forthright, populist sense of the class power they confront as members of a floating proletariat. "It was like they understood how everything worked and they were in charge of it," says the caretaker of the Mountain Manor about the condescending town bankers (106). In another story a developer, "sounding Yankee and superior," turns to stamping his foot in rage when confronted about the mud slide his projects have created ("He wasn't used to mountain people who would stand up to him") (116–117). An injured millworker, refused compensation by a "crooked" company doctor, knows no other mill will hire him because "all these plants work together against poor people" (152).

But oppression as Morgan presents it is by sex as well as class. Decades of work by feminist critics and scholars has exposed the invisibility of women in the official annals of governments, war, and trade, and has reconstituted woman as a subject of history. This tradition bears especially strongly on Morgan's social canvas, which already lacks the markers of a heroic masculine history. *The Mountains Won't Remember Us* is in the final instance woman's history, but woman's history, once again, of a complicated sort. A popular version of "herstory" presents women as the unsung heroines of the homeplace, guaranteeing human survival by their brute endurance, labor, and steadfastness. When Oprah Winfrey brought *Gap Creek* to a large public—making it the first of Morgan's books to sell widely—the publishing establishment and their representatives in the mainstream press struggled to pigeonhole him: if he won Oprah's endorsement, then he must write "women's fiction." For the marketers, the phrase seemed to indicate heart-lifting narratives of endurance in pioneer days—and indeed *Gap Creek* can be read this way; but that description will not suffice for *The Mountains Won't Remember Us*.

Most broadly, the stories record the pressures and demands put upon gender relations first by austere settlement conditions and then by a casual, proletarianized labor economy. "Martha Sue," the first of the five stories narrated by women, appears to be a wife's memoir, beginning with her young man's return from months in a Yankee prison camp, then gradually shifting to their courtship and marriage, his fitful, half-realized projects, the births of their children, and his obsession with charismatic religion, until it becomes clear that the narrator is speaking from her death bed and therefore not narrating her weak and vacillating husband's biography but delivering her own eulogy. This ingenious reversal allows the previously unnoticed and unspoken to rise into view, as the reader begins to grasp the specific contours of this woman's life and work and to notice the ways the story has been hers all along. Martha Sue, in other words, narrates her own social existence dialectically through the life of another until she's able to stand alone as a defined self; as we'll see soon, this strategy is repeated by other characters in the collection, including the narrator of the title novella.

In the last moments before beholding a "great distance closing in like comfort," Martha Sue sums up the relationship between men and women this way: "I want to say men and women are so different it's hard to believe they are the same race at all. Him and me has not been perfect mates. If it hadn't been [his religious fervor], it would have been something else. But being almost strangers we still brought comfort to one another at times" (73). Although women traditionally perform the work of social bonding and generational continuity in a community, these words express Morgan's women's profound sense—a sense profounder than the men's—of essential human solitude. Most often in his work, the men are the dreamers, and the women are the realists, who waken only slowly to the cost of yielding to male dreams. Sometimes that recognition is tragic, a realization of hopes diverted or subtly betrayed—if betrayed by men, then not so much by their perfidy as by their fecklessness or their inscrutability. Sometimes, though, Morgan's men are unredeemed rascals. In the comic masterpiece "Frog Level," a woman named Rachel Lessing surprises her husband in a brand-new shopping mall with another woman, confirming an old suspicion that he has always been both worthless and a cheat. Husband and wife embark on a sudden chase, she in her car, he fleeing recklessly in his red 4X4. At one point she catches him "hiding" between two huge semis at a rest stop off the highway (he escapes by pulling out onto the grass and crashing through picnickers); at another point, she blocks him in a supermarket parking lot (once again he escapes by overrunning the bar that holds shopping carts, dragging the clattering carts behind him). By focusing her energy on hunting her husband down and, after that, on destroying the mobile home they have shared, she breaks blindly but triumphantly loose from a lifetime of drift and deception, a decision that follows her wild drive over the scarred scenes of her past mistakes and dreams.

Between Martha Sue's resigned, qualified acceptance of the difference between men and women and Rachel Lessing's angry, exuberant exposure of an abusive heel lies the full range of sexual relationships explored in these stories. These relationships are inseparable, in turn, from the conditions of men's and women's work, which of course includes child-raising ("Martha Sue"); other female laborers in the collection include the caretaker of Mountain Manor, who in a passage that's also a satire on class power describes in detail the cleaning of a filthy bathroom, and the subject of "Death Crown," a retarded woman whose sole permitted function in her family has been the carrying of water. The nature of work is in turn inseparable from the texture of social life itself. What then is the relationship between the characters' economic and social subordination and their experience of work as a potential value?

As I've suggested, the social landscape of Morgan's fiction gives no sense of history as a product of conscious will, or of social change as a collective effort, or of tradition as a source of patriotic or regional pride. If anything, he's skeptical of organized attempts at human amelioration, locating transcendence (in classic American fashion) as an individual rather than a collective experience. His characters survive and endure not upon joining a common effort but, one almost wants to say, upon the point of abandonment. Because despite their obscurity and pain, all are survivors, nobly or otherwise—even those near the end of their lives who, typically, have strength left for an affirmation. In "Mack," the penultimate story, an eighty-five-year-old man keeps as his only companion a dog whose lively exuberance gives him the courage to keep going. One day, the old man becomes momentarily confused while crossing the busy highway outside his home:

> There are horns blaring and cars on all sides of me, but I can't see in what direction to go. If I could just sink down under it and let the traffic go on above my head it would be OK. And the noises I hear, beyond the horns and engines, are the thresh of the river, and a jet plane straight above, and water dripping through rocks in the ground far below. And there is a crisp sound, which is the crackle stars make on a cold clear night.
>
> "Pop, you can cross now." It is the man in the red car, leaning out his window. He motions for me to go ahead [175].

All this rushing, flowing, struggling and sinking, along with Mack's intimations of immortality, subtly suggest another river and another crossing—Bunyan's river of death, a type of the River Jordan which is also Pilgrim's last trial before entering the gates of heaven, and which he survives by the help of his companion Hopeful. But what Morgan's narrator finds on the other side is only the Promised Land of his own front yard, and the dog alive and well: "You can see by the way he holds his head when he runs he's ready to enjoy the rest of the day" (175).

Mack's highway is only one of the many thoroughfares in the stories, beginning with Poinsett's Bridge, which as I've mentioned will open the mountains not to torrents of rainwater but to the rush of commerce, travelers, wealthy tourists: the dizzying flood of cars that dodge the old man and his dog descend from that original bridge. These and similar episodes of difficult journeys and crossings flicker across the reader's mind, until they merge to form a persistent motif: the motif of forging one's way through mountain passes and highways, across rivers and years, sometimes losing oneself and sometimes saving oneself. Those recognitions become for Morgan's readers the flicker of history, which is also the cumulative effect of the countless parallels and repetitions that bind human lives across time and space in largely unconscious solidarity.

How far do Morgan's characters share the reader's sense of their fellowship over time? What do they inherit? By presenting lived experience up close, through the words and struggles of unhistorical people, Morgan cannot rely on the omniscient overview, say, of the Tolstoyan narrator, since his speakers voice only a shallow awareness of what came before; they have to struggle to make meaning of their lives, let alone appreciate their ancestors' achievements. The book's dedication to Morgan's father hails him as "*storyteller, rememberer*." The contradiction between dedication and title could not be more clear, pointing as it does to the dialectical movement in the stories between recalling and repudiating. In Toni Morrison's *Beloved*, the repressed history of slavery surfaces through maternal speech, an oral tradition passed on as "rememory" from mother to daughter; but in the end of that novel, the survival of the living requires the exorcism of the past in the form of the banished ghost, who in the great final sentences fades out as a series of hints and traces in the natural world. *The Mountains Won't Remember Us* shares Morrison's dual concern with memory and the letting go of memory. In the book's last sentences, Sharon, the female narrator of the title novella, appears to repudiate both history and memory, and therefore a major purpose of the book itself. "The fields where we work, and the mountains we look at, even the people coming after us, won't remember us at all," she notes in satisfaction (250).

Morgan embeds his characters in a temporal dimension that's incomplete, broken, shallow, or lost to sight, like the fossil record as Darwin described it one hundred and fifty years ago; it's the novelist's art to imply a whole greater than the memory of individuals, through the technique of structural echoes and variations. Those echoes suggest a vision not of collective progress but of many individual achievements whose traces constitute the ground of the present. The democracy of death in a mountain graveyard is repeated in Morgan's radical leveling of human events, by which he shows over and over again how the sacred inheres in the humble and the extraordinary in the ordinary; it's a radical vision, though without the hope on which radical politics usually depends. Memory is crucial to that vision; yet if the living owe the dead the tribute of memory, Sharon's startling statement reminds us that there is also a time to forget: the wish embodied in the anagram "asleep please" must also be a wish for release from memory. I'll return to this paradox once again at the end of my reading of Sharon's narrative, in which the themes of the other stories find a powerful culmination.

III

The novella "The Mountains Won't Remember Us" occupies the same place in its book as "The Dead" occupies in Joyce's *Dubliners*, and as it turns out, shares some of Joyce's themes. The protagonists of both stories are similarly preoccupied with the dead, and both experience a moment of shattering awareness upon a sudden encounter with a figure from the past—a moment whose endlessly rippling implications carry us backwards into the experience of the other stories. But Morgan's version is told by the person in Greta's position, and her Michael Furey—her first fiancé—is an Air Force engineer in World War II named Troy, who died when his B-17 crashed near a British airfield. It's a double story then, about the ghost sought in memory and about the seeker herself, who as we can guess from the start, is in some concealed sense the ultimate object of her quest ("And now the old woman is free to pursue her youth," she tells us in the first paragraph, in a casual pun). But this youth—her youth—is a story of loss, and she's had so many since then that she's come to define herself by her losses: in addition to Troy, the soldier, are her worthless first husband, who abandoned her, and her sons, who drifted away; her kindly second husband, who gave her the only genuinely happy years of her life and who died unexpectedly; and her family (her parents are gone, and siblings had she none). Morgan pens her around with losses until she's stripped to a bare singularity, like some doomed heroine—Niobe perhaps—except that her voice, chatty, resolute, and matter-of-fact, shows that she's a survivor rather than a heroic victim.

In present time, Sharon is recovering from an amputation, living temporarily in a nursing home, and taking her first painful steps on an artificial leg. Of course she feels tingling from her phantom limb and violent itching and soreness at the point of amputation; we understand soon enough that her artificial leg, painful and awkward to wear at first, is a transitional object, something to substitute for a separation, though what her leg will correspond to in her psychic life isn't yet clear. Surviving, nevertheless, will take all the force of will she can muster. Here's Sharon setting out on her first journey with her new leg, down the corridor of the nursing home:

> [The therapist] opens the door and I am out in the hall.... The corridor looks a mile long, down to the front desk, with obstacles like wheelchairs and laundry carts all along the way.... Sunlight falls through the front door on the desk, but the lighting in the hall is that peculiar gray fluorescent that makes you feel under water ....
>
> I take a step on the smooth floor, and keep my balance. But I see instantly what this is going to take. It is work, and I am weak from all the days of sitting, and lying in bed. It's all a matter of accommodation, of compensation [229].

Half-way through her journey, Sharon is blocked by a new patient in a wheelchair, Mrs. Klotz, who speaks all in a rush about her husband's stroke, their home in Florida, their interrupted vacation in the mountains: "'Some days his mind is clear as a bell,' she says. 'And the next day he thinks he's Franklin Roosevelt. He's just down the hall. You can talk to him if you don't believe me'" (230). It takes a page and a half for Sharon to complete her walk, exhausted, sweating, but happy. The corridor traffic, the "obstacles of wheelchairs and laundry carts," the garrulous old lady, and the smell of pee in the nursing home may not seem like hallmarks of a heroic journey, though if we recall Mack's aged owner's struggle across the flood of a modern highway, and the other moments of solitary, fragile daring in the various stories, we'll be able to read this episode the way it deserves. Sharon's walk, after all, is the test of whether she will survive, spiritually and physically.

Every heroic journey, of course, has its obstacles, but Mrs. Klotz, who makes her first and only appearance here, has another function than that of comic interrupter. Though essentially solitary, Sharon has always been surrounded by people, including those who obstruct and betray, those who come unbidden as helpers, and particularly those in need (her previous employers, the invalid Mrs. Berger and her joke-purveying husband, are cases in point). She has an outstanding capacity to comprehend need—intuiting by projecting into other minds how people think and feel—thus overcoming what she at one point calls her "silliness" and "selfishness." It's this capacity, along with the pain of loss, that drives her curiosity about Troy's last days; during the night he died, in fact, she had a waking vision of him in his plane, giving a long, sad look at her without meeting her gaze. This near-encounter across the boundary of life and death fires her determination to remember him; so does the shallowness of those who try to block remembrance. Her sister-in-law assures her that the Lord had His reasons for taking Troy away. "'Forget the past,' everybody said. 'Don't look back,' the preacher said" (185). She finds herself at a growing distance from the energetic souls around her, whose religion guarantees progress so long as one lives mindlessly in the present moment—very much the spirit of the tacky houses and smoggy highways and other marks of prosperity that are spreading over the land. By refusing either to forget the dead or to trust the purposes of these people's God, Sharon also refuses to shut down the rich inner life with its unexpressed needs that, it turns out much later, will sustain her. But for the time being, the future belongs to the shallow in spirit; Sharon's life, it seems, ended in 1943, without the means to "jump-start" it again. Another, more ruthless, agent of oblivion is her first husband, who, pathologically jealous of the young man's memory, systematically destroys the only possessions of Troy's she's been allowed to keep: a group of oil paintings, which he incinerates in the fireplace, and some boxes of arrowheads, collected years before. The bonfire cruelly repeats the manner of the airman's death and perhaps also suggests the pun in his name (like the ancient city, Troy went down in flames during war), though I find a more suggestive link in the fact that Troy is also a celebrated archaeological site.

Troy's collection of arrowheads, by connecting personal memory with archaeology, represent one of Morgan's most brilliant touches. Troy used to gather them from the old creek bottom that he'd loved as a boy, near the spot he'd hoped someday to build a farm. Years later, Sharon returns to the spot with her half-grown boys where, it turns out, memory gives her new eyes, recovering not only what was lost but what she'd never noticed: "It was as though I saw for the first time the valley along the river, the mountains and the stream he had painted in those pictures Charles had burned." They don't find any fresh arrowheads, but she does gain another clue to Troy's personality: "it wasn't until I took my sons down into the fields to look for arrowheads that I saw how hard he must have worked over the years and how skilled he must have been at finding arrowheads" (196). It turns out that Troy and his friends had sought out the arrowheads for their size and colors, then traded them like marbles. All human things circulate, Morgan reminds us again and again, in a double act of preservation and oblivion: the ancient tools, honed with precise skill by nameless hunters, re-appear as commodities in a boy's game of prowess through possession. On first seeing them in Troy's boxes, Sharon recalls: "In some pill-boxes he had put the tiny arrow points used for shooting birds, some no bigger than a tooth, so you wondered how the Indians fixed them on arrows" (181). But for Morgan's reader, the forgetting is less complete: in an earlier story, settlers creep up to an Indian camp and set fire to their sleeping victims—the very people, perhaps, who fashioned the arrowheads.

Abandoned a second time by death, Sharon, now an aging widow, returns to Troy's memory again, driven this time not by loss but by curiosity. Through months of inquiries, she learns that although he was officially listed as a mechanic, Troy had in fact been flying secret missions over Germany. But she is hungry for more than this: she wants details, eyewitness testimony, a clue to his state of mind. The photostatic documents that come from Army archives contain facts without illumination; when she tries to re-establish contact with Troy's army buddy, who had been turned from her home by Charles years before, her letter comes back unanswered. She reaches, as she puts it, a "dead end." But what does she want to know, after all? Morgan subtly controls our growing awareness of the ironic discrepancy between her research question (her curiosity about the exact circumstances of a loved one's death) and the deeper desire that's in some sense covered by her specific researches—the desire to know the truth of her relationship with Troy and her meaning in his life. But by blocking access to the further encounters and scraps of information that would fuel a more conventional plot, Morgan underscores in the most uncompromising way Sharon's profound experience of her essential solitude. Perhaps she is longing for some form of encounter across the years—a word or revelation, perhaps, that would answer her psychic vision of the night Troy died. But Sharon has burned his letters, and in any case, it's unclear what could be revealed. At this point we might ask, like Gertrude Stein, what was the question?

In a bold move, Morgan switches to a nameless omniscient narrator—for the only time in the book—who describes first-hand the facts of Troy's final days that Sharon will never know. We learn first-hand from this nameless narrator about the preparations for Allied raids over Germany; the mixture Troy felt of exhaustion, terror, and exhilaration; the nocturnal scavenging for machine parts; the cold, the mud, and the darkness—especially the darkness, since British days are cloudy and short, and most of the work must be done under cover of night. Hardest of all is that the radar scanner is unreliable. "[M]ost of the time you'll have to do your best with screen patterns that are partly ambiguous," an officer explains (240). On a practice mission over Scotland, Troy can only make out "wavy, frothy lines" on the screen, and then a "confusing mass of lines and specks" (242). Instead of the castle they are aiming for, they hit a mountain; as the report says, "Partial Success. The designated target was not hit, but the mistaken target was hit with remarkable accuracy" (242). But the bombing of Schweinfurt is a success, and as Troy flies back to England—the flight he will never complete—he is already "asleep behind his oxygen mask" (247).

It's difficult to describe, or even to account for, the power of this section. One can go a little ways by noting, first, an attention to details so convincing in their mundane sharpness (the corners of buildings worn down by Army trucks banging into them [237]), their psychological quirkiness (the pilot's habit of talking in vague sexual metaphor [243]), their harshness (American soldiers threatening other American soldiers over their rights to scavenged plane parts; the spray of brains across damaged metal [238–39]), and plausibility ("It was happening like it was supposed to, but it was happening to somebody else" [245]) that the man long dead flashes for a moment to life. This is what Sharon longs to glimpse, and the reader as well, who by this point cares enough about Troy to see him, at last, up close. What gives these pages their dream-like vividness is not surprise but the shock of recognition: this looks like the Troy we might expect, the Troy we might recognize in ourselves. But they do something else as well: they recall in a few consummating paragraphs the book's leitmotif—the motif of forging one's way without help, through mountain passes and highways, across rivers and years, sometimes losing oneself and sometimes saving oneself. Troy is one who saved himself, having faced death with terror and exhilaration and with everything to lose; it's good to know that and to remember it.

But the lines on the radar are frothy, and a lake can be mistaken for a castle: this is the story of Troy's last days, and it's the story of Sharon's life, which, in the final astonishing moment of "The Mountains Won't Forget Us," closes with his ghostly return—but not in the way we might expect.

Suddenly we are back in the nursing home, on the night before Sharon's release. A figure appears at the door, unspeaking. Scanning its face, Sharon sees only shadow, yet she knows from his height that it is Troy—and the feeling that wells up in her is anger: "You left me on my own," she says. "You left me and I didn't know what to do." Staring into the darkness that bears Troy's shape, her anger impels a flood of realizations that bear upon the reader as well. On and on they come, with her tears, until she dreads she has "gone too far," as though offending the specter and not her own crumbling defenses—realizations about his probable feelings for her fifty years ago, his family's attitude to her, and above all, her own responses:

> "I don't think you ever wanted to get married. I think you liked the idea, but you didn't want to make love to me. You liked airplanes better, and the thrill of the war. What woman could compete with a war for a man's attention? Or maybe I wasn't good enough. Were you looking for somebody better? Your family thought their glorious Troy could do better than little Sharon?"
>
> I have gone too far. I don't know where these things are coming from [249].

His face remains in the dark: he does not look at her, he does not touch her.

In "Mack," the story of the old man and the dog, the narrator's survival depends on a half-imagined relationship, since he partly observes and partly projects the dog's irrepressible power of joy—the power, we might say, that's not "really" in either the narrator or the dog but emerges as a joint product, a real thing. Sharon by contrast constructs a non-living Other which becomes the means for her to speak, revealing for the first time in her life herself to herself. Having gained a God's-eye view on Troy's last thoughts and experiences, the reader has some means to judge the accuracy of Sharon's words. Before this moment, her most burning questions were whether he really planned to buy that farmland and if he thought about her in the last days; the answers we learn are, in order, yes and sort of ("Sometimes he realized he had forgotten her face.... It was the fatigue. He had trouble remembering lots of things" [244]). But this does not mean Troy wouldn't, in the end, have come to love Sharon; nor does it mean that Troy was the love of her life, gone forever. Morgan leaves the emphasis throughout on Sharon's questions (there are three in the paragraph quoted above) rather than certainties. The epiphany, for all its shattering power, hovers between a genuine realization and a position constructed so that Sharon has the power to move on. Because she must let Troy go in order to move on. But who is the "you" she addresses? Troy does not look at her, he does not touch her, because he is not there; but his absence (the darkness in the room) becomes for her a thing that does not respond, thus repeating the act of abandonment of which she accuses him at long last, after nearly fifty years: You left me and I didn't know what to do. The words are cathartic in the strict Aristotelian sense—the feelings, brought up, are purged—and this is the feeling, more perhaps than Troy and the possibilities he stood for, that Sharon must acknowledge and then abandon, like a severed limb. All passion spent, she will sleep the sleep of the blessed; tomorrow she will leave the nursing home for her own home and garden in the hills: "The thermal belt is a zone in the valleys near the foot of the mountain where the spring comes early and the autumn late. I've read the explanation but can't remember exactly."

American Romantic writers have always held out the possibility of a sublime self-sufficiency attained by being true to oneself. Robert Morgan's heroes typically find self-affirmation through dauntless, solitary perseverance. There's correspondingly little space in his work for the possibility of *social* solutions; his dreamers, the ones who might provide the social solutions, often come to naught, leaving the enduring work of the world to those who use tools well and grow stronger after losses. Sharon in "The Mountains Won't Remember Us" returns home alone and at peace, having repudiated her remaining human obligation, to the memory of a man long dead; but that peace comes only out of profound experiences of separateness, abandonment, and betrayal—experiences that are bound up with her vulnerability as a woman living in a marginal economy. And her final self-sufficiency entails at the same time a surrender of self inseparable from a spiritual apprehension—one that, like her newfound ability to forget, is nevertheless at the farthest remove from her friend's religion of blithe getting-on. This response, we might note, is both similar and dissimilar to the spiritual transformation of Gabriel Conroy in "The Dead." "It hardly pained him now to realize how poor a part he, her husband, had played in his wife's life" (225), Joyce's narrator notes (with possible exaggeration), a realization that impels Gabriel, by temporarily eradicating his ego, to encompass within his unbounded consciousness the regions of the dead. "The only thing alive is me," Sharon says after Troy's figure has vanished in silence, strong enough at last to accept the harshest truths about her past and then to forget them. There is a time to remember, a time to forget, and a time to be forgotten. The mountains are non-human and silent; by living in their shadow now, instead of Troy's, she accepts their oblivion with something like relief: "The fields where we work, and the mountains we look at, even the people coming after us, won't remember us at all. And it's better that way" (250). Transforming her experience of abandonment into positive, spiritual acceptance, Sharon speaks with supreme humility not for herself alone but for a race of men whose labor is all that survives them and whose traces, in the end, form but a part of the earth's history.

Notes

1. Duke Senior's words spoken in the forest of Arden in *As You Like It* (Act II, Scene i, lines 16–17) receive many echoes in Romantic writers. Morgan's fullest expression of this idea appears in his lecture "Nature Is a Stranger Yet": "More like Emerson or Whitman than I realized at first, I have often seen nature itself as language, and the land as a text written on by runoff and wind, by floods and by time. And I have been intrigued by the way people inscribe their ambitions and greed, their dreams and pretensions, on the landscape. But just as mysterious are the ways we interpret the signs and signatures of nature. It is the essence of the human to see the accidental and incidental, the arbitrary and coincidental, as a correspondence, as message" (36). The lecture was delivered at Roanoke College on April 15, 1999, printed in *The Jordan Lectures 1998–1999* (n.p.), and is now available on the author's website. For the purpose of the pres.ent essay, the most important sentence is the second, since I argue that to read the earth in *The Mountains Won 't Remember Us* is to read the history of human activities as inscribed in the landscape.

2. Erich Auerbach's *Mimesis* (translated by Willard R. Trask, Princeton University Press, 1953) is the classic discussion of the way European literature reflects class relationships through stylistic levels—a linguistic hierarchy that, of course, breaks down when the narrator is himself or herself a colloquial speaker. My wording echoes Hemingway's often-noted remark that modem American fiction writers descend from *Huckleberry Finn*. Hemingway's own style does not of course descend from Huck's; it's an artfully contrived plain style derived from middleclass journalism, not from rural or working-class speech. See my "Views from Above and Below: George Eliot and Fakir Mohan Senapati" (Diacritics 37.4 [winter 2007], pp. 56–77), where I suggest that a literary view from below—which is how I read Morgan's fiction—is only possible once the authority of a learned, class-marked style has been qualified or abandoned.

3. The relationship between oral history and the processes and meanings of work were memorably demonstrated in Studs Terkel's *Working* (Avon, 1975), an anthology of interviews that became a bestseller and was later the subject of a Broadway musical. I'm not aware of other writers who have exploited in fiction the forms and subjects of the oral narrative to the extent Morgan has.

Works Cited

Joyce, James. *Dubliners*. New York: Penguin, 1992.

Morgan, Robert. *Good Measure: Essays, Interviews, and Notes on Poetry*. Baton Rouge: Louisiana State University Press, 1993.

______. *The Mountains Won't Remember Us*. Atlanta: Peachtree, 1992.

______. "Nature Is a Stranger Yet." *Robert Morgan Official Author Website*. 17 Sept. 2008.

______. *The Strange Attractor: New and Selected Poems*. Baton Rouge: Louisiana State University Press, 2004.

Blood Soil Field

The Physicality of The Balm of Gilead Tree

SUZANNE BOOKER-CANFIELD

The Balm of Gilead Tree (1999), Robert Morgan's third book of short fiction, expresses in its spare and lyrical stories the spirit of American Romanticism so notable in the ten volumes of poetry he published before it. Not only does the four-century time span provide an epic sweep of the American experience, it also underscores the interconnectedness of time with the land and people of the Blue Ridge Mountains. Time spirals—repeating its patterns of challenges, temptations, and hardships—from the mid-sixteenth century to the end of the twentieth. Time appears to write its story both on the land of the Blue Ridge Mountains and on the people who live there. Just as the Indians trod on the same paths that wild game had cleared, the first European explorers appropriate those same trails, altering them forever. Morgan draws parallels between the trails trampled on the land and the tracks written on the mountain people themselves, underscoring the inextricable relationship between the individual and the natural world. In a framework that ostensibly celebrates innocence and free will, the stories reveal a land haunted by the past and sometimes condemned to repeat its mistakes. Morgan is attracted to patterns of reduplication, linkage, and chiasmus in formal poems, employing such verse forms as terza rima, villanelle, or chant royal. The cyclical structure of time in *The Balm of Gilead Tree* provides him with an opportunity to create some of the same effects, presented as subtle echoes of the past, in a series of interwoven and emphatically physical stories hewn from the Blue Ridge Mountains and its people.

The Balm of Gilead Tree places Morgan in the tradition of American Romanticism, especially that of Ralph Waldo Emerson, Henry David Thoreau, and Walt Whitman. Expressed overtly in the theme of reverence for the land, such Romanticism can also be seen in Morgan's treatment of the phenomenal world as text. Celebrating the pantheism and stoicism of rural life, Morgan enlarges, in the form of seventeen intertwined stories, the Romantic framework so carefully laid out in his poetry. In unadorned language, he defamiliarizes the Puritan symbology that became the focus of the early American Romantics. In *Nature*, Emerson announces that the writer should "pierce rotten diction" and "fasten again words to visible things" (*Essential Writings* 16). Language itself becomes physical for Emerson, as he makes words analogous to nature by envisioning language as "fossil poetry" (296). In *The Balm of Gilead Tree*, Morgan, too, parses nature as logos, just as he had in the poem "Buffalo Trace," in which nature writes a story on peaks and paths that "ebbed back into the horizon / and back of the stars" (*Orchard Country* 6). Thus,

Morgan continues the trajectory of American Romanticism—tracing history as written on both the landscape and the common man, heeding the Stoics' directive to follow nature, and making the phenomenal world sacred.

In "Murals" and "Poinsett's Bridge," Morgan provides, by extended analogies with stonemasonry and painting, his own artistic credo. "Murals," the story of Gardner, a Works Progress Administration painter whose work on a mural in a mountain post office is interrupted by America's entry into World War II, echoes Morgan's own semiotic experiments. Gardner recalls how, as a boy, he "tried to imagine the relationship between specific things out in the woods and fields, a rock, a particular tree, a spring hidden in the cedars, with the great world in general," wondering "which was truer for him, the smell of cow stalls when he milked, or the discussion of milk ... in his health book" (198). And, whereas most of his contemporaries had no trouble rendering automobiles or "the energy of the industrial sublime," Gardner struggled with the modern but excelled at animals, landscape, and "his human figures, huge men in overalls hurling shovels, women in plain dresses" (186–87). Gardner's plan to become better at drawing machinery involves rendering it from memory "as if he were designing a woodcut using the fewest lines," with "each bolder and plainer than the one before" (187). Morgan's appreciation for brevity and concision, a consequence of his work in poetry where every line has to matter, resonates in Gardner's method. Grappling with how to paint a combine harvester authentically, for instance, he reflects on the machine's significance: "It connects man and earth, present and future, steel and muscle" (191). For Morgan, this seems to be the task of the writer, especially in *The Balm of Gilead Tree*. Gardner, defying attempts to stop the mural painting in order to provide space to sell war bonds, works alone on a scaffold in hot and humid conditions and feels compelled to finish the combine before leaving, hopeful that the mural will not just be painted over by the government. Within the logic of both the story and the collection, however, the trace of his brush strokes, like that of the traces marked by the paths of animals and the indigenous mountain population, will most certainly be overlaid.

Morgan's solitary artist need not always use a brush, however. In "Poinsett's Bridge," set just after the War of 1812, Morgan provides another portrait of the artist, working alone atop a scaffold and longing for his work to stand the test of time. Jones, the self-taught craftsman, relates the pivotal point in the learning of his trade. Fearful that he would not finish the firebox he was trying to build, he recounts his artistic break: "I seen in my pile a rock that was perfect for a cornerstone, and another that would fit against it in a line with just a little chipping" and eventually "put the cornerstone in place" (29–30). The analogy becomes even more revelatory: "best of all was the way you could rough out a line, running a string or a rule along the edge to see how it would line up, so when you backed away you saw the wall was straight in spite of gaps and bulges" (30). Here, the work of the stonemason and that of the writer converge. "Breaking the rocks to get flat edges that would fit so you don't hardly have to use any mortar," Jones finds "they just stay together where they're laid" (30–31). Like a writer, he describes the difficulty of "finding the new and just arrangement so they would stay" (31). The crafted final product must resemble a natural one. In fact, Morgan has noted that in exemplary fiction "the language itself can become almost invisible" (West 55–56). This is the effect the stonemason has achieved with his firebox: a natural arrangement that will endure. Looking back, Jones says his work is "still in plumb and holding together after more than sixty years" (*Balm* 30). For Morgan, then, whether the medium is stone or word, the artist tries to achieve something elemental and ageless by following nature, shaping it to fit together in new ways, emphasizing both the plain and the bold, and connecting human beings to the world around them.

Like Emerson, Morgan endorses a direct and essential relationship to nature. The mountain people of Morgan's fiction understand this in a way incomprehensible to outsiders. Their awareness and fear of nature's power can be viewed as primitive or naïve. As the British stonemason in "Poinsett's Bridge" charges, "You mountain folk are so superstitious.... All you ever do is worry about lightning, panthers, snakes, floods, winds, and landslides" (39). By the end of the book, however, this seems less a pattern of superstition than of wisdom. Morgan's mountain people, who often yoke divinity to the power of the observable world, understand nature's formidable power: "When the Lord talks, he talks big" (39). Such big words are spoken through the natural world.

Throughout *The Balm of Gilead Tree*, Morgan also captures the cyclical pattern of the seasons. Beginning with the first story, "The Tracks of Chief de Soto," which opens in the "moon of new leaves," the vernal periods instill hope (1). In "Little Willie," the adored three-year-old comes to the family "about tater planting time"; in the same story, we read that Celia "always loved the spring because you feel like starting over and doing things right" (90). Both Little Willie and Alice in "Death Crown," the innocents of the collection, die in autumn. In "A Brightness New and Welcoming," after his release from a Union prisoner-of-war camp, Woodruff walks from a train station in Greenville, South Carolina, to bring a companion's widow, Louise, her husband's watch. Woodruff goes up into the highlands and the season of rebirth: "The higher he got the newer the leaves on the trees. On the mountain the grass was green but shorter. He was climbing back into early spring" (128). As he ascends and travels back phenologically, Woodruff moves toward a destination that is equally interior—creating himself anew, gaining the strength needed for the encounter with the widow and his home. Throughout the collection, the return of spring, real or imagined, leads to characters' spiritual rejuvenescence and emphasizes a correspondence between human and nonhuman life.

For Morgan, this often means the intermingling of the animal and the vegetal, the blood and the soil. From the first page of the book, the Native American female narrator of "The Tracks of Chief de Soto" announces, "We always planted in the Blood Soil Field near the valley's head" (1). In fact, blood and soil begin and end this collection and bind all the tales in between, sometimes telling both new and ancient stories at once. Earlier in his career, in his essay "The Cubist of Memory," Morgan noted, "I like the sense that the continent has been written on by glaciers, earthquakes, floods, buffalo, Indians, and hunters. The soil is haunted by the Cherokee and the Iroquois.... Looking for new ground to clear we find Old Fields" (*Good Measure* 10). Again and again, Morgan's characters walk the same paths of a defined geographical area of the southern Appalachian Mountains. In "Poinsett's Bridge," the trails of the animals and the Indians have been usurped by the wealthy Kentucky lowlanders returning from Charleston, driving their herds of animals through the turnpike. That same Poinsett's Bridge becomes the place where John and Louise hold hands for the first time in "A Brightness New and Welcoming" (117–18). The paths of the Indians become the trails of the lowlanders and eventually, in "The Ratchet," the highways "crowded with Cadillacs from Florida ... and produce trucks from Atlanta" (266). Ironically, the Dark Corner of upstate South Carolina that Senator Poinsett declares will be opened to the state for commerce becomes, more than a century later, the area where most of the blockaders live. In the *New York Times Book Review*, David L.

Ulin fittingly calls Morgan's collection "a psychic history of the Blue Ridge Mountains" (par. 2). Such a label underscores Morgan's conflation of the human and natural worlds. The stories intertwine and reverberate; time circles back to the same location, presenting new choices and hardships. Hence the lives of the characters in *The Balm of Gilead Tree* draw equally upon blood and soil, man and nature.

From the ritual of the burning of stalks and brush from the prior year to that of correlating the planting times with specific phases of the moon, the cultivation of the earth is deeply spiritual and tactile. Purple Grass, the narrator of "The Tracks of Chief de Soto," explains, "I knew the soil would bless the corn if I scratched and caressed it" (*Balm* 2). Worry about planting, especially planting corn, becomes a motif throughout the collection. Powell, the Confederate deserter in "A Brightness New and Welcoming," tells his pregnant wife Louise, "I'll be back in time to put in crops next year" (113). The relationship with the soil remains deeply sensory. On a warm March day, "A breeze crept out of the south smelling of new grass and fresh plowed ground," drawing Powell's mind to his wife, who would be "unable to break the fields and put in a crop" and praying that he would come "now that it's corn planting time" (115). Likewise, in "Dark Corner," as Daddy Branch returns home to North Carolina from Texas, his dying thoughts revert to the atavistic ritual of planting: the unnamed narrator, one of his daughters, says, "I don't think he knowed where he was. He kept talking all night about farming and planting corn. He said it was time to plant the corn" (170). In "1916 Flood," the disarray of the fields mirrors the confusion of Raleigh, the eleven-year-old narrator, still haunted by his mother's death four years earlier. After eleven consecutive days and nights of rain, there were mudslides in the mountains, and the fields "were festering with weeds" (172). The baulks of the corn had not been plowed since mid–June, and Raleigh awakes feeling guilty about the rain because "they had not been able to work in the fields that needed hoeing so badly" (175). In "The Welcome," one of the first things that Dutch notices when he returns from a Nazi prisoner of war camp is that most of the fields have been planted with corn except for the Corbin place, "where last year's stubble and corn stalks sparkled in the sun" (220). Cultivating fields harmonizes characters' efforts with the natural cycle of decay and renewal, thus wedding the human and nonhuman worlds.

The counterpoint to this reverence for the soil and the rituals of planting can be seen in the equally pervasive act of digging, mining, and exploiting the land. "'I am looking for the bright rocks,'" announces Ferdinand de Soto in the first story (6). Morgan reimagines the story of de Soto's 1540 expedition from the western Florida panhandle up through Georgia and South Carolina in search of Cofitachique, a land fabled for its gold. Historically, de Soto met the Lady of Cofitachique, who offered strands of pearls as a peace offering. Taking them and then holding her hostage, he stopped his northward expedition, replete with hundreds of captive native bearers, in the Appalachian Mountains.

The cycle of extraction begins. In the story, despite the protestation that he comes in peace, de Soto quickly reveals his intention: "'I have been told there is a city of bright rocks in these mountains'" (6). He forces the women, who had been left alone in their village, to look for gold both by coercion and by promising them a pearl from the ornate carved chest he commandeered from Ocala, a character Morgan bases on the historical Lady of Cofitachique. The narrator laments that either the women must show de Soto where the shining stones, the "tears of the sun," come from or "he would kill us all" (10). The white men, the "hair-faces," who invaded their camp, force the women to dig ceaselessly and whip those who stop working. Morgan juxtaposes the careful Native American soil husbandry with the reckless digging de Soto demands in his attempt to extract mineral wealth and move on. As a result of de Soto, "All the valley was confusion. Soon the banks and stream were nothing but mud" (12). When de Soto and his men leave, the women try to erase the memory both of the despoiled village, whose sacred fire had been extinguished during the mayhem, and of de Soto and his men: "All the tracks of the hair-faces and other tracks will be gone" (23). Crawling on their knees, the women scrape the ground, carrying old dirt out and bringing new dirt in, so that it appeared "completely changed" and so that the "houses seemed to have been set down on new ground" (23). To adapt Morgan's terminology from "The Cubist of Memory," this "new ground" proves to be simply "Old Fields": the tracks of de Soto and his men cannot be erased.

These invasive returns to the Old Fields link avarice with exploitation of the natural world. Echoing Chief de Soto's fervent digging, Mr. Kuykendall, the eighty-year-old husband of the attractive sixteen-year-old Falba, blindfolds his slave and takes him out to bury his treasure in the woods to safeguard it. Digging, whether to unearth or to bury treasure, carries on through the generations. In "The Welcome," Dutch returns from a Nazi prison camp and longs to go back to the "pit his great-grandpa had dug, looking for zircons" (215). However, the saddest echo of de Soto's frantic digging comes near the end of the collection. In "The Bullnoser," most of the riches of the high mountain land have been plundered. The value of the land becomes not what can be dug out of it. Rather, with his bullnoser, T.J. is "'burying poisons and chemicals'" (299). Profit derives no longer from exploiting the natural treasures but from using the land to bury toxic waste. From de Soto and his men all the way to T.J. and his trailer park, digging equates with greed and marks the eternal return to the site where blood mixed with the soil.

The land also serves a spiritual purpose. Morgan concludes an early poem, "Warm Winter Day," with the line, "You must go into the wilderness alone" (*Red Owl* 65). And that is precisely what the characters in *The Balm of Gilead Tree* discover. In addition to the natural treasures found in the mountain wilderness, the woods often serve as the locus of rebirth, the place to start anew. This classic American "errand into the wilderness"—to use seventeenth-century Puritan minister Samuel Danforth's phrase (notably employed by historian Perry Miller)—does not hinge on the Christian rebirth of the unregenerate. Rather, it involves seeking refuge from a host of desperate circumstances. The narrator of "The Tracks of de Soto" thinks "of running into the woods" when the strange, hair-faced men arrive (*Balm* 5). In "Kuykendall's Gold," after the sixteen-year-old Falba realizes she has been sold by her father for fifty dollars to become the mistress of Mr. Burns, she escapes in the direction of the "blue mountains" toward which Pa and her brothers were headed: "I knowed that's where they was going, into the dark wilderness where they was a free land, and where nobody knowed who Pa was" (54). Heading west meant the opportunity to start over.

Fleeing into the woods does not always offer a safe renewal, however. Echoing the typological view of the woods from Puritan America, when Falba follows Mr. Kuykendall and his slave, she remarks, "The woods is so different at night it might as well be another world. The stars and the limbs and the shine from the creek get all tangled up" (62). At night, these woods recall the otherworldliness of those in Hawthorne's "Young Goodman Brown." Seeing Mr. Kuykendall talking to Theo in the distance, Falba relates, "It was like they was praying or performing some witch's service" (63). As with de Soto's lingering tracks, "people would say these woods was haunted in the future" and "would say they seen Mr. Kuykendall's ghost looking for his gold along the Pheasant Branch" (84). In spite of its being "haunted," Morgan would nonetheless seem to agree with Henry David Thoreau that "we need the tonic of wildness" (*Walden* 216). Falba recalls, "It made me feel better to get out in the laurels sometimes and listen to the birds and look for periwinkles and pretty rocks in the branch" (*Balm* 62). Below the limpid mountain sky, the wilderness provides a chance for Morgan's characters to escape, to begin anew, or just to feel better, yet mystery and danger seem to lurk in every thicket and hollow.

Peril notwithstanding, the mountain wilderness is often a refuge. In "Pisgah," Nelse and Mossy bell, the poor children from high on the mountain, find on their first day at school that the children and bullies taunt them and kick dirt at them while they try to eat their meager lunches. In this story, the woods have a sacred power, as in Morgan's poem "Broomsedge," in which the land sings a song "like the faint / music of our ancestors ... / who tell with bending blade / and downy seed everything we / know and nothing we remember / at this poorest elevation" (*Sigodlin* 31). When the potential of a skirmish provides a diversion, Mossy Bell and Nelse stand up and run off into the pine forest, never to return; they consider the condition at school more abject than their poverty at home. In those woods, Nelse later finds a fawn and carries it with him as he tries to negotiate for coffee and food from Old Salem, the bilious "skinflint" owner of the general store where his mother could not pay her bill (*Balm* 141). Intrigued by the fawn, a salesman and a man in uniform try to buy it, bidding up the price from one dollar to seven. Suddenly Nelse has enough money to pay his mother's debt and get what the family needed, aided by the support of some loggers admonishing Old Salem to "treat him square" (140–41). Thus, woods provide both safe haven and sustenance.

Characters learn that visibility is often vulnerability. Reversing the westward march of American literature, the Branch family, in "Dark Corner," tries to return to the mountains after pursuing the vain hope of gold on a tract of land granted to the narrator's great-grandfather after the Mexican War. After enduring the shame of being kicked off the train at Greenville and taken to the police for not having tickets, the Branch family finally sets out on foot for Asheville: "It was such a relief to get out of town finally, into the country where there wasn't somebody watching us every step" (150). For many characters, the woods offer a reprieve from the sense of being watched and judged by those with more power.

Sometimes the characters turn to the woods to discover something about themselves and discover painful truths. In "Tailgunner," the protagonist, Jones, goes to one of his favorite spots—a stretch of pine woods now targeted by developers: "In the shade of the pines he felt more himself, as though he was closer to a self he had lost in the war and never recovered" (232–33). For reasons he could not explain, "the peacefulness of the trees reminded him of instants of great danger and sickness," and brought him closer "to some bedrock definition, some value" (233). Similarly, in his *Journals*, Thoreau emphasizes a dualism between man and nature: "He is constraint, she is freedom to me. He makes me wish for another world. She makes me content with this" (*Thoreau's Writing* 445). Jones enters the woods of his childhood only to find they had been replaced in his minds by German woods he had stood in during the war. Confirming Thoreau's human-nature dichotomy, man's intrusion into nature means that Jones can no longer find the tonic wildness of the place he associated with freedom, as it now conjures memories of constraint. Certainly, the sense of the importance of escape from man resounds in *The Balm of Gilead Tree*; however, in the contest between man and nature, Morgan seems more sanguine about humankind, even with all its problems. The wilderness provides more than a place of retreat: it allows the characters to discover something fundamental about themselves.

At other times, they seek forgiveness in an unforgiving world. In "1916 Flood," Grandpa asks Raleigh, a young boy mourning his mother's death four years prior, to run to Poplar Springs in search of a wagon to carry back a corpse washed up by the flood. The boy, disturbed by dreams that his mother's casket has been dislodged and opened by the flood waters, traces the reason for this nightmare to his unwillingness to kiss his dead mother goodbye when she was in the coffin. Fearing that he will see her body as the flood finally subsides, he is elated to find that the corpse is someone else: "He could not remember when he had felt such a thrill of speed.... For the first time he heard the locusts in the woods ... chanting 'pharaoh, pharaoh,' as Grandpa said they would, remembering the plague in Egypt" (183). Morgan's allusion to the plague of locusts in Exodus reveals Raleigh's sense of being delivered from despair, of feeling "he could outrun all troubles and fears" (183). Perhaps this, more than any other reason, is why Morgan's characters are drawn to the wilderness, the Promised Land.

With each generation, each cycle of seasons, the landscape becomes increasingly altered by those who inhabit it. By the late twentieth century, the setting for "A Taxpayer & A Citizen," the narrator, like Raleigh, sees the woods as a place where she can outrun her troubles: "I knew I had to get out of there. I didn't have time to think.... If I could make it back to my car I might get away, might get off on a dirt road and disappear into the woods" (312). Jumping off the shoulder of the road and into a ditch, she runs through litter and weeds, recalling how as a child she played hide and seek: "I'd disappear into the brush and nobody could find me" (313). This action adumbrates the final story, "The Balm of Gilead Tree," in which the protagonist tries to outrun a helicopter, knowing "if they landed I could try to run for the woods at the other end of the orchard" (334). In Morgan's stories, then, the woods offer both a spiritual and physical refuge.

If wilderness provides the chance for a new beginning or an escape from the problems of civilization, the periphery between settled land and that wilderness becomes the *axis mundi* for Morgan's fiction. He sets many of his poems at the threshold of the wilderness, even titling one of his books *At the Edge of the Orchard Country*. Just as Thoreau writes in *Walden* that his unconventional, "half-cultivated" beanfield was "the connecting link between wild and cultivated fields," so too does Morgan give special status to that border (Thoreau 109). In his poem "The Hollow," Morgan writes of the first Blue Ridge settlers and their appreciation of the "mountain haze," which he compares to "a screen / ... to keep them hidden from disease / and god and government / and even time" (*Groundwork* 1). In *The Balm of Gilead Tree*, Morgan reveals how that screen has been penetrated, perhaps even from the first time de Soto and his men "came marching right up the trail and through the edge of Blood Soil Field" (4). In "The Transfigured Body: Notes from a Journal," Morgan professes, "I believe in the anarchic and creative soil, and stick to the fringes of society, out where it comes into collision with nature" (*Good Measure* 115). Such borders serve as loci of conflict in this collection and, in fact, in the corpus of his work.

Yet these shimmering, numinous thresholds between civilization and wilderness mark sacred spaces. In "Little Willie," when Celia has Judd and Steven bury the young runaway slave who had become a part of their family, she has him placed near the family row, "but off to the side a little, next to the edge of the woods" (107). Similarly, in "A Brightness New & Welcoming," Woodruff journeys to return to Louise the watch of her dead husband, and when "he reached the peach country at the edge of the hills," he stops his journey to try to interpret the three-note song of a mockingbird that has followed him and to "watch the petals in the breeze" (127–28). Morgan associates the periphery with an even more obvious power of beneficence in "Dark Corner." It is at this threshold that the Branch family stops to rest because the dying father cannot make it any farther. During the night, the cold, tired, and hungry daughter awakes to a voice "at the edge of the laurels" (170). She finds help in the form of the moonshiner and Good Samaritan Zander Gosnell, who comes to her aid, helping tend her father and later gathering the community to drive the corpse to the mountaintop for a proper burial. And, in "The Welcome," Dutch, the former Nazi prisoner, hearkens back to Jones in "Tailgunner." Overwhelmed by the welcome he receives, Dutch longs for that "bedrock definition" that Jones searches for in the woods. Dutch wants to "walk to the edge of the yard and stand in the woods and try to feel like he was really here" (216). Eventually, he "slipped into the edge of the woods," where he saw a spider's web and "pissed on the web until the strands looked decorated with amber beads" (217). In this act, Dutch adorns the spider's skilled design as both mark this sacred space.

These threshold spaces are not static, however. In "Tailgunner," Jones, reflecting forty years after the war, laments that when he and Lorna bought their house, "the development was at the edge of open country" but that things had changed: "there were new houses with carports and wooden fences all the way down the road, and they were building more where the fields had been bulldozed into sandy lots" (231). The ability to find that bedrock definition seems to erode as quickly as the land is demolished, but the longing to outrun fears and troubles remains, as seen most vividly in the final story, "The Balm of Gilead Tree." The mythic edge of the orchard country takes on a grisly air as the site of a plane crash. The narrator recalls, "When I broke through the tall weeds I was at the edge of a field of apple trees.... The orchard seemed to be full of bodies and pieces of the wreck" (333). In this Edenic periphery mounded with corpses, it seems that the mountain haze has, echoing "The Hollow," failed to insulate its inhabitants from god or government or time.

If the landscape is etched with human stories, it is also marked with the divine as well. Morgan's pantheism, with its debt to transcendentalism, allows him to give full voice to Emerson's notion of mankind as an extension of God, in which "everyone makes his own religion, his own God" (*Journals* 179). Morgan would seem to share the absolute personal value of moral law that Emerson announces in "The American Scholar": "We walk on our own feet, we will work with our own hands, we will speak our own minds" (*Essential Writings* 59). This is precisely what Morgan's most iconic protagonists choose to do.

In these echoes of Emerson, Morgan suggests that any divine message will come from the simple majesty of the earth. In "The Tracks of Chief de Soto," Ocala tells the women "about the Chief Spirit who loved us and had sent them to us with a message"; wanting to know what the message is, she reflects, "I never was sure, except that we were supposed to love the Chief Spirit and do what the black dressed men wanted" (*Balm* 8). Whereas the ostensibly Christian de Soto placed their faith in the coruscating rocks that left them spellbound, after the conquistadors leave, the Indian women capture a more authentic religion from the "flat rocks from the stream," used to smooth the dirt until "[t]he ground shone white in the midday sun" (23). The contrast between these minerals—garish gold and lowly stone—embodies much of Morgan's ethos. Exposing the hypocrisy of de Soto and his progeny, Morgan returns to the tradition of the Book of Nature that arose out of the early Christian church. As Saint Ephrem the Syrian wrote in the fourth century, "I considered the Word of the Creator, /and likened it / to the rock that marched / with the people of Israel in the wilderness" (qtd. in Graves 122). In this sense, Morgan's characters turn not to the Word made flesh but to the Word made rock. In an interview titled "The Rush of Language," he says, "Our first poets evolved a tradition of celebrating nature and reading nature as a mirror of the self, as an image or language of the soul" (*Good Measure* 157). This also aligns with Emerson's assertion in *Nature* that "the happiest man is he who learns from nature the lesson of worship" (*Essential Writings* 32). For Morgan, the divine resides in rocks and soil and blood, awaiting any reader of nature.

Morgan makes that lesson of worship vivid in these stories. "A Brightness New & Welcoming" begins with a chalice of sorts—two South Carolinians being given a dipper full of water from a bucket. This communal experience makes Powell's thoughts turn to the spring at home. It was formed by a kind of natural trinity: "There were at least three fountains coming together," and the water "tasted of quartz rock deep under the mountain" (109). Looking into the pool when sipping the water seemed "like watching an hourglass that never ran out of grains, a source feeding tirelessly as time, the flow running long before he ever saw or bought the acres and long after he left them," causing him to conclude that "nothing made him feel the vastness of time as much as the spring" (110). Powell, a sort of anti–Narcissus, gains spiritual nourishment from the spring water, which "was touched by all the mineral wealth it had passed through, the gold and rubies, silver and emeralds in the deep veins," forming "a cold rainbow on the tongue" (109). As Thoreau argues, "God exhibits himself to the walker in a frosted bush today, as much as in a burning one to Moses of old" (*Journals* 102). For Powell, the rainbow created by the richness of geologic time provides its own kind of covenant. The natural trinity of the spring, with its powers to revive and renew, stands in contrast to the "terrible shame and conviction" that he feels "as he walked up to the altar" at the revival at which he was saved (*Balm* 119). Yet, back out in nature on his walk home "and as he lay in the loft listening to the katydids, he was at peace, and in a brightness new and welcoming" (119). When taking Powell's watch back to Louise, Woodruff stops by the spring, takes the gourd from its stick, and drinks: "The tart cold taste seemed to come from the deepest part of the mountain, from the beginning of the world" (129). The taste of rock binds him to the divine as the salvific power of nature transports him back to creation.

For Morgan's characters, the problems with organized religion, on the other hand, can be a matter of life or death. In "Dark Corner," the Branch family sold its house in Asheville because Daddy "wanted to get away from the fuss and backbiting in the Baptist church" (151). After a falling out at church over who was to be the new preacher, Daddy "just up and sold his little dab of land" to move to Texas where the family lost everything (162). The ordeal weakens him so that he eventually cannot finish the last part of the journey back to the mountains. Although this repercussion is extreme, the stories often reveal the benighted views of the local churches. Morgan retells his poem "Death Crown" in a story by the same name. In it, Ellen comes to be at the bedside of Alice, an old, dying woman whose intellectual growth stopped around age three because of a brain infection. Ellen, whose father was a preacher, wonders if Alice has been saved. Ellen recalls how her father had to fight members of his congregation only too willing "to condemn people that never had a chance to believe" (252). Ellen reasons that Alice will go to heaven, just like all the little children who had died early. As the death watch continues, the look of Alice's head reminds Ellen of the story of the death crown: "Old timers used to say that when a really good person ... is sick for a long time before they die, that the feathers in the pillow will knit themselves into a crown that fits the person's head" (256). Although the crown will not be found until after the death, its presence may be construed as "a certain sign of another crown in heaven" (256). Such "death crowns," these apotheoses of the natural world, are "woven so tight they never come apart and they shine like gold even though they're so light they might just as well be a ring of light" (256). If "the cold rainbow on the tongue" gave Powell solace in his death, here Alice's goodness shows how human beneficence can inspire a natural symbol of the divine.

References to organized religion recur throughout the stories more as aspects of memories rather than expressions of belief. During the perilous freefall down the curving mountain highway in "The Ratchet," Fred prays, "'Please Lord, help us'" (270). He had never prayed in front of his brother Albert before: "Albert didn't go to church, and they never talked about religion to each other since Fred had been saved when he was sixteen" (270). As the truck skids off the bridge and into the water: "Light flew at him all the way from the end of the world, and beyond" (274). The water, it seems, inspires a sense of the brevity of life and the vastness of time, just as it did for Powell.

The most disquieting connection between nature and Christianity occurs in the book's title story, "The Balm of Gilead Tree." As the narrator, a construction worker, loots the bodies of plane crash victims, Morgan appropriates Christian iconography for a bleak pragmatism. The serial rationalizations made by the protagonist convince him that his behavior is justified in order to have enough money to buy a filling station and to get his girlfriend Diane a beauty shop. Maintaining that he saw "dozens of people picking through the rows," his moral awareness nonetheless causes him to say, "I hoped I didn't see anybody I knew" (333). Here, Morgan recontextualizes religious symbology. This Eden, with its filled trees "loaded with green apples," makes the narrator think of his youth. Having been raised working on an apple orchard, he is sickened not at the staggering loss of life but rather at the loss of the fruit: "You grafted and fertilized, pruned and waited ... and still a late frost or early frost, a beetle or fungus, drought or wet summer, could ruin you. A hailstorm, a flood, a plane crash, a drop in market price, could wipe you out" (333). A plane crash becomes simply another manifestation of nature's power.

This paradise lost becomes his refuge from the police who are trying to stop the looting: "I crouched down behind an apple tree until the flashing lights were past. It made me think of those preachers' cars with loudspeakers" (335). Hiding from the police while trying to find a way to reach an expensive pink purse in the brush, he breaks off a twig and recognizes the scent as Balm of Gilead: "the bright spicy smell woke me up from the heat" and "smelled like both medicine and candy" (337). He tells himself that there "wasn't any reason to leave the money" for the volunteer firemen sweeping the area because it was "money that would never get to heaven or hell with the owners, or to the rightful heirs" (337). After enduring the hornets' stings to get a pink purse filled with cash, the narrator recalls, "I hunkered deeper under the sumacs and the Balm of Gilead trees" and "tried to quiet my breathing by chewing a twig" (338). Finding that the owner of the pink purse had been from Coral Gables seemed to legitimize his right to take it because the area "had been overrun by retirees from south Florida ever since I was a kid" (334). In the purse, he finds three thousand dollars in brand-new bills, justifying hornet bites to get it.

Biblical allusions abound as Morgan recasts Judeo-Christian symbolism. In Jeremiah, that prophet asks, "Is there no balm in Gilead? Is there no physician there? Why then is there no healing for the wound of my people?" He laments that though God offers a remedy to his people, they have not availed themselves of it (chapter 8, verse 22). In Morgan's postlapsarian Eden, the wounds of the people are indeed pervasive, but the balm makes the wounded whole financially, not spiritually. Notably the narrator avoids the naked bodies not because there would be no money on them but because they were "embarrassing." Everyone appears motivated by greed; even the patrol of volunteer firemen decide, "'Whatever we get we will divide up'" (339). As the U.S. Marshal helicopter tries to reveal his location to the forces on the ground, the narrator retreats into the orchard: "I chewed on the spicy twig in my nervousness.... The medicine smell of the Balm of Gilead woke me up a little from my worry" (340). It serves as the salve the narrator needs to escape with the stolen money.

With its snakes and fruit trees, its naked bodies and temptations, the story's allusions to Eden proliferate. Trying to lose the chopper overhead, the narrator dives into brush, but a water moccasin "plunged into the ditch ahead of me," into water "cloudy with chemicals and moss" (341). The deputy was too afraid of chiggers, ticks, snakes, and spiders to pursue him deep into the sumac bushes, so it is only from the sky that the narrator can be seen. He hides in a ditch as "wind from the blades shook the leaves of the Balm of Gilead trees" (342). Though nature is still a refuge, the rimed fields have been symbolically replaced by "white chemical frost" (344). When two teenage looters provide a diversion for the deputy, he makes a run for it: "I ran like I used to as a kid through the orchard, throwing myself into every stride, thrusting my chest out and pushing the edge of the world ahead of me"; soon, he says, "I would be home free" (344). The latter phrase hints at a return to childhood innocence, but given the context, Morgan sends a much more ambiguous message about the human condition and its collisions with nature.

In many of these stories, the beauty and violence of the natural world corresponds with the pleasure and pain written on the human body. For Morgan, the body's cartography becomes as telling as the fossil poetry found in nature. In addition to the specific and sublime descriptions of the natural world, he connects the seventeen stories through an attention to the physical acts of the body; in doing so, his model shifts from that of Emerson to that of Walt Whitman, who writes in the Preface to *Leaves of Grass*, "[Y]our very flesh shall be a great poem" (717). The blending of the human and natural worlds occurs throughout the collection. For instance, the scent of wood and tears can combine in an almost-Proustian fashion. In "A Brightness New &Welcoming," the memory of being saved comes to Powell indirectly, in "the way his tears wet the pine wood and made it smell of resin" when the preacher asked him if he was ready to be saved (*Balm* 119). And, in "1916 Flood," after Grandpa tells seven-year-old Raleigh that Mama has died of the measles, he "ran down the hill to the orchard and cried with his face against an apple tree, his tears smearing on the lichen soot of the bark" (181). Amidst the flood four years later, the narrator reveals, "the woods today smelled like that tree" (181). The particular olfactory cue to memory shows how subtly Morgan conflates the somatic and natural elements.

For Morgan, the needs of the body can be as powerful and uncontrollable as a flash flood or a mudslide. In "Death Crown," Ellen reflects on the tyrannical claims of hunger: "The belly don't know any shame or any rules except its own" (253). In fact, Morgan announces those rules of the belly in the very first story, in which de Soto and his men perplex the narrator: "If they were gods they still ate like men. They ate like we ate on feast days. They ate until they belched and broke wind" (7). Throughout the stories, the passage of time manifests itself for the characters first in the imperious demands of hunger. In "Kuykendall's Gold," Falba, Pa, and her brothers are forced to steal a goose for food to sustain them as they walk into the mountains: "We roasted that goose and eat it in the middle of the evening like we had never eat nothing before" (55). Hunger wipes the slate clean each day. Likewise, in "Dark Corner," as the Branch family travels back to Asheville, the narrator recalls the hunger that prompted them to move from Texas, where each passing week they had less to eat: "I dreamed the world was a breast we sucked from, and sometimes the breast went dry" (153). In this allusion to John Steinbeck, Morgan counterpoints the Joads' treacherous westward journey with the Branch family's equally difficult eastward journey.

Thirst, too, is omnipresent. Whether quenched by a dip from a spring or a swig of alcohol, drinking provides a spiritual uplift. "The Tracks of Chief de Soto" describes Dionysian celebrations in which the characters drink bowls of red "laughing water," translated by Ocala as "berries changed into medicine" (8). Surprised by her unplanned dancing and celebration, the young narrator describes the effects of the alcohol: "I felt warmed by the laughing water, and lifted, as though in a foaming pool. I felt the wind rushing into my head, roaring past my ears and pushing me high into the sky" (20). Another source of uplift comes in the form of coffee. When the Branch family, cold and hopeless, needs a place to spend the night, they stop by a churchyard and sleep in the meeting house, figuring that "the Lord said he would provide" (156). Aware that it is the last of their coffee, Mama proceeds to make it into a form of communion. From behind the altar she takes a bucket and dipper used by the preacher "when he got all hot and sweaty preaching" (156–57). The smell of coffee raises their spirits, "It was like the fumes theirselves made us feel better" (157). As they drink hot coffee out of the dipper, the discouraged family laughs, feeling "happy and silly" as it "warmed the mud inside our bones, and the soil in our blood" (157–58). The salutary effects of the coffee reconnect them with nature, mingling figurative blood and soil and recalling the Blood Soil Field where it all began.

Renewed, the Branch family presses on, but when Daddy's cough gets worse, the narrator goes to borrow a dipper of water from a house they pass. The owner of the house, Mrs. Lindsay, insists, "'You all come right in and set down,'" and gives them water, coffee, biscuits and jelly, sweet potatoes, and sourwood honey for Daddy (160). Later, as Daddy's cough gets worse, the moonshiner Zander Gosnell offers him a sip of whiskey. As they try to make it to the North Carolina state line, Daddy gives out. In the middle of the night, Zander arrives with a jug, and finding Daddy dead, gets friends to lay him out and make a coffin for him. Drink unites the family with themselves, with others, and with nature. Symbolically, they bury him at Double Springs Cemetery at the top of the mountain.

Drink also serves as the conduit between Dutch, the returning POW in "The Welcome," and his old life. After abandoning the celebration in his honor and heading to the edge of the woods, he finds that his old friends Roger and Mitchell have followed him, and they give him some cheap rye: "as the liquid sank into his belly he felt the world get lighter," and "the sunlight was a little brighter" (217). Out of obligation, he returns to the picnic. Mama presents him with banana pudding and coconut cake, his two favorite desserts, but all he wants is another drink to make him "feel lighter" (218). Leaving with his old friends, he gets just that: "The second drink tasted even sweeter to Dutch, and he felt the extra illumination in his veins" (219). The alcohol creates the feeling of "a great weight shift within, independent of the way his body moved ... as if great masses were trading sides in his head" (221). The old friends get drunk and start dropping large rocks off the side of the mountain: "He was clearing off the top of the mountain. It was satisfying to get rid of all the rocks in sight, as if he was putting the world in order" (224). Working his body, getting sweaty and dirty, Dutch feels a lot more like himself, finding this to be "the best welcome yet" (224). Drink and work reintegrate him into his former world.

Yet the effects of alcohol are not always salubrious. In the later stories, alcohol results in both pleasure and pain. When the prisoners in "Sleepy Gap" steal sips of hidden moonshine during their work detail, the narrator notes that it "burned like ether, and seethed like soda water" (279). The men work their way toward the jug one by one and take a sip. When all have enjoyed a drink, they work their way back again: "Everybody moved slower and my arms felt so light they seemed to float" (279). Unfortunately, the glint of the jug in the sun catches the attention of the guard, and Mike, whose cousin had left the jug for him, pays a high price for the momentary transport to freedom. Likewise, the medicinal effects of alcohol in "A Brightness New & Welcoming" and "Dark Corner" seem a distant memory in "The Bullnoser" as Carlie and her unemployed son drink beer in their mountain trailer while she watches her soap opera. As he walks outside, he talks about how difficult it is to go out into the sun after drinking: "It's like the light presses against you and pushes you around. And you don't feel like doing anything either" (291). For them, the alcohol no longer lifts: it pushes.

Similarly, shared drinking provides only a momentary boost in "A Taxpayer & A Citizen." After initiating a divorce from her adulterous husband, the narrator drinks a bottle of wine with her friend Charlane and reflects, "I never left Charlane but what I was feeling better" (305). However, the deleterious effects come quickly. Despite the narrator's confidence that "sometimes a drink or two improves my driving, makes me looser, more in control," she is pulled over for driving under the influence (305). This unleashes a host of psychological and physiological forces. Her fear and paranoia cause her to try to make a run for it. Finally caught in the midst of a highway with cars from both directions swerving to miss her, she discovers that the body has a forceful two-way traffic of its own. The narrator likens its virulence to a force of nature: "What rammed up into my throat was driven like a jolt of lightning. It came with no warning, and I tasted the sour wine and crumbs of cheese and crackers in the back of my mouth and in my nose" (318). When she tries to lean over, the officer mistakes it as another attempt to escape, and jerks her around "so the puke went right onto the front of his shirt and down onto his crotch" (318). With the second convulsion she reifies the problems in her life: "I wanted to heave out all the poison and pain I had taken in. I wanted to throw up the confusion and frustration, the humiliation that Larry had given me.... I vomited again and again" (318). Afterward, she finds that "the sickness had scrubbed the world and made it firm again" (319). Although the cleansing improved her physiological situation, the story closes with her under arrest and being taken to the jail.

Foulness and decay recur through the collection. In his essay "The Cubist of Memory," Morgan asserts, "The stuff of poetry is compost, human as well as vegetable, verbal and cultural; but it is the prospect of rising from the rot and ruin that empowers the statement and embodiment of the words" (*Good Measure* 10). He translates that subject to prose in this collection, especially in "A Brightness New & Welcoming." Reminiscent of Whitman's *Drum-Taps*, the story focuses on the ruin and putrescence of war. Powell's fever makes it seem as if his flesh were cooking on his bones. In his somatic civil war, "all the sweating, all the diarrhea, the vomiting, left no scent in his nostrils"; others say, "Tarheel can't help his stink" (*Balm* 111). Morgan yokes the land and the people in fetid detail:

"beyond the sick area was the yard where all the others lived, with puddles here and there full of urine and excrement, rotting rags," which were manageable when they were frozen over, but "when thaw came the depression filled and turned putrid" (112–13). The experience convinces Powell not just that the war was wrong but that something had been wrong since creation, that wrong is simply the nature of things.

The sense of gastric distress repeats itself again and again throughout these stories. Jones, the World War II tailgunner "hoped he would not throw up" as the plane ascended because there is "nothing like frozen puke in your compartment" (228). Forty years later, "the smell of gas on his hands made him faintly nauseous" and when "he tasted the margarine, rancid in his throat," he stops "to inhale the fumes of fresh pine, hoping they would make his chest feel better" (232). As he tries to comprehend why he alone survived the attack by a Messerschmitt, he recalls being told, "'You are sitting in the hind end of death'" (242). Morgan emphasizes Jones's physical location at the rear of the plane: "In the ass of each of them sat some tailgunner like himself, cramped and trying to keep his fingers warm" (227). When he ejects, he becomes human excrement, waste of war, settling into a German cabbage patch. Living things die, and dead things rot. This is the simple logic of nature. Decomposition marks not an end but a beginning as carbon and nitrogen and phosphorus nourish new life.

Morgan's attention to visceral detail makes man no more than compost, a metaphor Emerson and Thoreau would have applauded. In the poem "Fall," Morgan writes, "Yes, I too, ... / believe we have passed / a hundred times through the guts of an earthworm / and bless those transformations" (*Land Diving* 60). The cyclical process of transformation at times changes direction: in "The Welcome," Dutch says, "The bouncing truck made me belch the watery oatmeal we had for breakfast," concluding, "it tasted better the second time" (*Balm* 277). In "The Ratchet," brothers Fred and Albert face death in a runaway truck careening down the mountain and trying to make it across the bridge. At that point, Fred thinks about God and family while at the same time, "Without thinking he had reached into his pants and held onto himself" then "pulled his hand out and smelled his crotch, his own shit" (*Balm* 273). For Morgan, this physiological liability testifies as eloquently as the Emersonian Oversoul to the meshing of the human and the divine, though in terms Emerson would be unlikely to use.

Despite the constant flux of these transformations, time can also write on the body indelibly. Mutilation of the body begins with the first European explorers and carries on throughout the four centuries covered in the collection. De Soto's men whip the women who stop digging for gold, and "each of the Appalachee men was tied to a tree and whipped until his back bled" (17). After de Soto and his men leave, the women set about recreating their village. Clearly, the notion that they can erase the tracks of de Soto proves illusory because the narrator finds "red spots like tracks down my arms," the corporeal evidence that he had brought the plague from Europe to their village (25). Other physical reminders of the price of European settlement recur in "Little Willie" as the broken blisters on the feet of the runaway slave mother. The tracks of the tragic implication of slavery provoke in Celia a moral conclusion akin to that of Huck Finn: "But looking at them wore-out people hunkered down you couldn't have done nothing else. It wouldn't have been Christian not to feed them, law or no law. I seen we was in trouble one way or another.... It was one mother speaking to another" (94). The physical manifestation of the turmoil of trying to bring her family to safety told the story.

Sometimes the body is violently inscribed. The warden of "Sleepy Gap" announces,

"Ain't no man that can't be broke, and I will do whatever it takes to break him" (275). He lives up to his word, supposedly to get the prisoner's "mind right so he could respect hisself," and his carceral sadism proves unbounded (276). Mike, the moonshiner whose cousin left the jug of whiskey on the hill, bears the fierce punishment: "His buttocks was crossed by welts big as bloodworms and nightcrawlers" and "blood run off his back and mixed with sweat and shit on his legs" so that "when the warden hit him, blood and shit and sweat flung off" (284–85). Acceding to the power of the warden, Mike finally utters the necessary words: "I'm broke" (285). As in Kafka's "In the Penal Colony," the warden writes a message into the flesh. That message goes back to the violence of de Soto, the Union prison camps, and the unspoken events that Dutch and Jones endured at the hands of the Nazis.

In the corporeal dialectic, the pain of torture is no more prominent than the pleasure of sexuality, although it is often one-sided. In "Kuykendall's Gold," Falba's father, who first sold her for fifty dollars to Mr. Burns, later takes a hundred dollars from Mr. Kuykendall to move on farther west. The sixteen-year-old beauty knows that she has to use her body to her advantage. When Kuykendall asks her if she knows how to draw a pint, she responds, "I know how to do whatever is needed," which proves true of her character, although not in the way suggested (58). Morgan imbues the story with sexual symbolism. As she searches for where her elderly husband keeps his gold, she eventually finds it in the shot bag hanging in the room: "I lifted the flap and looked in, and seen the lead balls. But I stuck my fingers into the pouch and felt something flat and colder than lead. They was gold pieces under the shot" (60). Leaving the gold untouched, except for a single splurge on an opal ring, Falba follows her husband to watch what he does with the money.

Again, Morgan makes the money an extension of the body. Falba observes that Mr. Kuykendall's "delight as he counted out the gold pieces" is like "his face when he put his hands on my ninnies and when I pleasured him the most," concluding that "the counting out that was part of the pleasure, like the work of love" (64). With this knowledge, Falba reflects, "I felt like I knowed him for the first time" (64). Nonetheless, Falba becomes infatuated with the hunter Homer Hopps, "the handsomest feller" she has ever seen, whom she describes as the epitome of male sexuality: "He leaned his gun on the table and had squirrel tails sticking out of his pockets" (67). The gun metaphor recurs. When Hopps touches her, "It was like somebody had throwed powder in my blood and I was half asleep and half trembling" (68). The authority of her body makes her feel powerless to control it: "I wouldn't have cared if Mr. Kuykendall and all the ladies from the church had come out to watch us.... I couldn't have stopped him if I'd knowed it would cost me a million years in hell" (69). Even so, Morgan emphasizes the care Falba gives to her husband while his health is failing, her loyalty and her knowledge that when faced with his physical decay, "the only thing to do was to look right at the ugliness of it" (73). Her pragmatism and feeling of usefulness in nurturing her husband stops her affair with Hopps, even if all the ladies from the church could not.

Sexuality becomes less natural as time progresses. In "A Brightness New and Welcoming," Powell recalls how he too enjoyed being with his wife near the spring, where he met her at dark: "Sometimes they used the cot in the laurels, in the early evening, with katydids loud in the woods around and stars prickling through the canopy above" (121). By the end of *The Balm of Gilead Tree*, however, this unity of the human and natural worlds disjoins, and references to sexuality occur with no attempts to put them in the context of nature. In "A Taxpayer & A Citizen," the sublime plenitude of Powell's memories is replaced by the drunken narrator's paranoid belief that the state trooper "wanted to hold me in some remote place as a sex slave, someone to torture in kinky ways" (315). The cycle of the temporal structure returns in different fashions, writing its story on both the phenomenal and physiological worlds.

Time marks diminutions with each repetition of its cycle. By end of the collection, the resolve that reminds the Confederate soldier Powell, "It was no good to hanker," seems to have dissipated (114). Whether for money, beer, cigarettes, a filling station, or a beauty shop, the desire to be rewarded can be as palpable as the watch on the corpse of the crash victim, "still cool from the air conditioning in the plane" (327). In "The Bullnoser," Grandpa's statement to T.J. about animal husbandry—"'Got to keep your breeding stock up, otherwise a family will run to ruin in two generations'"—certainly seems valid when comparing T.J., Carley, and Riley to the earlier inhabitants of their mountains (293). What begins as the song of a mockingbird ends as MTV. What starts as an Indian village with a sacred fire ends as a trailer park development with a satellite dish. What begins as Falba's thought that "things can't get no worse than this" morphs into Jones's prison camp realism, "When you think it's bad ... just remember it can get a *lot* worse" (55, 237). Yet, despite the grimness, Morgan expresses the strength and capaciousness of the mountain people rather than articulating their late-twentieth-century anomie.

In both his prose and poetry, Morgan's writing continues the tradition of American Romanticism, linking lives over time both by the fossilized stories written in the lush but unforgiving landscape of the Blue Ridge Mountains and by the tales chronicled in the bodies of the characters themselves. All of them dwell near the Blood Soil Field, where animal, vegetable, and mineral unite. Despite its uneasy optimism about progress, *The Balm of Gilead Tree* appears more of a celebration of human resilience than an indictment of human failings. For the most part, his characters seem, like Jones in Poinsett's Bridge, guided by the belief that "there ain't nothing a man can't do if he just takes time to study it out" (38). Morgan writes, "Poetry always points in the direction of the ultimate metaphor, suggesting that in some fantastic way everything is the same thing" (*Good Measure* 116). In that sense, *The Balm of Gilead Tree* resembles a poem, with its elaborate patterns of linkage, reduplication, and chiasmus supporting that ultimate metaphor and collapsing the boundaries between time, space, and man.

Works Cited

Emerson, Ralph Waldo. *The Essential Writings of Ralph Waldo Emerson.* Ed. Brooks Atkinson. New York: Modern Library, 2000.

_____. *The Journals and Miscellaneous Notebooks of Ralph Waldo Emerson.* Ed. William H. Gilman et al. Vol. 3. Cambridge: Harvard University Press, 1963.

_____. *Ralph Waldo Emerson.* Ed. Richard Poirier. Oxford Authors Series. Oxford: Oxford University Press, 1990.

Graves, Michael. *Biblical Interpretation in the Early Church.* Fortress Press, 2017.

Morgan, Robert. *At the Edge of the Orchard Country.* Middletown, CT: Wesleyan University Press, 1987.

_____. *The Balm of Gilead Tree: New and Selected Stories.* Frankfort, KY: Gnomon Press, 1999.

_____. *Bronze Age.* Emory, VA: Iron Mountain Press, 1981.

_____. *Good Measure: Essays, Interviews, and Notes on Poetry.* Baton Rouge: Louisiana State University Press, 1993.

_____. *Groundwork.* Frankfort, KY: Gnomon Press, 1979.

_____. *Land Diving.* Baton Rouge: Louisiana State University Press, 1976.

_____. *Red Owl.* New York: W. W. Norton, 1972.

______. *Sigodlin.* Middletown, CT: Wesleyan University Press, 1990.
Thoreau, Henry David. *Walden and Civil Disobedience.* Ed. Sherman Paul. Boston: Houghton Mifflin, 1960.
______. *The Writings of Henry David Thoreau: Journal IV.* Ed. Bradford Torrey. Boston and New York: Houghton Mifflin, 1906.
Ulin, David L. "Blue Ridge Tales." Rev. of *The Balm of Gilead Tree: New and Selected Stories,* by Robert Morgan. *New York Times Book Review* 30 Jan. 2000.
West, Robert. "The Art of Far and Near: An Interview with Robert Morgan." *Carolina Quarterly* 49.3 (1997). pp. 46–68.
Whitman, Walt. "Preface 1855—*Leaves of Grass,* First Edition." *Leaves of Grass: Authoritative Texts, Prefaces, Whitman on His Art, Criticism.* Ed. Scully Bradley and Harold W. Blodgett. New York: W. W. Norton, 1973.

"The Little Clearing of Now"

Storytellers in The Hinterlands

REBECCA GODWIN

In the first section of Morgan's *The Hinterlands: A Mountain Tale in Three Parts* (1994), narrator Petal Jarvis Richards articulates the essence of humans' love of story. Speaking to her grandchildren, she explains that her direct ancestral knowledge is limited to her grandparents, with family of previous generations being "lost in the fog and dust," reduced to "a name here, a fact there, a rumor." To her grandchildren's children, her own existence will seem as shadowy. "We are isolated in the little clearing of now, and all the rest is tangled woods and thickets nobody much remembers. I always said it's how you enjoy that little opening in the wilderness that counts. That's all you have a chance to do. That's why I'm telling you this story" (14). Her metaphor evokes the key elements forming the core of this collection of three tales: place, time, and storytelling itself. With the western Carolina frontier as their subject, three generations of storytellers in *The Hinterlands* entertain with wonderfully vivid and often humorous tales that not only describe the late eighteenth- and early nineteenth-century Blue Ridge Mountains landscape but also teach lessons in how to live, focusing on the human connection that lies at the heart of storytelling's purpose and appeal.

Robert Morgan, like many southern writers, credits his family for his own storytelling flair. In an interview with Jeff Daniel Marion, Morgan explains that while his mother "taught [him] a sense of delight in the small and the ordinary," his father was "a brilliant talker, who ... turned [him] toward an early love of language" (*Good Measure* 127). Writing of his father's impact on his poetry, Morgan in an essay titled "Work and Poetry, The Father Tongue" reflects that his father never seemed entirely comfortable in the twentieth-century world into which he was born in 1905. "Daddy seemed an anachronism. He appeared to belong to an earlier century, to a world of hunting and trapping, of storytelling," to the "frontier past" (7) that Morgan explores in *The Hinterlands* as well as in his chronicle of legendary frontiersman Daniel Boone in *Boone: A Biography* (2007). His father's delight in the rituals and rhythms of work, his recitation of poems memorized in grade school, and his love of the outdoors and of telling stories set "way back yonder" inform Morgan's sensibility to language and narrative, and a specific memory that he recounts in this *Southern Review* essay bears a striking resemblance to the literal and metaphoric subject of these three mountain tales—roads. One Saturday in 1956, Morgan's father drives his son high into the Pisgah Mountains in his new Studebaker truck, traveling newly rebuilt Highway 64, the first modern road that twelve-year-old Morgan has seen. At this time interested in a career in civil engineering, Morgan finds his imagination captured by the highway itself as well as by the history his father points out—the trail he followed as a teenager and the Canadian balsams gracing the North Carolina mountains since the last Ice Age. This memory relates directly to *The Hinterlands*, where making pathways for connections, from place to place and from generation to generation, is a dominant theme. Its three mountain tales, called "The Trace," "The Road," and "The Turnpike," share one pioneer family's trailblazing story. Morgan explicitly incorporates his own family storytelling tradition, relying on Blue Ridge language and folklore to create spirited mountain voices reminiscent of those who made him into a lover of words.

Even though different voices tell the stories of *The Hinterlands*, common narrative techniques link these three tales spanning seventy-three years. Each narrator looks back to an earlier time, relaying memories to an implied audience of grandchildren never called by name but addressed directly from time to time. Each narrative also centers on the storyteller's seeking or getting a marriage partner, thus making *The Hinterlands* a series of love stories, in a way, stories about building marriages along with building roads. These mountain storytellers explore work, intimacy, and family relationships as well as their own hearts. Their narratives connect the outer landscape to the inner, showing how strength and daring develop from the need to settle an unsettled land.

The first storyteller in *The Hinterlands* is a woman, one who delights in the details of a pioneer woman's life even as she claims the adventurous spirit of the frontier male explorer. Before she tells the story of keeping house and giving birth alone in the backwoods, Petal Jarvis turns Horace Greeley's "Go West, Young Man" on its head. Breaking the myth of male wanderlust, this strong young woman explains in the very first paragraph of "The Trace," set in 1772, that "every young girl dreamed of running off to the West." Yes, she quickly integrates the more passive, feminine notion that "Every girl has a dream of being carried off to some better place, by a big handsome feller" (3). But her explanation that people naturally think their lives will be better if they start over in a new place, away from people who know their past failures or mediocrity, articulates the universality of humans' desire for change and challenge. "I've heard it said men like to up and move on and women want to nest and stay. But I've never noticed it was so. I've seen just as many women as men with a hanker to move on, to light out and try a new place. Couldn't have been so many people settled here if the women didn't want to come too," she declares (4). Here, she does not stress women's willingness to be carried but their desire to go. Particularly in this first story, Morgan debunks the gender stereotypes associated with early pioneers, honoring women's role in America's settlement, as he does in his later book *Boone: A Biography*. In *Boone*, in fact, as he speaks explicitly of the hard life Daniel Boone's wife Rebecca endured, Morgan refers to feminist critic Annette Kolodny's examination of women's experiences on the American frontiers in *The Land Before Her* (1984), a text that informs his understanding that "women made it possible to claim and hold land in Kentucky and elsewhere" during the period of settlement (*Boone* 313). In "The Trace," Petal Jarvis makes that same point as she illustrates that she is, in many ways, a stronger character than her husband.

Petal's introduction of her husband, Realus Richards, expresses her sexual attraction to him while revealing a vigor that sustains her when he fails her later on. Wanting her listening grandchildren to understand human longing, Petal acknowledges the masculine magnetism that draws her to the young Realus, who has the look "real men have": their "shoulders are broad, it's true. But you see it most in their chest and waist, and the power in their upper legs showing right through the cloth or buckskin" (5). Shortly after she first sees Realus, his presence in church generates a reaction calling to mind the merger of sexuality and religious ecstasy that Morgan writes about in *The Truest Pleasure* and other works, both fiction and poetry: "It made my skin prickle all over me, under my dress and down to my ankles. I told myself it was the excitement of the service, but I knowed better" (20). Her description of Realus's physical appeal establishes Petal as an honest, self-revealing narrator eager to help her grandchildren understand all of human nature. She turns promptly to another aspect of her makeup when she shares the memory of throwing hog slops at a preacher's son trying to steal pigs from her father's pen. She hits him with her bucket, the slops covering his face, and she is "trembling with madness and excitement" as she defends her family's property (17). This story of her verve circulates among the community, making men see her as a potentially "dangerous woman," a suspicion she does not try to dispel. Instead, she continues to flout stereotypes, frequenting the blacksmith shop because she enjoys it although she realizes that "women are not supposed to like the place a blacksmith works." When Realus tries to compliment her by saying the shop is "too dirty ... for a lady," she retorts, "Women has to work in all kinds of dirt.... Men just want them to look pretty and clean, like they don't spend their time scrubbing and washing diapers" (19). Her forthrightness fits her for life as a pioneering woman, Realus recognizes, but her candor does not elicit the same honesty from him.

For Realus Richards deceives Petal Jarvis when he marries her on the pretense of taking her to the West. Courting Petal, he paints the West as Edenic, with blue meadows, plentiful deer grazing in glades, valleys full of buffalo, woods full of turkeys, a land "covered with chestnuts and huckleberries and elderberries" where he has already built a cabin on the "prettiest ground you ever seen" (11). Petal dreams of living "off in the promised land of the Holston" (14), a tributary of the Tennessee River running through Upper East Tennessee and Southwest Virginia. Petal assumes when she marries Realus that she is going "all the way to the Holston" (25), all the way "out into the new country" (26). Realizing that her parents will not grant permission for her to go to an unfamiliar, most likely treacherous place, Petal elopes with Realus in the middle of the night. And although she soon suspects that they are not following the road to the Holston, she trusts him when he insists that she is just "all mixed up" (33). Wiping away the tears his accusation elicits, she draws on her fortitude and integrity: "I would foller my man to the West, as I had promised to do" (34). Her reason for telling the story of her husband's deception, which becomes clear only near the end of her tale, again relates to her desire to educate her grandchildren, as she discloses when she describes waking up on the cold ground after she and Realus spend their first night together in the woods: "That's the way it goes, grandchildren. You do things in the rush of newness and surprise, and in the gray morning you have to pick up and start all over again" (37). Part of Petal's eventual starting over involves her coming to terms with her husband's ruse, which she discovers eight years into their union.

Realus's initial deception, of course, necessitates further duplicity during those eight years of marriage. He essentially lies to Petal about getting a cow, letting her wonder how he will get one when they supposedly will be so far from any other settlers who might sell them an animal. Unable to break his cover about their location when a pioneering couple comes by their house, he sends the strangers away by telling them that he and Petal have had smallpox, pretending to Petal that he fears the people will rob them. One of most troublesome untruths Realus backs himself into comes when Petal is almost ready to deliver their first baby. Having no neighbor women to consult and inexperienced in the process of giving birth, Petal asks Realus to find her a midwife. He leaves home for two days, pretending to look for a granny woman. During his absence, Petal gives birth alone. Her childbirth story, creating one of the most vivid scenes of *The Hinterlands*, illustrates the tenacity and courage that characterize her throughout "The Trace."

Morgan bases the account of Petal's birthing her first child on a true story told by his maternal grandfather, R.H. Levi, about his own grandmother Beddingfield, left alone during the Civil War:

> One night a panther climbed up on the house and screamed and tried to jump down the stick-and-clay chimney. She built up the fire to keep the cat away but realized she didn't have enough wood to feed the blaze all night. As she looked around the cabin in terror she saw there was nothing to burn but her furniture. The panther had killed her cur dog just outside the door and clawed on the door itself before jumping on the roof. All through the night she broke up chairs and fed the pieces to the flames. She even had to burn up the breadboard carved from a wide piece of yellow poplar, and the ladder leading up to the loft ["Autobiographical Essay" 261].

Morgan translates the basic details of this family story into a wrenching childbirth scene. Left alone while Realus supposedly rides fifty miles to a settlement to find a midwife, Petal finds herself without enough wood or water in the house to last through her labor, which begins soon after Realus departs. Returning from the spring, she has to run from a panther, who claws all night at the chimney, trying to get into the cabin. Knowing she must keep the fire going so the smoke will deter the cat's efforts, Petal finally breaks off the stumps their one bench is pegged to, burning them so that she can leave the bench propped against the door to keep the panther from entering that way. Morgan's description of her physical pain and her anger at Realus pays tribute to his ability to imagine a laboring woman's point of view: "It was your Grandpa that left me with not even a gun and no firewood to last the night, and no granny woman to help, and nobody to explain what I needed to do. It was your Grandpa that took me off into the wilderness and got me with a baby and then didn't find a midwife." Like the practical woman she is, Petal puts her anger to good use:

> My frustration come to a point right then. I seen that stump like it was your Grandpa's head, and I hauled off with both legs and kicked it. It was like I gripped the boards with my back and kicked. I would have killed Realus had he been there. But I felt that stump give a little. I kicked again and the pegs broke and the stump rolled off by the hearth [80].

Petal's description of the labor pangs and childbirth following this burst of passion rivals Ivy Rowe's lyrical description of birthing Joli in Lee Smith's *Fair and Tender Ladies*, a scene critics have described as validating this feminine experience whose details have been largely absent from canonical literature. Ivy's memory of her "bones parting" for the "splashing" and the sweet smell of blood (Smith 144) parallel Petal's sense that she had "shot [herself] through a tunnel of pain" as the baby "worked its back through like a weasel coming out of a burrow," giving her the "wonderfullest feeling" that enables her to bite the bloody umbilical cord in two (82). Morgan allows Petal eleven pages to tell her childbirth story, from the time her water breaks until she cleans up the dirty sheets and enjoys the dreamy sleep that follows birth. Her details help her audience, both grandchildren and readers, to appreciate that women can embody the Emersonian ideal of self-reliance as well as men.

Perhaps Petal's self-sufficiency adds to her initial resentment when she learns that Realus has lied to her for eight years about the location of their homestead. Looking back on the youthful years of their marriage as she narrates their life for her grandchildren, the older storyteller Petal recounts Realus's attempts to control her when she and the children go for walks: "Don't go away so far.... You might get lost or run into Indians.... I don't want you to go too far from the house. I forbid you to go far from the clearing" (105). But Petal does wander across meadows and branches, and one day when she and the children follow the river bank to pick foxgrapes, they go miles and miles from home, until the shape of a mountain peak looks familiar to Petal and a cowbell's tinkle "was like something [she] knowed but just couldn't name" (110). When she recognizes her Daddy's cow Bess, her confusion over the cow's being in the West quickly gives way to an epiphany: she has lived for eight years just over the mountain from her parents. She eagerly continues to their home, full of excitement and turmoil as they welcome her and the grandchildren they thought they would never see. "I could see I was going to have to tell my story," she says, though she hates to validate her Daddy's disapproval of Realus (115). Ironically, neither her father nor her brother says a word when she explains that she was "tricked into thinking we was in the West" (116). In fact, they turn away from Petal, obviously reverting to male bonding as they recognize that Realus tricked Petal in an effort to play the role of brave frontiersman taking his new wife west to unknown lands. Petal is angry enough to contemplate not returning to "such a lying polecat" as Realus (118).

At her childhood home, Petal hears stories of the outside world that open her eyes to the isolation Realus has imposed upon her. The American Revolution is raging around her, right in the mountains, and her own brother has returned from the war because of fever. Neighbors have died fighting against the British king. Families have been driven out of the community for being Tories. In despair about her husband's deceit, Petal considers, but then decides against, staying at the settlement with her parents. She chooses instead to confront Realus with her new knowledge. Her choice affirms the character she has illustrated throughout her story, one of vigor and responsibility. And when she gets back to the home she built with Realus, she needs that strength of character as much as she ever has.

The last portion of "The Trace" attests to Morgan's narrative control, as Petal's story of her return home builds suspense that keeps listeners predicting and fearing outcomes. As she and her children cross the mountain, they encounter drunken Indians who have butchered Old Bess, one of them wearing a red plaid shirt and black hat belonging to Realus. Arriving at their cabin, they find no Realus but a muddle of their belongings strewn across the yard, where the marauding Indians have killed and eaten their fowl. Realistic Petal begins the work of restoring order to her home, finding Old Daisy and milking her, all the while worrying that Realus has fallen victim to the Indians. The tension builds as she finds, the next morning, a corpse tied to a scarecrow frame, emitting a sickening stench. Petal realizes that "they wasn't nothing to do" but cut the corpse from the frame and give it a decent burial (139). So that's exactly what she does, working alone until she gets that body on a sheet. Eventually, her oldest child Wallace helps her to drag the body on a timber sled to the cemetery they started with Eller, the third Richards child who dies from milk poisoning. Describing all this gruesome work, Petal insinuates that the big, smelly corpse could be Realus and that she is hiding that identity from her children by sending them back to the house until she has the body wrapped in a sheet. Her narrative strategy teases her audience, even when she thinks about being mad at Realus, her "sudden hatred" (139) of him for not being there to help her spurring her on to cut the rags off the dead body. "Bone-chilled thinking of not seeing him no more" (143), she leads listeners to wonder whether her anger perhaps stems from grief and fear of being alone. This story-within-the-story, like that of Petal's first childbirth, exhibits her excellent storytelling skills: she manages pacing and vivid sensory description while withholding telling details, thus keeping her audience intrigued.

Although the title of this first story, "The Trace," relates logically to the entire book's subject of building roads for settlers' movement into the back country, the work that Petal does to bury this man, who turns out not to be Realus but another man killed by the Indians, presents a possible double meaning. When Petal lights upon the idea of pulling the timber sled to the field so that she and her son can use it to haul the corpse to the graveyard, she does the work of a draft animal, hooking the sled's trace chains over her shoulders and pulling the sled behind her. This scene provides a symbol of Petal's hard labor throughout the novella, helping Realus to clear land for crops while keeping her family fed and clothed. The image reinforces Petal's work ethic as well as her secondary status in her eighteenth-century world, her subjugation to her husband's decision that she will remain isolated from the community connections she needs.

The ending of this last episode within "The Trace" reinforces the tale's depiction of both Realus's and Petal's essential natures, particularly as they relate to the thematic issue of community. Realus reappears during the night, standing by the barn as a ghostly figure, leaving Petal to wonder at his identity and fear for her children's safety. When she finally determines that the figure is her husband, her anger reignites. "It riled me anew that he was afeared to face me," she admits, realizing he must know that she has discovered his deception about where they live (144). She mentally reviews a litany of wrongs, such as his leaving her alone to birth her first child. "I wanted to hear what he would say about all those times I had gone without a woman to talk to and my own Mama just across the mountains, no more than fifteen miles away" (145). As her emotion gives way to the reason that has helped her to make a successful pioneering life, Petal again reviews her options for her future. If she leaves him, she will have to raise her children alone "like a widow woman." She recognizes the limitations placed on women, even strong women, at this time: "Realus could go off to the west and start a new place and new family. A man could just vanish into the wilderness and clear him up a new place and find another wife." The unspoken parallel is that women cannot. Once more, Petal's strength of character and practicality prevail. "I was going to have to forgive Realus," she concedes (145). Again, she takes action, leading pathetic Realus back to the house, extending the physical touch of friendship and human connection that form a core of this book.

Connection has been Petal Richards' need throughout her marriage to Realus, something she has craved during her isolation from a larger community. Women "just want to go gallivanting" and "to socialize," Realus once claims when Petal asks to go into the settlements to trade eggs and honey to buy things for her home (90). He does not allow her to accompany him when he travels every four or five months to buy tree saplings or livestock. He wants to keep her ignorant of their whereabouts, but also his restrictions on her movements reflect the eighteenth-century expectation that women stay in the home rather than mingle in public spaces. Petal tells Realus outright that she wants to talk to the woman traveling with her husband past their homestead, but Realus protects his own lies rather than allow her that connection. The sprig of myrtle that this woman leaves for Petal to plant represents the continuity that she instinctively knows this isolated wife must need. And Petal's insight into the connection the myrtle symbolizes resonates in the final words of her story.

Petal's forgiveness of Realus takes on a spiritual dimension despite it showing her practical ability to see that her life as a single mother in the eighteenth-century hinterlands will be dismal. This spiritual element assumes a concrete form in the church she and her children pass on the way back home from her parents' settlement. The children, unfamiliar with church, question her about the purpose of people's gathering to worship. She replies, "to show they're a community" (121). Her recognition that community is absolutely essential to human existence prompts her forgiveness of the imperfect Realus, who, she rationalizes, probably lied about taking her to the West because he feared that she would not go with him unless he promised to fulfill her romantic dreams of adventure. When she touches Realus to signal her forgiveness at the end of "The Trace," her feelings go much beyond the sexual attraction that drew her to Realus as a young girl. "I seen that when I touched your Grandpa with love, it was like I was touching all the people back through the ages, through all their love and affection" (149). She reminds her listening grandchildren that she and Realus will be with them as they mature and begin their own families. "Don't worry if you don't understand. I don't think the young is meant to.... But I wanted to tell you anyway, so's you'll remember it after I'm long gone" (149). Petal's forgiveness of Realus, tied not to organized religion but to the human communion the church building represents, intertwines with her understanding of story's connective purpose in the final image she shares with her grandchildren. Although Realus is dead at the time of her storytelling, she returns, to end her saga, to the morning after she forgave his deceit. He brings her a branch of witch hazel in full blossom, noting that witch hazel blooms in late fall and winter after other plants have gone dormant, thus symbolizing possibility, the fact that "they's always another chance" (150). His gesture thanks Petal for pardoning his dishonesty, and Petal's ending her narrative with this gift shows her grandchildren that forgiveness generates connection and community, "the most precious thing" that humans need (59).

Morgan gives Petal Richards the longest storytelling time in *The Hinterlands*, perhaps nodding to his own observation that "women make exceptionally good storytellers because they notice details ... and especially because, unlike many of his male characters, women are quite willing to talk about their relationships and feelings" (Conway 284). This gender distinction in fact shows up in "The Trace," not only in Realus's silence about the location of their homestead but also in Petal's announcement to her grandchildren that their Grandpa "always had trouble speaking his affections" (149). But as he moves to the second and third stories in *The Hinterlands*, Morgan gives the men their chance to share their mountain voices. And while they may not share their feelings as explicitly or frequently as Petal, their stories certainly offer the details that depict the early American landscape as well as the spirit of the place they are settling. Their narratives also disclose the same focus on connection that Petal Richards so effectively expresses as a central purpose of the storytelling tradition.

The storyteller in "The Road" is Realus and Petal's grandson Solomon Richards, son of their oldest child, Wallace. Adapting Petal's strategy of addressing his direct audience not by name but by "son," Solomon tells his grandson the story of building a road through Douthat's Gap to facilitate travel from South Carolina into North Carolina, all the way to Asheville. "I was going to let a little light into Dark Corner," he remembers (162), referring to the mountain wilderness of upper South Carolina just where North Carolina and

South Carolina meet. A young man of nineteen when settlers' talk of building a road into the mountains captures his imagination, he becomes at the same time enamored of a young lady whom he identifies as the girl he will marry before he even knows her name. These dreams intertwine and spur him to action: "The vision of building the road became joined with romance in my mind. They got so tangled up I couldn't think of one without the other. No, sir, building the road was the same as winning Mary. Marrying your Grandma was the same as finding a roadway into the mountains" (158). The journey of romance in "The Road" offers few intimate details about the relationship between Solomon and his bride but focuses instead on the hard but humorous journey he takes to win her hand. Like his grandmother Petal, Solomon tells his story to teach his grandson the value of work and determination, providing a philosophy of life in his entertaining travel log.

Morgan again uses family lore in "The Road," illustrating Petal's theory of story as the means by which humans understand their ancestors and their history. Weaving tall tales and mountain legends into the true story of Solomon Jones, husband of Morgan's maternal great-great-grandmother's sister (Conway 284), Morgan creates in "The Road" a rollicking trailblazing journey charting the adventures Solomon encounters while holding the tail of his sow named Sue, recording the oral folk tradition that holding a pig's tail will help a man to chart a direct course, for the pig will take the shortest route possible to its feeding trough. While Petal's story in "The Trace" covers eight years of her relationship with Realus, "The Road" focuses on one day's journey. As Solomon and Sue blaze a trail through the mountain wilderness, they encounter and overcome a series of obstacles, both natural and human, leading their one-day trip to become a metaphor for life's trials. Along the way, Solomon reveals his respect for nature and other humans, and in telling the adventure story to his grandson, the old man Solomon makes sure that the young man understands that the most important part of being a human being lies in helping others, making connections that allow a community to form.

Telling a tale of 1816, Solomon Richards uses the same traits of eighteenth- and nineteenth-century Appalachian dialect as Petal, showing Morgan's authentic reflection of his storytellers' time and place. Both Solomon and his grandmother illustrate several nonstandard verb forms documented in Walt Wolfram and Donna Christian's *Appalachian Speech* as grammatical features of Appalachian English (79–85). They regularize irregular verbs, for instance, using *-ed* past tense forms in "knowed" (Morgan, "The Road" 88, 161), "catched" (106), and "throwed" (183), and they use nonstandard participial forms in "had give" (81), "have took" (181), and "I seen" (159). Another trait of the language, the uninflected base verb appearing as the simple past tense, occurs in "come" for "came" (56), "eat" for "ate" (62), and "run" for "ran," as when Solomon hits a beagle with his hatchet and "it squealed and run off into the brush" (176). Petal and Solomon also modify unstressed *-ow's* at the ends of words to *-er's*, as in "feller" (153) and "foller" (168), demonstrating an aspect of the Appalachian English phonological system quite evident to outsiders (Wolfram and Christian 66), and they call panthers "painters" (73, 243), following the rural working class Appalachian vernacular. To win the hand of Mary McPherson, the daughter of a local college teacher from Scotland, Solomon reads every evening by the firelight, educating himself beyond his few weeks of formal schooling; aware of her "proper speech" (165), Solomon measures his words carefully when he first meets her, "trying to talk the way people in town talked" (164). But his natural speech patterns govern his storytelling, reflecting the oral culture that Morgan portrays in these tales.

Mainly, "The Road" entertains with its episodic series of obstacles that Solomon and Sue encounter when they leave Aunt Willa's and Uncle Rufus's house to survey a path through Douthat's Gap to Cedar Mountain, a trip Solomon makes after signing up shareholders willing to back his plan to build a toll road. The image of this young man running behind a pig, bending over to hold its tail while trying to hack notches in trees to mark the trail, might undercut the seriousness of his purpose, to establish himself in a business so that Mary's father will allow her to marry him, if it weren't for the older storyteller's direct addresses to his grandson listener. As Solomon answers the child's implied questions about Indians or offers advice about human nature, he helps his audience to understand that he tells this story of his misadventures at his own expense. In parts, it seems almost a tall tale, especially in its hero's constant escapes from dangerous situations. But in the end, its humor gives way to an unmistakably realistic drama that allows Solomon to learn a lesson in humanity, one enabling him to re-evaluate the "vanity" that he admits set him on his journey with Sue (171).

Much like Phoenix Jackson in Eudora Welty's "A Worn Path," Solomon overcomes obstacle after obstacle as he lets himself be dragged by a hungry pig through mountain woods and clearings, but his encounters are both more dangerous and more amusing than Welty's determined protagonist's. Sue fights off a pack of beagle dogs before she guides Solomon into the Dark Corner moonshine blockaders' camp. Morgan admits that some of his own relatives spent time in the penitentiary in the 1940s and 1950s for making moonshine in Chestnut Springs in South Carolina, "in the Dark Corner" ("Noble" 5), and he uses this history here in "The Road," naming "Morgans" as one of the Dark Corner families that was "always fussing and feuding" (182). Solomon paints a hilarious scene as he describes Sue's getting drunk by gorging herself on the mash that keeps the blockaders' hogs "drunk half the time, grunting happy and fat" (183). After they finally escape this riotous skirmish (with Sue dashing through the middle of the blockaders' tent, bringing it down around her while the astounded blockaders point their guns but decide that they cannot shoot a crazy man with a drunk pig), Sue runs straightaway toward a water falls, prompting Solomon to think, "The sow seemed bent on suicide" (189). His narrative voice throughout the tale maintains this same droll humor, reflecting a take-what-comes attitude reminiscent of Petal's more solemn voice exuding the same patience and can-do spirit.

As Solomon tells about his confrontations with other obstacles—a Cherokee Indian, a group of bathing Melungeon girls whose old woman supervisor runs a needle though his lip, a preacher who tries to talk him out of building the road, a bear who scares Sue into releasing her bowels as Solomon runs behind her, a raggedy family that tries to kill Sue for their supper, a "frog rain" storm that drops toad frogs among the puddles and hailstones, a black spider, a rabid panther, lead miners who threaten to shoot him and Sue—he lets his narrative meander between past events and present time addresses to his grandson listener. He moves from action-filled, dangerous yet comic scenes sometimes intimating the outlandishness of Southwest humor (especially when Sue frequently breaks wind in his face) to reflective, philosophical commentary, particularly on the value of work and on the humanity of those he meets during his trek. Like his grandmother Petal, he teaches through his tales his deep understanding of life: that animals, such as the pig Sue, the bear, and even the rabid panther, are to be respected and treated with dignity; that people, who are not good or bad but some of both, should try to see others' points of view; that people everywhere have the same basic needs and desires; that humans are not always in control of events; that "everybody's life is hard" and "the only thing that can get you through so much messiness and grief is a plan" (257). The plan he espouses entails work and determination. "We have to believe we can do great things even to accomplish little things," he tells his grandson (276). And his descriptions of work explain how he and his family made the roads through the hard mountain landscape: "that's what work really is, something difficult, something to fill up the time. Every day is a long day if you don't have work to do. Every hour is long unless you have something that has to be done" (230). Like Petal, Solomon shows himself to be a philosopher-storyteller, one who makes explicit his intent not just to entertain but to instruct.

Also like Petal, Solomon arrives near the end of his story at a place where he is faced with a choice, and the decision he makes is influenced not only by his grandmother's obvious influence but also by his encounter with an old mountain man he assumes to be Tracker Thomas, a mysterious fellow who supposedly came into the Carolina and Tennessee mountains when Daniel Boone was scouting those hills. This gentleman further opens Solomon's eyes to the beauty of the world around him, to the apple orchard that Solomon has not noticed, and to the vastness of time that humans can hardly understand. Tracker Thomas is himself a storyteller, relishing the way his older perspective enlightens Solomon, who has not thought before of the people who might have lived in the mountains before the Cherokee. His sad but resigned prediction of road-building's ultimate destruction of the wilderness does not convince the young Solomon to give up on his road project but does seem to resonate with the older, storytelling Solomon: "And next thing we'll have is wagons and dust, peddlers, new ground cleared and gullies washing every holler. The game will be gone, like the Indians is gone." Despite Tracker Thomas's despair over Solomon's project, he extends a token of human connection, a gold piece that he deems "might be of use" to the young man (250). With this gold piece in his pocket, Solomon continues onward to his final destination.

That final destination within the framework of "The Road," however, is not his home on Cedar Mountain, the place that will mark his and Sue's fulfillment of their goal of surveying a route for a road. Solomon gets sidetracked and lets the need to help someone else take precedence over his own ambition. Coming across a boy who has been bitten by a snake, Solomon stops to assist, cutting the boy's flesh with his hatchet, risking his own safety by sucking the poison out of the boy's hand, and finally carrying the boy to his home. He says, "I thought about my road and my plans and I seen they wouldn't be worth nothing if I couldn't stop and help somebody bit by a rattler. They wasn't no road that important" (278). Ironically, in forgetting himself, Solomon achieves success, for Sue continues her journey and makes it back to Cedar Mountain, according to people who see her "heading lickety for Cedar Mountain" (286). The last lines of "The Road" signify that Solomon's destination is not a physical space but an understanding of his place in the world. As Solomon pulls from his pocket the gold nugget given to him by Tracker Thomas and watches it sparkle in the moonlight, he remembers the millions of butterflies that fly through the gap periodically. His reverie evokes his grandmother's belief in the kinship of humans and of humans with other creatures of the beautiful mountain landscape, suggesting that her lessons in community will endure.

The last storyteller in *The Hinterlands* is David Richards, Solomon's son and Petal's great-grandson, who describes in "The Turnpike" the 1845 rebuilding of the road that Solomon Richards eventually builds based on the survey he and Sue complete in "The Road." This very short tale continues the first two stories' narrative premise—a grandparent talking to a grandchild—although this listener is an adult granddaughter. Its community awareness shifts to an explicit social and environmental consciousness, and it ends, fittingly, with love, as young David arrives at the home of his betrothed.

The notion of story that Petal introduces to her grandchildren as she begins *The Hinterlands* comes full circle in "The Turnpike" in David's reference to hearing about his "Great-grandma Petal Richards staying up all night to keep a painter from coming down the chimney" the night his Grandpa was born (299). As he passes this story to his granddaughter, he illustrates Petal's explanation of story's appeal: it allows us to connect with humans, especially family, that we will never know, thus providing a comforting sense of our place in the world. In "The Turnpike," David's granddaughter wants to hear his own panther story, as signaled in his reply to her implied prompting, "I'm *coming* to the painter, girl" (298). David's monologue, like that of his father Solomon and his great-grandmother Petal, achieves the effect of dialogue as it repeats a listener's question or incorporates it into a response. This strategy reflects the fact that story is, after all, a dialogue—a conversation among generations, a way to exchange values through folklore and actual events.

David's panther story mimics the folklore story Solomon tells in "The Road," about a panther's stalking a young, betrothed girl traveling home with fresh meat from a hog killing. She drops all the meat and then pieces of her clothing to distract the panther, dashing into her house to realize she has arrived stark naked. David experiences practically the same fate in "The Turnpike." Returning after the turnpike-opening ceremony to his boarding house, run by his betrothed Miss Lewis's family, he sheds his clothing piece by piece to divert Old Tryfoot, a famous panther attracted to the barbecue smell on his hands. David explains the evolution of story into myth as he introduces the legend of the big three-footed cat: "You know how stories like that will start on their own and grow" (300). Like the young girl in the story Solomon recounts in "The Road," David bursts into his beloved's parlor wearing only his drawers and one wrist cuff, ending a hilarious journey (one marked by the throwing of galluses and trousers) in a warm and safe environment. Here, Morgan the storyteller uses the panther tale to create a vivid sense of place as he threads mountain folklore through all three narratives.

The sense of place is portrayed most dramatically in "The Turnpike," the only story in *The Hinterlands* describing the actual work of building a road, in David's depiction of his turnpike's destructive effects on the landscape. David paints himself as a nineteenth-century environmentalist as he explains his theory of road building: "you have to work with the soil and rock and slope you find," making an effort to "make your idea fit the place you're working on" (311). He expresses dismay that his partners do not save the wood they cut, and his despair at the raping of the land is palpable: "After they got through clearing the right-of-way, it looked like a storm had hit the mountain and broke off all the trees.... And the ground looked ugly as the mange where it was exposed" (317). He tries to stop workers from dumping dirt down the mountainside, killing bushes and trees, realizing that "the whole mountain begun to look like it had been hit by a landslide or flood.... It looked like we had shoveled out half the mountain and throwed it on the trees below" (321). When a long summer rain comes, the bank above the road caves in, and two slides of ruptured dirt cover up all the progress made on the road. David regrets the ecological disaster: "It seemed impossible this was the beautiful gap where we had started working a few months before. The whole mountain was filth and waste, like a wound festering and running its corruption down the slope. It made me mad all over again just to look at what we had done" (326). He implies to his granddaughter that he wants to be a good steward of the land, and in telling her this story, he passes on a plea for environmental protection.

David's distress over the destruction of the natural landscape mirrors his anguish over the inhumane behavior he witnesses toward black and white convicts working on the road, gangs probably treated no better than the slaves who built Solomon's road years before. He vehemently dislikes the warden's inhumanity, feeling sickened by the man's leaving a convict lying passed out after whipping him until his back is raw and bloody. David, in a supervisory position, digs with the convict gangs despite his co-supervisor's admonition that he should not "work with prisoners" (319). These incidents show David's deep sense of human community, a value he learned from his father Solomon, who learned it from his grandmother Petal and the stories she told to him. His integrity and work ethic color everything he does in this story—showing the convicts how to dig straight so they will take pride in their own work, declining money from Mr. Lance because Lance is guilty of usury, and even taking on the job of building the turnpike when his father Solomon is too sick from a stroke to do it. All David's actions reinforce the fact that the voices in *The Hinterlands* mean to convey the absolute supremacy of community. They use their storytelling skills to share the generosity of spirit they enjoy.

David shows this desire to communicate with others especially poignantly in his addresses to his audience, his adult granddaughter. Calling her "honey" and "sweetheart" and "my child," he spends more time than the first two narrators in this collection talking to his listener about her own life. His granddaughter has a baby but no husband, and David throughout comforts her and shows his boundless love. He tells her, "They will be another boy come to love you, and your baby. You've got to see this through" (306). "I know how you feel," he says as he reflects that all people encounter hard places that seem impossible to get around. He adds, "That's why I'm telling you this. When your heart is about broke, ain't nothing helps but knowing other people have their troubles too. That, and getting on with your work. Here, don't cry" (307). He further consoles his granddaughter by ending his story with his happy arrival at his beloved Miss Lewis's home, where she laughs at his near-nakedness, seeing beyond the moment's embarrassment and signaling her own understanding of humans' need for meaningful connection. His ending shows his granddaughter the possibility of "another chance," as Petal shows her grandchildren when she describes Realus's gift of late-blooming witch hazel at the end of "The Trace."

Robert Morgan shares Petal Richards' understanding of the purpose of story. He sees it as the way we connect with our past, thus getting "a firmer sense of ourselves through knowing what has come before." In the modern world of Internet and television, he surmises,

> we want to catch in words a world all but gone. We tend to write best about cultures that have almost melted into the past. The blue valleys, the fog-haunted coves, the tireless milky waterfalls are still there, but the people, the people with wisdom in their hands and humility in their hearts, have slipped away forever, unless we can find them in our own words , and in our own hands and hearts ["Autobiographical Essay," 286].

Morgan finds with his words in *The Hinterlands* Petal, Solomon, and David Richards, three humble, wise, hard-working storytellers representing the early settlers of the Appalachian Mountains, the mountains Morgan knew as a child. His own upbringing on a one-horse farm in the mountains close to Zirconia, North Carolina, with the Green River meandering nearby, surely ingrained in him a love of Southern Appalachian geography and history that is palpable in *The Hinterlands,* as in all his creative work. His Welsh ancestors settled in these mountains in the eighteenth century, and the family homeplace sits still on land cleared by his maternal great-great-grandfather in 1840 (Conway 276). This landscape thus embodies the past for Morgan, becoming a concrete, though not stable, emblem of earlier times. In describing so well the spirit of these late eighteenth- to mid-nineteenth-century Southern Appalachian mountains, Morgan paints a true American literary landscape. His three mountain voices, authentic Appalachian storytellers, want to show us the texture of their place and time as they teach us, too, to connect with our own. That's why they're telling us this story.

Works Cited

Conway, Cecilia. "Robert Morgan's Mountain Voice and Lucid Prose." *An American Vein: Critical Readings in Appalachian Literature.* Ed. Danny L. Miller, Sharon Hatfield, and Gurney Norman. Athens: Ohio University Press, 2005. pp. 275–89.
Morgan, Robert. "Autobiographical Essay." *Contemporary Authors.* Vol 201. Farmington Hills, MI: Gale, 2002. pp. 258–86.
_____. *Boone: A Biography.* Chapel Hill, NC: Algonquin Books, 2007.
_____. *The Hinterlands.* Winston-Salem, NC: John F. Blair, 1994.
_____. "Interview by Jeff Daniel Marion." *Good Measure: Essays, Interviews, and Notes on Poetry.* Baton Rouge: Louisiana State University Press, 1993. pp. 127–30.
_____. "A Noble and Dangerous Tradition." *The Algonkian* 14 (2001): pp. 4–5.
_____. "Work and Poetry, The Father Tongue." *Southern Review* 31.1 (1995): pp. 161–80.
Smith, Lee. *Fair and Tender Ladies.* New York: Ballantine Books, 1988.

Faith, Sex, Talk, and Work

The Cornerstones of Community in The Truest Pleasure *and* This Rock

George Hovis

The first time Ginny Peace Powell, *The Truest Pleasure*'s narrator, attends a Holiness revival, she hears the presiding minister describe their worship as "the fellowship of time with eternity" and as "the communion of the flesh with the spirit" (5). Reverend McKinney's words help to explain the appeal of Holiness worship to Ginny and the other Appalachian congregants. Both *The Truest Pleasure* and its sequel, *This Rock,* are religious novels in that not only do they address the perennial religious questions that have faced humanity—for example, the relationship of flesh to spirit and of time to eternity—but they do so within the explicit context of a lived religious experience situated in a specific historical context—that of Baptists and Pentecostal Holiness revivalists in the North Carolina mountains. Nevertheless, these religious questions are subsumed by the novels' more pervasive concern with community. Taking the grammatical subjects, unmodified by dependent clauses, from Reverend McKinney's statements about worship (excerpted above), the most essential aspects of their worship are more simply "fellowship" and "communion." And it is the possibilities for these states of being—and the frustrations to their fulfillment—with which these two novels most concern themselves.

In a novel by Morgan's fellow North Carolina writer Fred Chappell, we are told that "to be well spoken is not in the tradition of the Appalachian mountaineer, whose sometimes inscrutable taciturnity is locally regarded as a virtue having something to do with valor and manliness" (183). These words aptly describe Tom Powell, the mountaineer Ginny Peace marries, and it is Tom's taciturnity that most challenges their marriage and Ginny's personal fulfillment. *The Truest Pleasure* chronicles the struggles of this couple to communicate and the ways that their communication is facilitated and frustrated by family and faith. Unlike *Gap Creek*'s portrayal of Hank and Julie Richards's struggle against nature to establish a homestead, the Peace farm is a model of the abundance possible on a middle-sized yeoman farm around the turn of the twentieth century in western North Carolina. With its seasonally appointed chores, the farm provides a bucolic setting for the marital and familial discord that threatens to rend irreparably the lives of the Peace and Powell families. The necessity of perpetually discovering ways to rebuild fellowship and communion within this family is intensified by the family's relative isolation. All of *The Truest Pleasure's* major characters are related by blood or marriage, and nearly every scene is set on the family farm—with the exception of Ginny's several adventures to the Holiness services and her one business trip to town.

In his landmark study of yeoman farmers throughout the antebellum South, *Plain Folk of the Old South* (1949), historian Frank Owsley attributes the isolation of most southerners into family groups to the "rural environment of the Old South," which contributed to the relative isolation of kinship groups. According to Owsley, these extended families "worked together, hunted together, went to church and parties together, and expected to be buried together and to come to judgment together on the Last Day" (95). As Ronald Eller notes, throughout the Appalachian South, geography intensified such clannishness, as "houses were seldom constructed within sight of each other but, instead, were spread out, each in its own separate hollow or cove. Solitude and privacy were such dominant cultural values that they fostered dispersed settlement patterns and the continual penetration of the deeper mountain wilderness long after the passing of the frontier" (25–26). Several pages later, Eller discusses the "familism" that characterized Appalachian farming culture, observing that in "preindustrial Appalachia, as in most traditional rural societies, the family was the central organizing force of social life.... Obligations to the family came first, and this economic condition created intense family loyalties that not only insured the survival of the group, but also provided a strong feeling of security and belonging for individuals" (28–29). Not surprisingly, the two sets of values Eller attributes to Appalachians—familism on one hand and solitude and privacy on the other—often come into conflict, and this conflict underlies the broader tensions in both *The Truest Pleasure* and *This Rock.*

Ginny calls attention to her family's isolation, when she accompanies her father to town to talk with a lawyer about a property dispute, reflecting that it has been a year since she last visited town and that she "hated to go to town for it made [her] feel dizzy and lost to be among so many people" (257). The family's prosperity very much depends upon the farm's proximity to town, since nearly all of her husband's farming is "done for the village trade" (186). Tom sells to the mill workers the farm's surplus of corded wood, molasses, and hogs (186). While Ginny recognizes the importance of this revenue, she also at least partly appreciates the threat of the mill village and what it represents to her family's way of life. The way that the mill economy insinuates itself into the isolated subsistence farm economy and family structure is represented by the mill whistle, which blows not according to patterns of seasonal daylight but with the regularity of clockwork at seven a.m., noon, and mid-evening. The mill whistle pierces the quiet like "a hawk calling across the mountain" and it "washe[s] up the river valley" (186). Just as Tom comes to depend upon income from the mill, Ginny learns to depend upon the whistle to order their daily lives, until she realizes that "soon it come to seem like something we had heard all our lives" (186). Although the mill never provides a setting for the novel—indeed, Ginny points out that she has "never seen inside the cotton mill" (186)—its presence just over the mountain ridge points out that this is a society on the brink of major economic and social change.[1] Robert Morgan has confessed that he "and a lot of other people" are writing about "the mountain past," because they feel they "are very quickly losing it" and they "want to recapture it" (Harmon 14). In another interview, Morgan notes that he seems "to have been called to write about a world that's mostly gone now: Southern Appalachia of eighty, one hundred, one hundred and fifty years ago. Those lives were dominated by the church, the family, and marriage, and when you write about that world, you have to focus your story there" ("A Conversation" 70).

In order to understand the familial dynamics of this past world, it is necessary to explore its daily life, which is largely constituted by a rich variety of labors. One of the most persistent emphases throughout Morgan's fiction and poetry is work, which remains true in *The Truest Pleasure*. The novel recounts (often in exacting detail) the processes involved in a wide range of farm labor, including boiling molasses, pulling fodder, pressing cider, canning peaches, predicting the weather, trout fishing, birthing a baby, fighting a brush fire, fighting illnesses (in particular pneumonia and typhoid fever), building a spring house, and cultivating a wide variety of crops, including strawberries, melons, and corn. Very often these labors are collective, creating social opportunities for members of Ginny's extended family. On an occasion when she is canning peaches with her perennially feuding sister and sister-in-law, Ginny remarks, "I've noticed that when people work together they sooner or later get more friendly. It's natural that once you are sweating and straining together you begin to feel like a team. Even Lily and Florrie started to act agreeable as we worked that morning" (161). In the antebellum diary of North Carolina yeoman Basil Thomasson, farm work is described as a joint enterprise that involves members of multiple generations. In his Introduction to Thomasson's diary, Paul Escott observes that the family economy "functioned almost as a unit across two generations" (xix). Such is certainly the case on the Peace farm in *The Truest Pleasure*. When Tom Powell marries into the family and moves into the Peace homestead, he works tirelessly to achieve numerous improvements, and frequently Tom works with either his father-in-law or his brother-in-law. Furthermore, in a letter to her brother Locke, Ginny reflects on how when she looks at the yard, at the trees planted there by her great-grandfather and then pruned by her husband, she thinks about how "people work together across time, just as sure as if we was all together" (248).

If work provides a cohesive force within this family, it also frequently creates opportunities for interpersonal tensions and separateness. After Ginny delivers a child and later when she is bedridden with pneumonia, Tom hires her sister Florrie to come over and do the housework. Ginny suspects her sister and her husband of developing a sexual attraction—created by their working together—and, to prevent its further development, Ginny asks Florrie to leave and no longer work in her house. Whenever Tom is angry with Ginny, he works all the harder and stays away from home, working late into the evening, coming home to sleep separately in the loft above their bedroom. Stephanie McCurry has written insightfully about the ways that women's work was often undervalued on the yeoman farm.[2] In *The Truest Pleasure,* Morgan explores the deeper truth of how few people, regardless of gender, sufficiently value the work of a spouse or other family members. When Ginny thinks of Tom's work, she as often suspects him of greed for profits or resents his time away from home, as she does appreciate his work's contribution to the family. In fact, only after Tom's death is Ginny able to look beyond her resentments and accept his work as "gifts" (334).

On an occasion when Ginny again defies his wishes by leaving home to attend a Holiness revival, he threatens her life by blasting a shotgun into the air. In light of this scene, Tom's work provides a safety valve, allowing him—especially during the periods when he and Ginny are abstaining from sex with each other—to channel potentially violent and anarchic forces into the creation of further order. Notwithstanding these positive benefits, however, his work also contains powerfully destructive forces, especially when considered within the context of their marriage. His long absences from home exacerbate the alienation he and Ginny experience, making it easier for them to brood in their respective silences. On at least two occasions, his overzealousness for work (and greed for its profits) leads to violent devastation of land and flesh. Both events, one early in the novel and the other near its end, begin with his processing of sorghum into molasses, a hot, physically challenging job, but one that produces the majority of Tom's cash income. On the first occasion, Tom simply overreaches, attempting a job larger than he can physically handle alone; as a result, he falls into the boiling molasses, which burns his face, chest, and arms and attracts a swarm of yellow jackets, which begin feasting on the molasses and then end up stinging him after he tries to bat them away. Years later, Tom and his father-in-law make a batch of molasses during an autumn drought; against their better judgment, they try to produce one last batch of the season, only to let the fire escape into the grass and then into the forest, causing major damage but eventually burning itself out. In his efforts to contain the fire and save his property, Tom again overreaches, working so hard that he overheats and develops a case of cholera morbus, followed by a fatal bout with typhoid fever.

As the fire rages out of control, Ginny panics, trying to look after her children while seeking her elderly father in order to prevent him from overworking himself to the point of death. But Ginny's Pa understands his human limitations—a wisdom informed by his spiritual life. Just as he has never put the work that his son-in-law does into improving the property and maximizing a surplus for cash profits, he also is not willing to risk his life beyond reasonable limits to stop the unstoppable fire. Ginny finds him sitting in the spring, and they both survive the fire by bathing themselves. As they cool themselves with spring water, Ginny watches in awe as the fire rages overhead (288–89). Both Ginny and her Pa share the same Holiness faith, and this image of father and daughter together surviving the baptism of fire while administering to themselves the baptism of water is one of the most beautiful images in a novel full of such beauty. Unlike Tom, who vainly tries to fight nature, who resists the threat that nature brings to the order he has so many years labored to create, both Ginny and her Pa know the wisdom of not attempting to fight nature. This is the very same instinct that terrifies Tom but binds Ginny to her Pa and brother Joe in their shared experience of Holiness spirituality.

During her first brush arbor revival, Ginny feels herself transformed, allowing the joy and praise of creation in her to express itself, at the same time that she witnesses the "praise" of others express itself in ways natural to each individual. Ginny worships by "speaking in tongues," "shouting," and "holy dancing," while Ronnie Carter, "known as a barker," likes to "run out to a tree," grab it "with both hands" and howl "like a dog at the moon. Nobody knowed why he did it. It was his way of showing joy. Everybody has their own way of being happy" (190). Leaping George, whom Ginny describes as inhibited and withdrawn before a service, is moved by the Holy Spirit to "jump over stumps and chairs. He leapfrogged people praying and once at Crossroads he jumped all the way over the pulpit" (190). "I believe people have a taste for food and for loving," Ginny concludes, "but those are just echoes of the taste for divine love. Humans was put here to experience that love, and to praise" (191). Although Ginny enjoys sublime moments of meditation while wandering alone in nature, she has a natural hunger for the transformations she finds possible only in collective worship and under the conditions peculiar to the Holiness brush arbor services. For Ginny, religious worship services "always went better in the woods ... among the trees and elements. It was like houses and too much light killed the Spirit. There was a secret and a mystery to meeting in the woods. In the lanternlight you could feel the Spirit moving. It was good to get away from the greed and spite of everyday life" (189). In agreement, her father says, "They should build a rock church.... Except then it would get just like all the other churches" (15). Ginny's Pa understands that the humbleness of the brush arbor is an essential element in producing the necessary humility and receptivity among the worshippers, so that they can collectively open themselves to the Holy Spirit and to each other.

One of Ginny's physical responses to worship manifests bodily this humility. On the occasion of her first "fire baptism," once she has made her way to the preacher at the altar, she drops to the sawdust and begins wallowing on the ground. This is the sort of behavior that southern writers have enjoyed satirizing ever since Twain and George Washington Harris and other frontier humorists began lampooning religious revivals during the nineteenth century. But Morgan's account is utterly free of satire and a treatment of the worshippers as grotesques. Rather, he accepts the legitimacy of this form of worship and penetrates the gestures to understand the psychological state that accompanies the outward show. Reflecting upon her possession by the Holy Spirit, Ginny explains that the "only way to show humility was to wallow like a mare. I had to stretch out and shed my vanity.... Turning, I felt pulled underground, deeper and deeper into humility. Only by turning could I reach the center" (9). The allusions here to varieties of animal life gradually descend the evolutionary chain from a mare wallowing in the dirt, to a snake shedding its skin, to a worm burrowing in the earth. After collectively shedding their vanity and their inhibitions, the congregation, filled with the Spirit, gather down at the altar by Preacher McKinney, with their knees upon the earth. The preacher encourages them to squeeze together in a group hug and to adhere to the commandment that they "have love one to another." He then begins a prayer: "Lord, we will get right down here in the dirt in our humbleness to you.... We ain't got no pride, and our strength comes from you" (11). This humility is somewhat offset by the preacher's boasting of their exclusive access to the Spirit. In addition to rejecting the sufficiency of "water baptism" espoused by Baptists, he makes the humble nature of the brush arbor a point of pride: "The Spirit is right here.... It is not in some dryhide Baptist church and not in Greenville. It is not in some fine building, and not in Washington, D.C., or New York City. It is right here in this brush arbor tonight, and it is here to change our lives" (7). No doubt, it is such statements as these that elicit the ire of other members of the community and that result in its outlaw element setting fire to the brush arbor while the congregants are inside, shouting the challenge, "It's the baptism of fire" (13).

If Ginny's account of her own spiritual life convinces the most rabid skeptic that whatever she feels is not faked for outward show, her sister-in-law Lily, whom Ginny accuses of being "vainer about her clothes than any woman in the valley" (7), appears less free of suspicion, even though Ginny never suspects Lily or anyone else of being duplicitous during worship. When Lily walks toward the preacher "shivering and shuddering," while her "whole body [is] dancing in spasms and seizures," the act serves for Ginny as a clear demonstration that Lily has "cut ties to being stiff and vain, to being prideful and full of self-regard" (7). However, Lily's later explanation that she wears her best clothes to church "out of respect to Jesus and the Holy Spirit" (100) is the kind of line that might draw a snicker from those suspicious of the authenticity of Pentecostal Holiness worship. Likewise, after Ginny is first moved by the Spirit, Lily's affirmation that Ginny "had a true baptism" suggests the obvious possibility that such a baptism is often faked. In fact, the novel begins with a challenge to the services' authenticity made by Ginny's sister Florrie and her brother Locke (who, of course, shares a name with the great champion of rationalism). After Florrie asks if Ginny, Pa, Joe, and Lily are attending "the kind of service where women roll on the ground," Locke asks, "Who do they roll on the ground with?" (1). And, when Lily praises a new Holiness minister, saying that everywhere Preacher Carver goes "the number of saved increases" (101), Ginny's usually laconic husband, Tom, responds, "I've heard that everywhere he goes the population increases about nine months later" (102).

The confusion of sexual passion and religious ecstasy appears frequently in the worship services themselves. For example, following Ginny's fire baptism, when Preacher McKinney encourages the group hug, Ginny becomes aware of a hand squeezing her breast, although she can't see who it is and doesn't "much care" (12). "We was so close," she notes, "everybody was touching somebody. We swayed as one body when the preacher prayed" (12). Again, it is hard to read this scene and not be reminded of similar moments in camp meetings lampooned by Harris and Twain. But Ginny's account of her own spiritual experiences, even when they are charged with a powerful sexual subtext, is utterly devoid of such bawdy humor. Consider, for example, her description of a brush arbor service she attends after she has married and become a nursing mother:

> I guess I did a kind of dance, swaying among the people. I didn't notice I had moved across the sawdust to the front, still holding the baby. Jewel had woke up and screamed but I hardly noticed. Milk come out of my breasts and soaked down the front of my dress, but I didn't pay it any attention.
>
> It was only when I got to the front of the tent and turned that I saw how Tom looked at me. I was feeling the sweet inner burning of the Spirit. I felt I was floating up above my life. But Tom looked shocked and scared. He come forward and took Jewel, and jerked me by the wrist out of the tent into the dark [116].

Ginny's hunger for Holiness worship remains a major conflict in her marriage with Tom until his death. Looking back, she says, "I know he hated me for shouting in front of other people, dancing in front of other men. I know he felt betrayed in some intimate way" (195). Although Ginny declares that she has never been sexually interested in preachers, her dependence on the minister for "the spark" that ignites the worship service suggests that perhaps at least subconsciously the visiting ministers do become confused with paramours. When she explains why the preacherless services held in Joe's home failed, she says, "With just family and neighbors it never did take off. We needed a force from outside" (128). The same nearly universal human taboo against incest that charges the social outsider with sexual potency here provides the visiting preacher with the power to invoke the Holy Spirit. The adventure (sexual, spiritual, or otherwise) of the brush arbor services is further enhanced by their being the only frequent setting away from the farm that Ginny recalls in her narrative. Recalling the way she felt during one especially spirited revival, Ginny remarks, "It was like falling in love with everybody, being married to the world" (123). That this revival accompanies a period of bitter feuding with Tom helps to explain his feeling of abandonment.

Typically, when Ginny comments consciously on the similarity of sexual passion and religious ecstasy, she does so in the context of her relationship with her husband. On one occasion, they are making love the day after Ginny has read *The Song of Solomon*, and passages from the scripture pass through her mind while she is experiencing sexual ecstasy, prompting her later to reflect that "the thrill of loving was almost the same as communion with the Spirit" (130). This episode of lovemaking occurs during a "new stage" in Ginny and Tom's sexual relationship, when they move beyond lovemaking—as Ginny describes it—as merely "something our flesh did, only slightly connected to us as people. Now we met, at least at times, as the people we truly was" (131). This passage calls to mind Preacher McKinney's description of worship as "the communion of flesh with spirit" (5). Also, Ginny uses the language of faith to describe this new stage in their relationship, calling it "a new dispensation" (132).

If Ginny and Tom open to each other through shared sexual passion, outside the bedroom their differing values and methods of coping with everyday fears tend to close off lines of communication. Although she never shirks her share of farm work, Ginny repeats throughout the novel her belief that the purpose of life is to "praise" and to experience joy and pleasure. Tom, however, single-mindedly trusts hard work. She craves the ecstatic release from fear and pursuit of joy that accompanies Holiness worship, whereas he finds solace and safety in the accumulated fruits of labor. When she is frequently angry with her husband, Ginny accuses Tom's hard work as evidence of his greed. Control of the family savings becomes a major obstacle, and when Ginny gives money to a traveling preacher and to a family suffering from typhoid, Tom accuses her of destroying everything for which he has worked. Ginny recalls, "He acted like I had gone crazy and he couldn't trust me. He acted like I wanted to steal his money, to hurt him where he was most tender" (135). Afterward, Tom hoards his savings, and immediately after his death Ginny finds hidden in his loft the four hundred dollars he has worked to amass during his life. During a period of harmony in their marriage, Ginny finds herself helping Tom in the fields and thinking like him: "I thought of every squash as so many pennies, and every row as so many quarters. I saw green leaves turning into dimes, and gold roots and veins in leaves turning into silver dollars. Every bit of soil come to promise its secret of money" (173). Because such a view of nature is at odds with her usual pantheistic tendency, she more often sees his materialism as evidence of a lack of real faith. "Sometimes," she says, "I don't think he believes anything at all. I think he is trying to stuff all the wealth of the fields and weather into a bag of money.... But I know that's not really so, for he loves the place itself too, and the work itself" (245).

If only after Tom's death, Ginny does ultimately gain a sustained compassionate insight into her husband's rage for order. Weeks after she writes to Locke, who is working as a nurse in California, she receives a letter from her brother in which he tries to help her understand their mother's fear (and thus Tom's fear) of Holiness worship, which so depends upon the faithful completely surrendering control to the unpredictable movement of the Holy Spirit. The letter arrives after Locke witnessed a terrible earthquake and while Ginny is nursing her dying husband. Locke writes,

> I think the biggest problem we all have is our fear. We live in fear of sickness and pain, and big losses.... Almost everything we do is for reassurance. I guess what Mama feared most and Tom fears most is loss of control and reason. It scares them to see a husband or wife go out of control. If somebody that close to them can lose their willpower and dignity then they might also.
>
> We never understand another person's ecstasy. Watching intense joy in somebody else is repugnant to us, even somebody else's sexual pleasure is unsavory to us. And a fit of ecstasy at a service, the loss of control in speaking in tongues or rolling on the ground, must seem embarrassing as watching somebody in the spasms of sex. It could be seen as a loss of humanness, of the faculties that make us human.
>
> For somebody like Tom that is a price too great to pay. All his life he has felt little control over anything except his work. Sister, no one wants a spouse to escape to a place of their own [304–305].

Whereas Locke (and elsewhere Ginny) makes the connection between sexual and spiritual ecstasy, it is perhaps this very connection that most threatens Tom.

Ginny tries to explain to him her hunger for Holiness worship, saying, "The Lord wants us to be happy … not all troubled and angry. Not riled up most of the time" (96). He sarcastically retorts, "You mean like the Happyland colony?" (96). Ginny recalls the so-named group of freed slaves, who left Mississippi after the "Confederate War" to settle there in the mountains. And she remembers their leaders, a preacher and his wife, who were the "king" and "queen" of the "community they named The Kingdom of Happyland" (96). Tom has a more visceral memory of the settlement. As a boy he grew up near the community and would hear their nighttime meetings, and the "hollering and screaming" that accompanied their dancing (96). Ginny, out of sympathy with their style of praise, argues that perhaps they were "happy not to be slaves anymore," but Tom asserts that these "ordinary people," with whom he worked and respected "in the daytime," at night during their services "went wild" (96). "They was supposed to be Christians," Tom continues, "but they hollered and leaped around like crazy people. Sometimes the women would take down their dresses and dance naked, shaking theirselves in the lantern light. They used skulls and blood in their services. I think some of it was voodoo…. It was heathen stuff…. They looked like they was having fits" (97). Ginny shows tolerance, saying, "Everybody worships different," but she feels it necessary to tell her husband, "Don't nobody take off their clothes at our services…. At least I've never heard of it" (97). This latter qualification suggests that, based on her experience, nakedness at the Holiness services is not completely beyond the realm of possibility, if the Spirit were to move in that direction.

Just as Ginny suspects her mother of fearing "any display of joy" (240), she has heard other women say that "you wasn't supposed to show pleasure [during sex], or a man would take advantage" (227). Defiantly, she asserts her right to self-expression, saying, "I didn't care. I was thirty-six and felt like a girl…. I didn't care how much pleasure I showed" (227). Ginny's ability to abandon self-restraint, which Tom hates to witness at the public worship services, is arguably the very attribute that makes his wife such a pleasurable companion in bed. Similarly, although Ginny frequently criticizes the near monomania of Tom's farm labor, during sex she approvingly observes that "he put his mind to loving the way he did to other work. Everything he did was careful and right." This observation leads her to speculate that "Tom was special," or unique, in his lovemaking habits (88–89).

Just as Tom differs with Ginny and most of her family on the issue of religion, he suspects their loquaciousness of deceit, even if unintended. Contrary to the image of the taciturn Appalachian farmer (so typified by Tom), Ginny's Pa loves to talk and read—proclivities that his children have inherited. In the evening they frequently indulge in family stories and regularly read to each other from the Greenville newspaper reports from the Spanish-American War. Into this love of both print and oral cultures marries Tom, who is lulled to sleep in the evening by the music of his wife's voice as she reads the paper. Ginny reflects on the difference between Tom and the rest of her family:

> Tom saw words as commitments he did not want to make unless he had to. I think he felt any verbal commitment was over-commitment. I know he thought most talk was a mistake. "People get in trouble talking," he liked to say. "It's the tongue that destroys you."
>
> I think he believed human honesty was in the arms and hands, in a strong back. That's why he was such a good lover. He had confidence in anything done with his body. "Nobody can talk for ten minutes without telling a lie," he would say. I don't know where he had heard that, but he would repeat it from time to time. Since Pa and me and Joe and Florrie and Locke all liked to talk, it was an accusation [98].

Ginny's love of language is essentially the poet's love of the concrete words themselves. She recalls being young and "always falling in love with a word, or phrase, with a particular image or sentence" (126). Hours she would spend poring over words in a big Webster's dictionary her father brought home after selling hams in Augusta, Georgia. In those days she made "lists of words and facts" and thrilled at the way the "color and strangeness of a word would trigger a feeling," producing a "sweetness that stayed with" her (127). She recalls how one time she fell in love with the description of Christ's Transfiguration from the book of Mark. She searched for accounts of the Transfiguration in other gospels but discovered that "no other pattern of words had the same effect" and that, furthermore, with repetition the thrill associated with the words "wore off" (127).

Ginny's love of language is closely associated with both her spirituality and her love of nature. She recalls the day she "fell in love with the shoals" when she was "standing with her feet in the water" and it "was like the water was talking, quoting scripture or muttering a poem" (125). Unlike Tom's tendency to abstract nature into the financial gain he can extract from the land, Ginny is enamored of the physical world itself. And similarly, it is not the abstract idea conveyed by language but, rather, the music of the words and the sensory world they evoke that most appeal to her. Her love of language calls to mind Morgan's assessment of his own involvement with poetry early in his career, a time when he sought to write about "elemental things," about "simple objects" such as "metals" and "insects" ("Art" 47). "The ideal poem for me when I was twenty-five," he remarks, "would have been a poem that really evoked a sense of, say, evaporation, the elemental process" ("Art" 47). Paradoxically, he has also remarked that he "can't imagine poetry without some sense of worlds beyond the merely physical" and that "perhaps poetry is the unifier, seeing at once the spiritual and the physical" (Harmon 16). This same unifying impulse appears powerfully in Ginny, the lover of language, who savors the physical sensation of speaking in tongues while manifesting through the bodily act of speaking the presence of the Holy Spirit.

Just as Ginny only fully appreciates the gift of her husband's labor after his death, Tom seems not fully to appreciate the gift of his wife's voice, even though it is her capacity for expression that accounts for their union in the first place. According to Ginny's account, they became engaged after surviving what anyone acquainted with the rudiments of astronomy could only view as an unnaturally spectacular description of a meteor shower. After declaring that the meteors must be "a sign" and then failing to engage him in speculation about what the sign foretells, Ginny hopefully suggests that it could be a "sign for us," to which he laconically responds, "Could be." "And that," she concludes, "was our engagement" (53).

Similarly, later in their marriage, in what for Ginny must be the apex of their sexual lives together, she is so moved by passion that she begins speaking in tongues and then afterward realizes that this is the first time she has ever done so outside of a worship service. "It was a higher kind of talk," she recalls. "I didn't know what I was saying, but I saw what was visited upon me was a gift. 'Tom!' I said, and my mouth flew like a bird and my tongue soared. I gripped and sung out and didn't hardly know what I was doing. I was on a long journey that went on and on over banks and gullies, valleys and mountains of flowers. The whole world was coming to us in the dark" (178). Where she arrives at the end of this journey requires some explication. When she was a girl of seventeen and had still not menstruated, her father took her to a Native American healer, whose prescription involved giving her a secret name, which only she could ever know, and the advice of imagining herself as a "pigeon high on a tree or flying over the valley ... flying hundreds of miles, of flying close to the sun and over rivers" (68). When she is speaking in tongues at the climax of her passion with Tom, she reaches a moment of recognition:

> And then I saw what we had been going toward. Everything swung around like compass needles pointing in the same direction. It was in the eye of a pigeon setting high on a tree at the mountaintop. The eye was still as a puddle with no wind. It was still at the center of the whirl and clutter of things.
> "This is what was meant," I said.
> Tom still didn't say anything.
> "This is really the place," I said. "Ain't it?"
> "Yeah," Tom said. It was all he said, but it was enough.

Of course, without her private knowledge of her past, Tom cannot understand her question, but his simple affirmation and his acceptance of her speaking in tongues while they make love allows her to experience this discovery of self—within a sexual union—toward which her life has been moving. If outside the bedroom their temperaments are usually incompatible, inside the bedroom they become complementary. During lovemaking, the very aspects of each other's characters that most inflame the other become the source of shared joy.

Although the marriage of Ginny and Tom serves as the novel's primary focus, the contextualization of that marriage within the extended family is of at least equal importance. In an interview with *Image* magazine, Robert Morgan has remarked that community gives people "a greater intelligence" ("A Conversation" 71). This perspective is manifested in the conclusion of *The Truest Pleasure* as Ginny watches her husband die and is overwhelmed by anger and regret, which conspire to alienate her in her grief. The threat of despair and alienation are made more tangible by the fact that Ginny is the only person in the house awake during the early morning hours when Tom dies. She is rescued from despair largely by interpreting her current emotions within the epistolary dialogue she has recently pursued with her brother Locke, who is geographically separated from the family. Ginny initiated this dialogue with a letter she sent Locke prior to her husband's illness, in which she sought to understand Tom's resentment of her choice to attend Holiness revivals, just as Ginny and Locke's mother had opposed their father's delight in Holiness worship. Ginny's letter is a lengthy and nuanced appeal for understanding, and Locke's reply is an equally intelligent and comprehensive consideration of her questions. As Ginny meditates upon her brother's insights into her marriage, she is able to see for the first time how she has resisted considering her husband's work an act of service to the family. That she recognizes her error only after Tom's death adds to the pathos of the novel's ending, and yet the sadness is tempered by Ginny's triumph over fear and regret, by her ability—aided by family—to turn away from her own habitual anger toward her husband and to accept "his gifts" of work (334).

This Rock begins over a decade later, and now that Ginny has reached early middle age, work has become more important to her than sexual pleasure or even divinely inspired ecstasy. In the letter to her brother near the end of *The Truest Pleasure*, she shows how she had already been moving toward this readjustment of values: "There's great pleasure in loving, just like the poets said. But what keeps you going day after day through spurts and quirks, fits of temper and irritations, is the steady work" (241). Early in *This Rock* Ginny confesses guilt for shirking her duty as a mother when her children were young by indulging in the Pentecostal Holiness revivals that produced strife in her marriage. Even though she still yearns for this form of worship and for sexual love, she makes the decision not to pursue these desires in order more fully to dedicate herself to the labor of raising her children, especially her boys Moody and Muir, who are now navigating the treacherous passage from adolescence into adulthood.

Since first becoming a mother, Ginny harbored the dream that one of her sons would become a preacher, and when at the age of sixteen Muir embraces that ambition for himself, her allegiance to him grows stronger, whereas her quickness to judge her wayward older son, Moody, and to "expect almost nothing" of him (296), results in his progressively greater distance from the family and his sinking deeper into the outlaw trade of bootlegging. As the novel progresses, Muir temporarily abandons the dream of becoming a preacher only to replace it with the dream of single-handedly designing and building a stone church on the mountaintop, a plot twist Robert Morgan acknowledges being inspired by the life of Saint Francis ("A Conversation" 68). Meanwhile, Moody pursues his own journey, sinking to new depths of depravity and being nearly murdered by his boss, Peg Early, when she detects his practice of cutting her whiskey with water. Ultimately, though, inspired by his brother's dream of building a new church on the hill, Moody makes tentative steps toward greater social responsibility and toward seeking a renewed communion with his family. As in *The Truest Pleasure,* work and religion play crucial roles in producing a narrative dynamic built upon familial strife and reconciliation.

This Rock is told in the alternating first-person voices of Ginny and Muir, with the son's voice occupying the majority of its pages and his story dominating the action of the novel. This is an initiation story and one that hinges upon Muir's discovery of his true profession. Ginny broods over her favorite's many false starts, as he embarrasses himself attempting to preach, joins his moonshiner brother on a midnight haul in which he is nearly caught by the law, temporarily cripples himself while trapping fur in the wilderness beyond his farm, and fails in his courtship of the neighbor girl Annie Richards. Often Ginny can only guess at the extent of his failures, which Muir fully confesses to the readers: how he nearly drowns while trapping furs on eastern North Carolina's Tar River, becomes frightened away from pursuing the fur trade in Canada by the automobile traffic and gangsters he meets on his way northward through Ohio, and even how he makes a fool of himself while serving as pallbearer for a friend.

The scene at Hicks's funeral exemplifies the muted slapstick we often find in this novel. Muir is wearing his one suit, of which he is overly proud, only to have it drenched and muddied by the thunderstorm that douses the graveside funeral. When he slips in the mud, he loses hold of the coffin, and—because he inadequately screwed down the lid—Hicks's body rolls onto the muddy ground beside the grave. A scene that similarly combines slapstick humor with genuine pathos occurs earlier when Muir, the mountaineer most comfortable alone in the wilderness checking his traps, attempts to navigate the busy, noisy streets of Ohio's cities. In one particularly nerve-wracking stretch of road, he discovers an irresistible urge to relieve his bowels, and only after driving through miles of urban development does he find a suitable place to do so: a small stand of trees where he squats in the limited privacy the grove affords. Even the boat scene on the Tar River, although potentially fatal, is not without its comic moments. In each of these failures, Muir responds with a combination of humiliation and a child-man's impotent rage.

In both *This Rock* and *The Truest Pleasure,* anger management is a persistent theme and marker of maturation. Morgan distinguishes—by gender—causes and manifestations of anger. Ginny's anger simmers over weeks and months and arises primarily due to suspicions of disloyalty (when, for example, she witnesses an alliance forming between her sister and husband) and when her personal freedom is unfairly limited (as when Tom seeks to prohibit her from attending the Holiness services or when an attorney threatens her family's continued use of their own property). By comparison, Muir's anger flares when his work is frustrated, a motif established in the novel's opening pages, when as boys Moody destroys the log cabin Muir is building in the woods behind their house. Just as *The Truest Pleasure* portrays the ways that Tom is able to channel the potentially destructive force of anger into his labor, Muir discovers this strategy as well—especially in the novel's "second reading" when he begins clearing the mountaintop to build a church:

> There is a rage that comes on you when you look at woods that need to be cleared. Oak trees and poplar trees stand in the way of the open place you want to make. A man with an axe looks at the woods all around him ... and feels the tightening of a fight in his guts. It must be the way our grandfathers felt when they faced the raw wilderness a hundred years ago.
>
> The shadows of thickets make you mad. The must and mold of the leaf floor rile you. With your two hands and an axe you want to let in the sunlight. You want to chew up the forest and spit it out as mulch [214].

Among Muir's noblest character traits are those he inherited from his father: persistence and a capacity for hard labor. But, after he discovers that someone has destroyed his initial work on the church's foundation, he flies into a rage, comes home and brutally beats his drunken brother on Christmas Eve and then flees in humiliation into the wilderness.

His ambition is to travel west all the way to Black Balsam Mountain, far away from his family and community. The vision that turns him around bears a strong resemblance to the passage quoted at length above. At the furthest extent of his wandering, he comes upon a mountain that has been stripped of its timber by the Sunburst Lumber Company, leaving a mountainside that has "been slashed and looked ugly as a mangy dog" (251). Afterward, he encounters a company "ranger" who threatens him with a rifle, only later to fall victim to the company's own ingenuity. As the ranger climbs into the log flume to try to dislodge a length of timber, the workers above send another log down the chute, which fatally wounds the ranger, while Muir looks on passively. Muir's assessment of the effects of the timber industry on the landscape resonate throughout the scene of the logging disaster. He remarks, "They'd ruined the mountain, but they showed they was experts at their work" (253–54). This remark shows Muir's dawning realization that meaningful work requires more than ingenuity and effort and that one's spiritual approach to the work informs the outcome. He again demonstrates his fitful receptivity to this lesson when, working with Hank Richards on construction of the mountaintop church, he affirms the older, more experienced carpenter's lessons not to rush but to work with patient care and humility.

The death of the logging ranger and its result of turning Muir back on track toward his call to build the church echoes an earlier tragedy, which first led to the vision of the church on the hill. Muir arranges a date with Annie Richards to attend the circus, but before the show at the fairgrounds, they join the throngs along Main Street to watch the regional marching bands usher the circus into town. Jumbo the elephant is intended as the high point of the parade, but unfortunately Jumbo is suffering under what appears to be sustained stress—and likely torture—which culminates in Jumbo's trampling an automobile and then the auto's owner, as the man attempts to protect his property. The county and city officials become embroiled in a contestation of authority over the case, and several days later Muir and Annie and younger siblings return to watch the climax of events as a railroad crane is brought along the tracks to the fairground and a chain is placed around the elephant's neck, and then the crane is used to hoist the elephant off the ground, performing an execution by hanging. Just as the earlier parade of subdued and caged animals through Main Street demonstrated man's mastery over nature—the elephant's execution extends that message to the throngs of onlookers, who cannot help but be awed, as is Muir, by the technological power demonstrated by the railroad crane. Muir recalls seeing "the great body swung on the chain like a mountain tore loose, a hunk of the earth ripped out" (203). This comparison of a suffering creature to a destroyed mountain resembles Muir's description (quoted earlier) of a mountainside stripped of timber compared to a mangy dog. In both instances, Muir recoils at a vision of how man's labors can be channeled toward destructive purposes.

Early in *The Truest Pleasure,* Ginny and Tom's courtship exposes them to several destructive natural phenomena of a similar capacity to provoke awe. Together they survive the rush of an enraged bull, the pursuit of a tornado, and a singularly destructive meteor shower. In each case, the survived spectacle is a natural phenomenon that produces greater identification and interdependence between the two young people. And, ultimately, the meteor shower produces their engagement at Ginny's initiative. The courtship of Muir and Annie similarly exposes them to two destructive spectacles: the circus elephant's destruction of the auto and its driver, and then days later the execution of the elephant by hanging. However, unlike the natural phenomena encountered by Muir's parents during their courtship, the spectacles witnessed by Muir and Annie both result from mankind's desire to tame—and ultimately destroy—nature. Instead of bonding the couple, the elephant's execution has the opposite effect—because Annie insists that Muir prevent the destruction, and he is incapable of doing so. Instead of at least making a heroic gesture (as his father did while courting his mother by pursuing her hat into the pasture of the dangerous bull), Muir responds with impotence and horrified paralysis.

Only much later, while recovering from the spectacle by walking in the woods alone, does Muir begin to imagine a heroic response to the destructive force he has witnessed. After accidentally discovering Moody's stash of liquor and bootlegging money, the normally abstaining Muir drinks enough of the moonshine to help inspire his vision of a church on the mountain and to provoke his oath to himself and his God to build it. Another source of the vision is the recurring memory of the familiar "panic" (204) he witnessed in the elephant's eye prior to its trampling of the auto and its driver and then during its execution by hanging. Muir reflects upon the characteristics he shares with the elephant—notably his clumsiness and his tendency to "blunder around and hurt people" until, like the beast, he is "guilty" and "trapped" and "nobody is able to help" him (205). Muir's words demonstrate how fear and alienation lead to destruction, a truth that the actions of the novel's primary villain reinforce.

Preacher Liner currently presides as minister over the Baptist church the Powell family attends, a church Muir's grandfather built for the community, just as Muir would now renew that covenant with a new church on the mountain. However, ever since the Peaces were first ostracized for their attendance at the brush arbor Holiness revivals, Preacher Liner has continued to suspect the Peace and Powell families of potential mutiny (an apt metaphor, given the novel's frequent comparison of church structures to ships). Although he attributes his opposition to Muir's building of a new church to the fear that it could "splinter" the congregation (212), Preacher Liner's deeper motive is a fear of losing personal control, power, and status. When Muir tells the preacher of his plans, Preacher Liner leans over Muir "like he was pushing [him] away" (211). The preacher shifts around "in the dark the way a boxer or wrestler might" and warns Muir of the "sin of pride" and points out that his plans might be "the devil's work" and insists that he submit to "Baptist discipline" (212–13, 271). Referring to Muir's family's history of attending Pentecostal Holiness revivals, Preacher Liner says, "All my life I have fought off Pentecostals from breaking up my church, and I won't let it happen again" (214). That Preacher Liner is motivated primarily by fear is reinforced by his physical similarity to the terrified, destructive elephant. Muir repeatedly describes the preacher as a big man who uses his bulk to intimidate, and Muir says that Preacher Liner's eyes are "the color of tobacco juice" (212), the very same language he uses to describe Jumbo's tears (192) just before the elephant tramples the driver and his roadster.

In the pure Calvinist tradition, Preacher Liner's sermons rely upon fear tactics and threats of hellfire and brimstone, and such fear-inspired worship is indirectly responsible for the construction of a new church, even if Muir and Ginny do not fully understand it to be. Muir muses that "Preacher Liner acted like he was the boss. All I could think of was that a new church would change the spirit of the community, and Mama agreed. But she said the whole membership would have to vote, after I told them what I was planning" (209). In her own gentle way, Ginny warns her son of the sin of pride and the danger of repeating Preacher Liner's anti-democratic error of imposing his will upon the community. Even if Muir and Ginny do not fully realize it when Muir begins construction, the vision of a church on a hill represents more than the dream of inspiring geography and architecture; it represents a vision of redirected governance and worship for their congregation.

Of his own spiritual journey and his adolescent resistance to religion based upon fear, Robert Morgan remarks,

> From the time I was an undergraduate at Chapel Hill, I have been drawn to Episcopalian and Anglican services because of the great difference between a liturgical church and an evangelical church. I was raised in a church where the whole point of life was to go out and get people saved, to bring them into the flock. Even back then, I was attracted to the idea of a church where worship is not a matter of being saved or lost, but of everyday participation in a process ["A Conversation" 67].

Even if the Pentecostal Holiness and Baptist churches chronicled in these two novels both exemplify the "evangelical" church in which Morgan was reared, none of the major church-going characters in *This Rock*—with the notable exception of Preacher Liner—overtly practices a faith that is motivated by fear of perdition. Ginny seeks in religious worship ecstatic release and a heightened sense of communion with God and her fellow man, and despite her constant desire that her son Moody undergo a conversion experience, the conversion she desires for Moody involves a holistic life change and is not explicitly identified with religious conversion. Moreover, after the renegade Moody is shot and killed by a deputy sheriff, the substantial grief expressed by Ginny and Muir is in no way amplified by a fear for his soul's destiny. And their defiance of Preacher Liner's readiness to judge "the state of his soul" (297) or to determine "who is a Christian and who ain't" (298) constitutes a rejection of the evangelical doctrine Liner represents. When Fay, Ginny's youngest child, realizes that Moody won't be given a funeral in the Green River Baptist church, she is the only one in the family to articulate a fear that this exclusion may imply that he will "go to hell" (298). The reader is meant to assume that the other, older, members of the family have a faith that it is in some fundamental way too mature to share the young girl's fear.

Muir represents perhaps the furthest departure from the evangelical tradition. One of his childhood memories is of his mother speaking in tongues, which he found terrifying and likens to "the teeth of a saw in [his] ears" (102). He recalls bursting into tears at the sight of her holy dancing and later his inability to look at his mother for days (103). In his first attempt at preaching, he remarks that no Baptist minister ever "reads" a sermon, but when three years later he begins receiving the invitation to preach revivals, he painstakingly prepares sermons ahead of time, rather than trusting purely in divine inspiration. Furthermore, despite his rearing in the Baptist church and his ultimate service as minister to such churches, Muir's religious *ideas* more closely resemble those found within the liturgical tradition—in, for example, the Anglican church to which Morgan has been drawn. Despite its ostensibly friendly portrait of Southern Baptists, *This Rock* actually critiques the fundamental basis of the evangelical tradition, identifying Preacher Liner as the patriarchal, demagogic Baptist minister who drives and is driven by fear. Preacher Liner's fear-mongering ultimately produces destruction and divisiveness, despite his oft-proclaimed mission to prevent Muir from dividing the community with his heretical actions and ideas.

Muir's neighbor, Hank Richards, an experienced carpenter and a deacon at the church, joins Muir in his defiance of Preacher Liner and begins helping Muir build the church. Hank provides the encouragement that Muir's father might have offered, had he lived, and he provides the example of an experienced worker—physically and spiritually. Hank encourages Muir to give preaching another chance, proclaiming that a "preacher don't have to be perfect.... Nobody in this world is perfect. A preacher only gives what he has, all of what he has.... What a preacher is, and what a preacher does, is as important as what he says in the pulpit.... For a preacher his whole life is his witness and his sermon" (302). In his neighborly helpfulness and in his emphasis in this advice upon good works and right action, Hank reflects the values of the liturgical church, as opposed to the evangelical church's emphasis upon right belief and the rhetorical power of the Word as manifested in the preacher's ability to win converts.

Although Moody never actually goes so far as to help Muir build his church, he does begin to applaud from the sidelines Muir's willingness to undertake such an audacious dream and to do so in opposition to the wishes of authority figures such as Preacher Liner and the board of deacons. After the foundation of Muir's church is destroyed, Moody even pursues and challenges the culprits, whom he alone understands to be established bootleggers in the region, men who resent his taking black market share from them. His confrontation results in his accidental killing of the rival bootlegger Zack Willard, and subsequently Moody flees from the law, only to be shot down by a deputy sheriff after hiding for weeks in the mountain fastnesses. After receiving the news of her son's death, Ginny responds with the grief-stricken and Calvinistic statement, "Moody's anger was in his blood.... It was like all his life I had seen this moment coming" (296). Indeed, in her account of his childhood delivered throughout *The Truest Pleasure*, Moody's one recurring statement is of an eager desire to shoot outlaws. In becoming an outlaw himself, it seems, he finally found his opportunity. But when Moody invites his own demise by pointing a pistol at a deputy sheriff—who has broken his promise not to follow Moody's cousin U.G. into the wilderness after the outlier—the reader is invited to question society's clear delineations of outlaw and law-keeper.

Moody's ghost lingers in the years ahead, challenging his family's and community's inclination to dichotomize humanity as sinners and saints. Long after Muir preaches Moody's funeral in the unfinished church, the construction of which Muir will eventually abandon, Ginny and her neighbors report seeing or hearing Moody around the abandoned structure on the mountaintop. The ghost's "snicker" resembles for Ginny the way Moody used to laugh "to show how bad he was" (321–22). The presence of such laughter within the church produces a dissonance that Ginny continues to explore throughout the novel's epilogue, observing how with time the unfinished church is said to be "haunted" and then later "cursed." Moody's life and death force Ginny to confront her own tendency to accept the clear dichotomy of Muir as the obedient, hard-working child and Moody as the wayward, lazy one, and she begins to understand her own complicity in producing this dichotomy. Her final words of the novel observe in all people this general tendency to dichotomize; in an effort to understand how the church her son built came to be called cursed, she observes, "I think people want to believe there is places in the world that is cursed. It reminds them there is things they can't see with their eyes wide open in broad daylight, and makes them feel other places may be blessed" (323).

This human tendency to dichotomize and to do so as a pretext for destructive violence—either physical or ideological violence—underlies the evangelical church's basic dogma of heaven and hell. Within its self-identified mission of saving mankind from hell is a desire to elevate its own membership to a status of ultimate privilege. Preacher Liner upholds this sense of the Baptist church's mission when he prohibits Moody's funeral service from being held in Green River Baptist Church, arguing that the church has to "take a stand against lawlessness" (298). Preacher Liner points out that Moody was not a member of the church and that, furthermore, neither is Ginny. Upon checking church records, he has discovered that her membership was never reinstated after it was revoked years earlier for her attendance at Pentecostal brush arbor services. Despite Preacher Liner's repeated emphasis throughout the novel that he will not allow Muir, in building the new church, to divide his congregation, it is the preacher himself who achieves this destructive end.

After Preacher Liner bars the Powells from holding Moody's funeral in their church, Muir declares that he will preach the service himself in the church he is building on the hill, a gesture that Ginny finds symbolically appropriate, since like Moody's maturation, the new church is unfinished (300). In his address to the group gathered to pay their last respects to Moody, Muir affirms that there is "a great lesson to be learned from Moody's life and from his death" (309), and certainly a large measure of that lesson is the error of dividing a community with an evangelical theology devoted to placing human beings into categories of "saved" and "damned." Muir tells the mourners that Moody "was a sinner, as each and every one of us is a sinner.... The good news, the gospel, is that there is grace for us all, and forgiveness for us all, and love for us all. Not just for the pious and perfect, but for the liars also, for the cheaters, and for the doubters, for the violent and them tore by anger and fear and hate" (309). These last mentioned sins are ones that Muir knows intimately, as he must understand his own complicity in his brother's death. By his violent attack upon his drunken and sleeping brother on Christmas Eve, in which he falsely accused Moody of destroying the new church's foundation, Muir arguably initiated Moody's crusade to discover and punish the true offenders.

While preaching Moody's funeral sermon in the unfinished church, Muir realizes that the purpose of a sermon is to "spirit up and strengthen people. There wasn't no other reason to preach.... A sermon was to bring us together in a feeling of community and fellowship. A sermon was to show people how they supported each other and was important to each other. A sermon was to show people how they could be sustained, how they could be better people" (314). Were Preacher Liner present to hear Muir's sermon, he would no doubt consider it highly heretical. As his own sermons demonstrate, the primary purpose of a sermon within the evangelical tradition is to make clear to mankind its utter depravity and need of God's grace, provoking repentance and salvation. Muir's first attempt to preach, at the age of sixteen in the Green River Baptist Church, demonstrates the effects of that church's theology; fully ego-invested, Muir dreams of distinguishing himself as a big voice in the community (and of winning Annie Richards's affection). But, at the same time, he fears failure and humiliation. When in the back pew Moody loudly passes wind, Muir's fears choke him and he leaves the pulpit mortified and then for weeks distances himself from the congregation, while they will continue to hear Preacher Liner clarify for them Sunday after Sunday the individual choice between heaven and hell, between sanctification and sin, between saintly success and abysmal solitary failure.

By contrast, when he preaches Moody's funeral sermon, Muir overcomes his self-consciousness by becoming "part of a ceremony. I was not there as myself only," he realizes, "but as a minister in the ceremony of the funeral. Whatever I said, it was the ritual of the funeral that was important.... It was the power of the occasion, and the ancient words and everlasting truths, that was important" (307). This statement echoes Morgan's personal affirmation of the liturgical service with its emphasis on "everyday participation in a process" that defines the community of believers. Muir's sermon's emphasis on a shared ritual also echoes Morgan's more general interest in preserving a connection to the processes of farm work from a century ago. Just as the participant in the liturgical service reenacts the rituals practiced by the faithful centuries earlier, following the old-time practices of farm labor enacts what Morgan recognizes as life's "sacramental" possibilities, of which his readers are made more fully aware by their vicarious participation in both religious and labor practices. In an interview with *Image* magazine, he asserts,

> I think that people at their best feel their lives are sacramental. To write about people at their best, you have to show that their marriages, their work, and their cooperation with other people are sacramental. Love, after all, is both a physical and a spiritual thing.
>
> I think one of the things we're in danger of losing because of the way we live in the contemporary world—sitting at our computers, driving on the expressway, going to the big shopping malls—is knowing who our physical neighbors are. At their very best people are not just individuals, but part of the family and the community. The community gives them a greater intelligence. Once people learn to be of service to others, they've risen to a new level. Escaping from fear and mere selfishness is what humanity is about ["A Conversation" 71].

Although Morgan says that he was attracted to the liturgical services of Anglican and Episcopal churches he attended after leaving the mountains to attend college, his fiction clearly demonstrates the liturgical elements of the evangelical services he attended growing up on Green River. The tension between the evangelical and liturgical aspects of these services expresses itself in one of the final images Ginny leaves the reader with in *This Rock*'s epilogue. According to Ginny, coon hunters report hearing noises around the unfinished church on the mountaintop, which breeds rumors about the nature of those haunting noises: "Some said it was the voice of a preacher hollering about fire and damnation. Others said it was voices singing like a choir from long ago still harmonizing from the grave" (321). In these two possibilities, the raging, evangelizing, alienating, solitary preacher is contrasted with the communal and "harmonizing" voices of a choir, singing in the same voices heard generations ago, preserved intact to sustain the contemporary listener and to inspire in her a vision of community.

Ginny's and Muir's participation in the life processes of their community results in Muir's abandonment of his work on the church in the spring of the year following Moody's winter funeral, when both he and his mother realize, "[T]he fields had to be broke if we was to eat" (319). Throughout the following summer, Muir spends any spare time from farm work not building the church but reading his Bible and constructing the sermons he will preach at the various area churches that issue invitations after word spreads of his moving sermon at his brother's funeral. Only after renouncing personal ambition for the pulpit does he genuinely hear "the call" to the ministry. Ginny offers her assessment of his first revival sermon, preached months after Moody's funeral, remarking that, despite his inexperience, you "could see he had something. He had a spark in his voice that connected with the congregation. And he got the rhythm of speaking, which is the best sign of a true preacher" (320). As in *The Truest Pleasure,* here again Ginny is most moved by the sensory experience of the Gospel, by the hearing of the poetic rhythm of the language, more than the ideas contained therein. And she betrays the evangelical's emphasis upon salvation, attributing as evidence of Muir's early promise in the pulpit that "four people was saved ... and three was reclaimed" (321).

The gospel account of the Transfiguration provides for Ginny and Muir a shared source of inspiration while delineating the differing values of their personal faiths. As previously mentioned, in *The Truest Pleasure,* Ginny recalls how the account of the Transfiguration from the Gospel of Mark was her favorite girlhood scripture, the words themselves possessing a magical transformative power, while the same account found in the different language of the other synoptic gospels provided her little inspiration. Muir begins his preaching career with the failed sermon at Green River Baptist, preaching on the same subject, but basing his message on the account found in the book of Matthew and emphasizing not the Transfiguration of Christ but Peter's response to it, which was to propose the erection of three tabernacles, honoring Jesus, Moses, and Elijah (*This Rock* 19, 271). Ginny's spiritual journey leads her repeatedly to seek an elevated, spiritually clarified view of life and community; Muir's journey leads him relentlessly to seek his proper profession, the way he can best work to serve his community.

The tension between Ginny's and Muir's personal faiths reflects a deep, pre–Christian dichotomy, between Dionysian and Apollonian inclinations. Ginny seeks intoxication with the Spirit and expression of her natural impulses in the night-time brush-arbor services. Her words of praise for God and creation are spontaneous and beyond her control. By contrast, Muir, like his father, seeks relentlessly to impose order on creation. He seeks to create order in language in the preparation of sermons, and he resists entropy in building his church by moving the stones from the creek bed to the top of the mountain. In contrast to the brush arbor and the evening services held there, the stone church Muir builds is high on the mountaintop, close to the heavens and bathed in sunlight.

In the same way that Ginny's and Muir's explorations of faith are in dialogue with each other, and just as their alternating narratives throughout *This Rock* provide a deepening understanding of the world of that novel, *The Truest Pleasure* and *This Rock* provide a richer experience when considered as two parts of a whole. If *The Truest Pleasure* chronicles a wide range of farm labors, *This Rock* takes as its principle theme a celebration of labor, of human endeavor. Whereas the former novel investigates the relationship of sexuality and work within a family, sexual desire in the latter is thoroughly sublimated, as Muir channels his desire for Annie Richards into his pursuit of a proper profession. *This Rock* serves as a sequel to *The Truest Pleasure* in the best sense—offering an antiphonal call-and-response, never merely duplicating but always balancing, echoing but challenging. Each novel deepens the other's inquiry of those timeless questions of faith and work and body and spirit. Although either novel stands alone as a worthy object of study, read together they achieve—as Morgan says of individuals within a community—"a greater intelligence."

Notes

1. For a helpful introduction to the economic and social changes brought to western North Carolina with the advent of the textile industry, see Jacquelyn Dowd Hall, et al., *Like a Family: The Making of a Southern Cotton Mill World* (Chapel Hill: University of North Carolina Press, 1987); and Ronald Eller, *Miners, Millhands, and Mountaineers: Industrialization of the Appalachian South, 1880–1930* (Knoxville: University of Tennessee Press, 1982).

2. See Stephanie McCurry, "Producing Dependence: Women, Work, and Yeoman Households in Low-Country South Carolina," in *Neither Lady nor Slave: Working Women of the Old South*, eds. Susanna Delfino and Michele Gillespie (Chapel Hill: University of North Carolina Press, 2002), pp. 55–71.

Works Cited

Chappell, Fred. *Look Back All the Green Valley.* New York: Picador, 1999.

Eller, Ronald. *Miners, Millhands, and Mountaineers: Industrialization of the Appalachian South, 1880–1930.* Knoxville: University of Tennessee Press, 1982.

Escott, Paul D. Introduction. *North Carolina Yeoman: The Diary of Basil Armstrong Thomasson.* By Basil Armstrong Thomasson. Athens: University of Georgia Press, 1996.

Hall, Jacquelyn Dowd, James Leloudis, Robert Korstad, Mary Murphy, Lu Ann Jones, and Christopher B. Daly. *Like a Family: The Making of a Southern Cotton Mill World.* Chapel Hill: University of North Carolina Press, 1987; New York: Norton, 1989.

McCurry, Stephanie. "Producing Dependence: Women, Work, and Yeoman Households in Low-Country South Carolina." *Neither Lady nor Slave: Working Women of the Old South.* Eds. Susanna Delfino and Michele Gillespie. Chapel Hill: University of North Carolina Press, 2002. pp. 55–71.

Morgan, Robert. "The Art of Far and Near: An Interview with Robert Morgan." With Robert West. *The Carolina Quarterly,* 49.3 (Summer 1997) pp. 46–68.

_____. "A Conversation with Robert Morgan." Interview with Sheryl Cornett. *Image: A Journal of the Arts & Religion,* 43 (September 2004): pp. 65–76.

_____. "Conversation with William Harmon." 1990. *Good Measure: Essays, Interviews, and Notes on Poetry.* Baton Rouge: Louisiana State University Press, 1993. pp. 158–70.

_____. *Gap Creek.* Chapel Hill, North Carolina: Algonquin, 1999.

_____. *This Rock.* 2001. Rpt. Scribner's, 2002.

_____. *The Truest Pleasure.* 1995. Rpt. Chapel Hill, North Carolina: Algonquin, 1998.

Owsley, Frank L. *Plain Folk of the Old South.* Baton Rouge: Louisiana State University Press, 1949.

The Work of Love in *Gap Creek*

Martha Greene Eads

In reflecting on his career as university teacher, poet, and novelist, Robert Morgan confesses that he "went off to college to escape the hard work of the mountain farm" (Bizarro and Bizarro 181). Born in 1944, Morgan grew up in the Green River community near Asheville in western North Carolina, raising pole beans with his parents and his sister. The detailed accounts of work his poetry and fiction provide come from his first-hand knowledge of carrying water, tending field crops, and slaughtering hogs and chickens on a one-horse farm—chores he thought he was leaving behind when he enrolled at Emory College at Oxford at age sixteen. After transferring to North Carolina State University to study mathematics and engineering and then to the University of North Carolina to graduate with a BA in English, Morgan earned an MFA in creative writing at the University of North Carolina at Greensboro in 1968. He has taught poetry- and fiction-writing at Cornell University since 1971, where he has been surprised by "how often [he] returned to descriptions of work and narratives about work." He explains, "[O]ver the years, I got so interested in describing how people do work, how they experience work, what we might call 'the poetics of work,' that it occurred to me that work is our most definitive activity, that we define ourselves through our work, not through our leisure activities" (Bizarro and Bizarro 181–82).

Among the many characters who illustrate Morgan's conviction about work's significance, Julie Harmon Richards, the protagonist of his 1999 novel *Gap Creek*, is perhaps the most memorable. Seventeen-year-old Julie falls in love with Hank Richards at first sight and marries him after a one-day courtship and a month-long engagement. She is ill at ease during their first meeting, thrilled by his good looks and obvious physical strength but embarrassed for him to see her barefoot and cutting wood. Julie hopes that Hank will be a partner in if not a rescuer from the back-breaking work she has had to do since her father developed consumption and died. "Hank's look," she confides to the reader, "filled me with something that was sweeter than the sweetest sleep when you are tired" (36). Julie quickly learns, however, that her first year of marriage to Hank will be anything but restful. By the end of the book's third chapter, a little less than a quarter of the way through the novel, she says, "Marriage was different from what I expected. Like all girls I imagined something wonderful, and it was wonderful, in most ways, but in different ways from what I had thought. Mama had always said that marriage is like everything else: it is work, hard work" (48).

In making Julie's marriage the site of her hardest work, *Gap Creek* places her in a world in which physical labor becomes redemptive. Although he never romanticizes "the hard work of the mountain farm" in *Gap Creek*, work that he himself left behind in becoming a Cornell professor, Morgan nevertheless communicates a keen appreciation of its benefits. Julie matures because she is able to tap emotional and spiritual resources that are increasingly hard to come by in contemporary urban and suburban settings: the disciplines wrought by performing hard physical labor over time as well as practical forms of support from neighbors in a rural community.

Gap Creek's appreciative treatment of the work of farming in community illustrates philosopher Norman Wirzba's argument in "Vocation in Pianissimo: The Loss and Recovery of Vocation in Contemporary Life." Wirzba points out that "vocation (from the Latin *vocare*, which means 'to call') refers to a person's calling and thus presupposes a life lived in response to a summons (vocation) from another" (16). Wirzba extols Martin Buber's vision of the authentic life as "dialogical": "one in which the lives of others—whether plant, animal, human, or divine—intersect meaningfully with our own so that the course of our living is adjusted to be more responsive to their rightful claims and needs" (17). Warning that the self-absorption contemporary Western culture promotes makes listening to others difficult, Wirzba explains that the pursuit of professional success keeps people on the move and thus never "beholden or accountable to a reality—whether community, region, or God—greater than [them]selves" (17). In particular, Wirzba warns against urbanization's "overriding temptation ... to forget that we are biological beings enmeshed in biological processes that are vulnerable to exhaustion and destruction" (18).

Robert Morgan appears to agree with this assessment, having stated in a 2004 *Image* interview that "one of the things we're in danger of losing because of the way we live in the contemporary world—sitting at our computers, driving on the expressway, going to the big shopping malls—is knowing who our physical neighbors are" (71). He continues:

> At their very best people are not just individuals, but part of the family and the community. The community gives them greater intelligence.... I think in our society we feel a great fear of other people—because it's a dangerous society sometimes—and we've lost the sense of community that includes service to others, working together. Once people learn to be of service to others, they've risen to a new level. Escaping from fear and mere selfishness is what humanity is about [71].

In *Gap Creek*, he provides a corrective to this situation, showing through Julie how the hard work of farming attunes an individual to her natural environment and subsequently makes her responsive to it and to the people around her. In this setting, Julie's marriage refines her character further, presenting her with striking challenges, but with blessings as well.

Basing its plot on the lives of his maternal grandparents, Morgan situates *Gap Creek* on isolated farms in the Blue Ridge mountains at the turn of the last century. In her parents' home and then on the Pendergast farm where she and Hank settle after their marriage, Julie Harmon Richards faces continual reminders of her "enmeshment in biological processes that are vulnerable to exhaustion and destruction" (18). Not only must Julie tend crops, care for animals, and chop wood to stay warm in winter, but she also watches as intestinal worms strangle her little brother Masenier. In *Gap Creek*'s opening lines, Julie declares, "I know about Masenier because I was there. I seen him die" (1). By the end of the second chapter, young Julie has also witnessed her father's torturous death from tuberculosis. After she marries, she faces fire, flood, and childbirth, all in the midst of carrying out her ongoing farming duties. Because she is so much at the mercy of her natural environment, Julie must respond to the call of crops, livestock, family members, and neighbors. The work of responding often exhausts her, but it also disciplines her and gives her a deep sense of purpose.

When *Gap Creek* opens, Julie has been doing hard work for years, work that her parents use to define her role in the family. "Whatever man marries you will be the lucky one," Julie's papa says, "[f]or you're the best of my girls, the best one" (21). Her mother is more matter-of-fact about Julie's bearing more of the family load than her sisters do. "Julie can work like a man," she declares on one occasion as the teenager unloads firewood (4). When Julie questions her father's plan to have her help him carry the gravely ill Masenier to a doctor down the mountain, her mother says, "[Y]ou're the strongest one in the family, and everybody has to do what they can" (8). Later, when Julie informs her newly widowed mother that she has accepted Hank's marriage proposal, the older woman wonders aloud, "Who is going to do the work around here?" (48). Eventually, her mother relents, and her genuine concern for Julie's well-being becomes evident even as she frets over losing her best laborer.

Julie has internalized her parents' expectations, taking pride in her role even as she resents it. Repeatedly, she tells the reader that some task "fell to me" or "was up to me" (3, 18, 23, 23, 28, 32, 81) and that she might as well get on with doing it (18, 33, 57, 60, 74, 81, 284). She takes grudging satisfaction in providing her parents and siblings with firewood (4) and journeying in bitter winter to fetch cornmeal with her older sister Lou, the only other family member who will take on "outside" chores (5). She stubbornly carries out tasks she dreads, such as hauling her dying brother down the mountain. "I was still mad that I had to carry him," she recounts, "and that give me more strength" (10). Still, she recognizes ruefully that the work she does may disqualify her from marrying. She tells Lou that she hopes no man ever sees them using the crosscut saw "[b]ecause he would never think of us as ladies.... I don't want to be looked on like a field hand" (20). Their conversation continues:

> "Maybe that's what some man would want," Lou said.
> "No man that I would want," I said.... "Any man that just wanted a woman who could cook and bring in firewood would either be a cripple or too old to be any count" [20].

Julie's observations are purely speculative at this point; she stays too busy to primp, much less to enter a courtship. "[W]hat was the good of thinking about boys when Papa needed me to help him," she wonders, "and my hands was so rough from holding an axe or shovel or hoe handle I didn't want any boy to see them, much less hold them and feel the calluses and swelled knuckles" (22). When Papa dies, Julie seems destined to remain single in order to become the head of the Harmon household.

Julie is too naïve to realize that her willingness and ability to work make her just the kind of woman handsome Hank Richards wants to marry. Julie recounts that when they first met, her "hair had come unpinned when [she] wiped the sweat off [her] forehead. [Her] face was hot and there was big rings of sweat under [her] armpits" from pulling the crosscut saw (33). Even so, Hank tips his hat and gives her a look that signals keen interest. When he shows up at the Harmons' church a few days later and accompanies the family home for Sunday dinner, Julie's awkwardness does not dissuade him. "You are an unusual person," he tells her. "I couldn't think of any way I had been unusual except to splash coffee on his britches," Julie confesses, but she accepts his kiss (42). As they walk around the Harmon farm, Hank asks about the well-tended fields, "Who did all that work?" When she tells him, he replies, "You will make somebody a good wife" (45). Her response reveals her hopes: "You will make somebody a good husband" (44). She confides in the reader, "I hoped he didn't think I had cut all the tops in the cornfield by myself. I was a little ashamed of all the hard work I had to do" (45). Julie never dreams that for Hank, her resourcefulness is not a source of shame but rather an indication of her being an especially promising marital prospect.

Of course, Julie sizes up Hank as a worker, too. The best-looking man Julie has ever seen, Hank is "tanned dark from working in the fields all summer. But the thing that first caught [her] notice was his shoulders. He had the straightest, widest shoulders, and you could tell how powerful he was, and how much he could lift" (33). After Sunday dinner during Hank's first visit, Julie fantasizes about working alongside him. She says, "For I knowed that more than anything in the world I wanted to be married to Hank Richards. I wanted to live in a house with just him and me, and I wanted to help him work in the fields and raise chickens and pick apples to dry in the sun for winter. It seemed too much to hope for that I could be with him day after day, night after night" (44). When he offers to come help slaughter the Harmons' hog, Julie chooses not to reveal that she is capable of doing the work herself. Having a strong man's help promises to be a welcome relief.

The haste with which Hank and Julie marry and move away takes them far from the Harmon household by hog-killing time, but Hank fails to help Julie with that task when they are newlyweds rooming with the cantankerous Mr. Pendergast. From the outset, their living arrangement is far harder on Julie than on Hank, for he leaves for work in a brick-kiln each day while she earns their room and board by cooking and cleaning for their lewd landlord. Having to butcher Mr. Pendergast's hog without Hank's help, however, reveals just how sorry Julie's lot is. Although he says that both he and Julie will help Mr. Pendergast slaughter the animal, Hank goes to the kiln, and Julie ends up taking the lead in the gruesome process. In the midst of describing the event, Julie complains briefly, "I'd always hated butchering hogs, and here I was married and doing it again" (83). When Mr. Pendergast marvels that he has "never seen a woman work like you," Julie responds, "Work ain't nothing but work" (84). Even though she resents doing the heavy jobs she thought she would escape after marrying, Julie never shirks.

Hank's visiting mother, Ma Richards, reveals how Hank's upbringing has made him less responsible than Julie. Over lunch during a break from rendering lard during hog-killing day, Ma Richards tells Julie,

> "I spoiled Hank because he was so little.... I fed him better and never made him work hard as the other boys. That's why he growed up so big." "Hank works hard," [Julie] said.
>
> "He works hard, but he don't finish what he starts," Ma said. "He loses his temper too easily. The hard work is staying with a job till it's done" [90].

Ma's words prove prophetic, as Hank's lack of "stick-to-it-iveness" becomes the source of some of his and Julie's most serious problems.

Although Julie is often disappointed to find herself working alone and even harder than she did before marriage, work nevertheless provides her with certain satisfactions. On her first morning at Mr. Pendergast's, for example, she is initially discouraged by the prospect of living in and caring for his filthy house. She considers going home to her mother and sisters, almost wishing she "could go out and work in the fields or woods.... It was the thought of work that cleared [her] head a little. If [she were] going to have to work so hard anyway," she muses, "[she] might as well be working for Hank and [her]self.

[She] might as well work where [she] was, now that [she] was down on Gap Creek" (57). After making the bed (which Mr. Pendergast had mischievously rigged to collapse during the newlyweds' first night together), Julie takes on her most daunting task: doing the old man's nasty laundry. She describes its ardors in detail:

> It took me four trips just to carry Mr. Pendergast's clothes out to the wash table. With my arms loaded I tried not to smell all that sour cloth and soiled long handles. But when you have a filthy job the only thing to do is jump in and get it done. Won't hurt your hands to get them dirty; you can always wash them. The quicker I got the clothes in the boiling water the quicker I would be done....
>
> Much as you hate it, washing makes you feel you're starting out new. You have put your face in the smoke and steam, and your hands in the dirty slick water. And then you lift the pieces out and rinse them in fresh water and wring them out in the wind....
>
> When the washing was done I felt a little better. For even Mr. Pendergast and his grumpy manners couldn't keep me from getting things done. I didn't know what to say to him, but if washing his stale clothes was part of my job, then I had done it. If waiting on him was part of my married life, then I had got it started this morning [60–61].

Having long seen herself as someone who "gets things done," Julie's characteristic conscientiousness in her new role as housewife enables her to tackle an exceedingly unpleasant task.

Morgan suggests that Julie's labor on this occasion is somehow transfigurative. He has Julie recount, "The washing hung on the line like a whole army marching in the sunlight. Where the underwear hung and the shirts hung it looked like angels and not soldiers. But they didn't make any noise. The sun behind the cloth made them blinding" (62).[1] Devotional writer Kathleen Norris makes similar observations in her 1998 book *The Quotidian Mysteries: Laundry, Liturgy and "Women's Work,"* writing, "As for laundry, I might characterize it as approaching the moral realm; there are days when it seems a miracle to be able to make dirty things clean. I once wrote an article on laundry, specifically the joys of hanging clothes on the line to dry, and sent it to the *New York Times Magazine*" (15). Norris elaborates:

> Even if we do not make ... glorious poems out of our ordinary experiences, arranging Easter lilies or making salad, we are free to contemplate both emptiness and fullness, absence and presence in the everyday circumstances of our lives. No less a saint than Therese of Lisieux admitted in her *Story of a Soul* that Christ was most abundantly present to her not "during my hours of prayer ... but rather in the midst of my *daily* occupations" [emphasis added] [14].

Although he does not present Julie's doing laundry in such explicitly religious terms, Morgan uses the washday scene to illustrate his claim that "insofar as we have any wisdom, it's probably in our work—the way we sustain ourselves, the way we get through, is in the work we do and in the satisfaction of a job well done—probably the greatest satisfaction that people have.... It's their work that gives them a sense of who they are—of their worth—and probably helps them to get through day after day" (Bizarro and Bizarro 182).

Work is the most consistent element, day after day, in the next year of Julie's life. When she becomes pregnant and battles morning sickness, she continues to find surprising satisfaction in heavy physical labor. In this scene, Morgan establishes more overtly the link between Julie's labors and her spiritual life. Describing the pleasure she takes in scrubbing the floor, Julie says, "It made me feel strong to get down on my knees on those rough boards. It was like a morning prayer, kneeling on the cold boards and crawling backwards to rub away dirt with the rag. That's when I felt how much it meant to have a home, a place to live in day after day and night after night" (122). As much as she dislikes her mother-in-law, Julie embodies Ma Richards' declaration that "the good Lord made the world so we could earn our joy, … [b]ut it's no guarantee we'll ever be happy" (90). Julie seldom experiences the kind of happiness most twenty-first-century readers would seek, but she does find satisfaction—even spiritual joy—in her work.

In her essay on such work, ethicist Beverly Wildung Harrison suggests that its profound theological significance has become more difficult to appreciate since the nineteenth century. Noting that women in non-industrialized societies bear most of the responsibility for the tasks that sustain daily life, Harrison categorizes their labor as "the most human and most valuable and most basic of all the works of human love—the work of human communication, of caring and nurturance, of tending the personal bonds of community" (217).[2] According to Harrison, however, recent Christian practice has come to prize the intellectual life, largely dismissing "the activity of sustaining daily life as mundane and unimportant religiously" (215). Arguing that *doing* loving work is as significant as *being* a devout and contemplative person, Harrison asserts that "[o]ur world and our faith are transformed, for good or for ill through human activity" (216). She continues, "Women have been the doers of life-sustaining things, the 'copers,' those who have understood that the reception of the gift of life is no inert thing, that to receive this gift is to be engaged in its tending, constantly" (215). Morgan shows Julie, again and again, coping: taking step after step with the dying Masenier in her arms, repeatedly emptying her ailing father's bedpan, chopping wood, cooking meals, and now scrubbing her landlord's clothes. In so doing, she is also undertaking what Harrison calls "the deepening and extension of human relations" (218).

This intersection of labor and love enables Julie on several occasions to delight in the human fellowship of work. On the day cranky Ma Richards makes her pronouncement about "earning our joy," she and Julie and the odious Mr. Pendergast share a companionable meal after laboring together over the hog carcass. Julie observes, "People eating together felt bound to each other, like it says in the Bible about the breaking of bread.… I don't know what brought us together in such a fine fellowship unless it was just the tenderloin and grits and coffee, and maybe the work of hog killing. But it was like we formed a special kinship in the kitchen, at the table piled with tubs and dishpans of pork fat" (88, 90). Julie shares a similar kinship with her sister Lou when Lou, her new husband Garland, and the girls' little sister Carolyn come to visit and Lou and Julie do housework together (177, 179). She even experiences it with Hank when he helps her and Carolyn noisily clean the kitchen to give Lou and Garland privacy on their wedding night: "'Everything will be clean and fresh in the morning,' Hank said and glanced up at the ceiling. Then he looked at [Julie] and grinned. It had been weeks since [she] had seen him grin" (187). Working together in a dishwashing assembly line helps bring the estranged couple together for an evening.

Sometimes, however, work functions as Julie's only solace during emotional upheaval. Near the beginning of the book, as her father is dying, she escapes the house to split wood in the windy night. Absorbing herself in the task, she describes its noise and activity:

> It was a satisfying sound. I brought the axe down again, and with a crackle the wood separated into halves and fell apart.… Much as I hated to split wood, here I was doing it. I didn't know what else to do.… I was beginning to sweat, and my dress was sticking to my back under the

> coat. The wood fell apart like I knowed where to touch the nerve at its center with its blade. I aimed for the heart of a cut end and hit it. The wood cracked itself, and cracked again [30].

Breaking the heart of the wood enables Julie to escape, if only briefly, the heartbreak of losing her father. Later, when Mr. Pendergast suffers fatal burns in a grease-fire on hog-killing day, Julie pours herself into caring for him and then preparing his body for burial. Blaming herself for the fire, she says, "It was my job to do what I could to help, to make up for the bad I'd done.... There was so much to be done, and I had to work my way through it. But the more I done the calmer I got" (99, 110). After Hank strikes her for naïvely giving money to a con man, Julie finds a measure of comfort in washing dishes:

> The hot soapy water felt good on my hands and wrists. I buried my arms up to the elbows in the steaming pan and put my face close to the dishpan to feel the warmth on my chin and neck. I wished I could sink my whole body in a tub of hot, soapy water. I needed to soak myself and cleanse myself. I needed to melt away the stain of shame. I scrubbed each knife and fork, each glass and dish and bowl. I rinsed them in a pan of fresh water and dried them with a clean towel [132].

Julie cannot wash away the shame of her mistake or Hank's abuse, but she can use work to distract herself and to deal with her emotions. All the while, she is developing fortitude and self-discipline, virtues she needs in her marriage to Hank.

Morgan eventually reveals that Hank's deepening despair is, at least in part, the product of his not working. For weeks after being fired for striking a supervisor, Hank pretends to Julie that he was laid off because the brick-making project was complete. He does some hunting but more sulking while Julie works and tries to avoid him in his worst moods. He finally confesses to her that hitting his boss "was not the Christian thing to do" and frets that "nobody will ever hire [him] again" (267). The young couple face their leanest days as the birth of their baby approaches, living on eggs and grits and then nearly starving when a predator kills their laying hens.

Malnourished, Julie barely has the strength to take on the hardest physical work she has done yet: laboring to deliver her daughter. Alone while Hank goes to fetch his mother, Julie steels herself with corn whiskey and sets up a space to labor in the kitchen because it will be easier than the other rooms to clean afterward. Initially, she thinks of the pain, "I can't stand this much suffering. I can't do this all by myself" (282). In characteristic fashion, though, she soon accepts her assignment, praying to Jesus for mercy. She explains,

> Even though I didn't know how much further, it was certain I had a long way to go before I was done. It was a full day's work. And I remembered that's what they called giving birth: labor. I was in the *labor* of giving birth. It was hard labor. I would try to think of it as work and not as pain. I had a mountain of work ahead of me. I might as well pitch in. There was no way I could get out of it. There was no way I wanted to get out of it.
>
> This is *my* work, I though. This is the work only I can do. This is work meant for me from the beginning of time. And this is work leading me in an endless chain of people all the way to the end of time. Other women have done their work down the course of the years, and now it's my turn. There's nothing to do but take hold of the pain and wrestle with it. It was not a choice to give in....
>
> This is what it means to be a human being, to labor and to hurt, I thought [284].

When the baby comes, a tiny girl, Julie feels both pride and peace. "I had done all the work myself and I wasn't afraid anymore," she says (287).

Soon she discovers, however, that she cannot do the work of nursing her child. Gravely ill from childbed fever, Julie has no milk. Hank attempts to feed the baby milk from an eye-dropper and sugar water from a bottle, but she fails to thrive. Julie agonizes as she hears her piteous cries, saying, "She was my baby and she was hungry, and there wasn't nothing I could do about it. I was the one that was supposed to feed her, and there wasn't nobody else to do it. I hated myself for not having milk" (290). As little Delia continues to decline, Julie observes, "There's nothing that makes you feel as helpless as a baby that's sick. It's your job to do something about it, but you don't know what" (306). For the first time in her young life, Julie's willingness to work exceeds her physical strength for a task that only she can do.

Julie's "failure" as a mother becomes, however, a surprising occasion for grace. As she battles illness, she has a near-death vision of a Christ-like figure she associates with her father, standing in a hilltop meadow. She describes their encounter:

> "I have come to show you my love," he said.
>
> "Why have you come to me?" I said. I felt how shameful I was. I hadn't even been able to nurse my baby.
>
> "Because you have shown the truest love," Papa said.
>
> "How?" I said. My knees was shaking.
>
> "Because you have loved others more than yourself," he said.
>
> "I done what I had to do," I said.
>
> "You are one of the blessed," he said.... "I have come to tell you, you will live," Papa said. "You will live and you will continue to work and to love."
>
> "That sounds simple," I said. "Simple and hard." They was two words that fit my life, the life I had lived. Ever since I could remember, the work had been hard, work I often hated [300].

And Julie does return to life, to consciousness, to work and to love.

Grace works in Hank through Julie's incapacity. When he first returns to Julie and the newborn Delia, having turned back in anxiety halfway to his mother's house, all he can do is make pessimistic pronouncements about the baby's frail appearance. Worried that he will be angry with her for being sick, Julie nevertheless succumbs to her illness and observes from her delirium how Hank rises to the occasion: getting milk from the neighbors, preparing a shoebox-bed for the baby, trying to feed her while tending to Julie, too. As she listens to him singing "By Jordan's Stormy Banks" while he labors over the washboard, Julie thinks, "Hank had never washed clothes before, but now he had no choice" (294). Describing the tenderness with which he diapers his daughter, she says, "Hank's hands was too big for that kind of work, but he was doing his best. I seen there was things about Hank I couldn't have guessed" (296). For the first time in their marriage, Julie depends on Hank.

Through taking on more of the work of their home and farm, Hank, like the women Beverly Wildung Harrison describes, comes to "[understand] that the reception of the gift of life is no inert thing, that to receive this gift is to be engaged in its tending, constantly" (215). In so doing, he also develops remarkable insight about human relationships. When Ma Richards returns and she and Julie quarrel, Hank shows surprising maturity in counseling them to reconcile. Julie marvels,

> I had never heard him talk so dignified and wise. It was usually him losing his temper and me holding mine. But here he was sounding like a deacon that led in prayer and was the head of the family. His calm moved me more than anything else had. I felt proud that he was a man I could rely on and trust. He was not only the father of my baby, who had took care of the baby, but he could show me what to do when I got all worked up and beside myself with disappointment and resentment. It was like Hank had got a lot older [305].

When little Delia dies, Julie discovers she can turn to him for comfort. "I couldn't bear such grief on my own," she explains. Also for the first time, she has someone to share the work of grieving.

In the months that follow, Hank and Julie share the farm's physical work, too. She does turn to solitary labor for solace as she always has, scrubbing the floor, washing clothes, hoeing potatoes, polishing windows. "It seemed I didn't have control over nothing in the world except the work I done. I couldn't make nothing right, but I could make the floor and the dishes shine," she remembers. "I want to make one little place in the world as bright and tight as a crystal, I thought. I want to make one tiny place as fit as it can be" (309–10). As she plants and tends more crops, Hank warns her that she is likely to kill herself. "But he didn't say it ugly," Julie says, and "Hank worked on the place as hard as I did" (311). Together, they pull fodder, dry apples, and cure meat for the winter. "You take pride," Julie says, "in how you can keep things together with no money and just hard work" (317). In spite of—because of—their shared grief, Julie and Hank come to share the productive, satisfying life she had dreamed of before their marriage.

Although they still live in relative isolation at Gap Creek, Hank and Julie's relationship extends further into their community. Having begun to go to church during Julie's pregnancy, they had benefited during the difficult winter from budding friendships with Preacher and Mrs. Gibbs and two older women who visit Julie, bringing jellies and baby clothes. In the summer after Delia's death, the young couple are finally able to reciprocate, reaching out to their neighbors. Julie explains:

> The more I worked the more I had to work. I would give the preacher potatoes and carrots instead of any tithe. And I would help anybody else I could. I would give people that passed on the road new taters and squash.... While we worked that summer we attended every prayer meeting and church service, every singing and dinner on the grounds. I carried taters and cider and canned preserves to shutins and old folks. I made jelly and canned beans and peaches and tomato juice. I canned blackberry juice and grape juice. The days was thick and cluttered with grief, and I fought my way through every minute with work. I wrestled with every job like it was a demon, or an angel.... It was my sweat and my effort that made that time possible [310, 311–12].

Hank even makes peace with Timmy Gosnell, a vicious drunk who has hounded them since Mr. Pendergast's death. Instead of threatening Timmy as he once did, Hank prays aloud for him in his presence, thus driving Timmy away. Julie recounts, "Hank looked at me and grinned. He had changed since last winter. He had knowed what to do to get rid of Timmy without hurting him. I hugged him with my elbows and wrists, since my hands was so dirty they would smear on his wet shirt" (316). In their life of grief and love and work, Hank and Julie forge a deeper marital relationship as they relate more to their neighbors.

While *Gap Creek* is not an overtly religious book, its characterizations dramatize Christian conversion through work. Although he had been active in church during his youth, Hank only develops a robust faith through suffering and, ultimately, through laboring. Morgan also shows how Julie's work necessitates and sustains her maturing Christian commitment. Her religious faith buds when Preacher and Mrs. Gibbs visit her and Hank over Christmas, just after the farm has flooded and Hank has suffered an emotional breakdown. When Hank remarks bitterly to the Preacher that "Christians have to work as hard as anybody else," the older man responds, "They have to work as hard, ... but it means more" (240). Julie observes, "It struck me that he didn't say Christians enjoyed work more, or had it any easier. But saying that their work meant more sounded more than just talk. It sounded like the truth, or at least the truth as he knew it" (240). At church the following Sunday, New Year's Day, Preacher Gibbs tells his congregation, "The Lord is with us as we go about our work. He is with us when we milk the cow or chop wood.... He is with the mother who nurses her child, and he is with the mother who loses her child" (244). Moved by the pastor's message, Julie walks to the altar and prays, "Lord, make me worthy to have a baby and raise it. Life with Hank is going to be hard, as everybody's life is hard. Give me the strength to face the pain, and to eat the pain like bread. And give me the sense to know joy and to accept joy. For I know I'm weak and can't sustain my life alone. Teach me to accept what is give to me" (247). When Preacher Gibbs asks her, "Do you dedicate your life to [Jesus'] will and glory and his work?," Julie answers, "I do" (247). Julie's commitment to do God's work is renewed in her dream after Delia's birth.

When the book ends, Julie and Hank have no expectation of living an easier life; their only certainty is that more hard work lies ahead. They have, however, proven in their first year of marriage their capacity to work individually and as a team, to help and be helped by their neighbors, and to find grace and healing in their work and their relationship with one another. Julie's hardest work has been in her marriage, but Hank is now shouldering his half of that responsibility.

When asked directly about the relationship between work and marriage, Morgan offers observations that confirm and illuminate his exploration of the subject in *Gap Creek*. "All experience that's well done has to be taken as work," he begins. "Even people who fall deeply in love who don't [take marriage as work] can't make it. Building a good marriage is like building a house; it never ends!" He observes that marriage goes through many stages, pointing as example to a married woman in the 1946 film *The Best Years of Our Lives* who tells her young adult daughter that she and her husband have fallen out and back in love with each other over the course of their marriage.

Morgan notes, however, that a cultural shift over the twentieth century has yielded what he calls a "'me-culture'" that undermines stability in marriage. He continues:

> Marriage [used to be seen] as part of the community. Add to that a religious, sacramental sense—different from our contemporary romantic view of marriage. I remember people in the community [where I grew up] who didn't even go to church regularly but would show up to dig a grave. Today, there's not that sense of obligation. Now, marriage is for your gratification, not to serve spouse, children, community. Now, the talk is about how to get what you want. Sometimes, that's good, but how do we learn the most important thing against our own will? [Morgan]

Sociologist and Johns Hopkins University professor Andrew J. Cherlin concurs with Morgan's assessment, noting that "[m]arriage today, like the rest of our lives, is about personal satisfaction." Cherlin's observation comes in response to a 2007 Pew Research Center survey in which a majority of Americans pronounced "mutual happiness and fulfillment" to be marriage's main purpose ("To Be Happy" A1).

Morgan's acknowledgment that getting "what you want," however, can be good points to one of several challenges *Gap Creek* poses to those who would use it to reflect on work, marriage, and community. Few readers will regard Hank and Julie's isolation, primitive living conditions, and unrelenting hard work as desirable circumstances, helpful though they may be in the characters' formation of virtues and cultivation of life-giving faith. Norman Wirzba could have been writing about *Gap Creek* when he admits that "[i]t would be foolish, as well as supremely ungrateful, to suggest that [modern] forms of liberation are bad. Nobody wants to go back to a world in which vast segments of the population—women, rural folk, ethnic and racial minorities, the handicapped and mentally ill—had no say over the course of their lives" (18). In turn-of-the-century rural North Carolina, Julie has few if any options for escape, even if Hank were to have become habitually physically abusive. As a woman, her vocational choices are even more circumscribed than his, a reality certain to disturb those of us who have benefited from the women's movement.

Even so, Morgan notes that the majority of readers who express appreciation for *Gap Creek* are women. They recognize that the novel is far more than a book about an overworked housewife. In its sensitive characterization of Julie, the novel honors vast numbers of women and men whose circumstances require them to make the best of work they often—or always—find less than fulfilling. The book demonstrates that even humble, virtually back-breaking labor can offer its own deep satisfactions. To twenty-first-century readers, *Gap Creek* offers an imaginative alternative to the modern life Wirzba laments, in which "even as we exalted the autonomy of the individual, we relegated our freedom to paths of alienation, disenchantment, boredom, and anxiety" (18). Of course, Morgan provides no actual prescription for a life worth living today; we cannot go back in time, even if we wanted to. The novel does challenge us, though, to re-think our notions about what constitutes meaningful work and what constitutes meaningful marriage in a society that tempts us to ignore the claims of nature and our neighbors.

Notes

1. Morgan's treatment of this homely task is reminiscent of Richard Wilbur's early poem "Love Calls Us to the Things of This World," in which the soul "cries, 'Oh, let there be nothing on earth but laundry, / Nothing but rosy hands in the rising steam / And clear dances done in the sight of heaven.'" *Collected Poems 1943–2004* (New York: Harcourt, 2004), p. 307.

2. In describing his grandparents' work, which informs *Gap Creek* and several of his other novels, Morgan acknowledges that the men worked hard but that "the women would have to get up and start the fire, cook the breakfast, milk the cow, and then go out and work in the fields, often, with the men, and come back and fix dinner—not to mention all the work of looking after the children. That has been forgotten to some extent. We have so many modern conveniences. Women still work very hard, but they don't have to carry water from the spring if they're going to wash clothes; they don't have to carry wood to start a fire under the pot, carry the clothes and wash them on a washboard" (Bizarro and Bizarro p. 179).

Works Cited

Bizarro, Patrick, and Resa Crane Bizarro. "'The Poetics of Work': An Interview with Robert Morgan." *North Carolina Literary Review* 10 (2001): pp. 173–90.

Cornett, Sheryl. "A Conversation with Robert Morgan." *Image* 43 (Fall 2004): pp. 65–76.

Harrison, Beverly Wildung. "The Power of Anger in the Work of Love: Christian Ethics for Women and Other Strangers." In *Weaving the Visions: New Patterns in Feminist Spirituality*. Eds. Judith Plaskow and Carol P. Christ. New York: Harper and Row, 1989. pp. 214–225.

Morgan, Robert. *Gap Creek*. New York: Scribner, 2000. Chapel Hill: Algonquin, 1999.

_____. Interview with the author. Ferrum College, Ferrum, VA. 8 June 2004.

Norris, Kathleen. *The Quotidian Mysteries: Laundry, Liturgy and "Women's Work."* New York: Paulist Press, 1998.

St. George, Donna. "To Be Happy in Marriage, Baby Carriage Not Required." *The Washington Post* 1 July 2007: pp. A1+.

Wilbur, Richard. *Collected Poems 1943–2004*. New York: Harcourt, 2004.

Wirzba, Norman. "Vocation in Pianissimo: The Loss and Recovery of Vocation in Contemporary Life." *The Cresset* 68:4 (Easter 2005): pp. 16–21.

Tunes from the "Madrigal of Time" in *Brave Enemies*

HARRIETTE C. BUCHANAN

Several poems near the end of Robert Morgan's *Topsoil Road* (2000) deal with types of traditional mountain music. "History's Madrigal" tells how the "old woods" are preferred by fiddle and dulcimer makers for their "truer and deeper / music" as if the woods themselves had "stored up the knowledge of / passing seasons" of "bird call and love / moan, news of wars and mourning" so that

> ... century
> speaks to century and history
> dissolves history across the long
> and tangled madrigal of time [48].

The "madrigal of time" is a useful image for discussing Morgan's novel of the American Revolution, *Brave Enemies* (2003). This novel can be heard as a madrigal sung by the two main characters Josie Summers and John Trethman as they struggle to find themselves and each other during the civil chaos of the winter of 1780–81. Their paths meet and diverge as the vagaries of war sweep them up, finally enabling their reunion after the Battle of Cowpens.

As a musical form, the madrigal is composed of two or more voices that may move in chordal or contrapuntal style. The form, established in fourteenth-century Italy, uses two voices, with an upper part that is "more elaborately ornamented than the lower. The poem consists of one to four stanzas of three lines each and a two-line closing section called the *ritornello*" (Ammer 187). This description of the structure of the ancient Italian form of the madrigal interestingly and accurately describes the structure of *Brave Enemies*. There are four major sections, each consisting of three or four chapters spoken by Josie and ending with a part titled "John Trethman" in which we hear John's voice in clear counterpoint to Josie's. The novel ends with two chapters spoken by Josie that form the climax and denouement to the story. Josie's chapters, or verses, speak in her simple straightforward voice. John's, however, reflect both his greater degree of education and his more abstract motives and goals. Together their madrigal voices tell personal stories of guilt, anguish, and the search for redemption and humility, all set against an ongoing percussive rumble of "news of wars and mourning" ("History's Madrigal").

The novel opens with a "Prologue," set in "*Spartan District, South Carolina, January 17, 1781*" (1). The narrator's first words are: "I was the only one nearby who wasn't running around" (1). These words describe battle confusion, with the narrator, whose identity we do not yet know, opposing a redcoat who seems to want to surrender. Both fire, and the redcoat falls dead as the narrator falls wounded. The "Prologue" captures our attention by describing the confusion of what the date and place reveal to be the decisive Battle of Cowpens in the American Revolution. We are also drawn into the story by the vividness with which the narrator describes both place and events. The narrator's connection to the place is both literal and literary:

> I don't even remember hitting the ground, but I do recall the smell of cow manure in the broom sedge. I reckon the Cowpens were just covered with cow piles and we'd been too busy that morning to notice them. Last thing I remember was the smell of broom sedge and frost down under the stink of smoke and blood. It was like I was sinking and there was nothing to hold me up, and the cow piles were turning gold [3–4].

The narrator hears the sounds of battle, men shouting, weapons firing, and bagpipes playing. As the battle winds down, visual images come into clearer focus. "Men lay all over the field, and prisoners were gathered in bunches huddled in the broom sedge. Flags lay in the weeds and peavines" (7). The smells of the smoke, blood, and cow piles; the sounds of the shouting, weapons, and bagpipes; the sights of the dead and wounded men, fallen flags, and weeds and peavines, vivify the scene through the narrator's attention to basic sensory details. The "Prologue" ends as the narrator, being tended by a Scottish Highland doctor, reveals her gender and pregnancy by asking, "Is my baby all right?" (12).

Chapter "One" opens with Josie Summers asking another question, "Did you ever see somebody stamp a terrapin, just stand over it and come down with a boot heel on its shell?" (13). This cruelty aptly describes Josie's stepfather Mr. Griffin who terrorizes both Josie and her mother as well as the apparently random cruelty of the war in piedmont North Carolina. When, at age 16, she is raped by Mr. Griffin and rejected by her mother, Josie kills Mr. Griffin, cuts her hair and, in Mr. Griffin's clothes, escapes disguised as a boy. Although we had not fully recognized it in the prologue, Josie's affiliation with and attachment to the earth is reinforced on her first night in the wilderness. She eventually realizes she cannot continue blundering in the dark. So, when Josie feels a branch, she follows it to the tree's trunk. "The tree was like a big friend comforting me in the dark, with its roots deep in the hill and the limbs high above. A current seemed to be flowing in the tree and from the tree. It was rooted deep in its place and was calm. I wanted to be calm and certain as the tree" (36). The next day, searching for food and shelter, Josie comes on a rowdy band of men, tarring and feathering a woman who proclaims her royalist sentiments. Frightened, Josie cautiously continues her search. Finally she sees a lantern and follows it to a small church. There she hears a young preacher invite the congregation to share their troubles and "comfort one another" (42). Compelled to speak, Josie says, "I have done wrong and I want you all to pray for me" (44). The preacher invokes prayer, saying, "Lord, help our brother to repent and forgive.... For only when we forgive can we be forgiven" (45). After the service, the preacher, seeing that the newcomer has nowhere to go, invites him home. They introduce themselves as John Trethman and Joseph Summers (48). On their way to John's cabin, they see the home of a loyalist being burned by a band disguised as Indians who have hanged the family from an oak tree.

In the first three segments of the novel, Josie has set the scene and introduced herself to us. The "Prologue" describes part of the Battle of Cowpens in January 1781. Chapters One and Two circle back, in a kind of flashback, to tell of Josie's life from the age of twelve to sixteen and of her flight from home shortly after the Battle of Kings Mountain in October 1780. In addition we have seen the connections between Josie and the earth.

Her awareness after being wounded at Cowpens of the smells of broom sedge, cow piles, smoke, and blood (3–4) as well as her sense of longing to connect with the rootedness and calm of the tree under which she had sheltered (36) all depict her as a creature of earth. Josie's naming the peavines among the weeds at the Cowpens reinforces her connection to earth and enhances our sense of her values by echoing Morgan's poem "Wild Peavines." In this poem, Morgan laments the loss of the wild peavines that once covered every landscape. He ends this poem by connecting the peavines with language:

> you must look through several valleys
> to find a sprig or strand of wild
> peavine curling on a weedstalk
> like some word from a lost language
> once flourishing on every tongue [*Topsoil Road* 7].

This earth connection is not only to the physical earth but also to the manner in which Josie relates to her environment through the words by which she names it. Josie's earthiness is also reinforced by our knowledge that at the Battle of Cowpens she is pregnant. Smoke and blood recur at the end of her first three verses in the images of the destroyed family. In addition we have seen Josie's struggles for survival in the wilderness and her guilt at killing Mr. Griffin, even though we clearly recognize the self-defense from which she acted.

John Trethman's first verse in the madrigal presents him as a creature of air. He opens with, "I always loved to watch clouds. Even as a boy … I could lie … for hours and watch the luminous shapes of mist and vapor drifting far above" (50). He adds that he imagined he "saw prophets and apostles from the Bible … staring at me." These visions merge into a sense of seeing "the face of God" or "Jesus soaring up there" (50, 51). In addition to displaying a vivid imagination, John's language tells us that he is a creature not only of air but also of a philosophical and religious turn of mind. This perception is borne out as we learn his history as a Wesleyan missionary with an itinerant circuit in the piedmont of North Carolina. John has come to the wilderness to bring word and song to the darkness. John's romantic idealism is evident when he describes part of his ministerial impulse: "I took out my flute and played to the trees and meadows, to the sunlight and breeze, or I opened my songbook and sang a carol for the foxes and deer in the thickets" (51). Although the ravages of war are all around, John vows to follow the advice of his superior, "to stay above the fray" and "not to take sides in this rebellion" (55). Determined to bring the light of Christianity "into the dark forest" (58), John Trethman slowly builds his ministry. Because he reads the newspapers as well as talks with all of his parishioners, whether they be royalist or rebel, we learn of the progress of the war in western North Carolina and northern South Carolina. John's first verse ends with a confrontation, during a barn raising, with royal soldiers. John resolutely declares himself a neutral "psalmodist and minister" (65), but Lieutenant Withnail says that such a role may be a "ruse" for a "messenger or spy" (66) and promises swift punishment if he finds that to be the case. John's tendency to see the apostles and even the face of God in the clouds as well as his desire to bring enlightenment to the wilderness indicate a sense of his own importance. His voice is that upper madrigal voice that is more elaborately ornamented than Josie's simpler, lower voice.

Josie's second verse begins with the burial of the burned-out loyalist family. As Joseph she becomes John's assistant, traveling with him when he visits his various congregations. They develop a routine, with John confident that Joseph has been sent to him to be Silas to his Paul (79–80). Then, one night, awakening Joseph to come see the northern lights, John touches a breast and discovers Josie's true identity. John flees in anger only to return physically ill. They reconnect as Josie nurses him back to health and they eventually make love. Unable to live in sin, John conducts a marriage ceremony that ends with their singing "Joy to the World." Josie tells us "The next few days were the happiest I had ever known" (104), but their happiness is short-lived. While traveling to one of their meeting houses, John and Josie are overtaken by a forest fire. John saves them by scooping a shallow trench in which he covers Josie's body with his own, but his back is badly burned as the fire passes over their heads. They return home to discover their cabin ransacked and the message "DEATH TO REBELS" written in charcoal on the mantel (113). The next day they are visited by a rebel troop who threaten that if they are hiding soldiers of the Crown they will be burned. Josie's second verse has introduced her to both personal joy and the growing threat from both sides in the war.

John Trethman's second verse returns to the burial of the loyalist family he and Joseph/Josie had seen the first night they met. In this section he tells his version of the belief that Joseph has been sent to be Silas to his Paul (119). John determines to teach Joseph the Gospel and "to sing harmonies with me" (120). John values music because "In those violent days I found no greater support and shield than music. Music soothed the hate and fear in the air.... Music seemed to calm and heal the air and the passing hours" (120). His discovery that Joseph is Josie evokes extreme anger, and, in a moment of candor, John confesses to us that his great weaknesses are anger and vanity. He elaborates that his vanity is less of appearance, although he would have liked to have had vestments, but "My vanity was more of talent, more of spoken word and sung note" (126). John's second verse ends with a warning that Lieutenant Withnail is asking about him, about any letters he sends or receives. Josie fears that his correspondence with his church superiors will brand him as a rebel spy.

Josie's third verse begins with their work after John's burns begin healing. Josie echoes John's comments about music at the first of this section. John has insisted they sing because "Song will help me heal" (133). Josie thinks, "When we sang, the music did seem to heal the hard moments of worry and fear. The music softened time and put things in order. The music sweetened the hours.... I saw that music fed us, nourished us the same as grits and bread did" (133). The peace and joy of song and love making are marred by quarrels as John probes to learn Josie's secrets and by more warnings that the redcoats want to arrest John. On Christmas Eve the redcoats finally come and Lieutenant Withnail arrests John, ties Josie to a tree, and fires the cabin. Josie despairs as John is led away and the fire burns hotly. "The logs got so hot they seemed to turn into a blinding liquid. Everything we had was burned up. John's flute was melted, and the coins I had stolen from Mama. My eyes stung and I had to turn my face away" (152). At this point, the madrigal structure of Morgan's novel assumes a more complex texture as the recurring images and themes subtly echo the pantoum structure of Morgan's poem "Audubon's Flute." Like Audubon, whose "silver pipe sings on his tongue," John has been "modeling a melody" "over calamus and brush country," heedless of human ear to hear (*The Strange Attractor* 100). Josie grieves these material losses as well as the loss of John and of the cabin that has been their refuge. Not knowing if she will ever see John again, Josie fights to save herself, freeing herself from the tree just as it, too, catches fire. She grabs the only available tool, an ax (here echoing the weapon with which she has liberated herself from Mr. Griffin) and flees barefoot into the night. After wandering for days with little food, Josie realizes that she is likely pregnant. Finally, caught trying to steal food from a military camp, Josie is brought before Captain Cox of the North Carolina militia and denies that she is a spy. Cox says, "Well, Joseph Summers, if you're not here to spy on us then you must be here to join us," to which Josie promptly replies, "Yes, sir" (170). Josie is issued a rifle, begins days of drill under the bullying Sergeant Gudger, and learns of a coming battle between the American General Morgan and the British Colonel Tarleton.

John Trethman's third verse opens with his anxiety over whether he will ever see Josie again. After Withnail's interrogation, John finally convinces the redcoats that he is only a minister and is drafted into the king's service as chaplain to Colonel Tarleton. John is able to accept this as part of "a larger plan I knew nothing about" to atone for his arguments with Josie and to minister to "these troubled and desperate men of Tarleton's legion" (178). John's ministry to Tarleton's men helps him to realize that he has much to learn from this unbidden experience:

> I was learning not to be so quick to judge, to be patient and willing to learn, from strangers and enemies, from anyone. I was learning to be humble and compassionate. And I was learning from my love for Josie, which sustained me. And I was learning to love my enemies, as we are told to do, and to see that there were no enemies, only brothers in need and confusion [180].

John finally meets Tarleton and observes his volatile personality that ranges from generous to vicious and tyrannical.

Josie's fourth verse begins with her adjustment to life as a foot soldier in the militia. She feels that this service is her opportunity to expiate her guilt about killing Mr. Griffin and to avenge what she is certain is John's death. Her challenges are hiding her gender and avoiding the dreadful Gudger who has figured out that she is not only female but pregnant. Cox's militia joins McDowell's and moves towards a camp at Grindal Shoals in upstate South Carolina. After several weeks of drilling, they spot Tarleton's dragoons across a river and pursue them toward a ford. Finally they make camp at Cowpens where General Morgan moves from campfire to campfire exhorting the men. Josie is scared but feels proud to be part of what she senses is an important moment of the war. She gazes around the campfire. "I'd never seen men so carried away, so thrilled. It was so strange to be there with them. I was excited and proud to be there, but mostly I was scared. It still didn't seem possible I could be in the militia" (242). Just as John is learning humility, Josie is beginning to find the connections between her concrete experiences and the larger meanings of life. "It came to me how every day has its own angle and pitch and smell. It's like every feeling has its own stink, its own size, different and surprising each time. There is a texture to the touch of every terrible thing" (243). January 17 dawns and the battle begins. Josie's group fires then engages in a wild retreat that suddenly stops when they turn to fight again, ending her fourth verse.

John Trethman's fourth verse begins with his recounting the weeks since his capture; he has thought constantly of Josie, of his service, and of the war. While he has "come to care for these men and respect them," John realizes more than ever "the hopelessness and futility of war" and that the "only true way was the way of peace ... only a message of love and peace could win" (271). He is sure that losing Josie and serving Tarleton are a penance, but he feels that there is "no greater honor than to pray with these men so far from home" (272). Lieutenant Withnail finally exacts revenge when he persuades a prostitute to arouse John then suddenly interrupts them by calling her to Tarleton's tent. John's vanity is punctured by this reminder of his humanity and humility. "I heard laughter outside as I pulled up my breeches, and terrible thunder shook the ground ... the fault was mostly mine, and the author of my embarrassment was my own ordinary frailty. I was made of common clay, and I had much to pray about. I had much to be humble about, and I still had much to learn" (280). These are John's final lyrics in the madrigal of *Brave Enemies*, reinforcing the theme of his journey from the intellectual recognition of his vanity of "talent" (126) to the earned humility of recognizing the humanity of the brave enemies to whom he is forced to minister and of recognizing his own human frailty.

Josie's final verse, composed of two chapters, brings the novel to its close and forms the *ritornello* of the madrigal. Chapter Thirteen is the crucial battle scene when the tide of war turns. Even Josie, whose primary struggle has been for survival, recognizes the significance of the moment:

> Sometimes I don't think time means anything. It was just an instant, but it could have been half a lifetime for the way things had turned. The field shifted in that moment, as the regulars and the volunteers turned and fired their barrage. The whole battle, maybe the whole war, turned around in a second. I can still smell the smoke from that moment, and the sweat of fear. There's a smell of gunpowder and blood and cow piles that's not like anything else.... I was a girl and I had been part of it all [285–6].

Historians agree that the Battle of Cowpens was, indeed, a turning point in the American Revolution (Edgar xvi). In the madrigal story of Josie's struggle to survive and to forgive herself and her mother for the crimes committed in the name of survival and of John's struggle with pride and vanity, the background drumroll of war has reached a crescendo.

Between chapters Thirteen and Fourteen is the incident reported in the "Prologue." Chapter Thirteen ends with a verbal cue to this with Josie's sentence: "I was the only one nearby that wasn't running around" (288). Chapter Fourteen begins where the Prologue ended and makes up the denouement of the story. Discovered as a woman with a wounded foot, Josie has been left behind with other wounded from both sides. She hears a preacher conducting funerals and singing and knows it must be John. Unable to make her keepers know what she means when she says she has to talk to the preacher, she despairs until finally John approaches the wagon in which she lies:

> John was walking straight toward me. He looked tall as a tree with the firelight behind him, and when he reached out toward me his arms were long wings of shadow and light stretching far across the camp to touch me. As he came closer I couldn't see his face, but he looked tall as an oak with the lit droplets of rain behind him, tall as a house, as he bent down to see me better [309].

This version of the madrigal of time concludes as the elements draw together. Josie's earth will join John's air as the firelight and rain droplets illuminate their reunion. Their journeys, separately and together, have brought Josie to redemption and acceptance, if not understanding, of the crimes in her life and John to true humility about his mission to be a "psalmodist and minister" (65). We are hopeful that Josie and John will be able, as John had preached earlier, to "Together ... step forward to the future" (81).

In the December 2000 commencement address at Appalachian State University, Robert Morgan indicated that as a boy he "connected wilderness and writing.... Text and wilderness mirrored each other and informed each other. The wilderness was a poem, and poems had the splendor and mystery and perhaps the danger of the wilderness" ("Commencement" 5). This address also tells of Morgan's youthful desire to "compose a poem or a piece of music as grand as [Cicero] mountain. It would be an epic, or something like an oratorio, or fantasia and fugue for organ" ("Commencement" 5–6). Morgan also tells of students in his creative writing classes who had learned about storytelling. They had learned to bring "their art to the level where a story is not so much a plot as about human connection, and not just about the conflict of good versus bad, but the conflict of loyalty with loyalty" ("Commencement" 7).

Brave Enemies: A Novel of the American Revolution is Morgan's musical composition that tells a story of human connections in which the characters wrestle with good and bad and with loyalties to one another as well as to political groups. The madrigal form in which two voices sing the story in an interwoven fashion has worked well as Josie and John tell their interconnecting versions of personal struggles played out against a drumroll formed by the personal vendettas and civil wars that were the American Revolution in piedmont North and South Carolina. Just as the Battle of Cowpens was a turning point of the American Revolution, it is a turning point for Josie and John as, from opposite sides of the battle lines, they expiate their personal sins and find redemption in reunion. Like the musicians playing fiddles and dulcimers made from antique woods, Morgan's story is a musical form in which

> ... century
> speaks to century and history
> dissolves history across the long
> and tangled madrigal of time ["History's Madrigal" 48].

Works Cited

Ammer, Christine. *Harper's Dictionary of Music*. 1972. New York: Barnes and Noble Books, 1973.

Edgar, Walter. *Partisans and Redcoats: The Southern Conflict that Turned the Tide of the American Revolution*. 2001. New York: Perennial, 2003.

Morgan, Robert. *Brave Enemies: A Novel of the American Revolution*. A Shannon Ravenel Book. Chapel Hill, NC: Algonquin Books of Chapel Hill, 2003.

_____. "Commencement." Unpublished manuscript of address. Appalachian State University, Boone, NC, December 16, 2000.

_____. *The Strange Attractor: New and Selected Poems*. Baton Rouge: Louisiana State University Press, 2004.

_____. *Topsoil Road: Poems*. Baton Rouge: Louisiana State University Press, 2000.

Acting in Faith

Robert Morgan's The Road from Gap Creek

THOMAS ALAN HOLMES

Told from the perspective of Annie Richards Powell, the younger daughter of Hank and Julie Richards, the events of Robert Morgan's *The Road from Gap Creek* (2013) depict how Annie comes to appreciate the personal engagement of acting in faith in everyday life. Annie achieves this perspective through comparing the accomplishments of two young men who play vital roles in her life and then determining her own direction. Her younger brother, Troy, a favorite of her family and her community, has applied his talent and drive toward many admirable achievements, and his death during his World War II service affects Annie's understanding of how a person can live a full but short life. Her growing and reluctant affection for Muir Powell invites her considerations of limitations imposed upon her as a woman in a restrictive social era, just as she witnesses Muir's call to preach and his struggles with established local church hierarchy. Breaking from convention, Annie comes to recognize that blessedness isn't some permanently attained, static state of being: it requires us to engage bravely with life, to "behave with a purpose."

In the 2012 paperback edition of *Gap Creek* (1999), which includes as a preview the first chapter of the soon-to-be-published *The Road from Gap Creek*, Morgan describes how his initial plans for a sequel to his novel were to continue with the voice of his protagonist, Julie Harmon Richards, only to realize that he needed a "fresh perspective":

> ... I saw Julie had already told her story. Her later life should be seen through the eyes and voice of her daughter Annie.
>
> Once I began to tell the story in Annie's voice I knew I'd made the right choice. Rather than going back, I was moving forward ... to the uncertainties of the future, the struggle to define one's self ... [*GC* 337–38].

Annie's struggles derive from the cumulative effect of having lost her younger brother, Troy, to war, her growing awareness of her mother's illness, and her developing love for Muir, an idealistic young man driven to find his own place, as the remote Appalachian community experiences the global upheavals of the Great Depression and the Second World War, the personal crises of poverty and death. Fully aware that Troy has been her mother's favorite child (*RfGC* 6), Annie nevertheless recognizes that Julie's constancy has preserved the family through its difficulties; the subsequent decline her mother suffers as Annie matures affects how the young woman determines her own place and opportunities.

As Annie matures, however, she often appears to have a secondary role in comparison to Troy and Muir. Troy seems to have a natural talent for just about everything: an artist, an athlete, a favorite of the community, handsome, determined, and successful, he lives an active, often self-determined life, falling in love, making strong friendships, acquiring skills as an artist and a mechanic, and appreciating the depth of his experiences. As the Richards family suffers their loss of him, Annie cannot help but contrast her comparatively limited possibilities with Troy's opportunities. Yet Annie also witnesses numerous failures on the part of Muir, a young man seven years her senior who eventually wins her heart. Muir, like Annie, struggles with both personal and societal expectations; he must learn that he can shape his own role in his home community, and he wins the community's respect only once he approaches their shared values in his own way. These two prominent figures in her life, Troy and Muir, serve as models by pursuing their ideals in the face of social expectations. While they have varying success in navigating these attempts, they nevertheless achieve full, complete self-definition, a state that eludes Annie for most of her life.

This discovery requires more than Annie's coping with imposed "women's roles," because Annie does not have the same isolation from the world that her mother has experienced. In *Gap Creek*, Julie spends much of her time alone, a fact most symbolically significant in her solitude while giving birth the first time, but emphasized repeatedly by her having little help to maintain her home and marriage as her husband, Hank, struggles to become a stronger man. Annie's experience differs, in that the woes of the world come to her. During the Great Depression, she watches as many suffering people pass by her home, some grateful for the meager help the Richards family can give, others conniving to get the best of them. As World War II approaches, a fighter plane crashes on the hillside near the Richards family's home. In spite of their community's relative remoteness, violent global upheavals affect them. For Morgan, Annie's turning from this destructiveness informs her fulfillment. In an interview concerning the recurrent theme of work in his fiction, Morgan considered,

> It is one of the mysteries of human life, and human history, that intelligent people, often ethical people, kill each other often and on such a scale.... Annie in *The Road from Gap Creek* is mystified by the paradox. So often people of extraordinary intelligence and culture ... have slaughtered each other wholesale, and many wars have been fought over issues of religion, which seems on the surface a contradiction. Even in our own time much terrorism is conducted in the name of fundamentalist religion.
>
> Obviously, we have not evolved as far from the killer apes as we like to believe [Godwin 17].

For a young woman strong in her faith but growing in awareness of human shortcomings, this immediacy of her experience that impersonal external forces affect her community may appear to be a shortcoming in itself. In many ways, the global facts of the Great Depression and the Second World War become difficult obstacles for the family to overcome, just as they have to survive the threat of typhoid as it makes its way through their community. When the difficult financial times hit, Annie finds relief that her family remains mostly self-sufficient on their farm, so while people in the big city have a great deal of suffering during the Great Depression, the Richards family endures yet another spate of lean times, trusting that they can persevere. When Mr. Bishop, who has contracted with Annie's father to build a house, shows up onsite and halts the work on the basis of his bankruptcy, his laughing at Mr. Richards's predicament prompts Annie's father to knock him down; Mr. Richards collects himself right away and helps the man up. The cause of the Great Depression remains a mystery to her ("Had somebody took all of the money and hid it?") [*RfGC* 80], but she sees the immediate effect her father's worry has on him. In a like manner, as the effects of the Second World War begin to reach her community, Annie rarely considers the reasons for the war. When neighbors and kin gather to offer the Richardses consolation soon after learning of Troy's death, the men's conversation begins to focus on warfare itself, leaving Annie to dismiss their childlike fascination with its machinery: "Their eyes light up and their faces glow when they talk about airplanes and guns and fighting" (*RfGC* 162). Annie finds it difficult to witness their quick shift from personal mourning to vicarious thrill.

For Annie, war remains immediate and personal. In the only mystical passage of her account, she describes how two weeks prior to learning of Troy's death she has "a dream.... Maybe not really a dream, more like a vision" (*RfGC* 10) in which, looking out the window before bedtime, Annie witnesses a scene where her sad-looking brother sits and then appears to become aware of her, about to speak. "[S]uddenly there was this roar, as if a thousand shotguns had gone off at once. And a whoosh of flame that covered everything as fast as lightning.... And then it was all gone." This vision disturbs Annie, because while experiencing it she wants "to see what happened. I wanted to reach out and save Troy" (*RfGC* 13), but the vision ends her feeling of immediacy, as if she could have reached through some numinous aperture to draw her brother out, as if through a doorway.

The personal nature of Annie's vision mirrors her mother Julie's vision on the mountaintop in *Gap Creek*, which occurs soon after the birth of her ailing daughter, Delia. While changing the baby, Julie's husband Hank imagines the infant's future, predicting a long life that will culminate with Revelation's foretold end of time, which Hank believes will occur at the end of the millennium: "This girl will start out in a shoebox by the fireplace and live to see Jesus bust out of the eastern sky in all his glory."

> "How can time come to an end?" I said in my head.
> "It will come to an end when the Word is fulfilled," Hank said.
> "Time can't end, for what would follow would be time too," I said.
> "Don't you believe the Bible?" Hank said. "Don't you know it says plain in Revelation that time will stop?"
> "But what comes after that will be more time," I said [*GC* 297].

One finds a disorienting ambiguity in this exchange, as Julie indicates that she does not ask aloud how time can end. Nevertheless, Hank's conventional interpretation of Scripture seems to respond to her unspoken question, and he continues by challenging her faith in the Bible. After this exchange, Morgan abruptly ends the scene and places Julie on the mountain, where she begins to follow a familiar voice she believes to be her father's. Finally, finding a man who resembles her father as a much younger person, Julie refers to him as "Papa," and he offers her comfort, assuring her that he has come because Julie has "shown the truest love ... [b]ecause you have loved others more than yourself." Referring to her as "one of the blessed," the vision of her father assures Julie that she will live and "continue to work and to love" (*GC* 299). He vanishes before Julie can ask about her baby's future, and the vision abruptly ends with Julie's awareness that she lies in her sickbed, covered with sweat and sick. While the section prior to the vision suggests that Julie's vision begins when she finds herself on the mountain, listening to a familiar voice, perhaps the beginning of Julie's altered state of consciousness begins when she asks the question about time "in [her] head." The vision of her father provides an oblique answer to that question.

In the wake of her baby's subsequent death, its premature state incapable of surviving with the basic remedies the Richards family has to offer, Julie turns to hard work and service to her church community as a means to cope with her grief. When Julie confides, "It was my sweat and my effort that made time possible" (*GC* 312), we see that she has answered the question she has not spoken aloud to Hank. Her experience tells her that she has a broader concept of time than the context of limited interpretation of Scripture; the fact of *Gap Creek*'s publication well after Hank believes time will end offers a super-textual reason to challenge his prediction of end times, as well. Julie's relationship with the church relies more on her active engagement in charity and good works rather than a rigid interpretation of the Bible; her state of being blessed relies on her ongoing process of blessing others through her good works.

While Julie does not share her vision with her husband, Annie does describe her vision of Troy to Muir, and he dismisses it. "He didn't like people to talk about superstitions. He said superstition showed a lack of faith" (*RfGC* 13), Annie says, unquestioning as is Muir about any distinctions between their shared faith and superstition. While Annie decides not to tell "another soul," she cannot help but consider the validity of what she has seen.

> In the Bible it said young men will see visions and old men will dream dreams. Didn't say nothing about girls or women. What bothered me most was how worried Troy looked.... And then as I played it over in my mind I remembered there was something else, something I'd forgot. After the flash and just before it all disappeared there was a smell for an instant, a smell like burnt paint or some burnt chemical ... like leather had been scorched, and maybe hair [*RfGC* 14].

Physically sick after this memory, Annie feels that her experience has been genuine, and her vision's occurring prior to her learning of Troy's death gives the specificity of the scent of her experience more credibility. Annie later does not want to dwell on the details of Troy's death, criticizing her older sister, Effie, for dwelling on the details of Troy's remains. "At least I have sense enough to try to help people and not rub their faces in shit," Annie says, adding, "Just because something hurts don't mean you have to drag it through the mud" (*RfGC* 121–22). Aside from the rare instance of profanity in the stories of the Richards family, Annie's two comments draw a clear contrast between the prurient indulgence of lingering on the wounds ("shit" and "mud") and one's attempts to soothe the grief of the bereaved. Like her mother, Annie feels the impulse to perform consoling actions during such difficult times.

Annie best articulates her understanding of accepting a role in one's life when she recalls the visit her maternal Aunt Lou and her husband make to the grieving Richards family, soon after their learning of Troy's death.

> As I watched Lou and Garland shaking hands and chatting and laughing with everybody it come to me how important acting was. What Lou and Garland was doing was acting. There was no way they could actually feel so light and cheerful coming to a place of bereavement at such an awful time. But instead of acting mournful and quiet, as would be natural, they knowed how to be lively and full of affection and humor. They hugged people and made teasing comments, like everything was all right and it was a happy get-together. It come to me that most of the smart things people do are a kind of playacting. It would be awful to just act the way we feel. Better to behave for a purpose, with good sense. Use our minds and not just our feelings of the moment. Act the way you need to. It was something I'd thought about before but never seen so clear [165].

In the course of describing this visit, Annie offers an overt articulation of a colloquialism Morgan exploits throughout *The Road from Gap Creek*: the reliance on the word "acting" to mean "behaving" ("It would be awful to just act the way we feel. Better to behave for a purpose ..."). In Annie's many reflections on social functions and expectations, she almost always discusses how people should "act," from the type of clothing they might wear to the sanctioned manners on particular occasions. Given Annie's professed interest in acting for the stage, her relating this behavior of her aunt and uncle to a type of necessary performance acknowledges that social interaction requires a seamless roleplaying, as we move from one situation to another. Such necessity ("Act the way you need to") functions as yet another responsibility taken on by smart, empathic people. As Annie has said of her brother's dog, Old Pat, "you could think she was almost human, except for her willingness to always be happy" (*RfGC* 21). Annie comes to understand that happiness requires action, and people must elect to take that action in hard times. Annie rejects happiness as a state of being and instead suggests that people best remain on their guard in their relationships. As she later states, "Most of the time you can't show how you really feel about people anyway. If we always spoke our minds we wouldn't have no friends at all, and no love, and the human race would die out" (*RfGC* 123). While it seems overdramatic to suggest that everyday civility will serve to preserve humanity, Annie holds that acting serves as the best means to hold family, community, and society together. In her analysis of Morgan's women narrators, Nicole Drewitz-Crockett praises Morgan's Petal Jarvis (*The Hinterlands*, 1994), Julie Richards, and Ginny Powell (*This Rock*, 2001) as "physically strong, hardworking, and knowledgeable about and appreciative of their surroundings," emphasizing their ability to "make a way in the wilderness or on the homestead" (118). While Annie does not face the challenge of literal wilderness, global events coerce her to brave a different frontier of modernity.

For Annie, however, these opportunities seem limited at best, and, as a younger girl, she tends to dwell on standards of living rather than on quality of life.

> I wanted a man who could take me places and was going places hisself. I wanted to travel, I wanted fine shoes and clothes. I didn't want to milk cows and pull fodder and go to an outdoor toilet. I wanted a man with a nice car. He didn't have to be rich. I didn't want a rich man necessarily. But he had to have a job and enough money to live on. I told myself I didn't want to marry no farmer where I'd have to work my fingers to the bone and live on soup beans in late winter the way Mama had done [31].

Annie's evident immaturity shows in her failure to consider how she feels about her future husband. Instead, she sees getting a husband as a means to escape a hard farm life of limited comfort, unsure of just how much money it would take to provide the life she wants. "Enough money to live on" sounds like subsistence earnings incompatible with "fine shoes and clothes" and a great deal of leisure travel. These vague youthful dreams contrast with her concrete descriptions of specific chores and getting by on the limited remaining beans from the previous harvest.

This understanding of poverty helps Annie to acknowledge her limited opportunity to pursue her own dreams of being an actress. Having been successful in a school play, Annie receives glowing encouragement from her drama teacher:

> I was in the school play in a few days and had a wonderful time staying after school for rehearsals. One of the boys that had a car would drive me home. And once Mr. Oswald drove me home just in time for supper. It was like jumping between different worlds to spend a day at school, and then rehearse the play, and then go home to shell corn for the chickens and gather eggs in the gloom of the henhouse. Moving between those worlds made me a little confused sometimes. But on the night of the play the audience loved me.
>
> "Did you ever think of being a actress?" Mr. Oswald said.

> "How does anybody become an actress?" I said.
>
> "You have to go somewhere and study," Mr. Oswald said. He said I should go to college to study speech and dramatics. He said I could be a teacher while I worked at becoming an actress. I would have to go somewhere there was a theater to act in. But even as he said it I knowed I wouldn't leave home. I didn't have enough money for new shoes for graduation, much less enough money to go to college [*RfGC* 82].

Inherent in Mr. Oswald's encouragement lie financial concerns that Annie would have to overcome to follow her dream. He recognizes the limited employment opportunities she would have; he assumes that she, like him, would have to teach to make ends meet, although he does not follow through with the immediate consideration that Annie would require training to become a teacher in a school system close enough to commercial theater where she might get a big break. Without intention, he makes Annie's potential career on stage seem even less of a likelihood, given that her training for another career would need to come first. He suggests how her goal slips even further from her grasp.

While one might offer Mr. Oswald a generous benefit of the doubt when it comes to his discussion of Annie's possible career—one hopes that teachers can avoid discouraging students from pursuing their creative interests—Annie has to acknowledge that poverty will curtail her pursuit of acting as a career. Regardless, she acknowledges that she does not feel ready to encounter the larger world on her own.

> ... I thought of being an actress. I knowed I could be an actress, for I felt more like myself when I was playing a part than I ever did when I was just being me. I never was sure who myself was. But if there was a part that had been wrote, then I knowed how to play that part. And I could learn any lines that anybody wrote.
>
> But to be an actress I had to go off to New York or Hollywood, a long way from home where I didn't know nobody. I'd have to leave home and go there as my nervous self. I didn't know how to play the part of somebody that is going off to study to be an actress. And I didn't have the money to go somewhere like that. The Depression had come, and there was no money for groceries, much less for traveling to some far-off place that would be expensive once you got there. I thought and thought about going away to be an actress, but I never did. The only part I would play would be myself, and that wasn't wrote too good [*RfGC* 202].

Annie has not reached the point of maturity where she could determine to write her own part. She finds herself defined and, in many ways, trapped within specific social parameters. Her insecurity in acknowledging such obstacles leads to her undercutting her own potential.

One recalls that Annie's experience with drama has come from her involvement in church and school plays. She has had limited experience with drama other than those plays, and her stage experience has enjoyed the encouraging indulgence of her family and neighbors. While she sometimes mentions going to movies, she never describes listening to radio shows or other forms of commercial, dramatic entertainment.

> I'd been in church plays at Christmastime and found how much I loved to go up on a stage and pretend to be somebody else from a different time and place, in different clothes. I always thought it was odd that I liked to take part in plays and act a part since I was too shy to ever get up in front of an audience, even a small group, and give a speech.... I found that if I put on a costume and become somebody else it wasn't hard at all to get up on a stage with people looking at me. In fact I enjoyed it [*RfGC* 199].

When Annie becomes "somebody else," she manages to escape her personal insecurity. Her association of drama with her school and with her church shapes her understanding of what it means to act well, because doing so remains in the purview of two of the strongest influences on her development; outside of her family, the church and school define most of her world. She expands her acting repertoire only a bit when she has the comparative independence of working in a town shop for a brief period before returning to her home, but church plays and school drama, both produced under the careful eye of propriety, will not permit her to expand her sense of self beyond acceptable boundaries.

This issue affects her view of her limited opportunities as a woman, especially as she considers what married life might hold for her. Annie often rejects the notion of losing her independence once she gets married, and her limited understanding of marriage leads to true trepidation: "I didn't want to be in the power of no man or boy" (*RfGC* 192), she says, emphasizing later, "I guess I was afraid of marriage too. I never wanted a man to handle me and force his way with me. I never wanted to be under the will of a man. I wasn't going to be the play toy of no man" (*RfGC* 209). When Annie explains what she means by being "under the will," she relates the anticipated experience of sexual intercourse—even that permitted by marriage—to her fear of public speaking:

> I'd never wanted to be in the power of no man. I didn't much want to be bothered by a man running his hands over me and having his way with me. Other girls said it didn't hurt and besides it was fun and some said loving was the most wonderful thing they'd ever done. And I was curious and attracted as any girl is. But I felt a dread also of laying night after night with a man and letting him do whatever he wanted to with me. I couldn't admit it even to myself that I was that timid. But the fact is I was. Nothing in the world scared me as much as the idea of having sex, unless it was the fear of having to make a speech in public [*RfGC* 211].

Annie's concern reveals itself in two significant ways. First, she refers to herself as a "girl" at this moment of her life, even though from the context she refers to young married women, and she assumes that the woman must be available to the man to submit to whatever he might will. Of course, at twenty-seven (*RfGC* 208), her status as "girl" in her community comes only from her not being married. Her comparison of her fear of sex to her fear of public speaking alludes to her other ideas about performance. She likes acting because she can be another person. She does not pursue a career in acting because she would have to be herself in that pursuit. Even when she accepts Muir's proposal, she insists that they keep their marriage secret so she can play the role of single daughter to pacify her mother. Once married to Muir, however, her ideas shaping her identity change: "...it come to me that a wedding night could also be things a woman done to a man. It could work both ways" (*RfGC* 218). She rejects the feared role of passive bride and takes on her role of a woman pursuing mutual gratification. She revises what she considers the prescribed role as a wife.

Yet marrying Muir places Annie in the predicament of having to serve a role that she despises, the preacher's wife:

> ... I didn't want to be no preacher's wife....
>
> All my life I'd seen how preacher's wives had to go to church and set quiet while their husbands preached. They had to smile at everybody and be friendly. But nobody paid much attention to them. They had to dress well but not too well. They had to eat dinner at other people's houses and compliment the cooks. Most had to work to support their husbands cause the churches paid them so little. Most preacher's wives was gray and mousy. That kind of life was not for me [*RfGC* 117].

Annie describes this role as if it were a bit part in a bad production, even down to poor costuming. But Annie implies a strong difference between this expected preacher's wife behavior and the loving behavior her Aunt Lou has shown during the Richards family's grieving. Aunt Lou and her husband feel the immediate need of that loving behavior, conducting themselves as they need to rather than as they are expected to. Annie's objection to the role of preacher's wife stems from her resistance to being assigned a bad role.

Annie's taking on the role of a preacher's wife parallels Muir's learning how to be a preacher. For a person strong in faith, Annie offers many criticisms of the conventional behavior of preachers. Annie considers church a vital part of her life. Soon after the Great Depression hits and she describes its effect on her father's morale, she says, "...a man that can't find work and don't have money to buy groceries or put in the collection plate at church or buy gas for his truck is humbled and ashamed" (*RfGC* 81). She considers church participation every bit as vital as home life and work, so a preacher who performs poorly hurts every aspect of a congregant's life; assurances of Heaven do not provide needed comfort to endure the suffering of this world. At one point, Annie goes so far as to ascribe mercenary motivations behind the hellfire sermons: "Preachers always see doom and tribulation. That's how they get people to come up to the altar and get saved and join their church and give their money to the collection. They get them scared and then they keep them scared" (76). The conventional pastor's greatest failing, according to Annie, occurs when preachers fail to comfort mourning families, as when Preacher Rice visits the afflicted Richards family upon their losing Troy:

> ...when a preacher comes to comfort you it always makes you feel worse.... For the preacher will say God's ways are mysterious and beyond our understanding. What seems unbearable to humans must be part of a plan. If something bad is an accident it's bad, but if it's part of a plan that's much worse. I've never understood why preachers think that is comforting. They make you feel so hopeless and stupid. For they remind you there's nothing you can do. Your suffering is all part of God's plan. You don't have control over nothing, no matter what you do. It makes you feel weak and sick in your bones, the way a bad fever does [*RfGC* 15–16].

Such platitudes, in Annie's view, perform the exact opposite of their intended effect. Annie believes that people look for hope in such situations, that they do not need their attention directed to their own weakness, their own inability to understand why such awful things happen and their own inability to prevent such awful things from happening. Preachers who do little more than accept the part of comforter and repeat platitudes serve as bad actors, having limited investment in their parts and failing to respond to their audiences.

Annie's reaction to the first church service following the news of her brother's death demonstrates the difference she finds between the conventions of religious practice and any genuine spiritual feeling. Annie feels some discord prior to the service, because her mother, Julie, refuses to attend with the family, the first time Annie can recall her mother's missing Sunday service when sickness does not cause her absence. Annie cheerfully places her only money, fifty cents, into the collection plate, and waits for the service to begin. After the preacher asks the congregation to hold the Richards family in its prayers, a mentally ill congregant, Edward Peace, claims the Richards family has incurred God's wrath. Although the preacher calms Peace, Annie sees the pastor's failure in his attempt to continue the otherwise rote ceremony, how his timing falters during the sermon, with his repeating lines and his failed invitation to bring repentant congregants to the altar. Leaving the service brings her relief:

> It seemed almost strange to me to come out of the church and see the trees and feel the wind. I was almost surprised to see the road and the fields, the parked cars and cattle in the pasture,

> and the gray and blue mountains, and everything going on about its business, like nothing had happened in the church, nothing had been said. There seemed little connection between the words inside the church and what went on outside. But the strangeness was not bad. In fact it was comforting, to see the peacefulness of the shrubbery and the parking lot, going on in time as always. It was both good and scary to see that time didn't stop for nothing. We might all be getting older, and a dear one was gone, but life and time went on, no matter about the talk of hell and heaven, sin and getting saved [155].

This passage deserves our attention because Annie understands that the words in the church are not of this world. Like the rote terms of comfort the preacher offers when he visits the Richards family after they first learn of Troy's death, the sermon fails to impress Annie with any reference to the immediate concerns of their lives. Walking outside, Annie finds comfort in the world around her, but it is not a natural world untouched by people. Her reference to "the peacefulness of the shrubbery and the parking lot" reveals an appreciation of how people participate in the continuation of the world, integrated with "the road and the fields, the parked cars and cattle in the pasture, and the gray and blue mountains." Annie's description shows us how she, from her position standing outside the church, permits her vision to stray from her immediate physical space to how she fits with the community just outside the church property and then, in turn, with the larger world. In his analysis of Morgan's poetry, John Lang describes how Walt Whitman's "Song of Myself," with its emphasis on the intrinsic interviability of the soul and the spirit, has influenced Morgan's work: "Such juxtaposition of the physical and spiritual is characteristic of Morgan's poetry, as is the movement from the abstract to the concrete and from the immanent to the transcendent" (75). Annie's transcendent moment proves such influence on Morgan's prose as well. Symbolically, the preacher's sermon has failed to accomplish what Annie can see for herself; the sermon's reliance on clichéd descriptions of the afterlife does not orient Annie in her love for people so much as her watching life go on outside the church. The preacher's failed sermon cannot encompass her spirit and the spirit of her community.

Muir must arrive at a similar understanding. Annie recalls Muir's first attempt to preach at her church, when he relies on abstractions and familiar terms from other sermons. Annie describes feeling deep sympathy for his predicament, "afraid as if I was the one standing up there trying to think of words to say, trying to find the rhythm of a sermon" (*RfGC* 38). His failure, punctuated with a disruption by his brother Moody, makes Muir feel disgraced, so much that when he later encounters Hank Richards in a scene in Morgan's *This Rock*, Muir doubts that he will preach again: "I'm afraid I ain't got the call." "The call might still come," Hank says. "The Lord's timing may be different than ours" (*TR* 68). Hank's parting words in the scene, "We don't have to do nothing fancy to serve the Lord" (*TR* 69), appear to influence Muir's approach to preaching. When Muir delivers Moody's funeral sermon, Annie recognizes that Muir offers a delivery all his own: "It was the honesty and plainness of his talk that surprised me. I'd never heard a preacher at a funeral talk like that. I think everybody was as surprised as me" (*RfGC* 116). Later, when Muir speaks at the funeral for his mother, Ginny, he concentrates on describing her good life, how she has performed specific acts that have demonstrated her faith:

> Muir had chose not to say the usual things preacher talk about at funerals. He didn't mention heaven and hell or the many mansions in the sky, the way preachers usually do. Instead he just give a long list of the things that Ginny had loved. It was the simplest funeral speech I'd ever heard, and maybe the best. He said Ginny had loved her house, her rose garden, and the stately

> junipers around the yard. She'd love sewing white blouses and making black skirts. She loved giving to the poor and coming to the aid of anyone in need. She'd nursed the sick and comforted the bereaved. She liked to set on the Sunset Rock beyond the pasture and watch the stars come out in the evening. She'd done that since she was a little girl [*RfGC* 239].

Muir's touching influence on the congregation comes from his emphasizing that their daily lives have meaning. Ginny has had the opportunity to practice her faith even in the limited confines of her being denied specific religious roles as a woman. She could practice her faith, influence the beliefs of her children as best she could, and interpret the world around her as an assurance of God's conscious and present blessing. Muir's sermon reveals his ability to recognize the good in the world as Annie has learned in her own way.

After the war, taking the pulpit, Muir's approach to delivering the sermon has changed, and Annie believes she sees how she has influenced him, as well.

> He was older now, and his work away from home during the war had matured him, and maybe marriage had matured him, too.... [I]t was partly acting, for I was certain he was nervous, though he didn't show it. Even his voice was soothing.
>
> Muir talked like a sermon was natural as rain falling on an April morning or the leaves turning yellow in the fall.... Even though he was my husband he didn't seem hardly like the nervous and excited man I'd knowed and lived with. He talked like the right words just come to him without effort. He was speaking his thoughts. It was not the way he talked at home. It was a different voice and a different manner. As I watched him I thought how he was like an actor, a good actor, playing the *role* of a preacher. Through practice, years of thought and study and practice, he'd learned the role. That was thrilling to me, for I'd always loved acting. I seen that we are always learning our roles, rehearsing our roles, and playing a part [*RfGC* 300–01].

In spite of their age difference and the ranges of their experiences, Annie finds a confirmation in her understanding of the value of good acts by seeing the benefits that Muir derives from them. Yet Annie understands the necessity of practice in Muir's making his sermons seem natural, the need to "act right." Annie discovers that one must build a repertoire of responses to meet the crises likely to come, if only to be prepared to assist others in their needs. Annie and Muir believe in the reward of the hereafter, but they see the necessity to celebrate the blessedness of this world, even when empathy remains the most one can offer.

Cecelia Conway praises Morgan's women narrators by saying he "comes into his own in the later and longer works after he shape shifts and begins writing convincingly and fully from a woman's point of view" (289). Annie's growth as a loving, engaged member of her community develops in a similar fashion. After struggling with the limitations of men's voices, she learns to cope with hardship by developing her role, rejecting ill-read and ill-interpreted stereotypes of being a bride and being a preacher's wife, instead writing a new role as she goes along. No longer bound by the clichés of tired church services, delighting in her husband's conscious practice of grace in his fulfilling his dream to become a preacher, Annie comes to appreciate blessedness as a way of life rather than a state of being. In the novel's final chapter, Annie, after weeks of laying in and concentrating on her newborn daughter, Angela, first sees Muir's church on the top of Meetinghouse Mountain. When she sees the steeple for the first time, it unites for her the human, natural, and spiritual world:

> It was the most beautiful thing, that steeple pointing straight to heaven. It made the mountain and the valley and the whole community seem to reach up to that point of hope, far above the sinkholes and mud and confusion of the everyday things [*RfGC* 316].

Annie senses that Muir has found the means to integrate these influences, just as she has experienced earlier when she has seen the busy world outside the dismissal of the failed funeral sermon for Troy. In the final scene, Annie later takes her toddler with her to share a picnic lunch with Muir as he continues to build a church on top of the mountain. Characteristically, Muir considers tradition:

> "Everybody will think it's funny to have a picnic on a workday," Muir said.
> "We have to eat lunch somewhere," I said. "Might as well be by the river."
> Angela started to cry with the sun in her eyes and I moved her to my side so she set in my shadow. The warm sunlight near the splashing water made me feel so easy I thought I could set there forever [318].

Annie's comment reminds us of the significance of the river as a symbol in her faith, and Morgan has her direct her husband to that spot, a significant indication that while Muir acts as head of the household, Annie's role as wife and mother serves as foundation of the household. Her last comment, moreover, echoes a key passage in Willa Cather's *My Ántonia*, where the orphan Jim finds some peace lying in his grandparents' Nebraska pumpkin patch:

> I kept as still as I could. Nothing happened. I did not expect anything to happen. I was something that lay under the sun and felt it, like the pumpkins, and I did not want to be anything more. I was entirely happy. Perhaps we feel like that when we die and become a part of something entire, whether it is sun and air, or goodness and knowledge. At any rate, that is happiness; to be dissolved into something complete and great. When it comes to one, it comes as naturally as sleep [Cather 18].

Of course, such moments of peaceful, loving stasis do not last forever, but those moments restore one's spirit in preparation for whatever may come. Annie's moment at the river serves more as a confirmation than a reward. Through the struggles of the Great Depression and the Second World War, through the heartbreaking losses of her brother and mother, Annie has found her role, to engage and nurture the blessedness around her, her own courageous life's work to "behave for a purpose."

Works Cited

Cather, Willa. *My Ántonia*. 1918. Boston: Houghton Mifflin Co., 1954.

Conway, Cecilia. "Robert Morgan's Mountain Voice and Lucid Prose." Miller, Danny E., Sharon Hatfield, and Gurney Norman, editors. *An American Vein: Critical Readings in Appalachian Literature*. Columbus: Ohio University Press, 2005. pp. 275–95.

Drewitz-Crockett, Nicole. "Authority, Details, and Intimacy: Southern Appalachian Women in Robert Morgan's Family Novels." *The Southern Quarterly* 47.3 (2010): pp. 117–28.

Godwin, Rebecca. "'After the fighting, the scars remain': An Interview with Robert Morgan on His War Literature." *North Carolina Literary Review* 23 (2014): pp. 6–17.

Herring, Gina. "Interview with Robert Morgan." *Appalachian Journal* 29 (2002): pp. 494–504.

Lang, John. *Six Poets from the Mountain South*. Baton Rouge: Louisiana State University Press, 2010.

Morgan, Robert. *Gap Creek*. 1999. Chapel Hill, NC: Algonquin Books, 2012.

______. *The Road from Gap Creek*. Chapel Hill, NC: Algonquin Books, 2013.

______. *This Rock*. 2001. Chapel Hill, NC: Algonquin Books, 2002.

Robert Morgan's Nonfiction Books

Crossing Over the Mountains

TED OLSON

An evanescent spirit of the past is present at the core of much of Robert Morgan's poetry, and a keen historical consciousness infuses his fiction. To Morgan, though, imaginative approaches to understanding the principal setting in virtually all his literary works (Appalachia) and the central theme of those works (the unique experience of living in Appalachia) ultimately proved limiting. After achieving considerable literary success in poetry and fiction through interpreting Appalachia from literary perspectives, Morgan yearned to explore the interactions of actual rather than fictional characters in a regional context. The characters that particularly interested him were historical figures of national significance whose renowned deeds on the Appalachian frontier had haunted him since his boyhood. It was therefore inevitable that, in his quest to understand the motivations of distinctively Appalachian yet indisputably national heroes, Morgan would turn to nonfiction. This mode of expression would allow him to ply his narrative and literary skills in service to the telling of stories of public ownership. Revealingly, in this quest he has to date employed not some contemporary, currently fashionable postmodern form of creative nonfiction; rather, he has exercised a classical style of prose balancing clear-eyed presentation of historically grounded narratives with traditional historiography.

Morgan's effort to understand American heroes of a provably Appalachian background has thus far culminated in the publication of two nonfiction books: *Boone: A Biography* (2007) and *Lions of the West: Heroes and Villains of the Westward Expansion* (2011). These are textured works of scholarship, containing cross-referenced interpretations of the lives and deeds of historical figures affiliated with late eighteenth- and early nineteenth-century Appalachia. The former book, of course, chronicles the life and accomplishments of the frontier hero Daniel Boone, while the latter book interweaves stories about such figures as Thomas Jefferson, Andrew Jackson, David Crockett, Sam Houston, and James K. Polk. At another level, Morgan's two nonfiction books offered the author the opportunity and the challenge to explore and chronicle the fact-bound Appalachian frontier as opposed to one that has been artistically reconstructed.

By his own reckoning, Morgan intentionally departed from his familiar Appalachian fictional realm because there were other Appalachian stories worthy of his telling. As he conveyed in that book's introduction, *Boone* was the logical next step for an author whose literary imagination had previously, and quite successfully, navigated passage from the abstractions of poetry to the more concretely rendered world of fiction. Morgan's realization of his need to turn to nonfiction occurred during the composition of his 2003 novel *Brave Enemies*, a work that rendered the backcountry experiences of Revolutionary War soldiers.

> It was writing the novel *Brave Enemies*, set in the American Revolution and culminating at the Battle of Cowpens in South Carolina in 1781, that led me back to Boone. As I did my research on the Revolutionary period in the Carolinas, I grew more and more preoccupied with life on the frontier, where white settlers mingled and fought with and learned from the Native populations. I came to see what an extraordinary story that was, the collision of different worlds right in my own backyard, as British confronted French, Indians fought Indians, white Regulators confronted the colonial government, and finally Americans fought the Crown. And through it all the thread of slavery stretched like a poison filament from earliest colonial times to the nineteenth century and Civil War.
>
> I found Boone a much more complex person than I had noticed before. Why was he remembered, romanticized, revered, and written about when many other figures on the Kentucky frontier were pretty much forgotten? I wanted to find out what it was about Daniel Boone that made him lodge in the memory of all who knew him and made so many want to tell his story. How was a scout and hunter turned into such an icon of American culture? [*Boone* xviii-xix]

Morgan rightly recognized that narratives based on historical events need to honor facts, but he also understood that such stories hold considerable mythic value. For an accomplished imaginative writer like Morgan, revisiting stories defined by existing documentation would pose a particular challenge, necessitating a balance between narrative and expository modes of discourse. Morgan's success in achieving such a balance can be illustrated through reference to the fact that *Boone* and *Lions of the West* received accolades in more or less equal measure from literary critics and historians.

Many Americans of Morgan's generation were drawn to Boone after witnessing the popular media's romanticized portrayal of that frontier hero during the 1960s (primarily conveyed through the hit television show starring Fess Parker, which was an effort to tap into the national audience Parker had garnered in the 1950s by portraying another Appalachian hero, David Crockett). Obviously aware of the representations of Boone circulating in American popular culture, Morgan's perspective on Boone was ultimately a personal one shaped after hearing his father's Boone-related stories and anecdotes while growing up in western North Carolina. Morgan's family believed there was direct kinship between their ancestors and Boone, and indeed Boone's mother was named Sarah Morgan. While his research never identified close genealogical ties between the families, Morgan nonetheless felt profound psychic connection to Boone and in his biographical study decided to add to the already voluminous written interpretations of that historical figure.

In his introduction to *Boone*, Morgan identifies the contributions of earlier biographers toward constructing (John Filson, the Rev. Timothy Flint), correcting (the Rev. John Mason Peck, Lyman Copeland Draper), or deconstructing (Archibald Henderson) the widely-held romanticized images of Boone. Morgan acknowledges the brilliant biographical work by such twentieth-century Boone scholars as John Bakeless, John Mack Faragher, and Michael A. Lofaro, and when Morgan challenges particular notions about Boone offered by such scholars, he does so without the vitriol of many academic historians—a fact that suggests he sees his own biography of Boone as being in collaboration, not competition, with these other scholars.

Morgan does make several noteworthy contributions to Boone scholarship. Elaborating upon a biographical detail overlooked by previous scholars, he explores the important role of Freemasonry in Boone's life. Morgan's most perceptive scholarly contribution may be his assessment of Boone's impact on such authors as William Wordsworth, Lord Byron, James Fenimore Cooper, Ralph Waldo Emerson, Henry David Thoreau, and Walt Whitman, and on such visual artists as Thomas Cole, Asher B. Durand, Frederick Church, and George Caleb Bingham. In recognizing and tracing the "anxiety of influence" of Boone on a range of British and American artistic figures, Morgan extends Boone's relevance: Morgan suggests that Boone should not only be viewed as a frontier hero, but should also be valued as an internationally relevant culture figure.

Boone was positively received within America's literary and scholarly communities. Authors ranging from Ron Rash and Richard Bausch contributed laudatory blurbs to the book's cover, as did such prominent scholars as John Shelton Reed, Daniel Blake Smith, and Michael Kammen. Smith's blurb encapsulated the contributions of Morgan's book: "A narrative tour de force.... Informed by serious scholarship and propelled by superb storytelling, Morgan's book captures the heart of an American original." Critical reviews in mainstream newspapers as well as in specialized academic periodicals were generally positive—and were at times rapturous—in their praise of Boone, leading to strong national sales. Reader responses on bookseller websites were typically enthusiastic, with many readers commenting that Morgan had elucidated distinctions between Boone the man and Boone the myth.

As impressive as *Boone* was in balancing narrative command and contextualization (as evidence of the latter, the book features 37 pages of research citations), Morgan's next nonfiction book, *Lions of the West*, is in some respects a greater achievement. To write the former book, Morgan was entering territory previously surveyed and explored; his main tasks were to identify features of Boone's world that had been overlooked and to interpret the consciousness of that one person. *Lions of the West*, though, required its author to tell multiple historical narratives and to represent a host of consciousnesses. Put another way, while *Boone* is a biography of a singular historical figure, *Lions of the West* is a history of an entire nation during one crucial phase in its development. Proving equal to that daunting task, Morgan in this later book exhibits comprehensive and at times innovative scholarship: the citation notes, indicating references to a wide range of scholarly and archival sources, add up to 42 pages, and Morgan's discussion of the Mexican War often draws upon the perspectives of Mexican historians.

While largely based on secondary sources, *Lions of the West* makes a solid contribution by virtue of its graceful melding of diverse historical materials and its authoritative storytelling. Indeed, the book lucidly draws connections between disparate historical figures whose lives intersected in matters of national expansion and legislation, but who otherwise had little in common in terms of personal experiences or political philosophies.

"The West" in the book's title refers mostly to the post–Revolution Southern U.S. territory west of the Appalachian crest and extending into present-day Texas (an area historically called "the Old Southwest"). Devoting individual chapters to such well-known denizens of the "West" as Crockett, Jackson, and Polk, and including a chapter on the heretofore neglected figure of Nicholas P. Trist (a key U.S. diplomat during the Mexican War who was related to Thomas Jefferson by marriage), Morgan in this book builds upon the historical coverage of Boone by exploring a later phase of American history, the first four decades of the nineteenth century. It was during this period that restless people from Appalachia and the Old Southwest—compelled to venture further westward because of overcrowding in settled areas and the possibility of riches in unclaimed territory—relocated to Texas and other areas west of the Mississippi River. Hence, *Lions of the West* links eighteenth-century Appalachian frontier history with the settling of the present-day U.S. Southwest and the usurpation of Texas after the Mexican War. That conflict has often been depicted as a contest resulting from the inevitable spread of a nation imbued with a sense of Manifest Destiny, yet Morgan's account of the Mexican War is commendably balanced, even nuanced. While he clearly respects the American leaders who settled the West, Morgan resists romanticizing them; instead, he sees and straightforwardly conveys strengths as well as weaknesses in their characters. He does not ignore or downplay the greed and violence associated with the historical events he confronts in the book, and he leaves no doubt that his own sympathies are firmly directed toward the victims of the westward expansion movement—the Native Americans.

In a short but helpful Prologue, Morgan explains his objectives with *Lions of the West*:

> With the exception of Nicholas P. Trist, the lives of all these men ... have been chronicled many times, often by outstanding historians and biographers. My hope is that recounting them briefly and in sequence here may create an integrated narrative where the separate lives link up and illuminate each other, making complex, extended events more accessible to readers in the twenty-first century. The discovery and exploration of the West is a large part of the story of who we are [xxii].

In creating an overarching yet trustworthy nonfiction narrative of his own region's role in the founding of the American nation, Morgan exhibits humility and restraint: he makes no claims that *Lions of the West* is a revisionist historical study of the frontier of Appalachia and the "Old Southwest." Eschewing the self-consciousness and stylistic trickery endemic to much contemporary nonfiction, Morgan crafts a direct and linear portrayal of a complex, shared historical experience. Neither romanticizing nor vilifying the characters whose nation-making deeds he recounts, Morgan avoids the pseudo-mythologizing often associated with popular history books and instead unapologetically chronicles the public actions of various historical personages, with psychologically credible analyses of their private motivations.

Interestingly, while *Boone* was lauded within literary as well as history communities, *Lions of the West* primarily garnered critical reactions from historians, sporting blurbs penned by such leading scholars as Daniel Walker Howe, Walter LaFeber, and Douglas Brinkley. And, collectively speaking, the reader responses posted online during the initial months of that book's publication evinced little of the ambivalence that a few readers had expressed toward *Boone*. Whereas the earlier book had covered some ground previously explored by other scholars, thus inviting carefully parsed comparisons, *Lions of the West* was generally admired for the sweep of its narrative—for the fact that its author had skillfully adventured into a widely unfamiliar terrain of history.

This degree of respect from leading historians suggests that both of Morgan's recent nonfiction books—while obviously engagingly written—should be appraised first and foremost as authoritative and insightful works of history. Like the pioneers he writes about, who crossed over the mountains to find new territories in which to settle without losing their Appalachian identities, Morgan in these two nonfiction books has ventured into and mastered a new and difficult terrain—the genre of formal history—without surrendering the distinctive literary qualities that have long empowered his poetry and his fiction.

Works Cited

Morgan, Robert. *Boone: A Biography*. Chapel Hill, NC: Algonquin Books of Chapel Hill, 2007.
_____. *Lions of the West: Heroes and Villains of the Westward Expansion*. Chapel Hill, NC: Algonquin Books of Chapel Hill, 2011.

IV

In His Own Words

A Sense of Place

Robert Morgan

I think my earliest memory is of waking and seeing stars so close and bright they seemed to brush my face. I'd gone to sleep in the hot church during prayer meeting and was being carried home on my father's shoulder. I was about two. I woke as we crossed the pasture, my mother and sister walking beside us, starlight sparkling on the dewy grass. The swaying as my father walked made the stars seem to wash and swim in a kind of dance around my head, close as fireflies and luminous moths. I had awakened in a world of shadows, whispering lights, crickets, the shout of a distant waterfall. I discovered night was a place all its own, very different from the day.

Recently I was asked to describe my sense of place in connection with my writing. My sense of physical place is very specific, not just regional but local, not even a county, not even a township, but the Green River Valley in Henderson County, North Carolina. It is about a square mile of land in the Blue Ridge Mountains where I grew up in the late 1940s and 1950s. The land had been bought by my great-great-grandpa Daniel Pace in 1838. It stretched from the black loam along the river across the pastures and hills to the rim of the Mount Olivet ridge. There was a peach orchard on top of the mountain, and apple, pear, cherry, and plum orchards on the hillsides. As a child I worked in the fields, hoeing corn or plowing with the horse in the loamy bottomlands. I hoed strawberries on the red clay upland patches, and gathered leaves for cowbedding in the woods. In my free time I could roam the pastures, climb trees in the woods, dig caves in the sides of the gullies, build ponds on the pasture branch. I knew intimately every ditch and pine thicket, and the place on Kimble Branch where some Indian craftsman had left thousands of chips as he made arrowheads. I caught June bugs and tied threads to their legs and let them fly like model airplanes. I knew the pits on the mountainsides where my great uncles had dug for zircons. My cousins and I slid down the mountainside on boards polished by the leaves. I knew the swimming holes in the river, the places where trout lurked in the creek, the gloomy outhouse. For all my life since, that place has served as the touchstone with which I compare other landscapes.

As I worked more and more in the fields I found many arrowheads and pieces of Indian pottery, a broken tomahawk. My father told me the Cherokees and other Indians had lived there, and that Green River was a translation of the Indian name for the stream. The very ground seemed haunted by the ghosts of the Indians. The shoals in the river seemed to mutter Indian names; the shadows in thickets were charged with their presence. The connection to Indians thrilled, deepened, and saddened my sense of the place.

But for me there is an equally important sense of place, for which I have no name, in the landscape of language. When I heard a phrase such as "the valley of the shadow of death" or "death where is thy sting" or "Before Abraham was I am" or "I am that I am" I knew it was a place I had to seek, where language had an intense luster, a strange and luminous vitality. I did not know how to get there, but I knew it was what I had to try for.

When I was older I found guideposts to that place in lines from Walt Whitman ("I look long and long") or Longfellow ("A boy's will is the wind's will") or Sandburg ("I listened to the wind counting its money and throwing it away"). In my search I found other guides in the music of Mozart, in *Look Homeward, Angel,* in the writing of Boris Pasternak, sometimes in film. When my sister Evangeline returned from a year at college with her freshman English textbook, I looked through that anthology of American literature and found a poem by Wallace Stevens called "Domination of Black." In that poem he talked about the fire turning inside a fireplace, and the leaves outside spinning, and the wheeling of the planets far overhead. I was stunned by the analogy of motion far and near, and the words, "I felt afraid. / And I heard the cry of the peacocks."

That was my first inkling of the connection between terror and the sublime. However scary it might be, I knew that was a place in the geography of language which I must make every effort to reach, however long it might take, whatever the cost.

It is important to remember that place primarily means people, the people on the land, the people who have been on the land. Our greatest interest in a place derives from those who are there, their struggles, failures, joys. A place is about stories, and stories are about encounters, people encountering people, encountering the elements, or fate. It has been said that stories are about conflicts, and I would add that the best stories are less about conflicts of good versus bad, than conflicts of loyalty, one good versus another good. It has also been said that stories are about connection as well as conflict, connections between people, between people and land, people and cultures. We read stories to connect with other people's lives, people often very different from ourselves, at least on the surface. And we write stories to connect with others, to feel part of the larger community of humanity. Stories help us to feel less alone. One of the glories of storytelling is that narratives can reach across boundaries of gender, age, ethnicity, race, religion, geography, and even time and, through translation, different languages. Stories help us connect with a sense of community, even a community across time.

To keep us reading, to earn its space and the time required for reading, a narrative must reward us on at least three levels. First is the local level, the quality of word choice and insight in each sentence, giving us the pleasure of recognition. Second is the sense of dynamics, that the story is going somewhere, that we are learning. Third, and perhaps most important, narrative has to have a sense of unfoldingness, of enlargement, of an architecture of connection as scattered threads and details and characters link up. That sense of wholeness is essential whether implicit or explicit.

One of my favorite quotes about writing is from the writer and critic Hollis Summers. He said, "The point of the story is always the point beside the point." That is, every good story surprises; it does not go where you expect it to go. The most significant vision is peripheral. In his poem "Merlin" Emerson writes, "We mount to paradise / by the stairway of surprise."

To know a place, to write about a place, it is important to know something about its history. For the past helps define, and certainly impinges on the present. We cannot begin to understand the South without knowing something of the racial history here, the long struggles, the vexed aftermath of the Civil War, the cotton mill culture, the extraordinary

Revolutionary War history of the region. It has been said that Americans are challenged by history, that we are descended from a gene pool of people uprooted from elsewhere, who looked to the future rather than to the past. That may indeed be a part of our pragmatic genius. But I don't know a single good writer who is not somehow engaged with the past, whether family history, regional history, ethnic history, oral history. Among the strengths of Southern writing are its intimacy with and candor about the past.

Once a reporter asked Eudora Welty why there were so many outstanding writers from Mississippi, even though that state was poor and always rated low in education and cultural resources. Ms. Welty hesitated for what seemed like a full minute. (She always said the right thing.) Finally she responded, "Perhaps we have more to explain."

Much of my writing is inspired not only by the place where I grew up in Henderson County, but by the stories I heard when I was growing up there. A few years ago I was interviewed at the farm on Green River. The interviewer looked around at the old barn and the corn patch by the river and said, "Tell me, I'm curious, how did you ever get from here to Cornell University, because practically speaking you can't get there from here." I told him I could understand why he thought that. After all we were poor, did not have a car or truck or tractor. We plowed with a horse and kept our milk and butter in the springhouse. My parents did not have a lot of formal education. But in fact I had some special advantages for a young writer. I grew up among wonderful storytellers. As we sat by the fireplace in winter, or on the porch on summer evenings, grownups told stories. My grandpa had a thousand stories about panthers, mad dogs, bears, ghosts. One of his favorites was about a man named Revis who built a cabin for his bride on the side of the mountain, using a flat rock there as a natural hearth. On their wedding night they built a big fire in the fireplace and went to bed, not knowing a huge nest of rattlesnakes were sleeping through the winter beneath the rock. As the rock warmed up they crawled out. When Revis got out of bed to investigate he was bitten by hundreds of snakes and died. A lovely story to tell kids at bedtime.

My mother had many stories about witchcraft, spells and charms, babies marked in the womb. Though my dad had only gone through the sixth grade he loved to read history, and to recount story after story about the family, the region, the Cherokee Indians, Daniel Boone, the Civil War, the Revolutionary War. He loved to describe the battle of Cowpens, and believed we were related to the victor, General Daniel Morgan.

When I began writing at NC State I wondered what I had to write about. My favorite authors wrote about London, Paris, Moscow. All I knew was the little farm in the Blue Ridge Mountains. It only came to me slowly, by trial and error, that I had a lot of material, the place and people I had known, the stories I heard while growing up, the stories of the Revolution and Civil War. And most important of all, I had the voices of those I'd known, the living idiom, the many voices of witness and testimony. My greatest breakthrough came when I found I could let my characters tell their own stories, and that their stories were not about me but about them, their world, their time, their words.

In the late winter and spring of 1989 I was attempting to write a novel about the life and death of an American soldier in World War II, based loosely on my Uncle Robert, who was killed in a B-17 crash in East Anglia on November 10, 1943. I studied his letters, service records, flight manuals, interviewed members of his bombardment group, pilots, bombardiers, navigators, and visited the site of the crash near Brome in Suffolk. But I got bogged down in all the technical details of strategic bombing, and couldn't get started. In frustration, I decided to create a fiancée for the soldier and let her tell part of the story. It was so scary to think of writing from the point of view of a woman. What did I know about how she would remember seeing her fiancé off to war, getting the telegram announcing his death? I told myself I would become like an actor, I would try to erase myself and give everything to the imagined character. By the time I got thirty pages into the story I knew it was the best thing I'd ever written. I had escaped from my world and voice into the fictive world. It became the novella *The Mountains Won't Remember Us*. That is perhaps the most important thing I've ever learned about fiction writing. Eudora Welty says in *One Writer's Beginnings* that we sometimes create our best characters by accident, but usually by going farthest from ourselves. She added that she had never intentionally put one of her opinions in the mouth of a character. I think I know just what she means. The best fiction is not reality transferred magically to the page, but an imagined world, created sentence by sentence and detail by detail, that magically seems absolutely real.

It was a surprise to me to discover that the more specific to a place, the more precisely local a story was, the more accessible it is to others. Exact detail, judiciously chosen, human struggle, deep emotion, are understandable by any literate reader. My most local, Appalachian work is the novel *Gap Creek*, which found thousands of readers in Germany, Holland, Australia, New Zealand, Canada. In that sense almost all narrative is local.

"No Writing in the Abstract"

An Interview

Robert M. West

In 1997 I interviewed Robert Morgan for *The Carolina Quarterly*, the literary magazine for which he'd served as fiction editor during his undergraduate years at UNC–Chapel Hill. Our long conversation—which focused on his poetry—appeared as "The Art of Far and Near" in the summer 1997 issue (volume 49, number 3). Ten years later Morgan had become far better known as a novelist, thanks particularly to the success of *Gap Creek*; during the same interval he had also published two other novels, a book of new and selected short stories, a book of new poems, and a book of new and selected poems. He was also nearly ready to publish his biography of Daniel Boone, after dedicating four years to that project. There was, then, plenty of new ground to cover in a new interview. We spoke at Morgan's Ithaca, New York, home, during the morning and early afternoon of June 22, 2007, a few days before *Boone*'s final corrections were due to the publisher.

West: Before *Boone*, you'd published nearly half a dozen novels and three short story collections. Did your experience writing prose fiction offer any advantages (or disadvantages) as you worked on your first biography?

Morgan: The experience of writing novels is obviously helpful, in terms of the narrative. Biography is very similar to a novel in that it's a story, it's a narrative. It's about somebody's life, life writing, and biography has always been very close to fiction writing in modern literature, though the biography has classical roots perhaps that the novel does not have: biography goes all the way back to the Greeks, to Plutarch and to other classical writers.

But yes, I think there was an advantage for me to have written novels and short stories because I had a sense of how you unfold a story. But having said that, the way you write a biography is substantially different in that you first do the research—you start collecting the facts you're going to use to build the narrative out of—you go and read the documents, you make copies of quotes, you assemble a lot of information. Once you've done that, though, then you call on your experience and your talent as a narrative writer and start putting it together into a story that's interesting, that has tension, a sense of dynamics; you want to give the reader a feeling that there's going to be some discoveries, there's mystery to it, there's romance. In the case of Daniel Boone, there's a lot of romance, he's such a romantic figure. You also have the advantage in writing about somebody like Boone of comparing the facts you've discovered to the folklore—in a sense the subject matter is already built into the facts, but also you have this parallel story, this comparative story of what you think of as the real Daniel Boone that you found in the documents, *and* the myth, the folklore, and the relationship between the two is part of the real interest of the story. I feel my subject in the Boone biography is as much the biography of the folklore as it is the biography of Boone himself. You look at the evolution of the mythology, of the folklore in the context of American history, in the evolution of American culture.

But I would never have written this biography as I have, had I not been a novelist, to begin with. As I would not have written novels as I did, had I not written a lot of poetry before that. One thing feeds into the next, and as a writer, you simply use what you know, and your experience as a writer, to write the book that you end up writing. But I think that almost everyone thinks of biography and novels as very close in some ways. You obviously don't have the freedom writing a biography that you do as a novelist, because you're sticking—insofar as possible—to the facts, to the quotes, to the language that your subject actually used, and to the language that historians and other writers have used in writing about your subject.

West: I do want to get back later to the way your poetry writing may have influenced your prose fiction writing, but first I'd like to probe that "insofar as possible." You said you stick to the quotes, you stick to the record as closely as you can, insofar as that's possible. What's the alternative? Did you find yourself trying to fill in some gaps in plausible ways, between events in the narrative as you discuss Boone's life?

Morgan: I think you inevitably end up filling in some things. You try to stick to the facts, and to the personality, as you understand the personality.

An example of where I certainly use my fiction-writing ability in writing the biography of Boone is with the most important period in his life: his first trip to Kentucky, 1769 to 1771. He stayed by himself in the wilderness most of the time—some of the time with his brother Squire—for almost two years. Historians and biographers have speculated on why he did not return to his family, to North Carolina, to the settlements, for supplies, and then go back to Kentucky. Well, I have a section of the biography where I speculate on that and *try* to get into his mind, based on what was said, what was later said and what he did. That is a kind of fiction writing, but it's fiction writing based on your understanding of the personality of your subject. And I stick with the facts as I know them: I don't change anything. I keep the dates, and actually spent a lot of time talking about the geology of Kentucky: the flora and fauna of Kentucky, what it might have looked like to somebody there, looking at it in its pristine state, relatively unaffected by Indians, who had been there for thousands of years. I speculate on comparisons between Boone's two years in the wilderness and Thoreau's two years at Walden, and Goethe's two years in Italy. These are the most important periods of these people's lives. Notice they're all romantic figures: I'm always looking at Boone in the context of romanticism, and the folklore of romanticism, and the importance of romanticism to European culture and American culture.

So I think to be a good biographer you have to speculate almost as a fiction writer would at certain points. But it's very important that you stick with the facts as they are known, and you don't start changing things around just to make the story more interesting, or to make it fit some concept you have of this person, or of the times. Part of the fun of writing a biography is to try to make your subject *alive* to the reader, just the way a character in a novel is alive. Biography means "life writing," and you succeed as a biographer if you can bring this person, the subject, alive for your reader, so they can live with this character, throughout reading the book.

West: Boone aside, do you have any favorite biographies?

Morgan: Oh, I have lots of favorite biographies. Probably the greatest biography I've ever read is Boswell's *Life of Johnson*. That is truly a literary masterpiece. It brings not only Johnson alive, but the world he lived in: the coffeehouses, the other writers, the editors, the politicians, the hangers-on.

I love biography and have read many of them. One of the literary biographies that has meant the most to me is Gay Wilson Allen's biography of Walt Whitman, *The Solitary Singer*. That also is a masterpiece, in the way it brings Whitman alive, as well as the culture in which he lived, his reading, his interest in arts, politics. I would guess that's one of the great literary biographies, certainly, in America. Obviously Edel's *Henry James*—his multivolume *Henry James*—is another.

We learn an enormous amount from good biographies about history, and about culture. It's a kind of history that focuses on people, and on a particular person, and on a particular time. Autobiography is probably just as important. Obviously *The Education of Henry Adams* is one of the great masterpieces of American literature—not only in the way it reveals the character and the development of Henry Adams' thought, but the way in which he brings the cultural world of his era, the literary world of his era, alive, and zeroes in on the complexities, the contradictions, the paradoxes of modern culture.

West: As you did the research for *Boone*, do you feel like you learned something important about the world beyond Boone—something important about Southern Appalachia, or about America in general?

Morgan: I would have to say I learned a lot from working on this project. Probably the overriding recognition for me has been the way Boone is at the very center of the story of American culture, and what I call the tragedy of contradictions of American culture. Boone is almost symbolic of this country, in that he was a part of the destruction of so much wilderness. And he is the best example I've encountered of the way in which American culture destroys what it loves most. He loved the Indians, the wilderness, the landscape of North America so much that he led people to come in and destroy it. It's a paradox I think that he recognized himself late in his life—that when he was younger, the wilderness of North America seemed so great, so endless, that it didn't seem possible you could ever clear it and destroy it, and later in Missouri he had to see that he had been an instrument—in fact he said as much—he realized he had been an instrument for the destruction of the Indians' hunting ground. He had had a hand in doing just exactly what he wanted to prevent, in a way. And I think this kind of paradox, tragic paradox, is at the very center of American history, and American culture. We love things and somehow end up destroying them. The environment, nature. So I came as I studied Boone to admire him more.

That is not typical of biographers. Usually, once you've seen warts and all, the closer you look, you know.... But Daniel Boone stands up remarkably well to closer scrutiny. His great failures were often the result of his generosity. He was a bad businessman partly because he simply wasn't aggressive enough. He wouldn't go to court to fight for his land claims. He gave away so much. He gave away money. He loaned money to people on no more security than their word, and that was usually not paid back. But he kept moving on because he did *not* want to fight it out in the commercial culture. The more I looked at him, the more I came to admire him, and also to pity him, caught in the greed and the rage to develop Kentucky, the Ohio Valley, and then Missouri. I believe that he thought when he was young and even when he was middle-aged that somehow he could live at peace with the Indians in the wilderness as a hunter. That's what he wanted most to do, and of course he found it was impossible—that once you go to the wilderness, other people follow you and eventually the Indians are driven out. He discovered that, certainly in Kentucky, that a wilderness without Indians is a contradiction in terms—that once the Indians are gone, it will be settled and cleared out, and there will be no wilderness. So I came to admire him, but also to feel sad about Boone. And I believe he felt sad about an awful lot of his life toward the end of it.

West: How did you shift from the notion of a book-length poem about Boone to a prose work on Boone?

Morgan: Well, in between my plans to write the poem about Boone and writing the biography, I had published five novels and three collections of short stories. I had become much more of a prose writer. But I also realized that I could handle the subject much better in prose than in poetry, because the subject demanded an enormous amount of detail. A vast amount of research, documents, quotes. The prose was a more flexible medium for investigating a life, and also bringing alive, trying to bring alive the culture of the frontier, the landscape of the frontier. To talk about the rivers, the keelboats, the flatboats, the way you trap furs, the way an Indian path looks, the way people built cabins, the way women made soap from the fat of animals. I needed a medium where I could put in that kind of detail, and keep the poetry of language, the cadence of good prose. I guess I think of all my writing in some sense as poetry, and I hope that the writing has some of the economy and precision, texture, cadence of poetry. But I didn't want to worry about line breaks and rhyme schemes, and that kind of thing. I wanted to make the reader feel absolutely intimate with the world of the eighteenth century. We're all aware that people wore buckskin and homespun cloth and Daniel Boone wore leggings made out of buckskin that Indian women had decorated with beads. I wanted to get in that kind of detail, to make it seem real. You *could* write a great poem about Daniel Boone, but I thought I just had a better chance of succeeding in prose.

West: It's just that sort of detail that so many readers seem to have found appealing in *Gap Creek*—the detail of how those people lived at the time. They wanted to hear what it's like to slaughter a hog. I think about what another poet turned fiction writer, Robert Penn Warren, did with another important figure on the American frontier, one who also had that contradictory aspect of destruction and preservation. Warren's portrait of Audubon is very elliptical: it omits just the sort of details that you're talking about including.

Morgan: Well, that's a poem I admire a great deal. I think he got a lot of the vision of Audubon in that, but it *is* to a great extent implicit. A poem by Warren even more detailed and just as memorable is *Brother to Dragons*, written I guess as a play or as a dramatic poem, about Jefferson's nephews. He really gives a sense of frontier life in that, and the world of slavery. Jefferson's nephews had murdered a slave. Warren is a writer I admire a great deal. And Audubon knew Boone: he claimed to have met him and to have hunted with him.

West: I'd wondered about the relationship between those two.

Morgan: Well, some historians think that Audubon never did meet him. Audubon didn't always stick to the truth: he loved to tell a good story. But I think he did. The problem was he said he met him in Kentucky, but that's almost impossible. He met him in Missouri, and later painted a portrait of Boone from memory. He didn't from life. But this is one of the great moments in American cultural history: the meeting of Daniel Boone, the greatest scout and frontiersman, and Audubon, the greatest artist, naturalist, both men of the romantic culture of America. It's thrilling to think of them actually meeting somewhere in the wilderness of Missouri and hunting together. Audubon says Boone showed him how to "bark" a squirrel, that is, to kill a squirrel without actually shooting it, but hitting the bark of a tree nearby, killing it with a concussion, so that the flesh is not damaged, the skin is not damaged. I share with Warren a fascination with history, which a lot of modern poets have not had. Certainly the New Critics have not encouraged the study of history. But in the case of Warren, you have this major New Critic and poet of that generation who is absolutely obsessed with history, primarily American history, and his best poetry is about historical things: "The Ballad of Billie Potts," *Audubon*, *Brother to Dragons*, *Chief Joseph of the Nez Perce*.

West: There you've got a figure who began really as a poet and then shifted mainly to writing prose fiction, though he did continue his poetry writing somewhat in that period. Then he shifted back to poetry.

Morgan: I should point out that Warren's first book was a biography. He began as a biographer. I believe it's a biography of John Brown.

West: Earlier, you mentioned briefly the fact that your poetry writing had affected your approach to prose writing. What's your sense of that? Is it just a matter of putting a priority on economy, or is it more complex than that?

Morgan: Well, my first publications were actually short stories. But writing poetry was absolutely essential to me, in many ways. For one thing, I had so much to learn about writing; I just had so far to go as a writer. And focusing on language in smaller units—short poems—enabled me to really begin to look at the quality of language, the texture of it, the sound of it. Economy. Precision. Rhythm. And to learn to get away from clichés, to get away from journalistic language. And try to find a new sound and a fresh diction.

So the poetry was valuable to me in itself, but also as a learning medium. By the time I had focused on writing poetry for a decade, I was just simply a much better writer: I knew a lot more about language, and what you could do with language, and what was worn out and what was effective. So I would never have been a prose writer, I think, had I not worked in poetry before. And I think that's true of so many American prose writers: Faulkner, Hemingway, and others really begin as poets and work for years in poetry.

But of course beyond that, there was the thrill of poetry itself. To be involved in the world of poetry, and to read poetry, and to write about it, and to read criticism of poetry, theory of poetics. So I wouldn't take anything for having spent those two decades primarily writing poetry and writing about it—teaching it, reading it, thinking about it, dreaming about it, theorizing about it. But having said that, once I decided to go back to prose fiction writing, in a sense I had to put that behind me and focus very hard on character development, drama, tension, and stripped-down language that was functional in terms of a narrative and was not particularly poetic. But I think since then I've incorporated a lot of things I've done in poetry into the prose, particularly when it's spoken by a character. One of the great breakthroughs for me as a writer of fiction was to learn to let my characters tell their own story. Once I had a living character telling her own story, she could be as poetic as she wanted to be. So it wasn't me writing poetically: it was them speaking poetically. I feel that almost all my fiction is voice-driven, and I can usually tell the story once I get a sense of the voice of the character who's narrating it. It's almost dramatic in that sense: it's the character telling their own story.

But also I think if you've read some of my poems and some of my fiction, you can see that in a sense they're cut from the same cloth: they're set in the same world, the same fascination with work, with the natural world, with agriculture, and in fact I have some short stories and poems with the same title, the same subject. And many of my prose stories have incorporated things that I've also addressed in the poems.

West: After working on prose fiction and focusing on that so intensely, do you feel your approach to poetry is different as a result? We've talked about the way poetry has informed your fiction writing, but is there a way fiction writing has informed your poetry?

Morgan: The way I think of poetry, yes, has been changed by writing fiction, in at least two ways. Having written a lot of prose narrative, I think more in terms of the voice of the poem than I did when I was a young poet. I thought in terms of metaphor and image and language and line breaks, strategic line breaks back then. Now I think of the poem as a more dramatic thing, or as a narrative act more, often.

But also as I worked on prose I came to consider much more the differences, the many possibilities of poetry and the possibilities of prose. And that led me much more to what we would call traditional form, including rhyme, and metrics. There are things you can do in rhyme and meter you simply cannot do in prose. The form is just a great deal of its power, of its meaning. I believe that poetry, including those devices, antedate prose, actually: our ancestors were born to love onomatopoeia, chanting. So my poetry of the past decade has been much more formal, but often it's been much more narrative too. My ideal of poetry now is to be able to write in traditional forms, including rhymed poems, in language that is absolutely contemporary, that's in no way literary—that is playing a game with some literary form, so you have complete arbitrariness on the one hand, of the form, and complete naturalness of the language and the voice, on the other. That's the thing that excites me most about poetry; it's the thing I love about, let's say, the poetry of Philip Larkin. That he's a formalist, he's a master of form, with a voice that is as contemporary as anything you can imagine in prose.

West: Right: he's very true to that English middle-class background, and that way of looking at the world, and that comes across in fairly common speech.

Morgan: But a poet like Richard Wilbur can also do that, you know, in an American voice. Formal perfection, while the idiom is very contemporary and conversational.

West: As I think about the strictly metrical poems you've published in recent years, it's occurred to me that for unrhymed metrical poems you prefer an iambic tetrameter line rather than the full pentameter of what we usually call blank verse. Is there something more appealing, or something that works for you in that slightly shorter line?

Morgan: I tend to think that for me, the pentameter line sounds more literary. That if you wanted to write in a voice that is very natural, and relaxed, that tetrameter seems to work better. I'm not sure exactly why, but some theorists of poetics say that the tetrameter line is almost a universal line of poetry in all languages—the four beats and the eight syllables, common meter, ballad meter, hymn meter, and I like that connection, that the eight-syllable line is just sort of a basic unit in poetry and always has been. You can very easily remember lines, rhymed lines, in tetrameter: "Whose woods these are, I think I know. / His house is in the village, though." But even when I was writing in syllabics and not in metrics, I loved the octosyllabic line. It just seems to work for me, you know: that short line, metrical but with long sentences flowing through it, and folded through it, so you have the voice, the cadence of the sentence, but you also have this almost ballad-length, hymn-length line that it's being passed through.

I've never stopped writing poetry. I've at certain periods in recent years written almost as much poetry as I used to. I haven't *published* as much. But I find poetry always thrilling to come back to, particularly in periods when I'm not writing fiction. And writing nonfiction seems to agree well with writing poetry. Working on the Boone biography, I worked alternately on poetry and at certain periods, when I finished a draft for instance, going back to revise a draft, to work on poetry. I can't imagine giving up writing poetry.

West: We've talked a little about the biography and poetry writing and novel writing, but we haven't quite touched on short story writing. I remember you saying to an audience at NC State that your novel writing had "ruined" you as a short story writer. You turned to Lee Smith, who was in the audience, and said, "Did you have the same experience?" and she immediately said, "Oh, yes." And I believe at the time you said that novel writing changes your sense of scale so much that coming back to that much shorter narrative was difficult. But I wonder what your perspective is on that now—if you would still say the same thing.

Morgan: I think I would still agree with that. A short story in some ways is closer to a poem than it is to a novel: it's a very tight form. And though it's not written in verse lines, it depends as much on implicitness, and extremely tight control, as poetry. And when you really get into writing short stories, you think in terms of the rondure, the trajectory of the story. It begins, it moves fast, it pulls you in, then it's over. Very much like poetry. There's nothing as thrilling as writing a short story when it works, because it's something you can finish in the foreseeable future. You know you can have the satisfaction, the gratification, of writing something that's finishable, in a week, or however long it takes you to do it. Eudora Welty said she wrote some of her stories in one day; I think Faulkner could write a story in one day. For most writers, it might take a week, or two weeks. But that is a really thrilling thing, to know you're telling a story, you're writing this form, you have it under control, it's developing as it should, and then it's landing on its feet at the end, in the right place.

That is so different from writing a novel, which is an exploration of a world of characters that just goes on and on, and keeps opening up in this larger form. You think about people, you think of them this way, you think of them that way. You have this story going on over here, you have another thread of the story going on over there. You have a sense that the two threads will come together at some point. Working on novels doesn't incapacitate you, obviously, because you can go back and write stories, but the more you focus on that larger form, and on opening and opening and opening this world and the characters, their struggles, the conflicts there, the harder it is to go back and think of something that's going to be over in ten pages, fifteen pages. And that depends on selection to such an extent. What you don't say in a short story is just as important as what you do. And that implicitness and that indirectness is very, very important for the story—particularly to the kind of short story, let's say, that Hemingway wrote, or Ray Carver wrote, what we call minimalism, which is a very poetic kind of form. All poetry's a kind of minimalism, I guess, in that sense.

That's what Lee probably meant: that you spend years thinking of novels, and thinking of the way you just get deeper and deeper and deeper into the character, and the personality of the character, into the relationships and the family—what Eudora Welty calls an "extended intimacy" between strangers, the reader and the characters. It's as though you have developed other muscles and other ways of thinking of narrative, also. The more you write novels, probably the harder it is to write short stories, and you notice with writers such as Hemingway and Faulkner and probably Eudora Welty also that most of their stories were written when they were younger, and after they have written lots of novels they tend to go *on* writing novels. Eudora Welty wrote a few stories toward the end of her life, but very few of them.

West: And I assume that also has to do with the greater commercial market for the novel than for the short story collection.

Morgan: The competition to publish short stories has always been intense, because there's so many people who write them, and so many *good* writers who write them. Even a hundred years ago it was hard to publish short stories, and it's still very hard. Because the market is very limited. These days it's mostly limited to literary quarterlies, with a few exceptions: *The New Yorker*, *Gentleman's Quarterly*. I think *The Atlantic Monthly* has quit publishing short fiction, for example. So it's really hard even for famous writers probably to publish short stories. I've always been thrilled when I got a short story in print, to think that someone would publish my short story. It's actually easier to publish poems—a lot easier—than it is to publish short stories, because they don't take up very much space. So many journals publish poems. The two hardest things to publish are *books* of poems and individual short stories in magazines.

West: In our interview ten years ago I asked you something along these lines, but a decade *has* passed, so I'll ask again: how has your sense of yourself as a Southern and/or Appalachian writer changed over the last forty years?

Morgan: Well, I think the recognition that I was an Appalachian writer came slowly. I never set out to be someone who wrote about the region I had grown up in. It's just that as I developed as a writer, that's what I had to write about: all the stories I had heard as a kid, and what I knew best was the farm there, and the land my great-great-grandpa Pace had bought back in 1838. I never thought of myself as an Appalachian writer, because "Appalachian" was not a word I really was familiar with. I thought of myself as somebody from the mountains. But in the past ten years I think it's changed very much. It's been a very good ten years for Southern Appalachian writing: there've been a lot of new writers come along, in both poetry and fiction, especially in fiction. I think this country is so big and so diverse that almost all writers have some sense of connection either to a region or to an ethnic group or racial connection, religious connection. I've never been bothered by being thought of as an Appalachian writer; I'm certainly from the region and have written a lot about it.

I believe as the years go by, American writing is going to become even more diverse. There's going to be even more multiplicity, and these labels actually could be of some use, to identify writers. They're somebody from the West Coast, or the Rocky Mountain region. The oldest school of writing I suppose is the New England one, in the 19th century; that was American writing at that time, because almost all the writing was done in the Northeast.

West: We all learned in school—in high school, at least, if not in college as well—that American literature was something produced almost entirely by Northeasterners.

Morgan: Right. Well, what was being left out, depending on the time, in the 19th century, were a number of Southern writers. Poe was the only one who really was in the canon, being taught in literature classes. But that was leaving out certainly somebody like William Gilmore Simms, who was really one of the major writers of his time. Both a poet and a fiction writer, primarily a fiction writer, but also a critic: he wrote quite a bit of critical work. And the poets we associate with Charleston, and with Russell's Magazine, such as Henry Timrod, Paul Hamilton Hayne, and most notably Sidney Lanier, who was the most famous in his lifetime. Sidney Lanier had a great reputation in the 19th century. It was Sidney Lanier who was asked to write the words to the centennial cantata to be performed in Philadelphia in 1876. Well, it was controversial at the time, because living just across the river in Camden was Walt Whitman, who had been the wound dresser in the Civil War, and Sidney Lanier had fought on the Confederate side. But he was well known, particularly in music circles: he was a flutist and a musician as well as a writer, and he was asked to write the words, as Richard Wilbur was asked to write the words to the bicentennial cantata. But they may have had in mind that not only was Sidney Lanier a musician, but he wrote formal poetry that could be more easily set to music than Whitman's free verse.

West: You've written a poem about Sidney Lanier; Andrew Hudgins has written an entire book in Lanier's voice. And yet there's a poet whose reputation seems dead now. Do you have any speculations why that would be?

Morgan: Literary fashion is something very hard to predict. Somebody can have an enormous reputation in one century and be forgotten in the next. I don't know the reason why. I think that in the age of the New Criticism, so many of the anthologists and editors of textbooks were from the South, that they may have given a certain prominence to Sidney Lanier and Henry Timrod that other editors might not have. For somebody my age we had the impression when we were in college that these were part of the academic canon, which they may not have been except for that factor. It's true that the greatest writing of the period is done in the Northeast. Dickinson and Whitman were leading poets. I myself have spent a lot more time teaching and reading Emerson and Thoreau than any Southern writers, except for Poe: I've read Poe a lot and taught him quite a bit.

But when we think of the real origins of the American literary imagination, we think of Emerson and the way Emerson and Thoreau combined the zeal, the spiritual zeal of New England with the naturalism of the Enlightenment. It's as though Boston and Philadelphia came together to create what we think of as Transcendental poetry, American poetry of the 19th century. The Southern writers were a little bit off that map. Poe consciously and explicitly opposed that type of writing: he called the Transcendentalists "the Frogpondians." They returned the compliment by calling him "the Jingle Man." He belonged to that other strand of romanticism that has something gothic in it—that we associate with the Coleridge of "Kubla Khan," of "Christabel," "The Rime of the Ancient Mariner," with Hawthorne, and to some extent Melville.

West: There are ways to pull together those New England writers, as you suggest. Do you think there's anything tying together Southern Appalachian writers, of recent times? As you said, recent years have been a great time for Southern Appalachian literature. When you think of people like Lee Smith, yourself, Charles Frazier, Charles Wright, Fred Chappell, Kathryn Stripling Byer, others—is there anything tying these people together other than a geography?

Morgan: You can certainly find common themes. Since Southern Appalachia is not famous for its big cultural institutions, we think of the subject of Southern Appalachian fiction primarily as family—community and family. Particularly families led by strong women. Almost any Southern Appalachian fiction writer you can think of, and also poets, usually focus on strong women characters: to some extent the culture I think was a rural matriarchy. But they usually also have in common a great interest in evoking the landscape, the natural world of the Southern Appalachians. In that way they are part of the larger picture of American romanticism, carried out through Frost, and Stevens, *and* a part of Southern writing. It's not exactly separate from Southern writing.

But you don't see the same preoccupation with, let's say, the Civil War, that you see in Deep Southern writing. The people in the mountains were as often Unionists as they were sympathizers with the Confederacy. There were not a lot of large plantations, and there were few slaves in the region. The Civil War affected the region, but mostly in terms of the violence of the outlaws, the bushwhackers, as portrayed in *Cold Mountain*, for example. The sense of identification the mountain people had was that they were isolated, even from the Deep South, and perhaps almost as much from the Deep South as from the Northeast, as far as that went. That they were people who lived back in the hollows, in the coves, along the ridges, and were descended from German people as well as Welsh and Scotch-Irish and English, and often had to some extent a separate culture, had their own denominations, churches.

The period that I've been most concerned with, writing about Daniel Boone, is the Revolutionary period, and the period just after, when the mountains were perceived as a barrier for the English-speaking colonists and settlers. Instead of moving into the mountains, the mountains were something to get over—so oddly enough, Kentucky and Tennessee were settled before much of the Blue Ridge and the Appalachian Mountains. To that extent, the settlement was done both from the East and from the West: people came back into the mountains from the valleys of Tennessee and Kentucky. The settlements there are not as old as some of those further west. There are things that the mountain people shared with mountain people and rural people in the Northeast—in Vermont and New Hampshire, say, or even Maine. There is a common Appalachian culture all up and down the chain, the rural mountain culture.

But having said that, I have to admit that this sense of identity of being south of the Mason-Dixon line, and a part of Southern states that seceded (or in the case of Kentucky, did not; it's considered a border state), has given the people of the Southern Appalachians a further sense of separateness. You're different from the lowland Southerners, you're different from the northern Appalachian people, you're different from the Midwest.... I think that does show up in the culture: a sense of isolation, of distance. And in the county you and I grew up in, there was the further sense of difference between the local, native people, and the more wealthy people who came up in the summers to Flat Rock, had great mansions. My ancestors must have had a sense of being very different, as small landholders and farmers, from these families with many slaves and servants, huge estates, at the summer places in the Flat Rock area.

West: Something that seems especially prominent in the Appalachian literature I'm familiar with is music. You've written poems about musical instruments, Frazier gives us Stobrod the fiddler in *Cold Mountain*, Kathryn Stripling Byer writes about ballad singing. Could you say something about your own interest in music, your background in music, its appearance in your work?

Morgan: Well, my interest in music and my background are fairly complicated to explain. I love music, and grew up loving it. When I was a really small person, I made up music in my head all the time, based on hymns I'd heard and snatches of music I heard on the radio, the popular music of the 1940s: the Chuck Wagon Gang, Sons of the Pioneers, kind of Western ballad music. When I started studying music in elementary school, I lost that ability to constantly sort of improvise, making up music in my head. I began to learn something about playing piano and to read notes. But I was exposed not to mountain music very much per se, maybe a little bit to ballad singing, but mostly to gospel music and hymn singing in church. My parents opposed any sort of music that was intended for square dances.

But what really complicates my history and relationship to music was that when I was about 13, I began to really seriously study piano and music, and learn something about the history of classical music and harmony and music theory. I wanted to be a composer—so that by the time I was 14 or 15 I knew an awful lot more about Mozart and Bach and Handel and Telemann than I knew about the Grand Ole Opry or Bill Monroe. I've always loved classical music. I probably prefer that to any other kind, if I have my choice. But I later came to appreciate much more what is called traditional music—dulcimer music, the ballad singing of the Southern Appalachians, and got very interested not only in the music, but in the instruments that were made there in the region. I have written a number of poems about selecting the wood and making dulcimers and banjos, fiddles. The fiddle was called the devil's instrument by the fundamentalists.

I have never met a poet who wasn't deeply involved in some way with music, whether it was playing it, composing it, singing it, or just listening to it and going to concerts. There may be such a poet; I have never met him or her. Poetry seems very close to music, and a love of poetry seems very close to a love of music. Most of the poets I know have a very sophisticated interest in music, in fact know quite a bit about it, whether it's jazz—in the case of Bill Matthews, a real expert on jazz, or traditional music, in the case of someone like Jim Wayne Miller, or classical music. I think it was Anthony Hecht who had studied to be an opera singer before he went to college. So I've been involved with music, but it's difficult to explain how growing up on a little farm in the Blue Ridge Mountains had a deep interest in classical and baroque music, and romantic and even modern music, far more than what we think of as popular music, folk music associated with a region.

West: That reminds me of the difficulty George Ella Lyon had getting her book *Catalpa* accepted by a publisher: she wasn't supposed to have a deep, abiding interest in an English modernist like Virginia Woolf, who's at the heart of several of those poems. Lyon's a Kentucky mountain woman, so she's not supposed to be interested in that sort of thing.

Morgan: Well, that is related to the larger issue of disappointing people's expectations. It's very hard to be a popular writer if you create a world that is very different from what people expect it to be. If you violate the stereotypes too much. And in the popular arts, such as the novel or film, you can see this at work all the time: you're not going to get a film made if it's *too* original. It is not going to have a large audience. If you're really good, you can somehow satisfy people's expectations, and stretch them a little bit, and teach them a little bit. But that's related also to the whole issue of language, which is a set of conventions and clichés; essentially that's why we understand each other. We're using very common phrases and the same words that have been used over and over again, have references in common. An artist, a poet, can stretch that, can vary it, surprise, but only so far. If you go too far, you're writing or speaking in idiolect and not a common language.

West: And yet you did that very well with Ginny in *The Truest Pleasure*. There's a character who's a poor mountain woman, but who's very literate, and the language with which she narrates the novel reflects that.

Morgan: I tried to keep a flavor of mountain speech—she is a mountain farm wife of a hundred years ago—but show her love of language and her literacy. She has a pretty big vocabulary. She has a larger range of reference than people would expect of somebody on a small farm in the Blue Ridge Mountains. And to see just how large that range of reference is compare her to Julie Harmon of *Gap Creek*, who lacks that education, who's not a reader, but who speaks in many ways similar in terms of grammar. They have many phrases in common, but one voice is *much* more simple than the other. One is much better educated.

That side of my family—my dad and his mother—loved to read, and they did have a large vocabulary. It would surprise you the bits of erudition they had. Whereas my other grandmother was not a reader; she was certainly literate, and could read, but she was also not a talker, and I tried to give a sense of that in the narration of *Gap Creek*. Julie is someone who doesn't much trust herself, who doesn't have a lot of confidence in her voice. But of course that's a kind of artistic trick, because the whole book is her telling us her story. She's got to go into the fairly complicated emotions of her life, her marriage, her struggle to survive, her experience of childbirth. But she says from time to time, "I don't talk good" or "I don't know how to tell you this," and then she goes ahead and tells the story. But in the case of Ginny Powell you really get a sense (I hope) of someone who relishes language, who loves to play with it and use interesting phrases, unexpected phrases.

West: She's a terrific narrator. I've taught that novel, and my students have liked it very much. I think they like the idea of somebody who has exceeded her circumstances, who's risen above the station that fate assigned her. I do want to be sure to ask you, speaking of growing up reading in the mountains, what books or what writers have meant the most to you?

Morgan: Well there are so many writers who've inspired me and entertained me and thrilled me over the years. At the very beginning, when I began to read and read and read on my own, it was Jack London and James Oliver Curwood, those stories of the Klondike, Alaska, the Northwest Territories, the Royal Canadian Mounted Police—I just loved those adventure stories of the far north and read all I could get my hands on.

But not too long after that, I discovered Thomas Wolfe and *Look Homeward, Angel*. And that's the book that really started me thinking about being a writer myself. If Thomas Wolfe could grow up in Asheville and could write a book about it and publish it and become a famous author, maybe I could write something set in western North Carolina—not in Asheville, but off in the mountains. And it never occurred to me then how different my background was from Thomas Wolfe's. I identified with him so closely, partly because we had the same birthday (October 3)—but I was very much of the countryside, and he was very much a town boy, or a city boy. He dreamed of escaping Asheville, and I dreamed of *reaching* Asheville. It was the city set on a hill, for me. So Thomas Wolfe, when I was about 14, 15, really meant a lot to me, as an example of somebody who could write about family and the region and the yearning to be an artist, to achieve, to escape the limitations of his community.

When I was about 15, I discovered—all these books I got from the Henderson County bookmobile, by the way, which came to Green River Church once every month, the first Monday afternoon of every month—I went out there one day and saw this huge book, thick book in maroon binding, that said *War and Peace*, by Leo Tolstoy. I had seen that book advertised in the Sears and Roebuck catalogue as the greatest novel ever written, so I figured, oh, that's the one I ought to read. I took it home and found it slow going at first, but then I got hooked on it and read the whole thing; in fact I read it twice. It's one of two books I've read all the way through—got to the last page and then flipped to the first page and started again. Tolstoy gave me a much greater sense of the possibilities of literature, the way fiction can re-create lives and allow the reader to share very complex lives and interrelationships between different people and different classes. One of the great sections of *War and Peace* portrays Pierre, the nobleman, the wealthy person's relationship on the trail going back out of Russia with Napoleon's army, with Platon Karataev, the peasant, the illiterate peasant, who Pierre decides is the wisest person he ever met, who teaches him the most.

Not very long after reading *War and Peace* I read a book that has always been one of my favorites, and that is *Doctor Zhivago*, by Boris Pasternak. It had just been translated. Pasternak was notorious; the Russians were so angry at him for having published the book. He won the Nobel Prize. I read that book very slowly, savoring these scenes of Russia before the Revolution. And the hero's a poet. And one of the glories of the novel is the sheaf of poems at the end of it. I think Pasternak among other things gave me the idea that you could be both a fiction writer and a poet. You could practice the art in prose and in verse, and those echo each other in *Doctor Zhivago*. You read a poem at the end, and you can see something about its source, because among other things there are discussions of poetics and modern poetry in the novel; it's also a text about poetics.

This takes me up to about the time I went to go to college, in 1961. The writer I was reading when I went to college, who meant the most to me, was probably Hemingway. I had just discovered Hemingway and was reading Hemingway every day. My dad and I went to the mailbox one day, I think it was July 3, 1961, got the newspaper, and the headline was "Ernest Hemingway Dead at 61." And I can remember that day as clearly as the day Kennedy was shot. It just seemed this incredible thing—the writer I'd loved most at that time was dead. Hemingway, I decided much later, influenced the way I write more than any other single writer. Not just in the way he wrote, but in the *ideal* of his writing: the concision, the economy, the precision, the unflinching look at pain or contradiction, his clipped dialogue. I'm not sure Hemingway ever lived up to his ideal of writing; nobody probably does. This is the man who said the best dialogue is that which reveals what is not said: that's a very high standard. But I didn't realize until thirty years later, when I was writing an essay on Hemingway for his centennial, a lecture for his centennial celebration, just how deeply he had influenced me as a writer, primarily in his ambition as a writer, the way he thought of writing, the way you write with such plainness and directness on the surface, and such subtlety and indirection under the surface.

There's always so much going on in a Hemingway story. He after all is I think the man who gave us the metaphor of the tip of the iceberg. I certainly don't consider him by any means my favorite writer, but as much as anybody, and probably more than just about anybody, his writing influenced the way I began to think about writing and the way I aspired to write when I was young. Much more than any Southern writer ever did. I love the brevity, the precision of Hemingway's prose. I think he's had an *enormous* impact on the way modern prose is written, both in English and in French; I think a lot of French writers have been influenced as well. His influence on prose style is as great as the influence of Imagism on poetry.

West: Yes, he's interesting to contrast with the great Southern writers. When you think of somebody like Wolfe or Faulkner, you have the example of the long, cascading sentence—with Wolfe especially, a rhapsodic utterance. But you were more drawn to the brevity, the concision of Hemingway.

Morgan: And the ideal of accuracy, and absolute honesty. I mean, not that there *is* any such thing as absolute honesty, but the *aspiration* of the artist to get to the heart of something, and to say it unflinchingly, to not turn away from the things that are painful and contradictory and difficult to understand. I mean I love Wolfe's writing, and I love

Faulkner's writing, but I don't know that that kind of writing has influenced me as much as Hemingway's.

And another writer I guess I see as kind of between those extremes would be Steinbeck. Steinbeck at his best is just about the best we have. I admire his ability to write about all kinds of people: educated people, uneducated people, politicians, farmers, beggars, hobos. To write from the point of view of women. I see Steinbeck as one of our truly major writers, even though he's not very fashionable in academia at the moment. I can't think of a novel in American literature I admire more than *The Grapes of Wrath*—both in its narrative and in its cinematic, poetic sections. His ability to evoke the landscape, the climate, the Depression, the Dust Bowl, the highways, and the social issues. I don't think it's necessary for a novelist to address social issues, but I think that Steinbeck does it about as well as anybody ever has.

West: And everything you just said about Steinbeck makes me wonder if you've ever had much response to Agee.

Morgan: I discovered Agee in college, and he's been one of my favorite writers ever since.

West: He's also a writer from the mountains.

Morgan: He's from the Tennessee mountains. My first encounter with James Agee was in the novel, posthumous novel, *A Death in the Family.* Which I read and just loved the sections where Rufus goes to visit the great-grandmother, I think they call her grandmaw—his writing is so precise and colorful, and also lyrical. It's certainly much more poetic than Hemingway, or even Steinbeck. But when I was a senior in college I think, I discovered *Let Us Now Praise Famous Men*, and looking at those photographs by Walker Evans and then reading the text. Not reading that book all the way through, it's not a book you just sit down and read from p. 1. It's a book you dip in to, because it's so rich you can't take but about 3–4 pages at a time. And you read, you know, the section on shoes, and the section on the sounds at night, and then the girl and the description of the baby and the description of going into town and the description of the young black couple and of the black church. It's unsurpassed, in terms of just the intensity of its writing and the clarity of its vision of the world of the 1930s in Alabama. It's also out of fashion now: I don't think it's a book that's read as much as it was when I was a student, but it's one of the great classics of American literature, and will never, never be out of print. And Walker Evans' photographs are so impressive, they will always be available.

Anything anybody writes about the real South, and poverty in the South, will in effect be a dialogue with James Agee and *Let Us Now Praise Famous Men*. He wrote many other things—he wrote screenplays, he wrote many reviews, he wrote about film, he wrote some short stories. I don't think anything he ever did later is quite as good as *Let Us Now Praise Famous Men*. It's a book I go back to just to read a few sentences from time to time, to see how somebody can *really* try to tell it all, and to get to the heart of things with absolute honesty.

West: What writers do you especially recommend to your students as examples, as models? You've just been discussing writers who have meant something to you. Who then do you suggest your aspiring writers, your writers-in-training, to study, to learn from?

Morgan: It's usually different with every single student, because you have no idea what writer will inspire or teach a particular young writer. But I often think in terms of what Yeats would call the anti-mask: you try to learn something from people who do something very different from you. If you have somebody who writes a very florid kind of prose, suggest that they read Hemingway or Ray Carver, or somebody who is an underwriter instead of an overwriter. If a student is just wild about Ray Carver you suggest that they read some maximalist short story writers. But I think that we learn the most about writing simply from doing it. I've never found it effective to say to a student, "Oh, you should read such-and-such; that will show you what you need to do." I do that sometimes, but mostly a young writer has to find their own way, and they find that simultaneously with finding their subject matter. You can't have really good writing until you are writing what is given to you to write about. The two things go together. There's no writing in the abstract.

One of the hardest things to learn as a young fiction writer is how to let your characters tell their own story and help you create their world. Because that's a very humble thing to do—in a sense, you have to let your characters teach you how to tell their story, which is going to be different from anybody else's story. There's not a model for all novels or for all short stories; every one is somewhat different. This is why I think extremely intellectual people usually have a lot of trouble writing fiction. Because they have ideas, abstractions, paradigms, patterns in mind, and can't find that passive gear one novelist described to me where you let the story unfold. Once you have living characters struggling (and all stories are about struggle), once you have the living characters, you just go with them and let them live and deal with their problems.

I think that there is no such thing as a writing teacher, it's more being a writing coach. You're there to tell somebody what you think they might do, but you're not giving them a body of information the way a history teacher is, or even a physics teacher, or a literature teacher. Writing is action, it's doing something. And being a teacher of writing is a lot more like being a tennis coach or a basketball coach than it is like being a professor of history. It's a humbling kind of thing: there's a fairly limited amount you can do for a young writer, actually. If they're really good, they will by writing and writing and writing and writing teach themselves to write. This doesn't mean that there's nothing you can do: you can certainly give them some critical feedback, and enthusiasm for what they're doing well, and that can be very useful.

What is *most* useful to a young writer is to find what I call the true reader or the authentic reader. It might be a teacher, or another writer; it might be a fellow student. But the history of literature is full of examples of the writers who kind of teach each other simply by being the first reader, the best reader. This is more true in poetry than it is in fiction. Wordsworth and Coleridge come together, Byron and Shelley, Goethe and Schiller, Marianne Moore and Elizabeth Bishop, Emerson and Thoreau, Sherwood Anderson and William Faulkner, Sherwood Anderson and Hemingway, Sherwood Anderson and Gertrude Stein. Anderson was a wonderful mentor and friend to writers, and had great enthusiasm for the work of his contemporaries. But when you're a young writer, all you need is one reader who can see not only what you're doing but what you're capable of. You don't need a big audience; you don't need a workshop. But you do need one reader, and then you can be a writer. Because you can't really be a writer until you have a reader. You do not write in complete isolation. As you never learn language in isolation: language is social, and we learn it from other people. We learn it to communicate with other people. A kid who grew up in isolation would never even learn to speak.

West: I often hear friends who teach creative writing complain that their students seem interested in writing but not necessarily interested in reading; that's one reason I asked about models. It's not hard to see how that could be a handicap. But I sometimes wonder, though, if there might be an opposite kind of handicap. And your comments almost confirm this. Might an aspiring writer do well *not* to read everything? Might it somehow handicap a writer to know all the possibilities, to the point of thinking, "Well, this has all been done before"?

Morgan: Well, I think you could be a wonderful student of literature and not be a particularly good writer. Some of the frustration I think for teachers is that they teach class after class, you know, semester after semester, and have this high expectation that their classes are going to be full of extremely talented and accomplished writers. This is simply an unreal expectation. Writing is extremely hard to do. It's less a matter of talent than of hard work; I mean, any writer will tell you that. It's mostly hard work. The expectation that a sophomore in college is going to be writing really exciting and accomplished things is unrealistic. It's wonderful if it happens, if you encounter one of those talents, as I have more than once. But in fact most people are not very good writers, because they simply will not do the work; they don't have the time to give to it. And they will never be really accomplished writers.

Because of our mass education system, we have this wonderful expectation that everybody who takes our class and gets a grade at the end is going to have learned to be a really good writer.... It's wonderful we think that, but it's a completely unreal expectation. Particularly when we're talking about creative writing, that somebody's going to be a poet just because they took a class at a university or something. The truth is that really good writing is so hard to do that the person who does it has got to commit hours and hours and weeks and months and years to mastering the art, and very few people are going to be crazy enough to do that. It's a very lonely kind of occupation. Anybody who's taught as long as I have knows that your classroom is just full of talent, that practically everybody there will have talent, and some people a lot of talent. But what will separate most of them from the people who really become accomplished novelists or poets is those years of dedication to mastering the art of writing, so that what you write is so good and so exciting that people want to read it, they want to give it to their friends, they recommend it to somebody, they say, "Have you read this?" That's very different, especially from the idea of teaching writing-as-therapy, for instance. Teaching writing as helping somebody get through a crisis or deal with their medical problems or their emotional problems is a fine thing, but that's *very* different from mastering an art to the level at which many are going to read, want to read, what they're writing.

West: Speaking of writing something that's so appealing that people say to their friends, "You have to read this," I wanted to be sure to ask about the effect on you of *Gap Creek*'s success—as a person, as a writer, or both. (I think of how Eliot distinguished between the writer as a person and the writer as a writer in *Tradition and the Individual Talent.*) How did your life change?

Morgan: Well, first let me say that when I published my first book of fiction, one of the pleasures was to discover the larger number of readers. All my books previous to that had been books of poetry. I think I'd had some really good response to my poetry, but that was almost always from other poets. If you got a fan letter, it was from a fellow poet, usually. When I started publishing short stories, and certainly when I published my first novel, I discovered I was getting fan letters from people who weren't necessarily writers, but people who just loved to read. So as a fiction writer you reach a much larger audience, and a somewhat different kind of audience. And that was thrilling, to think that you're writing something that people would enjoy so much they would write you letters, and they would go buy the book and buy it as a gift for other people.

Being chosen by Oprah was just an extension of that, at an astronomical level: her television audience is so big, that I suddenly discovered that instead of getting two fan letters a week, I was getting dozens a day, right after I was on the show. So the big difference for me was the thrill of having a much larger readership. I don't know about other writers, but for me that meant a lot, because the greatest honor you can receive as a writer is to be read. And to write something that seems to move other people, to delight them, to entertain them, is a very special thing. I've gotten dozens of letters from people saying they were going through chemotherapy, or even they were dying of cancer, and they wanted me to know that reading my work, especially *Gap Creek*, helped them get through the very hard time. I never got letters like that about the poems. And the three books that seemed to move people most are *The Truest Pleasure*, *Gap Creek*, and *This Rock*. Those novels are interrelated, with the same families. I've gotten a lot of letters about *Brave Enemies*, but that's a historical novel set in the Revolution, and has a somewhat different readership, though it's also a story of marriage.

I think that being chosen for the Oprah book club and being on *The New York Times* bestseller list for more than three months did not affect me the way it would have had I been younger. It would have changed my ideas about being a writer had I been younger. But being 55 years old, and having published several books of poems and several books of short stories and already several novels, my relationship to my writing was set. And I don't think it changed that much. I mean, the morning after I heard from Oprah I got up at five o'clock and worked, exactly the same as I had the day before. And after I was on the show, I kept working in the same way. For me the great thing was just simply the pleasure of having those additional readers, and having readers who were so appreciative of the book. I got thousands of letters from readers, and I'm still getting them. Not only from the South, but from all over the country, Canada, Europe, Australia, New Zealand, and from Scandinavia and Germany in particular. It's now gone through three editions—*Gap Creek* is in its third edition, not printing, but edition, in German.

West: I think it's to your credit that you didn't turn around and immediately write *Gap Creek* again. I can imagine many writers would say, "Well, this worked; let me do that again. Change the characters' names, have essentially the same plot structure. But *This Rock* is quite different: it's different in form, with the two narrators, and of course *Brave Enemies* is a very different project, not to mention the venture into biography with *Boone*. Was there any temptation to turn around and say, 'Ah, OK: here's *Gap Creek II*.'"

Morgan: I write first to amuse myself. If the story doesn't thrill me, entertain me, and move me, I don't expect it to move anybody else. But having said that, I do plan in the future to write a sequel to *Gap Creek*. I want to go back to Hank and Julie and take their story forward into their marriage. But I have all these other stories I want to write in the meantime. I have more projects than I can ever, ever write, things I've been thinking about for years and years. I've been planning a story about the World War II Air Force—Eighth Air Force B-17s—the past quarter-century, which I still have to write. I want to write something set in the Depression years leading into World War II.

But no, I've always done as a writer just what interested me. And if it works, if I can sell it, fine, and if it doesn't, I guess that's fine too: I'll just go on to something else. But by the time a book is published, I'm usually deep into the next book, so that the choice of the next project is not at all affected by the reception to a particular book. I'm way into completing another project, because it takes at least a year, a year and a half, to actually get a book out there in the bookstores, from the time you finish it, and often longer than that.

West: It's interesting that you mention all the projects you have in mind, that you're not sure you can get to them, because lately I've thought about a kind of circularity I see you working at. You know, when I look at your selected short stories, *The Balm of Gilead Tree*, the book's first sentence refers to "The year the hair-faces came to our village," and the book's last words are "Home free"; there's a sort of circularity there, with the idea of home. In your latest selected poems, *The Strange Attractor*, the book's first line is "We do not talk loud in forests," and the book's last words are "a love whisper." You mentioned the word "rondure" earlier, and there's that circularity at work as you reshape and consolidate your work in short fiction and poetry. Do you see any similar movement in your work in long fiction? Is there some sort of large structure, some sort of rondure there, something you would like eventually to get back to, or not?

Morgan: I think it's more an issue of the subject choosing me, rather than me choosing it. You get an idea for something, and of course most of the ideas that occur to me and ideas I write down in notebooks never become anything: they're never pursued and developed. But the more you write, the more you develop a sense of what has possibilities for you. And later I think we can see patterns in that, that the writer does not recognize at the time.

So much of writing is about recovering things you'd forgotten that you knew; Frost said that somewhere, and it's absolutely true. Writers tend to forget about what they've written, precisely because they want to go ahead and do something new. Often somebody who has recently read a novel of mine seems to know it better than I know it; I mean, after all it's been years since I wrote it and I've had other things on my mind. I go to book clubs, discussion groups, where people have very fresh in their minds, particularly *Gap Creek* and *The Truest Pleasure*, and a detail will come back to me, but it's often something I haven't thought of in a long time.

Emerson says that every day he does what there *is* to do, what he's called to do, assuming that it will have a shape overall. Emerson was a very wise man: he often says the profound thing. I've often thought of that: that you do what you feel you *can* do every day, what thrills you, what interests you, what you're curious about, what seems to have the mystery and the magic, and you let people worry about the overall shape of your work or your career later. I've never thought of writing one of these sagas, these sequences, you know, forty novels set in the same place. I think it would be interesting to do that, but it's too late. I started writing fiction too late to do that sort of thing. I think of books as more separate works, perhaps. But I can see that all the stories, the novels, and even the poems, are related by theme and by setting, and by language.

If you're really, really good as a poet, and you're really lucky, you might write half a dozen poems that people still read a hundred years later. So you know you're just writing thousands of poems, 'cause it's fun to write, and it's a great challenge and a thrill—but even if you're better and luckier than you ever really have a chance to be, you probably will only have a tiny handful of poems that are actually read years later. So in a sense I don't think we need to worry too much about number and quantity and productivity: it's much more about quality and about being as good as we can be. There are some exceptions: Dickens has many novels that are still read and in print. Tolstoy, often considered the greatest of all novelists, really has only two, right? Dostoevsky has a few more than that. Stendhal, who is about as good as anybody—I can't think of any novels better than *The Red and the Black* and *Charterhouse*—really is known for those two books. Balzac published about fifty; in English we only read about three, typically—maybe in France they read more than that. Henry James said he was the greatest fiction writer of all time, Balzac.

West: You're very generous at granting interviews, and you've done it for years and years and years—is there anything you can't believe somebody has never asked you? Or even better, something you've always dreaded they would?

Morgan: I think the kind of question, the kind of issue that is most worrisome for a writer my age is, What are you going to do in your old age? What are you going to do as you get older? You want to think about that, and you don't want to think about it. A few years ago, a graduate student said to me, Can you think of any really great novel written when the author was more than sixty years old? And I immediately said, "Oh sure." I started to try to think what it would be, and realized that Dostoevsky died when he was about sixty, and Tolstoy never wrote a great novel, a really great novel, after he was I guess fifty. And Dickens died at fifty-eight. Henry James published his last novel when he was sixty-one. George Eliot died at sixty or sixty-one. Faulkner certainly did all his greatest writing before he was fifty. So did Hemingway. Fitzgerald was dead in his forties. The only novel I could come up with in American lit was a short novel, *Billy Budd*, which apparently was written right toward the end of Melville's life. We don't know exactly when it was written, but it was apparently in his late sixties. But then we know that people are now living longer, and with a longer lifespan in the future, probably great novels will be written later in people's careers. Poets happily often do some of their best work in later years. There's the example of Thomas Hardy, who certainly continued to write some of his best poems, in his seventies and in his eighties. Stevens was going great guns into his seventies.

West: Yeats.

Morgan: Yeats kept writing and wrote some of his finest work in his last decade. Williams, I think, probably wrote some of his finer poems in his last decade.

West: [Noticing a fly has entered the room, quotes Emily Dickinson:] "And then it was / There interposed a Fly...."

Morgan: Saying it's time to stop.

A New Robert Morgan Bibliography

ROBERT M. WEST *and* JESSE GRAVES

I. Primary Sources

A. Books

1. Poetry Collections

Zirconia Poems. Northwood Narrows, NH: Lillabulero Press, 1969.
The Voice in the Crosshairs. Ithaca, NY: Angelfish Press, 1971.
Red Owl. New York: W. W. Norton, 1972.
Land Diving. Baton Rouge: Louisiana State University Press, 1976.
Trunk & Thicket. Fort Collins, CO: L'Epervier Press, 1978.
Groundwork. Frankfort, KY: Gnomon Press, 1979.
Bronze Age. Emory, VA: Iron Mountain Press, 1981.
At the Edge of the Orchard Country. Middletown, CT: Wesleyan University Press, 1987.
Sigodlin. Middletown, CT: Wesleyan University Press, 1990.
Green River: New and Selected Poems. Middletown, CT: Wesleyan University Press, 1991.
Wild Peavines. Frankfort, KY: Gnomon Press, 1996.
Topsoil Road. Baton Rouge: Louisiana State University Press, 2000.
The Strange Attractor: New and Selected Poems. Baton Rouge: Louisiana State University Press, 2004.
October Crossing. Frankfort, KY: Broadstone Books, 2009.
Terroir. New York: Penguin, 2011.
Dark Energy. New York: Penguin, 2015.

2. Short Story Collections

The Blue Valleys. Atlanta: Peachtree Publishers, 1989.
The Mountains Won't Remember Us. Atlanta: Peachtree Publishers, 1992.
The Balm of Gilead Tree: New and Selected Stories. Frankfort, KY: Gnomon Press, 1999.
As Rain Turns to Snow and Other Stories. Frankfort, KY: Broadstone Books, 2017.

3. Novels

The Hinterlands. Chapel Hill, NC: Algonquin Books, 1994.
The Truest Pleasure. Chapel Hill, NC: Algonquin Books, 1995.
Gap Creek. Chapel Hill, NC: Algonquin Books, 1999.
This Rock. Chapel Hill, NC: Algonquin Books, 2001.
Brave Enemies. Chapel Hill, NC: Algonquin Books, 2003.
The Road from Gap Creek. Chapel Hill, NC: Algonquin Books, 2013.
Chasing the North Star. Chapel Hill, NC: Algonquin Books, 2016.

4. Nonfiction Prose

Good Measure: Essays, Interviews, and Notes on Poetry. Baton Rouge: Louisiana State University Press, 1993.

Boone: A Biography. Chapel Hill, NC: Algonquin Books, 2007.
Lions of the West. Chapel Hill, NC: Algonquin Books, 2011.

B. Essays and Interviews Not Yet Collected

1. Essays

"Albert Bierstadt and the Millennium." *Voices in the Gallery: Writers on Art*. Rochester, NY: University of Rochester Press, 2001. pp. 129–32.

"The Sound of Our Speaking." Rev. of *An Ear in Bartram's Tree*, by Jonathan Williams. *The Nation* 6 Sept. 1971: pp. 188–90.

"The Reign of King Stork." Rev. of *Somewhere Is Such a Kingdom: Poems 1952–1971*, by Geoffrey Hill. *Parnassus* 4.2 (1976): pp. 31–48.

"Introduction" to *Out in the Country, Back Home*, by Jeff Daniel Marion. Winston-Salem, NC: Jackpine Press, 1976. pp. 7–8.

"Never Confuse a Fact with Truth: The Poetry of Miller Williams." *Mississippi Quarterly* 46.1 (1992–93): pp. 115–20.

"Work and Poetry, the Father Tongue." *Southern Review* 31 (1995): pp. 161–79.

"Thomas Hart Benton and the Thresholds of Expression." *The Store of Joys: Writers Celebrate the North Carolina Museum of Art's Fiftieth Anniversary*. Ed. Huston Paschal. Winston-Salem, NC: North Carolina Museum of Art Foundation, in association with John F. Blair, Publisher, 1997. pp. 68–70.

"Nature Is a Stranger Yet." The 1998 William H. and Jane Torrence Harder Lecture. Originally published in Cornell Plantations' *Plantations Magazine* (Winter-Spring 2000): pp. 2–19. Rpt. in *The Jordan Lectures 1998–1999*. With Wayne C. Booth. Salem, VA: Donald L. Jordan Endowment at Roanoke College, [1999].

"O Lost, and Found." *Thomas Wolfe Review* 24.2 (2000): pp. 3–9.

"Hemingway and the True Poetry of War." *War, Literature, and the Arts* 12.1 (2000): pp. 137–56.

"Appalachia." Part of a feature titled "Tell It on the Mountain" also including essays by Fred Chappell and Lee Smith. *Hemispheres* (United Airlines' magazine) (August 2000): pp. 104–05.

"You Can't Get There from Here." On Carl Sandburg. *Appalachian Journal* 28 (2001): pp. 222–26.

"Writing the Living Voice: The Achievement of Lee Smith." *Pembroke Magazine* 33 (2001): p. 182.

"Cormac McCarthy: The Novel Raised from the Dead." *Cormac McCarthy Journal* 1 (2002): pp. 12–25. Rpt in *Sacred Violence, Vol. I: Cormac McCarthy's Appalachian Works*. Ed. Wade Hall and Rick Wallach. El Paso: Texas Western Press, 2002. pp. 9–21.

"On 'Fasting.'" Commentary on a previously unpublished poem by A. R. Ammons. *Epoch* 52.3 (2003): p. 342.

"The Lunchroom Victory: A Memoir." *Crossroads: A Southern Culture Annual*. Ed. Ted Olson. Macon, GA: Mercer University Press, 2004. pp. 241–46.

"The Wisest Book I Read." [On Boris Pasternak's *Doctor Zhivago*.] *Remarkable Reads: 34 Writers and Their Adventures in Reading*. Ed. J. Peder Zane. New York: W. W. Norton, 2004. pp. 67–72.

"The Birth of Music from the Spirit of Comedy." Foreword to *More Lights Than One: On the Fiction of Fred Chappell*. Ed. Patrick Bizzaro. Baton Rouge: Louisiana State University Press, 2004. pp. ix-xiv.

"Concord Constructivist and Yankee Doodler: The Poetry of William Harmon." *Pembroke Magazine* 37 (2005): pp. 9–14.

"Coming Down from Pisgah." *Appalachian Heritage* 33.2 (2005): pp. 23–25.

2. Interviews

"A Conversation with Robert Morgan." With Donald Anderson. *Xavier Review* 12 (1992): pp. 17–38.

"An Interview with Robert Morgan." With David L. Elliott. *Chattahoochee Review* 13.2 (1993): pp. 78–97.

"An Interview with Robert Morgan." With Marti Garrison. *Bookpress: The Newspaper of the Literary Arts* [Ithaca, NY] 4 (1994): p. 11.

"Interview." With Tal Stanley. *Appalachian Journal* 23 (1996): pp. 276–92.

"The Art of Far and Near: An Interview with Robert Morgan." With Robert M. West. *Carolina Quarterly* 49.3 (1997): pp. 46–68.

"'The Poetics of Work': An Interview with Robert Morgan." With Patrick Bizzaro and Resa Crane Bizzaro. *North Carolina Literary Review* 10 (2001): pp. 173–90.

"Getting the Voices Right: A Conversation with Robert Morgan about *The Gardener's Son*." With Peter Josyph. On Cormac McCarthy's published screenplay *The Gardener's Son*. *Southern Quarterly* 40.1 (2001): pp. 121–31.

"An Interview with Robert Morgan." With Norbert Schürer. *Pembroke Magazine* 36 (2004): pp. 252–60.

"The Moral Ambiguity of That Time." With Resa Crane Bizzaro and Patrick Bizzaro. *Appalachian Heritage* 32.3 (2004): pp. 11–17.

"A Conversation with Robert Morgan." *Image* 43 (2004): pp. 65–76.
"'The Authentic Reader': An Interview with Robert Morgan." With Tessa Joseph. *Carolina Quarterly* 56.2–3 (2004): pp. 68–73.
"A Note on 'A Tale of the Ragged Mountains' by Edgar Allan Poe." *Appalachian Heritage* 39.2 (2011): p. 75.
"The More Mysterious: An Interview with Robert Morgan." With Jesse Graves. *Georgia Review* 66.1 (2012): pp. 65–87.
"'After the Fighting, the Scars Remain': An Interview with Robert Morgan on His War Literature." With Rebecca Godwin. *North Carolina Literary Review* 23 (2014): pp. 6–17.
"'To Connect with That Beyond Ourselves': An Interview with Robert Morgan." With Robert M. West. *Appalachian Journal* 44 (2016–2017): pp.132–41.

II. Secondary Sources

A. Book Chapters

Chappell, Fred. "An Idiom of Uncertainty: Southern Poetry Now." A review of five books of poems, including Morgan's *Sigodlin*. *A Way of Happening: Observations of Contemporary American Poetry*. New York: Picador USA, 1998. pp. 112–24.
Lang, John. "Robert Morgan: 'Mountains Speak in Tongues.'" *Six Poets from the Mountain South*. Baton Rouge: Louisiana State University Press, 2010. pp. 73–98.
Quillen, Rita Sims. "Robert Morgan." *Looking for Native Ground: Contemporary Appalachian Poetry*. Boone, NC: Appalachian Consortium Press, 1989. pp. 49–62.
Turner, Daniel Cross. "Many Returns: Forms of Nostalgia in the Poetry of the Contemporary South." A chapter on poems from *Topsoil Road* and work by five other poets. *Southern Crossings: Poetry, Memory, and the Transcultural South*. Knoxville: University of Tennessee Press, 2012. pp. 47–86.

B. Journal Articles and Essays in Books

Four journals have published Robert Morgan special issues. Jeff Daniel Marion, editor of *The Small Farm*, assembled its special issue on Morgan: issue no. 3, which appeared in 1976. Joe Mandel compiled for *Pembroke Magazine* "A Tribute to Robert Morgan": issue no. 35, which appeared in 2003. George Brosi, then editor of *Appalachian Heritage*, put together that journal's special issue: vol. 32, no. 3, which appeared in 2004. Jesse Graves edited a special issue on Morgan for *Southern Quarterly*: vol. 47, no. 3, which appeared in 2010. The following list includes the contents of those four special issues, additional journal articles, and essays collected in books.

Anderson, Maggie. "'Sentences of Light.'" An introduction to her poem "Letter to Robert Morgan from Denmark," which immediately follows. *Appalachian Heritage* 32.3 (2004): pp. 37–38.
Ashburn, Gwen McNeill. "Working without Nets: Early Twentieth-Century Mountain Women in Fiction." On two novels, including *Gap Creek*. *Journal of Kentucky Studies* 24 (2007): pp. 133–40.
Banks, Russell. "Bob Morgan at Chapel Hill." *Pembroke Magazine* 35 (2003): pp. 82–84.
Bherwani, Bhisham. "The Elegiac Strain in Robert Morgan's Poetry." *Yale Review* 105.1 (2017): pp. 80–106.
Bizzaro, Patrick. "Food as Commodity and Metaphor in *Gap Creek*: The Making of Julie." *Appalachian Heritage* 32.3 (2004): pp. 29–35.
Booker-Canfield, Suzanne. "'Middle Sea': Robert Morgan and a New American Romanticism." *Pembroke Magazine* 35 (2003): pp. 71–76.
______. "The 'Rush Toward the Horizon': The Geography of Land and Language in Robert Morgan's Recent Poetry." *Southern Quarterly* 47.3 (2010): pp. 36–44.
Bourne, Louis M. "On Metaphor and Its Use in the Poetry of Robert Morgan." *The Small Farm* 3 (1976): pp. 63–79.
Brosi, George. "Robert Morgan's Mountain Roots." *Appalachian Heritage* 32.3 (2004): pp. 8–9.
Buchanan, Harriette C. "Changing Contexts, Changing Textures: Robert Morgan's 'Murals' over Its Publication History." *Pembroke Magazine* 35 (2003): pp. 28–36
Chappell, Fred. "Double Language: Three Appalachian Poets." *Appalachian Journal* 8 (1980): pp. 55–59.
______. "Morgan's Things." *Appalachian Heritage* 32.3 (2004): pp. 19–26.
______. "A Prospect Newly Necessary." *The Small Farm* 3 (1976): pp. 49–53.
Conway, Cecelia. "Robert Morgan's Mountain Voice and Lucid Prose." *Appalachian Journal* 29 (2001–2002): pp. 180–99. Rpt. in *An American Vein: Critical Readings in Appalachian Literature*. Ed. Danny L. Miller, Sharon Hatfield, and Gurney Norman. Athens: Ohio University Press, 2005. pp. 275–95.
Denham, Robert D. "'Service Is Also Praise': Recognition in Robert Morgan's *The Truest Pleasure*." pp. 129–41.
Drewitz-Crockett, Nicole. "Authority, Details, and Intimacy: Southern Appalachian Women in Robert Morgan's Family Novels." *Southern Quarterly* 47.3 (2010): pp. 117–28.
Eads, Marti. "Feminist Forgiveness in Robert Morgan's 'The Trace.'" *Southern Quarterly* 47.3 (2010): pp. 151–61.

Einstein, Frank. "The Politics of Nostalgia: Uses of the Past in Recent Appalachian Poetry." *Appalachian Journal* 8 (1980): pp. 32–40.

Gilbert, Roger. "Sea and Mountains, Motion and Measure: The Complementary Poetics of A. R. Ammons and Robert Morgan." *Southern Quarterly* 47.3 (2010): pp. 71–90.

Graves, Jesse. "Editor's Introduction" to the "Robert Morgan Special Issue: A Community Across Time." *Southern Quarterly* 47.3 (2010): pp. 6–11.

______. "Formal Tendencies in the Poetry of Robert Morgan and Ron Rash." *Southern Quarterly* 45.1 (2007): pp. 78–86.

______. "Reading Robert Morgan's New Poems." An introduction to the twelve new poems by Morgan published in the issue. *Appalachian Journal* 44 (2017): pp. 142–43.

Grimes, Larry. "Echoes and Influences: A Comparative Study of Short Fiction by Ernest Hemingway and Robert Morgan." *Southern Quarterly* 47.3 (2010): pp. 98–116.

Harmon, William. "Robert Morgan's 'Mockingbird' in Company." *Southern Quarterly* 47.3 (2010): pp. 61–70.

______. "Robert Morgan's Pelagian Georgics: Twelve Essays." *Parnassus* 9.2 (1981): pp. 5–30.

Johnson, Don. "Robert Morgan's Alchemy: Listening to Time and Space." *Southern Quarterly* 47.3 (2010): pp. 45–52.

Lang, John. "Coming out from under Calvinism: Religious Motifs in Robert Morgan's Poetry." *Shenandoah* 42.2 (1992): pp. 46–60. Rpt. in *An American Vein: Critical Readings in Appalachian Literature*. Ed. Danny L. Miller, Sharon Hatfield, and Gurney Norman. Athens: Ohio University Press, 2005. pp. 261–74.

______. "'He Hoes Forever': Robert Morgan and the Pleasures of Work." *Pembroke Magazine* 31 (1999): pp. 221–27.

______. "Pro Tempore." Editor's introduction to the Robert Morgan issue. *Iron Mountain Review* 6.1 (1990): p. 2.

______. "Speaking Charmed Syllables: The Two-Fold Vision of *Topsoil Road*." *Pembroke Magazine* 35 (2003): pp. 16–21.

Liotta, P. H. "Robert Morgan: Genius as Music." *Southern Quarterly* 47.3 (2010): pp. 182–88.

______. "Pieces of the Morgenland: The Recent Achievements in Robert Morgan's Poetry." *Southern Literary Journal* 22 (1989): pp. 32–40.

Marion, Stephen. "Gleaning the Unsayable: The Terrain of Vision in Poems by Robert Morgan, Fred Chappell, and Jim Wayne Miller." *Mossy Creek Journal* 9 (1985): pp. 25–33.

______. "Morgan's Travels." *Iron Mountain Review* 6.1 (1990): pp. 24–25.

Matthews, William. "Some Notes on Robert Morgan's Poetry." *The Small Farm* 4/5 (1976/1977): pp. 88–92.

McFee, Michael. "'The Witness of Many Writings': Robert Morgan's Poetic Career." *Iron Mountain Review* 6.1 (1990): pp. 17–23. Rpt. in McFee's *The Napkin Manuscripts: Selected Essays and an Interview*. Knoxville: University of Tennessee Press, 2006. pp. 164–80.

Merod, J. B. "Robert Morgan's 'Wisdom-Lighted Islands.'" *The Small Farm* 3 (1976): pp. 54–62.

Murrell, Duncan. "Robert Morgan Speech: Facing Down Fear." *Pembroke Magazine* 35 (2003): pp. 22–26.

Perry, Lori A. Davis. "Becoming America." On Morgan's novel *Brave Enemies*. *War, Literature, and the Arts* 16 (2004): pp. 274–80.

Powell, Lynn. Rev. of *Dark Energy*. *Appalachian Journal* 43 (2015–16): pp. 100–02.

Rash, Tom. "The Poetry of Robert Morgan: An Appreciation." *Southern Quarterly* 47.3 (2010): pp. 53–60.

Schultz, Robert. "Recovering Pieces of the Morgenland." *Virginia Quarterly Review* 64 (1988): pp. 176–88.

Shurbutt, Sylvia Bailey. "Robert Morgan's Peripheral Vision: 'The Point Beside the Point' in *The Hinterlands*." *North Carolina Literary Review* 19 (2010): pp. 30–43.

Secreast, Donald. "The Gap in the Circuit." On *Gap Creek*. *World & I* 15.7 (2000): pp. 232+.

Smith, Newton. "Going Back to the Mountains from 'Topsoil Road': A Retrospective Look at Robert Morgan's Poetry." *Pembroke Magazine* 35 (2003): pp. 55–64.

Smith, Rebecca. "The Elemental in *The Truest Pleasure* and *Gap Creek*: Nature as Physical Force and Spiritual Metaphor." *Pembroke Magazine* 35 (2003): pp. 37–46.

Villiers, Regina. "Women in Robert Morgan's Short Fiction: A Study of *The Blue Valleys* and *The Mountains Won't Remember Us*." *Pembroke Magazine* 35 (2003): pp. 65–70.

Waage, Fred. "In the Non-Euclidean Mountains of Robert Morgan's Poetry." *Pembroke Magazine* 35 (2003): pp. 47–53.

Ward, David C. "'Morgenland': The Poetry of Robert Morgan." *North Carolina Literary Review* 6 (1997): pp. 124–29.

West, Robert M. "'Here's the Church, Here's the Steeple': Robert Morgan, Philip Larkin, and the Emptiness of Sacred Space." *Southern Quarterly* 47.3 (2010): pp. 91–97.

______. "A Study in Sharpening Contrast: Robert Morgan and the Distinction between Poetry and Prose." *Pembroke Magazine* 35 (2003): pp. 77–81.

______. "Toward 'Crystal-Tight Arrays': Teaching the Evolving Art of Robert Morgan's Poetry." In *Appalachia in the Classroom: Teaching the Region*. Ed. Theresa L. Burriss and Patricia M. Gantt. Athens: Ohio University Press, 2013. pp. 252–64.

Wilhelm, Randall Shawn. "Bricking the Text: The Builder in Robert Morgan's Mountain World." *Southern Quarterly* 47.3 (2010): pp. 142–50.

Williams, Mary C. "Inside-Outside in Robert Morgan's Poetry." *The Poetics of Appalachian Space*. Ed. Parks Lanier, Jr. Knoxville: University of Tennessee Press, 1991. pp. 149–60.
_____. "Place in Poetry: Preserving and Deconstructing Southern Mythology." *Pembroke Magazine* 20 (1988): pp. 124–31.
_____. "The Toolshed, the Feed Room, and the Potato Hole: Place in Robert Morgan's Poetry." *Iron Mountain Review* 6.1 (1990): pp. 26–30.

C. Selected Reviews

1. Poetry

Baker, David. "Heaven and Earth." Rev. of *Topsoil Road* and four books by other authors. *Poetry* Feb. 2003: pp. 285–97.
Barber, David. "Short Reviews." Rev. of *Green River: New and Selected Poems* and four books by other authors. *Poetry* July 1992: pp. 219–36.
Bateman, Claire. "Recent Poetry in the Carolinas." Rev. of *Sigodlin* and four books by other authors. *South Carolina Review* 25.1 (1992): pp. 149–57.
Bell, Marvin. "Five Books." Rev. of *Land Diving* and four books by other authors. *Poetry* Oct. 1978: pp. 45–55.
Burns, Gerald. "The One-Eyed Critic Is King." Rev. of *Trunk & Thicket* and two books by other authors. *Southwest Review* 64 (1979): 304–05.
Chitwood, Michael. "Mountains Make Fertile Ground." Rev. of *October Crossing* and Fred Chappell's *Shadow Box*. *The News and Observer* [Raleigh, NC] 13 Dec. 2009.
Cox, Wayne. Rev. of *Green River: New and Selected Poems*. *Southern Humanities Review* 27 (1993): pp. 402–04.
Eisiminger, Skip. "Topsoil Road." Rev. of *Topsoil Road*. *South Carolina Review* 33.2 (2001): pp. 181–82.
Fulton, Alice. "Main Things." Rev. of *At the Edge of the Orchard Country* and seven books by other authors. *Poetry* Jan. 1988: pp. 360–77.
Greene, Jonathan. Rev. of *Land Diving*. *Montemora* 5 (1979): pp. 263–65.
Howard, Ben. "World and Spirit, Body and Soul." Rev. of *Sigodlin* and three books by other authors. *Poetry* Sept. 1991: pp. 342–50.
Kniffel, Leonard. Rev. of *At the Edge of the Orchard Country*. *Library Journal* 1 Aug. 1987: p. 129.
Kooser, Ted. "Nine Recent Chapbooks." Rev. of *Wild Peavines* and eight chapbooks by other authors. *Georgia Review* 51 (1997): pp. 365–77.
Kuzma, Greg. Rev. of *Green River: New and Selected Poems*. *Prairie Schooner* 68.1 (1994): pp. 168–69.
Mason, Karen K. "The Regional Poet and the World." Rev. of *October Crossing* and *Terroir*, as well as two books by Scott Owens. *North Carolina Literary Review Online* (2013): pp. 78–84.
Powell, Lynn. Rev. of *Dark Energy*. *Appalachian Journal* 43 (2015–2016): pp. 100–02.
Ramsey, Paul. "In Praise of Makers: American Poetry in 1979." Rev. of *Groundwork* and six books by other authors. *Sewanee Review* 88 (1980): pp. 665–71.
Rev. [unsigned] of *Topsoil Road*. *Virginia Quarterly Review* 77.4 (2001): p. 147.
Slavitt, David R. "Expansions and Contractions." Rev. of *Green River: New and Selected Poems* and three books by other authors. *American Book Review* 15 (June/July 1993): pp. 19+.
West, Robert. "Putting It All Together." Rev. of *Dark Energy* and two books by other authors. *Asheville Poetry Review* 22.1 (2015): pp. 51–60.
_____. Rev. of *The Strange Attractor: New and Selected Poems*. *Appalachian Heritage* 32.4 (2004): pp. 80–81.
_____. Rev. of *Wild Peavines*. *Carolina Quarterly* 49.3 (1997): pp. 43–45.
Wier, Dara. "Five Longing for Immortality." Rev. of *Green River: New and Selected Poems* and three books by other authors. *Southern Review* 28 (1992): pp. 981–94.
Wilhelm, Randall. "Robert Morgan's 'Big Talk.'" Rev. of *Dark Energy* and the Press 53 reissue of *Sigodlin*. *North Carolina Literary Review Online* (2016): pp. 54–57.

2. Short Story Collections

Buchanan, Harriette. Rev. of *The Balm of Gilead Tree: New and Selected Stories*. *Southern Quarterly* 38.4 (2000): pp. 145–47.
Dale, Neal. "Mountain Talk Tuned to Unforgettable Music." Rev. of *The Mountains Won't Remember Us*. *Asheville Citizen-Times* [Asheville, NC] 2 Aug. 1992: p. 8L.
Herring, Gina. "Climbing Paradox Mountain: The Stories of Robert Morgan." Rev. of *The Balm of Gilead Tree: New and Selected Stories*. *Appalachian Journal* 27 (2000): pp. 260–71.
Kennedy, Joanne. Rev. of *The Blue Valleys*. *New York Times* 10 Dec. 1989, late ed., sec. 7: p. 32.
Knotts, Kristina L. Rev. of *As Rain Turns to Snow*. *North Carolina Literary Review Online* (2018): pp. 47–49.
McGraw Erin. Rev. of *The Mountains Won't Remember Us* and five books by other authors. *Georgia Review* 47 (1993): pp. 802–13.

Pattishall, Roy. "'Blue Valleys' Is a Touching Look at People of Southern Appalachia." Rev. of *The Blue Valleys. Atlanta Journal and the Atlanta Constitution* 3 Sept. 1989: p. L11.
Rash, Tom. "Short Fiction in the Carolinas." Rev. of *The Blue Valleys* and four other books by other authors. *South Carolina Review* 25.1 (1992): pp. 157–69.
Sawyer, Paul. "Appalachian Transits." Rev. of *The Mountains Won't Remember Us* and *The Hinterlands. Bookpress: The Newspaper of the Literary Arts* [Ithaca, NY] 4 April 1994: pp. 10–11, 17.
Steinberg, Sybil. Rev. of *The Balm of Gilead Tree: New and Selected Stories. Publishers Weekly* 13 Sept. 1999: pp. 61–62.
______. Rev. of *The Blue Valleys. Publishers Weekly* 31 Mar. 1989: p. 43.
______. Rev. of *The Mountains Won't Remember Us. Publishers Weekly* 27 Apr. 1992: pp. 253–54.
Ulin, David L. "Blue Ridge Tales." Rev. of *The Balm of Gilead Tree: New and Selected Stories. New York Times* 30 Jan. 2000, late ed., sec. 7: p. 23.

3. Novels

Angel, Karen. Rev. of *The Truest Pleasure. Washington Post Book World* 4 Feb. 1996, final ed.: p. X08.
Bausch, Richard. "Talkies: Two Southern Novels Draw on the Sounds of Historical Voices." Rev. of *The Truest Pleasure* and Myra McLarey's *Water from the Well. New York Times Book Review* 29 Oct. 1995: p. 20.
Blythe, Will. "Revolutionary Road." Rev. of *Brave Enemies. New York Times* 9 Nov. 2003, late ed., sec. 7: p. 21.
Charles, Ron. "The Labor Pains of Democracy." Rev. of *Brave Enemies* and Jimmy Carter's novel *The Hornet's Nest. Christian Science Monitor* 2 Dec. 2003: p. 14.
Conway, Cecelia. Rev. of *Brave Enemies. Appalachian Heritage* 32.3 (2004): pp. 84–88.
Cook, Thomas H. "In the Land of Make-Do." Rev. of *The Hinterlands. New York Times Book Review* 24 July 1994: p. 12.
Dale, Neal. "Morgan Looks at Marriage in the Mountains." Rev. of *The Truest Pleasure. Asheville Citizen-Times* [Asheville, NC] 8 Oct. 1995: p. 2L.
Dezern, Craig. "Characters' Interaction Drives 'Truest Pleasure.'" Rev. of *The Truest Pleasure. Chicago Tribune* 5 Jan. 1996, sec. 5: p. 3.
Dooley, Susan. "Backwoods Blues." Rev. of *Gap Creek. Washington Post Book World* 30 Jan. 2000, final ed.: p. X06.
Garner, Dwight. "This Old House." Rev. of *Gap Creek. New York Times* 10 Oct. 1999, late ed., sec. 7: p. 10.
Garrett, George. "Carolina Taleblazing." Rev. of *The Hinterlands. World and I.* Aug. 1994: pp. 314+.
Gibson, Sharan. "Robert Morgan's Pointless Novel, Meaningless Lives." Rev. of *This Rock. Houston Chronicle* 30 December 2001, 2 star ed., "Zest": p. 21.
Godwin, Rebecca. Rev. of *The Road from Gap Creek. Appalachian Heritage* 42.1 (2014): pp. 115–17.
Goldman, Judy. "Three Steely Characters Struggle on a Mountain." Rev. of *The Hinterlands. Chicago Tribune* 3 May 1994, sec. 5: p. 2.
Griffin, Emilie. "Restless in Appalachia." Rev. of *This Rock. America* 185 (15 Oct. 2001): pp. 38–40.
Helman, Scott W. "Morgan Never Gets 'Rock" Off Ground." Rev. of *This Rock. Boston Globe* 6 Sept. 2001, 3rd ed.: p. F6.
McCay, Mary A. "Mother Courage." Rev. of *Brave Enemies. Times-Picayune* [New Orleans] 19 Oct. 2003, Books: p. 8.
Metzgar, Lisa. "Growing Pains Palpable in 'Gap.'" Rev. of *Gap Creek. Denver Rocky Mountain News* 9 Dec. 1999, final ed.: p. 10D.
Mielke, Laura Lynn. Rev. of *The Truest Pleasure. Carolina Quarterly* 51.2 (1999): pp. 85–86.
Perrin, Noel. "Patriot Acts." Rev. of *Brave Enemies* and Jimmy Carter's novel *The Hornet's Nest. Washington Post Book World* 16 Nov. 2003, final ed.: T07. Also published as "Novels Presidential and Professional." *Chicago Sun-Times* 23 Nov. 2003: p. 14.
Rev. of *Chasing the North Star. Kirkus Reviews* 1 Feb 2016: p. 241.
Sanders, Erica. "Love and Death and Destiny." Rev. of *Gap Creek* and three books by other authors. *Washington Post Book World* 2 Jan. 2002, final ed.: p. C08.
Sawyer, Paul. "Appalachian Transits." Rev. of *The Mountains Won't Remember Us* and *The Hinterlands. Bookpress: The Newspaper of the Literary Arts* [Ithaca, NY] 4 April 1994: pp. 10–11, 17.
Steinberg, Sybil. Rev. of *Gap Creek. Publishers Weekly* 23 Aug. 1999: p. 46.
______. Rev. of *The Hinterlands. Publishers Weekly* Mar. 1994: p. 55.
______. Rev. of *The Truest Pleasure. Publishers Weekly* 24 July 1995: p. 48.
Swoboda, Victor. "Gap Creek Is Aflood with Tribulation." Rev. of *Gap Creek. Gazette* [Montreal] 11 Mar. 2000, final ed., Books and the Visual Arts: p. J4.
Whittemore, Katharine. "Unto the Hills." Rev. of *This Rock. New York Times* 14 Oct. 2001, late ed., sec. 7: p. 21.
Zaleski, Jeff. Rev. of *Brave Enemies. Publishers Weekly* 2 June 2003: p. 29.
______. Rev. of *This Rock. Publishers Weekly* 27 Aug. 2001: p. 56.

4. Nonfiction Prose

Bell, Madison Smartt. "At Home in Paradise." *New York Review of Books* 20 Dec. 2007 pp. 73–75.

Hale, Matthew Rainbow. Rev. of *Boone: A Biography. Mississippi Quarterly* 63.1–2 (2010): pp. 351–54.

Myers, D. G. "Whatever Became of Poet-Critics?" Rev. of *Good Measure: Essays, Interviews, and Notes on Poetry* and four books by other authors. *South Carolina Review* 27 (1994): pp. 354–62.

Olson, Ted. Rev. of *Boone: A Biography* and *Lions of the West. Journal of Appalachian Studies* 21.2 (2015): pp. 277–81.

E. Reference Book Articles

Conway, Cecelia. "Robert Morgan." *Dictionary of Literary Biography*. Vol. 292. Ed. Lisa Abney and Suzanne Disheroon-Green. Detroit: Gale, 2004. pp. 252–63.

Harmon, William. "Robert Morgan." *Contemporary Southern Poets, Dramatists, Essayists, and Novelists*. Ed. Robert Bain and Joseph M. Flora. Westport, CT: Greenwood, 1994. pp. 370–76.

______. "Robert Morgan." *Southern Writers: A New Biographical Dictionary*. Ed. Joseph Flora and Amber Vogel. Baton Rouge: Louisiana State University Press, 2006. pp. 91–92.

Jones, Roger D. "Robert Morgan." *Dictionary of Literary Biography*. Vol. 120. Ed. R. S. Gwynn. Detroit: Gale, 1992. pp. 213–19.

F. Bibliography

Lang, John. "A Robert Morgan Bibliography." *Iron Mountain Review* 6.1 (1990): pp. 31–32.

Reisman, Rosemary M. Canfield, and Suzanne Booker-Canfield. "Robert Morgan." *Contemporary Southern Men Fiction Writers: An Annotated Bibliography*. Lanham, MD: Scarecrow Press, 1998. pp. 298–305.

Wright, Stuart. "Robert Morgan: A Bibliographic Chronicle, 1963–81." *Bulletin of Bibliography* 39 (1982): pp. 121–31.

About the Contributors

Bhisham **Bherwani** is the author of three books of poetry—*The Second Night of the Spirit* (2009), *The Circling Canopy* (2014), and *Life in Peacetime* (2016)—as well as many essays and reviews on poets and poetry. He is also coeditor of *The Shrine Whose Shape I Am: The Collected Poetry of Samuel Menashe* (2019). As an undergraduate at Cornell University, he was enrolled in Robert Morgan's creative writing workshop. He has taught literature at the City University of New York.

Suzanne **Booker-Canfield** is an independent educational consultant. She received an MA from the University of North Carolina at Chapel Hill. During that time, she met Robert Morgan and published an interview with him in *The Carolina Quarterly*. She was a Richard M. Weaver Fellow at the University of Oxford and received a Ph.D. from the University of North Carolina at Greensboro, where she wrote her dissertation on Morgan's poetry. She has subsequently published other essays on his work.

Harriette C. **Buchanan** is a professor emeritus of interdisciplinary studies at Appalachian State University. Her interests are in southern American literature, especially the literature of Appalachia, particularly the work of Fred Chappell, John Ehle, and Robert Morgan, and in modern popular mysteries, particularly the work of women such as Marcia Muller, Sara Paretsky, Louise Penny, and Jacqueline Winspear.

Fred **Chappell** taught at the University of North Carolina at Greensboro before retiring as Burlington Industries Professor of English. He is the author of nine novels, including *Dagon* (1968), winner of the French Academy's Prix de Meilleur des Livres Étrangers, *I Am One of You Forever* (1985), and *A Shadow All of Light* (2016). Among his many books of poetry are the Bollingen Award–winning *Midquest: A Poem* (1981), *Shadow Box* (2009), and *As If It Were* (2019). He has also published books of short fiction and literary criticism.

Jim **Clark** served, before his retirement, as Elizabeth H. Jordan Professor of Southern Literature and as Chair of the Department of English and Modern Languages at Barton College. His books include two books of poems, *Dancing on Canaan's Ruins* (1983) and *Handiwork* (1998); *Notions: A Jim Clark Miscellany* (2007), and, as editor, *Fables in the Blood: The Selected Poems of Byron Herbert Reece* (2002).

Martha Greene **Eads**, professor of English at Eastern Mennonite University, studied literature and theology at Wake Forest University, the University of North Carolina at Chapel Hill, and the University of Durham (UK). She has taught at the North Carolina Correctional Center for Women and at Valparaiso University. Her research interests include English modernism and southern fiction. Her articles have appeared in *The Carolina Quarterly*, *Christianity and Literature*, *The Cresset*, and other venues.

Rebecca **Godwin**, professor of English and director of the Ragan Writing Center at Barton College, is author of *Gender Dynamics in the Fiction of Lee Smith* (1997). Her journal publications include essays on Thomas Wolfe, Robert Morgan, and Tim McLaurin; an essay on Fred Chappell's *Moments of Light* appeared in *More Lights Than One* (2004). She has served as chair of the North Carolina Writers Conference, and as president of the North Carolina Literary and Historical Association.

Jesse **Graves** is a professor of English at East Tennessee State University. He is the author of four collections of poetry: *Tennessee Landscape with Blighted Pine* (2012), *Basin Ghosts* (2014), *Specter Mountain* (with William Wright, 2018), and *Merciful Days* (2020). His work has been recognized with the James Still Award for Writing about the Appalachian South from the Fellowship of Southern Writers. He guest-edited the 2010 Robert Morgan special issue of *Southern Quarterly*.

William **Harmon** is the James Gordon Hanes Professor Emeritus in the Humanities at the University of North Carolina at Chapel Hill. Among his publications are *Time in Ezra Pound's Work* (1977), *The Oxford Book of American Light Verse* (1979) and *The Poetry Toolkit* (2012). His books of poetry include *Treasury Holiday* (1970), which won the Academy of American Poets' Lamont Poetry Prize and *Mutatis Mutandis* (1985), which won the Poetry Society of America's William Carlos Williams Award.

Thomas Alan **Holmes** is a professor of English at East Tennessee State University, where he also serves as Associate Dean for Curriculum and Interdisciplinary Studies. His scholarly and creative work has appeared in venues including *Appalachian Heritage, Appalachian Journal, South Atlantic Review, Pine Mountain Sand & Gravel, Still: The Journal*, and *Valparaiso Poetry Review*. With Jesse Graves and Ernest Lee, he is co-editor of *Jeff Daniel Marion: Poet on the Holston* (2016).

George **Hovis** is the author of *Vale of Humility: Plain Folk in Contemporary North Carolina Fiction* (2007) and a novel, *The Skin Artist* (2019). His short stories, poems, and essays have appeared in *Appalachian Heritage, The Carolina Quarterly, North Carolina Literary Review*, and elsewhere. A former president of the Thomas Wolfe Society, he is a professor of English at the State University of New York at Oneonta. In 2017 he received the SUNY Chancellor's Award for Excellence in Teaching.

Michael **McFee** is a professor of English at the University of North Carolina at Chapel Hill. His books of poems include *Sad Girl Sitting on a Running Board* (1991); *Shinemaster* (2006); and *We Were Once Here* (2017). He is the editor of *The Language They Speak Is Things to Eat* (1994) and *This Is Where We Live* (2000). He has received the North Carolina Award in Literature, the James Still Award for Writing about the Appalachian South, and UNC's James M. Johnston Award for Excellence in Teaching.

Robert **Morgan** is the Kappa Alpha Professor of English at Cornell University. Among his many poetry collections are *The Strange Attractor: New and Selected Poems* (2004), *Terroir* (2011), and *Dark Energy* (2015). A book on poetics, *Good Measure: Essays, Interviews, and Notes on Poetry* appeared in 1993. His collections of short fiction include *The Balm of Gilead Tree: New and Selected Stories* (1999) and *As Rain Turns to Snow and Other Stories* (2017). He is the author of seven novels, including *The Truest Pleasure* (1995), *Gap Creek* (1999), and *Brave Enemies* (2003). He is also the author of *Boone: A Biography* (2007) and *Lions of the West: Heroes and Villains of the Westward Expansion* (2011). Among his numerous awards are *Poetry's* Eunice Tietjens Prize, the James G. Hanes Poetry Prize from the Fellowship of Southern Writers, the North Carolina Award for Literature, and an Academy Award in Literature from the American Academy of Arts and Letters.

Ted **Olson** is a professor of Appalachian studies at East Tennessee State University, where he teaches courses on Appalachian music history. He is the author of *Blue Ridge Folklife* (1998) and editor of University of Tennessee Press's Charles K. Wolfe Music Series. He is also the editor of three books of work by and about James Still: *From the Mountain, From the Valley: New and Collected Poems* (2001); *The Hills Remember: The Collected Short Stories of James Still* (2012); and *James Still: Critical Essays on the Dean of Appalachian Literature* (2012).

Rita Sims **Quillen** is the author of two novels, *Hiding Ezra* (2005) and *Wayland* (2019). Her poetry collections include *Counting the Sums* (1995), *Her Secret Dream* (2007), *The Mad Farmer's Wife* (2016), and *Some Notes You Hold* (2020). Her critical study *Looking for Native Ground: Contemporary Appalachian Poetry* (1989) is the first book-length treatment of the subject. The present book reprints *Looking for Native Ground*'s chapter on Morgan.

Paul Lincoln **Sawyer** is a professor of English at Cornell University and the director of its Knight Institute for Writing in the Disciplines. He is the author of a book-length study of the Victorian man of letters John Ruskin: *Ruskin's Poetic Argument: The Design of the Major Works* (1985). He has also written on Martin Luther King, Jr., Mahatma Gandhi, Victorian science, and college writing programs.

Robert M. **West** is a professor of English at Mississippi State University and associate editor of *Mississippi Quarterly*. His publications include several on Morgan's poetry—essays, reviews, and interviews—in venues including *Appalachian Journal, Asheville Poetry Review, Southern Quarterly,* and *Appalachia in the Classroom: Teaching the Region* (2013). He is co-editor of *Succinct: The Broadstone Anthology of Short Poems* (2013) and editor of both volumes of T*he Complete Poems of A. R. Ammons* (2017).

Index